ILLINOIS
IN THE
WORLD WAR

———

EDITED BY
THEODORE CALVIN PEASE
UNIVERSITY OF ILLINOIS

———

VOLUME VI

ILLINOIS IN THE WORLD WAR

VOLUME VI

WAR DOCUMENTS
AND
ADDRESSES

EDITED BY

MARGUERITE EDITH JENISON

SECRETARY, WAR RECORDS SECTION
ILLINOIS STATE HISTORICAL LIBRARY

PUBLISHED BY THE
ILLINOIS STATE HISTORICAL LIBRARY
SPRINGFIELD, ILLINOIS
1923

ILLINOIS STATE REGISTER
SPRINGFIELD, ILLINOIS

CONTENTS

CONTENTS

CONTENTS

CONTENTS

CHAPTER

PAGE

CONTENTS

CONTENTS

CHAPTER

EDITOR'S PREFACE

The sixth volume of the series, Illinois in the World War, published by the War Records Section of the Illinois State Historical Library, consists of selected documents of various classes, speeches, resolutions, etc., regarding the activity of Illinois in the World War. Naturally this publication cannot be exhaustive. It merely puts in accessible form a selected body of source material illustrating the various phases of Illinois' contribution to the victory of 1918 and the mental reaction of the state and her leaders toward the war. As in the case of the preceding volume the plan for such a volume was sketched out by Dr. Wayne E. Stevens, secretary of the War Records Section, and his outline was revised, altered, and developed by his successor, Miss Marguerite E. Jenison, who has completed the task of publication.

This volume is the last of the publications of the War Records Section which it is thought advisable to make at the present time. Additional volumes of source material may be published in the series if the material is available and the demand becomes apparent. This and the preceding volume of the series serve only to clear the way for the future historian of the war. Definitive historical writing on all save the purely military phases of the war will have to be left to a generation that has not known the psychological excitement of the years 1914-1920.

THEODORE CALVIN PEASE

Urbana, Illinois
August 9, 1923

PREFACE

It has been the purpose of the War Records Section to assemble in this volume certain proclamations of the Governor, enactments of the General Assembly, speeches delivered by state officials and others, resolutions adopted at patriotic meetings and by various organizations, and similar material illustrative of activities undertaken in Illinois in mobilizing men and resources for participation in the war with Germany. The period covered extends from February 6, 1917, when the Fiftieth General Assembly was addressed by Governor Frank O. Lowden on the subject of the severing of diplomatic relations between the United States and Germany, after which the two houses adopted a joint resolution pledging support to the President "in maintaining the honor and dignity of our country," until July, 1919, by which time the Thirty-third Division and the One Hundred Forty-ninth Field Artillery, organizations into which the Illinois National Guard was converted upon entering the federal service, had returned from overseas, the Fifty-first General Assembly, which enacted some post-war legislation, had adjourned, and practically all of the civilian war agencies in the state had ceased operations.

With the exception of the Governor's proclamations and the laws and joint resolutions of the Fifty-first General Assembly, which have been collated with the originals on file in the office of the Secretary of State, the various sources from which the material here presented has been taken are indicated in the footnotes. The War Records Section is indebted to Governor Frank O. Lowden for supplying from his private papers stenographic reports of the addresses which he delivered during 1917-1919 relative to the war. The Chief Justice of the Supreme Court, William Howard Taft, kindly supplied the manuscript of the address which he delivered in Springfield on December 28, 1917, and Jacob M. Dickinson, former secretary of war, and Samuel Insull, chairman of the State Council of Defense of Illinois, furnished printed copies of their speeches of March 31, 1917, and January 18, 1919, respectively. Col. Henry

J. Reilly, commanding officer of the 149th Field Artillery, and
Carl Vrooman, assistant secretary of agriculture, revised for publication in this volume accounts of their speeches which originally
appeared in *Chicago Commerce*. A number of addresses are reprinted from newspaper accounts, but only when application to the
speaker revealed the fact that no manuscript copy was available.
The War Records Section is indebted to the following persons for
permission to reprint speeches from accounts in its possession: Mrs.
Theodore Roosevelt (addresses delivered by the late Theodore
Roosevelt in Chicago on April 28, 1917, and in Springfield on
August 26, 1918) ; Mrs. William Crawford Gorgas (address delivered in Chicago on October 26, 1917, by the late Surgeon General,
W. C. Gorgas) ; Newton D. Baker, secretary of war; Josephus
Daniels, secretary of the navy; W. G. McAdoo, secretary of the
treasury; Judge J. P. McGoorty, of Chicago; Arthur Reynolds, of
Chicago; Mrs. Joseph T. Bowen, of Chicago; Frank A. Vanderlip,
director of the National War Savings Committee; Hugh S. Magill,
director of the Illinois Centennial Celebration; Dean Eugene Davenport, of the College of Agriculture of the University of Illinois;
Colonel C. S. Bach, United States Army; Barney Cohen, director
of the Department of Labor, 1917-1921. For permission to reprint
three addresses from volumes of collected speeches, acknowledgment
is made to the following publishers: to the George H. Doran Company for permission to use "Wealth Enlisted in the Nation's Service,"
delivered by Josephus Daniels before the American Bankers' Association, Chicago, included in *The Navy and the Nation* (1919) ; to
the same publishers for permission to use "Victory demands Unity,"
an address by Samuel Gompers, Chicago, September 14, 1917, which
appeared in *American Labor and the War* (1919) ; and to the
Harvard University Press for permission to reprint "The War and
Discussion," an address delivered by Elihu Root in Chicago on
September 14, 1917, which is included in a volume of speeches by
Mr. Root, *The United States and the War, The Mission to Russia,
Political Addresses,* collected and edited by Robert Bacon and James
Brown Scott (1918).

In general the text of the material has been reproduced exactly
as it appears in the original except for a few omissions, chiefly men-

tion in speeches of controversial matters where both sides have not been presented somewhere in the volume. In those speeches reproduced from stenographic reports and newspaper accounts, errors which are clearly attributable to a stenographer or proofreader have been corrected; in other cases changes in the text have been indicated by brackets. The War Records Section is under obligation to Dr. Francis W. Shepardson, director of the Department of Registration and Education, 1917-1921, who at the request of Governor Lowden did some preliminary editing of the governor's speeches.

In every stage of the compilation of this volume, Dr. Theodore C. Pease, editor of the Illinois Historical Publications, has given advice and assistance which have been of inestimable service. Miss Lucille Kile and Miss Wilhelmina Luther, of the staff of the War Records Section, have aided in collating the manuscript and reading proof.

MARGUERITE EDITH JENISON

Urbana, Illinois
August 10, 1923

I. PUBLIC OPINION AND THE WAR

AN ADDRESS BY GOVERNOR FRANK O. LOWDEN[1]

Delivered before the Fiftieth General Assembly, State of Illinois, February 6, 1917.

Gentlemen of the Fiftieth General Assembly:

On Saturday, the third instant, the government at Washington severed our diplomatic relations with the German Empire. As your honorable body was not in session, and as it seemed to me important that Illinois should speak, and speak promptly, I made a formal statement to the public. I thought that this was an occasion when the time of doing the thing was as important as the thing itself. This statement was:

"A crisis in our international affairs is upon us. The President is charged, under the Constitution, with the conduct of our foreign relations. He has acted. It is the solemn duty of all Americans to rally to his support. I have no doubt but that the people of Illinois, of whatever party, whether native or naturalized, will measure up to their full duty in this emergency.

"I shall recommend that the General Assembly take action which will assure to the President the loyal support of Illinois."

In the crisis which has arisen, our security against possible war depends upon hearty and united action on the part of all our people. And if war is to be averted, it will be averted only through our presenting such a united front to the world that no nation will lightly incur our armed enmity.

The time has passed for discussing the steps which led to the breaking off of our diplomatic relations with the German Empire. The government—our government—has acted. Our duty is plain. Illinois would not be true to her past if she did not, at this time, give unqualified support to the President of the United States.

Almost fifty-six years ago another General Assembly of Illinois

[1] From a manuscript copy in the possession of Governor Lowden.

was in session. Fort Sumter had just been fired upon. Stephen A. Douglas, then a senator of the United States from Illinois, appeared before a joint session of the two houses of this Assembly to urge support of the Union cause. It was an historic occasion. Among other things, Douglas said:

"Now, permit me to say to the assembled Representatives and Senators of our beloved State, composed of men of both political parties, in my opinion it is your duty to lay aside, for the time being, your party creeds."

And so today, in the same spirit, let us lay aside our party creeds. And let us, whatever our sympathies as between the foreign warring nations, remember only that we are Americans. We all have foreign blood flowing in our veins and our sympathy with one or another of the belligerent peoples is but natural. But if we permit our sympathies with our kindred to become partiality for their governments, we are recreant to our own government. We may have many sympathies; we can have but one allegiance, and that allegiance is to the United States!

I earnestly recommend such action by your honorable body as that all men may know that the President of the United States, in this crisis, has the whole-hearted support of Illinois.

PLEDGE OF SUPPORT TO FEDERAL GOVERNMENT IN WAR WITH GERMANY

Senate Joint Resolution Number 8, Fiftieth General Assembly, State of Illinois.

WHEREAS, Diplomatic relations with the German Empire have been terminated by the action of our Government at Washington.

Therefore, be it resolved by the Senate of the State of Illinois, the House of Representatives concurring herein, That we pledge ourselves as representatives of the people of the State of Illinois to support the Government of the United States in maintaining the honor and dignity of our country, and that a copy of these resolutions be transmitted to the President of the United States.

Adopted by the Senate February 6, 1917.

Concurred in by the House of Representatives, February 6, 1917.

PRESIDENT'S ACKNOWLEDGMENT OF RESOLUTIONS OF SUPPORT[2]

Letter from President Wilson to the Secretary of the Senate of the Fiftieth General Assembly, State of Illinois.

THE WHITE HOUSE.
WASHINGTON.

February 12, 1917.

MY DEAR MR. PADDOCK: It was indeed generous of the Fiftieth General Assembly of Illinois to adopt a resolution pledging to the Government the support of the great Commonwealth in maintaining the honor and dignity of the United States, and, in acknowledging and thanking you for the copy of the resolution which you were good enough to send me, I want to convey to the members of both Houses an expression of my deep appreciation.

Cordially and sincerely yours,

WOODROW WILSON.

HON. JAMES H. PADDOCK,
    Secretary of the Senate,
      Springfield, Illinois.

RESOLUTIONS ADOPTED BY THE CHICAGO CITY COUNCIL, FEBRUARY 5, 1917[3]

It has become necessary for His Excellency, the President of the United States of America, to sever diplomatic relations with the imperial German government.

A grave situation fraught with perils of war between this country and Germany has arisen because of the necessity of upholding the rights of the United States and our honor in the councils of the nations.

This time of national crisis calls for the undivided loyalty of every American citizen and a determination on the part of every American to uphold our nation's chief executive.

We, the members of the city council of the city of Chicago, as the representatives of the citizens of this great city without regard

[2] *Journal of the Senate of the Fiftieth General Assembly* (Springfield, 1917), Feb. 20, 1917, page 371.

[3] *Chicago Tribune*, February 6, 1917.

to party line or national origin, but all as Americans and patriots, do hereby pledge to the President of the United States our loyalty and support.

The city clerk is hereby instructed to forward a copy of these resolutions to His Excellency, the President of the United States.

MESSAGE FROM EDMUND J. JAMES, PRESIDENT OF THE UNIVERSITY OF ILLINOIS, TO GOVERNOR FRANK O. LOWDEN, FEBRUARY 7, 1917[4]

I beg in the name of the trustees and faculty of the University of Illinois to tender you, and, through you, to the President of the United States, in the event of war, the facilities of the scientific and technical laboratories of the University of Illinois as an aid in solving such problems as the federal government may assign to us.

SINGING PATRIOTIC SONGS IN THE SCHOOLS— A PROCLAMATION

One of the great unifying, nationalizing influences is the singing of our National songs. Nothing so arouses and fixes a sound and patriotic sentiment as the teaching of these songs to our children and the singing of these songs by our children.

Upon the recommendation of the Superintendent of Public Instruction, and because I deem it especially appropriate at this time, I suggest that the week of February 19-23 be set aside as a week for the singing of National songs in the public and private schools of Illinois. It is desired that a special time be set aside on each day for the singing of the following songs and hymns:

"America"
"Star Spangled Banner"
"Hail, Columbia"
"Battle Hymn of the Republic"
"Battle Cry of Peace [Freedom]"
"Illinois"

[4] *Chicago Tribune*, February 8, 1917.

	IN WITNESS WHEREOF, I, FRANK O. LOWDEN, do hereunto
(SEAL)	set my hand and cause to be affixed the Great Seal of State this ninth day of February, A. D. 1917.

FRANK O. LOWDEN

By the Governor:

Governor

   LOUIS L. EMMERSON

     Secretary of State.

AN ADDRESS BY GOVERNOR FRANK O. LOWDEN[5]

Delivered at the laying of the cornerstone of the First Illinois Cavalry Armory, Chicago, February 22, 1917.

National defense is a subject uppermost in the public mind to-day. All men, excepting only the extreme pacifists, agree that our defense should be strengthened. How shall this be done? There are three methods before us: first, a professional army; second, a volunteer army; and third, a conscript army, or a combination of these.

There are two objections to a professional army. In the first place, our experience has shown that it is impossible to raise a professional army adequate to our national defense. Even with the martial ardor always aroused by the first call for troops, we lately found that we were unable to recruit our regular army to its full strength. Though we have employed bonuses to recruiting officers and to postmasters, though we have resorted to advertising methods which, in some instances, would have been condemned if employed by private business, our regiments are far from full. Even, however, if it were possible, would it be desirable? History tells us that a free government cannot safely rely upon a professional soldiery for its defense. A recent great writer has said: "A democracy which asserts the right of manhood suffrage, while denying the duty of manhood service, is living in a fool's paradise."

Our history and the history of the world prove that no nation in a great national crisis can depend solely upon volunteers. Such a

[5] *Illinois State Journal*, February 23, 1917.

(3)

system, if practicable, is unjust. When a nation's life is at stake, dependence cannot be had upon any system which is founded in injustice. Whatever is essential to a national perpetuity is a duty resting equally upon all the sons of the state. To rely upon volunteers for national defense is as idle a dream as it would be to rely upon voluntary contributions to defray the expenses of a war. If our citizenship is not worth what it costs to maintain it either in treasure or blood, it is worth nothing at all.

The logic of the situation seems to demand a system under which all able-bodied men are liable, equally and impartially, to military service. This means conscription in some form. Just how to inaugurate this is the difficult question. I myself can see no practical solution of the problem with the national guard left out. I realize that there has been much criticism of the national guard during the last few months. Much of this criticism, in my judgment, is unwarranted. The time consumed in converting state troops into national troops has been emphasized. This delay, however, wasn't the fault of the National Defense Act. The state troops were not mustered into the United States service under that act. Whatever other faults the act may have, under the provisions of that act, if we were called to the colors today, we could be mustered into the federal service within twenty-four hours after mobilization, for neither the property transfer nor the muster would now be necessary in changing the state troops into federal troops.

Aside, however, from this consideration, when you put the conscription into effect, whether under the Chamberlain act, or under any other plan, how will you officer the draw levies unless you have the national guard to draw upon? Under existing law it is provided that one regular army officer be assigned as instructor to each regimental organization and independent unit of the national guard. Surely one instructor for a regiment would accomplish little enough. This law entitles Illinois to but fourteen instructors, yet the army authorities have been unable to assign more than four at any one time for the guard of the entire state. There are national guard organizations scattered all over Illinois. They contain many competent commissioned and non-commissioned officers. These officers are known to the people of the state. In my opinion they would be indispensable in the training and instruction of new levies called out.

In this connection, I wish to call your attention to a very able paper read before the Commercial Club of this city by Major Abel Davis of the First Infantry, Illinois National Guard. He submits the most concrete and practicable plan I have seen for the creation of an adequate military force. Briefly, he would recruit the regular army to its maximum strength by conscription. He would make the national guard the second line of defense. He would provide for the training of a reserve force by conscription, the size of which should depend upon the national need and our ability to instruct them professionally. He would exempt from such conscription all those who are members of national guard organizations recognized and accepted by the federal government and those who are students in military schools or universities having recognized military instruction. By this exemption, those of natural military inclination would enlist in the national guard, thus enabling the national guard organizations to recruit to their maximum strength.

This is not the time for controversy between the national guard and the regular army. It is time, rather, for coöperation and coordination of all the forces within our boundaries that may be needed in the time of war.

AN ADDRESS BY JACOB M. DICKINSON[6]

Delivered at a patriotic rally held in Chicago on March 31, 1917.

This meeting is in response to a numerously signed call as follows:

"Our country is on the verge of war. The crisis demands immediate expression by all patriotic American citizens of their sentiments and desires. The undersigned request all loyal Americans WHO STAND UNCONDITIONALLY FOR THEIR COUNTRY AGAINST ALL OF ITS ENEMIES, AND WHO DESIRE TO URGE UPON CONGRESS AND THE PRESIDENT THAT THEY SHALL IMMEDI-

---

[6] From a printed copy of the speech supplied by the Honorable Jacob M. Dickinson, of Chicago. Mr. Dickinson was secretary of war under President Taft, March 4, 1909–May, 1911.

ATELY TAKE VIGOROUS AND EFFECTIVE STEPS
TO PROTECT AMERICAN LIVES AND PROPERTY
AND VINDICATE THE HONOR OF THE NATION
BY USING ALL OF ITS RESOURCES
to meet with us at the Auditorium Theatre, in the City of Chicago,
on Saturday, March 31, 1917, at 8:00 o'clock P.M., for the purpose
of taking such appropriate action as may be determined upon at
that time."

The reason for this meeting is manifest to all good Americans.
Our ships have been sunk and our citizens have been ruthlessly put
to death by the German government on the high seas, where they
were within their rights under recognized principles of international
law.

This call is predicated upon the same facts which caused the
President to call Congress to meet on April the third.

The essential idea of our national life is the association of a free
people together for mutual protection in the pursuit of life, liberty
and happiness. No nation can have the love and respect of its people
unless it is willing to hazard all for the fulfillment of this purpose.
German citizenship assured world-wide protection. American citizenship is in danger of becoming a term of world-wide contempt.

The United States must vindicate its right to be a nation by protecting the property and lives of its citizens against unjust aggression.
What deeper wrongs are we waiting for to stimulate us to action?
If the outrages already inflicted are not sufficient to arouse the spirit
of our people, then we are cravens, impervious to insult, and will in-
evitably sink into a Chinese pacifism and inconsequence as a nation
that will certainly invite despoilment of our hoarded wealth, the destruction of our cities, the devastation of our country, the desecration
of our national monuments, the violation of our women and the
deportation of our children into captivity.

All of these barbarisms have been and are now being enacted
in other lands.

The crime of war lust cannot justly be charged upon us. History refutes it. No other nation has done more to promote the
spirit of peace among nations and the establishment of tribunals for
the settlement of international differences without appeal to arms.

We have, more than any other nation, been parties to agreements involving questions once regarded as too vital to national life and honor to be the subject matter of arbitration. Under conditions frequently acute, we have repeatedly, by such methods, settled our controversies with Canada, have kept peace with her over a hundred years, and maintained the longest boundary line in the world separating nations, without either side having a fort or armament of any description.

We are the only nation that ever went to war solely in behalf of the rights and liberties of another people. After establishing Cuba in her independence at our own cost, we promptly withdrew our armies.

We have been the apostles of peace on earth and good will to men. We have so long and so constantly idealized peace, that there has sprung up in our midst a noxious parasite, not from the American soil, but attaching itself to the body politic from which it draws its existence and whose protection it enjoys. I mean those so-called pacifists, who, even in a crisis like this, when our citizens are being murdered on the high seas, exalt a general theory of humanitarianism above the country that shelters them, and who would denationalize us, deny every principle of patriotism, scoff at the monuments of our national heroes, and turn to the wall the pictures of Washington, Jackson, Lincoln and Grant, who, through war and the direct results of war, achieved their country's love and a place among those immortal few that were not born to die.

You have before you on this stage survivors of our wars who hazarded their lives for their country. Many of them bear the scars of wounds received while fighting your battles. If you approve such pacifism, then tear from their breasts the badges of honor with which a grateful country decorated them and let them go forth outcasts and pariahs, so that other sons of America may never earn by patriotic action the contempt of their countrymen.

Such pacifists try to terrify us with a cry of "militarism." If there be such a risk, I would take the chances and trust to the sense and strength of our people to deal with our own military, rather than suffer the degradation and outrage that will certainly come from foreign militarism if we proclaim the shameful doctrine of nonresistance.

This threat is a bogy to frighten those ignorant of our history. With us the civil has always dominated the military, except for short periods and in restricted territory when martial law was necessary.

The two men in our national life who most conspicuously embodied the military spirit were Grant and Jackson. When our Civil War closed under the leadership of Grant, although some at that time charged him with Caesarism, the army he led of a million men melted back into civil life, without the least disturbance to the body politic, and Grant became a civilian as renowned for his simplicity and modesty as he had been for his military genius.

Jackson at New Orleans, when our country was threatened, not only by foreign invaders, but by domestic foes, declared martial law and arrested some who opposed the public good and backed it by vaunting their foreign citizenship. Hall, a United States judge, issued for their release a writ of habeas corpus, which Jackson promptly disobeyed. When the great victory had been won and the invaders had been driven from American soil, the laurel-crowned hero voluntarily presented himself to the court and submitted to its jurisdiction. Though protesting against it as an injustice, he paid in the court a fine of one thousand dollars. Immediately thereafter he addressed his indignant soldiers and an exasperated populace, saying: "It is the highest duty and pride of all good men to pay their tribute of respect to the guardian of our civil liberties. Remember this last charge, as in a few days I expect to leave you. It may serve as a lesson to yourselves and posterity."

Some urge that we are wholly unprepared and should take no hostile action until we are adequately prepared. That means that we are either to submit without ever having redress, or that we are to prepare, and then, if necessary, go to war to vindicate our rights.

Such a course is abject submission, or a war by us with Germany after this war is over. That would be the quintessence of stupidity. If we fight we must act with those who now are fighting Germany. The result will be quicker and surer, the outlay and hazard less, we will be at the council board when the terms of peace are adjusted and will have friends and not stand isolated when the war is over.

If we have unsettled issues with Germany and have no part in the treaty of peace, then God help the United States! If we stand aloof and say that we have no part in the present war, then when the terms are bartered over, if Germany, pressed for concessions, shall make it a condition of yielding that she have a free hand in Mexico, Central and South America, why should the other nations, from whom we have isolated ourselves, be more careful for us than we have been for ourselves? Would they not, to gain an advantage, say that the question as to those countries and the United States does not concern them? We have already had knowledge of Germany's activities in Mexico through the Zimmerman note. If we undertake to carry on an independent war of our own, because we shrink from entangling alliances which Washington, under conditions wholly dissimilar, warned against, then we must prepare to have not only a navy equal to any in the world, but to maintain indefinitely a standing army that will impose an appalling burden of taxation and make us truly a military power. If the professional militarism of Europe shall be effectually crushed, such disarmament will follow as will greatly reduce military burdens and the way will be open to maintain peace by a League to Enforce Peace, or such other method as the wisdom of the nations may sanction.

Abhorrent as is war, we know that out of war has often come much for the healing of the nations. It was through war that the independence of this country and the republican form of government were established. Our nation, thus born, has stood amid the dark and gloom, when other countries were struggling against oppression, like a Pharos to guide them to a haven where there is no recognition of the alleged divine right to ride, booted and spurred, over the masses, and where government of the people, by the people, and for the people reigns supreme.

It was through war that the old controversy of the dissolution of the union by peaceable secession was forever settled, thereby removing the greatest obstacle to our national life. If war shall unhappily come to us now, under its intense heat the melting pot of America will throw off the dross and consolidate all of the true metal into a homogeneous citizenship, which will in fact, as well as in name, represent our national life. We have not the wisdom and vision comprehensive enough in its sweep to foretell by our partial knowledge of passing events what Providence has ordained, but if out of this Euro-

pean war shall come the abolition of hereditary power and the casting
of the House of Lords, the Hohenzollerns, and the Hapsburgs into
the scrap heap with the Romanoffs, and the establishment of the right
of the people to rule, this war, with all of its costs, will be a boon to
humanity.

. . . .

If we wage war with Germany, we should make it plain to the
German people at large that we do not regard them as responsible
for our differences, that we believe that it is a condition brought
about by their military rulers, that we bear them no malice, that we
would gladly welcome them to the sisterhood of republics, and that
if they shall achieve control of their own affairs, our contest with
them will soon be ended.

That we are in many ways unprepared for war we all now know.
We have persistently shut our eyes to our condition and thought that
we alone of all the nations of the world would be spared the scourge
of war. For this unpreparedness our whole people are responsible.
There were a few who forecast events and endeavored to arouse
them to a proper sense of danger, but the effort was vain.

That we can almost immediately evolve tremendous forces that
will potentially affect the result of the present war is manifest.
Through our finances, our factories, our shipping, our light sea craft,
aeroplanes and navy, we can soon become a powerful factor. The
question of putting troops in the field is more remote, but if the war
shall last a year we can accomplish much in that direction.

The only just way to impose the burden of national defense is
by universal training, and, when necessity shall arise, by universal
service. It is not democratic to leave the sacrifice to be borne alone
by volunteers. We should here and now let Congress know how we
stand on this question.

If we go in, it must be with all our might. We should have no
war, or should wage war to the limit of our power.

Ambassador Gerard, direct from Germany and a conference with
the President, is credited by the press as saying on Tuesday last in
a speech in New York, that: "Woodrow Wilson is the greatest
peace president we have ever had. But I am going to tell you something else. That is, before long you will find out that he will stand

before the world as the greatest war president that the United States of America ever had."

He has set a high mark. Washington and Lincoln were war presidents, and the world has pronounced them truly great. I love to hear of great men. My heart swells with pride and my soul is exalted when they are my countrymen. I am not so jealous of the reputation of Washington and Lincoln that I would not have another American surpass them. No one will rejoice more than I over the luster that such an achievement will shed over our country. No predecessor of President Wilson was ever confronted with graver or more complicated conditions. It has been repeatedly stated in the papers that he has an open mind. He himself has solicited the judgment of the people. We are here to make our response.

It is said that the President will merely present the facts to Congress and make no recommendation. I do not believe it. The American people look for leadership. They respond to the counsel of those whom they have put to the front on account of their confidence in their superior wisdom, vision and courage. We have been fortunate, for never has there been a crisis in our history when we did not have some great men to tell us what to do. Washington, against the opposition of the faint-hearted, established our independence. It was his leadership that carried through, against violent opposition, the adoption of our constitution. Jackson, amid a storm of opposition, pointed and led the way to the supremacy of the people over the banking power. Lincoln, struggling at first against an overwhelming majority, achieved the consolidation of our people into a nation and the abolition of slavery.

I believe that our President will lead courageously in a way that Americans who are lovers of their country can proudly follow.

AN ADDRESS BY JOHN P. McGOORTY, JUDGE OF THE CIRCUIT COURT FOR COOK COUNTY[7]

Delivered at a patriotic rally held in Chicago on March 31, 1917.

This is probably the greatest patriotic demonstration held in Chicago during the last fifty years. Valor receives a deserved tribute

[7] *Chicago Tribune*, April 1, 1917.

in having the veterans of the Civil and Spanish-American wars occupying the post of honor on this historic occasion. Although this wonderful assemblage may have a military aspect, its purpose is not to arouse a spirit of war, but to emphasize the imperative need of immediate and complete national preparedness.

There can be no doubt that the American people favor peace, but not peace at any price. For nearly three years we have witnessed the horrors of modern warfare. We cannot be unmindful of its terrible consequences. The sword should be the last resort, but rather the sword than dishonor. This is a time for prompt action, tempered by moderation and wisdom.

I believe the American nation is prepared to accept any eventuality in a manner worthy of its noblest traditions. The American public may differ as to whether the incoming Congress should declare for armed neutrality or a state of war. However we may differ as to procedure, I confidently believe the American people are united upon the paramount necessity of maintaining our country's honor, and defending, if need be, our country's flag.

In this crisis we should not forget that our foreign-born citizens have voluntarily adopted this country and assumed all of the obligations of citizenship for themselves and for their children. They cherish these United States as the land of opportunity and the foremost champion of civil and religious liberty. Fear not for the loyalty of America's adopted sons and daughters. In every battle for American independence and American honor the alien has heroically shown his love and devotion for his adopted country. From the very beginning of our country's history the foreign born have been an essential part of our national life and our national being. We are a composite people. In this supreme hour we must be a united people. When the final word is spoken, we will obey the call of our President and of our Congress. We will stand by—for we are one people. At this moment, whether we believe peace or war more desirable, we must prepare for an adequate national defense.

The necessary outlay attending even a brief war would probably excel the sum essential for such preparation as may even yet insure peace. It is admitted by experts that our navy and our army are undermanned. The last Congress failed to pass necessary appropriations for our national defense in this hour of our country's need.

No true American citizen can view such a situation with complacency. Today this great city of the middle west is ablaze with patriotism. There is no mistaking the temper of our people. I interpret their attitude as a demand that our representatives in Congress respond to the widespread desire for adequate preparedness, let the cost be what it may.

Our navy, as our first line of defense, should speedily become, in the words of our President, "incomparably the best in the world." We should have a trained citizen reserve force from which an efficient army can be quickly recruited.

Congress, in my opinion, should not longer defer enacting a law for universal compulsory military training for our young men. This is no time for slackers! The national guard should not continue to be the "goat." Washington found compulsory military service necessary to win the war for American independence. Notwithstanding the gallant response of the repeated calls for volunteers during the Civil War, Lincoln had to resort to conscription to insure victory.

Universal military training will inculcate a spirit of obedience and of service. There is no danger, in my opinion, that we will thus become a military nation. Such a possibility is opposed to the genius of our people.

Verging towards war, as we have been for many months, let us show that the spirit of valor and sacrifice of '76 and '61 still lives.

Let us prepare. May an all-wise God guide our councils aright. Let us in every crisis prove ourselves to be worthy of the priceless heritage of liberty, ready to pay the supreme sacrifice, if necessary, for its preservation.

AN ADDRESS BY GOVERNOR FRANK O. LOWDEN[8]

Delivered at a patriotic rally held in Chicago on March 31, 1917.

It is not a question of whether we prefer war or peace. If it were, this vast audience would acclaim peace. It has always been the policy of the American people to cultivate friendly relations with

[8] From a manuscript copy in the possession of Governor Lowden.

all the world. It is our true policy—it ought always to be our policy—to be just and honorable in our international relations and to make any concessions consistent with our vital interests in order to avoid war. But when war comes in spite of all our strivings for peace, the entire strength of the nation should be marshalled back of it. There is no middle ground. It is peace altogether or war altogether. You cannot have both at the same time. If it proves to be war, our main object ought to be to so mobilize our forces back of it as to accomplish most speedily and most certainly peace again. I share with the pacifist the horror [of] war, because my mind cannot appreciate fully its ugliness and woe; but I believe, if war is to come, that we should throw all of our resources of men and material into the scale in which the future destinies of America rest.

The strong man avoids, if possible, conflict with his fellow man. He shrinks from giving cause for offense. He sacrifices much to escape a clash. But if he fails to avoid the contest, he finds it the highest prudence to cast all prudence to the winds and to devote his entire strength to the cause. So let us have peace, if we can; but if we still believe that our revolutionary fathers were fighting humanity's battles, if we still visit and garland on Memorial Day the graves of our patriotic dead — and sometimes I doubt it in the evidence I see about me, if we still cherish our land and our flag as the best land and the best flag beneath the shining sun, sustained by an unwavering faith in the righteousness of our cause, we shall meet like men the issues which confront us.

Do we still believe in a government of the people, for the people and by the people? Do we wish still to maintain a democratic form of government? If so, if these great principles for which our fathers fought and died are still worth our while, no man within our borders, either rich or poor, of high or low degree, should be exempt from service at this crucial time, but owes his ability to serve his country in time of need. The flag does not protect simply those who fight beneath it, it protects all alike, and all owe a common duty to keep that flag.

It has been questioned by some of our friends that universal military training and service when need be might result in militarism. Your chairman has refuted, very clearly, that sophistry—I cannot hear that charge made in the presence of these veterans of the Civil War I see before me and around me without resenting it. If there ever in the history of any nation was a time when militarism would be a crime, if it ever is a crime, it is here. At the close of our Civil War you recall the grand review down Pennsylvania Avenue in Washington—I doubt not that some of you, my friends, participated in that—one day almost a million men, an unrivaled army of trained veterans, an army before which the eagles of Caesar and Napoleon mingling would have gone down in utter defeat; and the next day that army melted into the pursuits of peace and became the Grand Army of the Republic, as proficient in peace as it was in the days of war. I am opposed to militarism in the European sense of the word, but I want to tell you, my friends, that the only alternative to actual and universal military service is a professional army, and I call your attention to the fact that more republics have lost their liberty through a professional soldiery than from all other causes combined. I know of no one instance in all the history of the centuries in which a people has lost its liberties through a citizen soldiery passing automatically back and forth between the pursuits of peace and the army's ranks; I know of no one that has ever lost its liberty through an army based on universal military service.

We know that the greatest national tragedies have come from the decline of the military spirit. Our writers are fond of going back to China. Why go so far? The most conspicuous example I know of is the example of the Netherlands. In the seventeenth century, not long ago as great epochs in history are measured, the Netherlands were the richest country in Europe; they were the bankers of Europe; their argosies sailed every sea. But they became so immersed in their vast wealth and so soft in fiber that they could not bear the idea of bearing arms, and so they employed a professional army. Not long afterwards, the more virile nations of Europe passed them in the race for supremacy, and they became a province of France. About a hundred years ago they shook off their slothfulness and they began to build again. Profiting this time by the costly mistake of the centuries which had gone before, they provided for an army to be raised from all the people; and that snug little kingdom by the sea to this hour has maintained its neutrality in this world-wide war, which has been raging all about it.

We cannot read the history of the Dutch republic without think-ing upon every page of the analogy between that country and this. Let us also profit as the Hollanders of later generations did, by their earlier experience, and come to the heritage of the fathers, the robust thing, universal military training.

It may be said, it often is said, that we dare not make the experi-ment because of the large number of foreign-born citizens in our midst. I do not agree that this is a reason. I was in Chicago last on Washington's birthday, and one of the commanding officers of a regiment of the Illinois National Guard told me that upon their re-turn from Texas many American men and officers sought to get out of the service, but not one foreign-born or foreign descendent soldier, though that number included many German citizens. I would not have faith in the future of my country if I did not feel our citizens of foreign birth would be just as loyal to the flag as any native-born citizens. When it comes to that, we are all of foreign birth or for-eign descent. I wonder if there are any Indians in the audience— they are the only true Americans. Those veterans of ours have passed on the proposition that America can take the sons of every other coun-try on earth and make them into American citizens. They and their forbears came to America largely because they preferred our institu-tions to their own. They believe in the principle of self-government. When the bugle calls patriotic Americans to the colors, I expect to find them standing in the front rank as staunch and loyal as any men we have—those who were born in the Central Empires, and those whose forebears came from the Central Empires. It is not wise to challenge the patriotism before the time to prove any of our citizen-ship. I think I know something of the German character. During a part of my boyhood I lived in a German settlement. My comrades were German born, of my own age, and if it should be my occasion to go to France, I don't ask for any better comrades than those German boys of my early experiences.

There are several other speakers, and I must hurry along very fast. There are one or two other things I want to call your attention to. And one of them is, suppose we are all wrong, suppose in the moment, from some hidden and mysterious source, universal peace should come, what then? We would have had a burst of patriotism by use of military service that would be worth infinitely more than all it would cost.

It is time that something happened in this country to accentuate the sense of duty of the average citizen to his country. We have become absolutely indifferent to the obligations of citizenship. Danger manfully faced is half overcome. We treat our country as if it were some great horn of plenty, scattering among the people from a royal hand her precious gifts, and exacting nothing, not even an ordinary obedience, in return. Think of the importance of this idea, if every man were made to feel that his citizenship was so precious that he himself would pay some price for it. [To unite all] these different classes of citizens, to escape class distinctions along undesirable lines, there is no remedy before you so appropriate as universal military training. We never appreciate the dearest things unless they are hardly won, and I wonder if we will ever fully realize all the value of our citizenship until we all render some reasonable proper service to the state.

There is one case of preparedness which I think we out in this country ought to dwell upon. If this war has proven anything, it has proven that to mobilize your forces of food products is necessary, if you are going to win a great war. We hear on every hand of the necessity of mobilizing our industries, but we hear nothing of mobilizing the forces of our food production. This great war in Europe will probably go far; as men can see now, it will be determined by food conditions in the end, and nothing else. No one over there on either side feels the lack of munitions or a lack of men, but they all fear the specter of hunger stalking through every land.

The Mississippi Valley, where we are assembled tonight in this great city, is the granary of the country, and it seems to me that it is entirely proper that we not wait till it is too late, but that we now begin to plan to mobilize our forces of food production. Already we hear the suggestion of restricting food rations. That will not be necessary if we shall begin now to mobilize our future food supplies. It is safe to say that our food supplies could be doubled. The whole modern tendency has been to draw labor from the farm. Means must be promptly devised to insure the largest possible production of food supplies. It must be recognized that the boy or man who puts all his energies to the increased supply of food is as truly a soldier as he who, in uniform, fights in the ranks. We must, if need be, draw upon the youth of the cities and country who are under military age to keep the farms running to their fullest capacity.

One more suggestion, and then I will be through. I do not believe in extravagant statements, I do not believe in alarming statements, but as I said a moment ago, I do believe that when you manfully face a danger, that danger is half vanquished. I do believe with all my heart that we, particularly of this section of the country, do not appreciate the dangers with which we are confronted. The whole world is literally rotting on its base—disaster is in the air. The ability of nations to endure is being challenged on every hand, and if there were no cloud as large as a man's hand in the sky, I believe that prudence and patriotism would prepare against these unseen dangers which all men instinctively feel are all around us.

In such a cataclysm as that which grips the world, only the competent and strong may hope to endure. At such a time does patriotism nicely measure the degree of danger to our beloved land or coldly calculate its nearness in point of time? It is all or nothing; we cannot be half-hearted. We cannot go half way. We either shall vindicate our mission and show to all the world that a great people can govern themselves, or we shall become but an episode in the history of the world. The decision is upon us, every one. God grant that we may so decide that when, next May, we bear blossoms to our soldiers' graves, we may go without shame in our hearts. I thank you.

RESOLUTIONS ADOPTED AT PATRIOTIC RALLY, CHICAGO, MARCH 31, 1917[9]

WHEREAS, The nation is on the verge of war; and, whereas, American ships have been sunk on the high seas by the submarines of the imperial German government with the loss of American lives in

---

[9] *Chicago Tribune*, April 1, 1917. The resolutions were drafted by a committee of which Harry Pratt Judson, president of the University of Chicago, was chairman.

violation of specific and solemn treaty obligations and in violation of international law; therefore, we, citizens of Chicago, in mass meeting assembled, "with malice toward none, with charity for all, but with firmness in the right," do hereby resolve:

1. That as loyal Americans, without regard to political party lines, we approve the action of the President of the United States in severing diplomatic relations with the German Empire.

2. That we pledge our hearty support to the government in every act to protect the safety of our citizens, the honor of our nation, and the cause of freedom and democracy throughout the world.

3. That we urge Congress immediately to enact a law providing for universal obligatory military training and service, as the only efficient, just and democratic method of national defense.

4. That we urge Congress without delay to equip our existing troops and all troops to be raised with the most modern appliances of war, so that the equipment and effectiveness of our army and navy shall be second to none.

5. That if war occurs, we urge the government of the United States to conduct it with all the power of the nation.

6. That a committee, of which the presiding officer of this meeting shall be a member, be appointed by the chair to place these resolutions before the President of the United States and the proper committees of Congress and to urge the adoption of the policies declared therein.

MILITARY PREPAREDNESS

Senate Joint Resolution Number 16, Fiftieth General Assembly of the State of Illinois.

WHEREAS: It is essential that the United States of America, as one of the foremost nations of the world, should be prepared at all times to defend itself against attacks by hostile forces, to protect its citizens in the exercise of their just rights and privileges, and to prevent unwarranted curtailment or restriction of such rights and privileges; and

WHEREAS: The organization, in an emergency, of an army of untrained civilians to repel an invasion or to vindicate the nation's just rights or those of its citizens, works a great and severe hardship on such civilians in that they, without sufficient military training, may be called upon to meet a hostile army, highly trained and efficient in the art of making war; and

WHEREAS: A system of universal military training will not only prepare the citizens of this nation for efficient service in the event of war, but when properly administered, will promote the beneficial physical development of those subject to such training and will instill in the citizens of our country a sense of democracy, patriotism, discipline and responsibility to duty; and,

WHEREAS: The want or lack of such a system of universal military training may result in disaster to our country; now, therefore,

Be it resolved: by the Senate of the State of Illinois, the House of Representatives concurring therein, That the General Assembly of the State of Illinois, is in accord with and favors the principle of universal military training and requests our Senators and Representatives in Congress to employ every effort to secure the enactment by Congress of a law establishing in the United States of America a system of universal and compulsory military training, and that copies of this resolution be transmitted to our Senators and Representatives in Congress by the Secretary of State under seal of the State.

Adopted by the Senate March 27, 1917,

Concurred in by the House of Representatives April 5, 1917.

LABOR'S ENDORSEMENT OF THE UNITED STATES' PARTICIPATION IN THE WAR[10]

A declaration adopted by members of the Executive Council, American Federation of Labor, representatives of seventy-nine affiliated national and international unions and of five unaffiliated unions at a meeting called by Samuel Gompers, president of the American Federation of Labor and chairman of the Committee on Labor, Council of National Defense, in Washington, March 12, 1917; adopted by the Executive Board of the Illinois State Federation of Labor and the Joint Labor Legislative Board of Illinois on April 12, 1917.

We speak for millions of Americans. We are not a sect. We are not a party. We represent the organizations held together by the pressure of our common needs. We represent the part of the

[10] *Weekly News Letter* (Illinois State Federation of Labor), April 14, 1917.

nation closest to the fundamentals of life. Those we represent wield
the nation's tools and grapple with the forces that are brought under
control in our material civilization. The power and use of industrial tools is greater than the tools of war and will in time supersede
agencies of destruction.

A world war is on. The time has not yet come when war has
been abolished.

Whether we approve it or not, we must recognize that war is a
situation with which we must reckon. The present European war,
involving as it does the majority of civilized nations and affecting the
industry and commerce of the whole world, threatens at any moment
to draw all countries, including our own, into the conflict. Our
immediate problem, then, is to bring to bear upon war conditions instructive forethought, vision, principles of human welfare and conservation that should direct our course in every eventuality of life.
The way to avert war is to establish constructive agencies for justice
in times of peace and thus control for peace situations and forces that
might otherwise result in war.

The methods of modern warfare, its new tactics, its vast organization, both military and industrial, present problems vastly different from those of previous wars. But the nation's problems afford
an opportunity for the establishment of new freedom and wider opportunities for all the people. Modern warfare includes contests
between workshops, factories, the land, financial and transportation
resources of the countries involved; and necessarily applies to the
relations between employers and employes, and as our own country
now faces an impending peril, it is fitting that the masses of the
people of the United States should take counsel and determine what
course they shall pursue should a crisis arise necessitating the protection of our republic and defense of the ideals for which it stands.

In the struggle between the forces of democracy and special
privilege, for just and historic reasons the masses of the people necessarily represent the ideals and the institutions of democracy. There
is in organized society one potential organization whose purpose is to
further these ideals and institutions—the organized labor movement.

In no previous war has the organized labor movement taken a
directing part.

Labor has now reached an understanding of its right, of its power and resources, of its value and contributions to society, and must make definite constructive proposals.

It is timely that we frankly present experiences and conditions which in former times have prevented nations from benefiting by the voluntary, whole-hearted coöperation of wage-earners in war time, and then make suggestions how these hindrances to our national strength and vigor can be removed.

War has never put a stop to the necessity for struggle to establish and maintain industrial rights. Wage-earners in war times must, as has been said, keep one eye on the exploiters at home and the other upon the enemy threatening the national government. Such exploitation made it impossible for a warring nation to mobilize effectively its full strength for outward defense.

We maintain that it is the fundamental step in preparedness for the nation to set its own house in order and to establish at home justice in relations between men. Previous wars, for whatever purpose waged, developed new opportunities for exploiting wage-earners. Not only was there failure to recognize the necessity for protecting rights of workers that they might give that whole-hearted service to the country that can come only when every citizen enjoys rights, freedom and opportunity, but under guise of national necessity, Labor was stripped of its means of defense against enemies at home and was robbed of advantages, the protections, the guarantees of justice that had been achieved after ages of struggle. For these reasons workers have felt that no matter what the result of war, as wage-earners they generally lost.

In previous times Labor had no representatives in the councils authorized to deal with the conduct of war. The rights, interests and welfare of workers were autocratically sacrificed for the slogan of "national safety."

The European war has demonstrated the dependence of the governments upon the coöperation of the masses of the people. Since the masses perform indispensable service, it follows that they should have a voice in determining the conditions upon which they give service.

The workers of America make known their beliefs, their demands and their purposes through a voluntary agency which they have established—the organized labor movement. This agency is not only the representative of those who directly constitute it, but it is the representative of all those persons who have common problems and purposes, but who have not yet organized for their achievement.

Whether in peace or in war the organized labor movement seeks to make all else subordinate to human welfare and human opportunity. The labor movement stands as the defender of this principle and undertakes to protect the wealth-producers against the exorbitant greed of special interests, against profiteering, against exploitation, against the detestable methods of irresponsible greed, against the inhumanity and crime of heartless corporations and employers.

Labor demands the right in war times to be the recognized defender of wage-earners against the same forces which in former wars have made national necessity an excuse for more ruthless methods.

As the representatives of the wage-earners we assert that conditions of work and pay in government employment and in all occupations should conform to principles of human welfare and justice.

A nation can not make an effective defense against an outside danger if groups of citizens are asked to take part in a war though smarting with a sense of keen injustice inflicted by the government they are expected to and will defend.

The cornerstone of national defense is justice in fundamental relations of life—economic justice.

The one agency which accomplishes this for the workers is the organized labor movement. The greatest step that can be made for national defense is not to bind and throttle the organized labor movement but to afford its greatest scope and opportunity for voluntary effective coöperation in spirit and in action.

During the long period in which it has been establishing itself, the labor movement has become a dynamic force in organizing the human side of industry and commerce. It is a great social factor which must be recognized in all plans which affect wage-earners.

Whether planning for peace or war, the government must recognize the organized labor movement as the agency through which it must coöperate with wage-earners.

Industrial justice is the right of those living within our country. With this right there is associated obligation. In war time obligation takes the form of service in defense of the Republic against enemies.

We recognize that this service may be either military or industrial, both equally essential for national defense. We hold this to be incontrovertible, that the government which demands that men and women give their labor power, their bodies or their lives to its service should also demand the service, in the interest of these human beings, of all wealth and the products of human toil—property.

We hold that if workers may be asked in time of national peril or emergency to give more exhausting service than the principles of human welfare warrant, that service should be asked only when accompanied by increased guarantees and safeguards, and when the profits which the employer shall secure from the industry in which they are engaged have been limited to fixed percentages.

We declare that such determination of profits should be based on costs of processes actually needed for product.

Workers have no delusions regarding the policy which property owners and exploiting employers pursue in peace or in war, and they also recognize that wrapped up with the safety of this republic are ideals of democracy, a heritage which the masses of the people received from our forefathers, who fought that liberty might live in this country—a heritage that is to be maintained and handed down to each generation with undiminished power and usefulness.

The labor movement recognizes the value of freedom and it knows that freedom and rights can be maintained only by those willing to assert their claims and to defend their rights. The American labor movement has always opposed unnecessary conflicts and all wars for aggrandizement, exploitation and enslavement, and yet it has done its part in the world's revolutions, in the struggles to establish greater freedom, democratic institutions and ideals of human justice.

Our labor movement distrusts and protests against militarism, because it knows that militarism represents privilege and is the tool of special interests, exploiters and despots. But while it opposes militarism, it holds that it is the duty of a nation to defend itself against injustice and invasion.

The menace of militarism arises through isolating the defensive functions of the state from civic activities and from creating military agencies out of touch with masses of the people. Isolation is subversive to democracy—it harbors and nurtures the germs of arbitrary power.

The labor movement demand[s] that a clear differentiation be made against military service for the nation and police duty, and that military service should be carefully distinguished from service in industrial disputes.

We hold that industrial service shall be deemed equally meritorious as military service. Organization for industrial and commercial service is upon a different basis from military service—the civic ideals still dominate. This should be recognized in mobilizing for this purpose. The same voluntary institutions that organized industrial, commercial and transportation workers in times of peace will best take care of the same problems in time of war.

It is fundamental, therefore, that the government coöperate with the American organized labor movement for this purpose. Service in government factories and private establishments, in transportation agencies, all should conform to trade union standards.

The guarantees of human conservation should be recognized in war as well as in peace. Wherever changes in the organization of industry are necessary upon a war basis, they should be made in accord with plans agreed upon by representatives of the government and those engaged and employed in the industry. We recognize that in war, in certain employments requiring high skill, it is necessary to retain in industrial service the workers specially fitted therefor. In any eventuality when women may be employed, we insist that equal pay for equal work shall prevail without regard to sex.

Finally, in order to safeguard all the interests of the wageearners, organized labor should have representation on all agencies determining and administering policies for national defense. It is particularly important that organized labor should have representatives on all boards authorized to control publicity during war times. The workers have suffered much injustice in war times by limitations upon their right to speak freely and to secure publicity for their just grievances.

Organized labor has earned the right to make these demands.

It is the agency that, in all countries, stands for human rights and is the defender of the welfare and interests of the masses of the people. It is an agency that has international recognition which is not seeking to rob, exploit or corrupt foreign governments but instead seeks to maintain human rights and interests the world over, nor does it have to dispel suspicion nor prove its motives either at home or abroad.

The present war discloses the struggle between the institutions of democracy and those of autocracy. As a nation we should profit from the experiences of other nations. Democracy can not be established by patches upon an autocratic system. The foundations of civilized intercourse between individuals must be organized upon principles of democracy and scientific principles of human welfare. Then a national structure can be perfected in harmony with humanitarian idealism—a structure that will stand the tests of the necessities of peace or war.

We, the officers of the National and International Trade Unions of America, in national conference assembled in the capital of our nation, hereby pledge ourselves in peace or in war, in stress or in storm, to stand unreservedly by the standards of liberty and the safety and preservation of the institutions and ideals of our republic.

In this solemn hour of our nation's life, it is our earnest hope that our republic may be safeguarded in its unswerving desire for peace; that our people may be spared the horrors and the burdens of war; that they may have the opportunity to cultivate and develop the arts of peace, human brotherhood and a higher civilization.

But, despite all our endeavors and hopes, should our country be drawn into the maelstrom of the European conflict, we, with these ideals of liberty and justice herein declared, as the indispensable basis for national policies, offer our services to our country in every field of activity to defend, safeguard and preserve the Republic of the United States of America against its enemies, whomsoever they may be, and we call upon our fellow workers and fellow citizens in the holy name of Labor, Justice, Freedom and Humanity, to devotedly and patriotically give like service.

RESOLUTIONS ADOPTED BY THE SPRINGFIELD FEDERATION OF LABOR, APRIL 13, 1917[11]

WHEREAS, Congress has declared war against Germany and calls upon all patriotic citizens of the United States to support their country; and

WHEREAS, It behooves all loyal citizens to show their colors at this time, that they are for America first; therefore be it

Resolved, That the Springfield Federation of Labor endorse the action of executive council of the A. F. of L. to stand by President Wilson and his protective policy and offer our services to our country's cause.

RESOLUTIONS ADOPTED BY ILLINOIS STATE BAR ASSOCIATION, DANVILLE, JUNE 1, 1917[12]

WHEREAS, It has been reported that a former senator of the United States has declared that "we dishonored ourselves by declaring war without just and reasonable cause"; and

WHEREAS, The Congress of the United States has heretofore, after the President of our country had used every effort consistent with national honor to avert it, declared that a state of war exists; such declaration having been made only after the commission of a long list of insufferable outrages against our sovereignty, as reviewed by the President's message to Congress; and

WHEREAS, The attitude of the President and the action of Congress represent the deliberate judgment and the patriotic desire of the whole American people; and

WHEREAS, At a time when our people are making every sacrifice necessary for the maintenance of the principles of democracy for which our country stands, it is our duty to discountenance and condemn in unmistakable terms any statement or action not inspired by an unalloyed devotion to our country; therefore be it

Resolved by the Illinois State Bar Association in forty-first annual meeting assembled:

That we do hereby condemn such language and action as unpatriotic, disloyal, and treasonable;

[11] *Illinois State Journal,* April 14, 1917.
[12] *Chicago Tribune,* June 3, 1917.

That the message of the President, declaring that the "world must be made safe for democracy," and the action of Congress represented the highest expression of American ideals and meet with our earnest approval; and, be it further

Resolved, That we do pledge to the President our loyal support in the prosecution of the war and call upon all loyal citizens of the country to do likewise; and, be it further

Resolved, That a copy of this resolution be sent to the President.

AN ADDRESS BY THEODORE ROOSEVELT[13]

Delivered at a patriotic mass meeting in the Stockyards Auditorium, Chicago, April 28, 1917.

I come here tonight to appeal to the people of the great west, the people of the Mississippi Valley, the people who are the spiritual heirs of the men who stood behind Lincoln and Grant. You men and women who live beside the Great Lakes and on the lands drained by the Ohio, the Mississippi and the Missouri have always represented what is most intensely American in our national life. When once waked up to actual conditions, you have always stood with unfaltering courage and iron endurance for the national honor and the national interest.

I appeal to the sons and daughters of the men and women of the Civil War, to the grandsons and granddaughters of the pioneers; I appeal to the women as much as to the men, for our nation has risen level to every great crisis only because in every such crisis the courage of its women flamed as high as the courage of the men. I appeal to you to take the lead in making good the President's message of the second of this month, in which he set forth the reasons why it was our unescapable duty to make war upon Germany. It rests with us—with the American people—to make that message one of the great state documents of our history. Let us accept the lessons it teaches. Let us grasp what it says as to the frightful wrongs Germany has committed upon us and upon the weaker nations of mankind, and the damage she has wrought to the whole fabric of civilization and of international good faith and morality. Then let

[13] *Chicago Tribune,* April 29, 1917.

us steel our hearts and gird our loins to show that we are fit to
stand among the free people whose freedom is buttressed by their
self-reliant strength. Let us show by our deeds that we are fit to be
the heirs of the men who founded the republic, and of the men who
saved the republic, of the Continentals who followed Washington,
and of the men who wore the blue under Grant and the gray under
Lee.

But, mind you, the message, the speech, will amount to nothing
unless we make it good, and it can be made good only by the high
valor of our fighting men and by the resourceful and laborious
energy of the men and women who, with deeds, not merely words,
back up the fighting men.

We read the declaration of independence every Fourth of July
because, and only because, the soldiers of Washington made that
message good by their blood during the weary years of war that
followed. If, after writing the declaration of independence, the men
of '76 had failed with their bodies to make it good, it would be read
now only with contempt and derision.

Our children still learn how Patrick Henry spoke for the heart
of the American people when he said, "Give me liberty or give me
death," but this generation is thrilled by his words only because the
Americans of those days showed in very fact that they were ready to
accept death rather than lose their liberty.

In Lincoln's deathless Gettysburg speech and second inaugural
he solemnly pledged the honor of the American people to the hard
and perilous task of preserving the union and freeing the slaves. The
pledge was kept. The American people fought to a finish the war
which saved the union and freed the slave. If Lincoln and the men
and women behind him had wavered, if they had grown faint-hearted
and had shrunk from the fight, or had merely paid others to fight
for them, they would have earned for themselves and for us the scorn
of the nations of mankind.

The words of Lincoln will live forever only because they
were made good by the deeds of the fighting men.

So it is now. We can make the President's message of April
2 stand among the great state papers in our history; but we can do so

only if we make the message good; and we can make it good only if we fight with all our strength now, at once, if at the earliest possible moment we put the flag on the firing line and keep it there, over a constantly growing army, until the war closes by a peace which brings victory to the great cause of democracy and civilization, the great cause of justice and fair play among the peoples of the world.

We Americans are at war. Now let us fight. Let us make it a real war, not a dollar war. Let us show that we have the manhood to pay with our own bodies, and not merely to hire other men to pay with their bodies. Let us fight at once. Let us put the flag at the front now, at the earliest moment, and not merely announce that we are going to fight a year or two hence.

I most earnestly and heartily stand by the proposal of the President to raise an army on the principle of universal obligatory military training and military service, demanded as a right, not as a favor, from all the young men of the country capable of bearing arms. This is the principle I have long advocated with all fervor of conviction. It is the only really democratic principle on which permanently to shape the military policy of this country. To have it adopted as the permanent principle of our national military policy will be of incalculable service to our national peace and welfare. Moreover, if the war lasts, as well it may, for one or two or three years, the army, to see it through, must be raised in this fashion. It is vitally essential, both from the standpoint of fighting this war through to a successful conclusion, if it should last a long time, and from the standpoint of our permanent national safety and democratic welfare, that we should immediately inaugurate this principle and set about raising a great army in accordance therewith. Such an army will naturally need a long time to train, and at the earliest moment we should begin to devote our strength and energy to calling it into being and training it. This should be the task which we treat as of prime importance.

But most emphatically we should not rest content with this We should not rest content with merely preparing an army to act a year or eighteen months or two years hence. Let us put the flag on the firing line at the earliest possible moment, this summer, wherever our services are most needed—in France or Flanders or the Balkan peninsula.

It need only be a small army at first. But even a division would be better than nothing. Then we can constantly keep that division filled, and other divisions from time to time added to it, until a year hence, if the war continues, we have a really formidable fighting force at the front, a fighting force which will be steadily increased month by month, year by year, until the triumph comes. To do this it is necessary that we should appeal for volunteers, not in any way as substitute for, but as a supplement to the administration's plan for raising an army in accordance with the principle of obligatory universal service.

If the system of universal obligatory training and service had already been in existence here for a number of years, and if in other ways we had been prepared in advance, we could by this time have had an expeditionary force of 1,000,000 men under way for the front, ready to strike the finishing blow. But the system does not yet exist, and, necessarily, all kinds of preliminaries will have to be gone through before it can now be called into being and an effective army of large size raised under it. Therefore, to wait for it before really entering into the war means an indefinite delay, a delay that might bring us to the end, not merely of the campaign this year, but of the campaign next year before we can strike hard and effectively.

I wish to see this system of obligatory service used in order to make all men serve who ought to serve. It would be a capital mistake to use it in such a fashion as merely to prevent men rendering service when they wish to render it and can render it, and ought to render it.

Do not let anyone volunteer to stay at home. But do not hinder men, who, under conscription, would be entitled to stay at home, from volunteering to go to the front if they can render good service.

Under the bill proposed to Congress by the War Department, many millions of excellent fighting men would be exempt from service, while a long time would elapse before the others are sent to the front. Under these conditions we ought to use the volunteer system to fill the gap; it opens to us at once a great possibility; let it be used, and used exclusively, to give to those who would otherwise be exempt an opportunity to go to the front without claiming exemption.

Let me illustrate my meaning by a homely comparison. Every village ought to have a fire company. But if it commits the error of waiting until a fire starts before organizing the fire company, it will merely aggravate the situation by committing the further error of refusing to put out the fire until after the fire company is organized. The only wise thing to do is to put out the fire with the means that are handy, and then immediately organize the permanent fire company.

I most earnestly hope that we shall avoid any policy of delay. If we are true to our own souls, we shall show that, like our forefathers, we are willing to pay for our principles with our bodies and not merely with our dollars.

Congress has passed, without a dissenting vote, a bill to appropriate $7,000,000,000 as representing part of our contribution to the great war. This is fine, but only on condition that we also put our men into the fighting line. Half of this great sum is to go to the Allies; that is, it is to be spent by them in getting their men up against the German and Austrian and Turkish shells and bullets.

Now, we Americans have always prided ourselves on being able to do our own fighting. It is right to help others to fight in the common cause for which we are engaged. But it is even more necessary that we should fight ourselves.

We fight for our own rights. We fight for the right of mankind. This great struggle is fundamentally a struggle for the fundamentals of civilization and democracy. The future of the free institutions of the world is at stake. The free people who govern themselves are lined up against the governments which deny freedom to their people.

Our cause is the cause of humanity. But we also have bitter wrongs of our own which it is our duty to redress. Our women and children and unarmed men, going about their peaceful business, have been murdered on the high seas, not once, but again and again and again. With brutal insolence, after having for well nigh two years persevered in this policy, Germany has announced that she will continue it, at our expense and at the expense of other neutrals, more ruthlessly than ever.

The injury thus done to us as a nation is as great as the injury done to a man if a ruffian slaps his wife's face. In such case, if the man is a man, he does not wait and hire somebody else to fight for him; and it would be an evil thing, a lasting calamity to this country, if the war ended and found us merely preparing an army in safety at home, without having sent a man to the firing line; merely having paid some billions of dollars to other people so that with the bodies of their sons and brothers they might keep us in safety.

I ask that we send a fighting force over to the fighting line at the earliest possible moment, and I ask it in the name of our children and our children's children, so that they may hold their heads high over the memory of what this nation did in the world's great crisis.

I ask that we send a fighting force over to the fighting line at the material self-interest. I ask it for the sake of our self-respect, our self-esteem. Our children will have to read the history of what we have done during this war. Let us make the chapter that yet remains to be written one that our children shall read with pride; and they will read it only with a feeling of self-abasement unless they read that in the times that tried men's souls we have shown valor and endurance and proud indifference to life when the honor of the flag and the welfare of mankind were at stake.

Put the flag on the firing line, and valiant men behind it; and keep it there, sending over a constantly growing stream of valiant men to aid those who have first gone.

In the Civil War there were many men who went to the front to pay with their bodies for the high faith of their souls. There were some men who hired others to go as substitutes to the front. Which ones among these men are the ones to whom we look back with pride—those who faced the bullets or those who paid with dollars to buy the willingness and ability of other men to face them? There is no need to answer.

In exactly the same way there should be no need to answer now the question as to whether we are merely to spend billions of dollars to help others fight or to stand in the fighting line ourselves.

By all means spend the money. A prime essential is to furnish the Allies all the cargo ships they need for food and all the craft they need to help hunt down the submarines. By all means aid them with food and ships and money, and speedily; but do not stop there.

Show that we can fight as well as furnish dollars and vegetables to fighting men. At the earliest possible moment send an expeditionary force abroad, show our German foes and our allied friends that we are in this war in deadly earnest, that we have put the flag on the firing line and that we shall steadily increase the force behind that flag to any limit necessary in order to bring the peace of victory in this great contest for democracy, for civilization, and for the rights of free peoples.

Now that we are at war, let us make it a real war, not a make-believe war, not a war of limited liability. Germany has been in a state of war with us for two years, but so far we have only been at the receiving end of the game.

Some centuries ago the Black Earl Douglas led a Scotch king and a Scotch army against the English; and when the battle place was reached, the grim old fighter turned to the young king and said, "I have got you up to the ring, and now you must hop."

Let us apply this to ourselves! We have walked into the ring, and now we must fight. Fighting does not mean merely parrying. It means hard, aggressive hitting. No fight ever was won yet except by hitting. A good rule to remember is never to hit if it is possible to avoid it, but above all things never to hit soft. We have gone into the fight; we have determined to hit, and we must not hit soft.

Three months have passed since we broke off diplomatic relations with Germany. Read the history of the opening months of the war and you will get a vivid idea of what the German army would have done to us during those three months if we had had only our own unprepared strength to defend us. We owe our safety at this moment to the British fleet and the French and British armies. I, for one, am not content to rest under that kind of obligation, and I do not believe that my fellow countrymen are content to rest under it. I wish to see us owe our safety to our own strength and our own courage and to the respect we inspire in our foe. We shall inspire no respect if we merely try to parry that foe's blows and not to return them. The only way in which we can return them is by immediately sending an expeditionary force to fight in Europe, a force small at first, but steadily increased until it becomes so formidable that it can end the war. It would be a scandal and a shame if the war ended now with our part in it limited to having furnished dollars behind the shield of other men's bodies. We are in the war. Let us fight it through ourselves, with our own strength and courage, to triumphant conclusion.

So I ask that we at once send a force over to the fighting line primarily for our own sakes. Even if the Allies asked us merely to furnish them with money and foodstuffs, such a request would imply so galling a contempt for our manhood that I would with equal scorn refuse it; I would answer that in war as in peace I put the man above the dollar, and would not rest content to see America make this on her own part merely a dollar war, instead of a man's war.

But I speak of my personal knowledge when I say that of course the Allies eagerly desire to see us send a fighting force to the front at the earliest moment, and steadily increase its size. It would be absurd for us to expect them as suppliants to ask us to send over men; they would not assume such an attitude, and it would be unworthy of us to ask them such a question. I have already seen in the public press the statement from the French minister of war that he confidently expects us to send troops to the battle line. In a letter just received from James Bryce he urges me to support as "specially useful" two steps, of which the first one is "the dispatch of an American force to the theater of war. The moral effect of the appearance in the war line of an American force would be immense." From France, England, and Canada, from the highest sources, I have been told the same thing.

Our regular army is so small that such a force, if sent abroad at the earliest moment, ought to consist largely of volunteers. Of course, no incompetent men should be given commissions; but to refuse competent men commissions for fear of lack of strength of mind to refuse the incompetent is at the outset to confess incompetency to handle armies.

As for the persons who say that such a force of picked volunteers

(5)

could not be speedily trained, they show utter ignorance of what Canada and Australia have done. I have before me [a] statement made on behalf of one of the highest military authorities of Canada, as follows: "I can personally say that with the use of the Canadian system of intensive military training your announced plan to have Americans at the front in four months would be entirely practical."

By all means let us set our house in order here at home. Let us obey the President's exhortation and put a stop to waste. Let us do as he outlines in furnishing money and ships and food to the Allies. Let us furnish the warcraft necessary to hunt down the submarines wherever the British admiralty deems that this service can best be rendered and in whatever manner it desires.

Let us, if necessary by governmental action, see that the fullest use is made of the soil and the largest possible production obtained therefrom. Let us see that skilled workers are employed wherever they can do most good, and all our industrial establishments and transportation lines used to the utmost.

Let us see that there is no improper or excessive profit making by those whose business activities are stimulated by the war.

Let us, even in war time, strive efficiently, by legislation and administration and through the activities of private associations and organizations, to secure a larger social and industrial justice for the men who actually toil, the workingmen on the soil and in industry, the wage workers and the farmers, so that we may show by our deeds that this is their country, the country of all of us, where the welfare of every honest and hard-working man is the prime object of government, where the flag means justice, and fair play, and reasonable equality of opportunity to all, and where, in consequence, we have a right to expect, and, if necessary, to exact, from all the fullest measure of loyal service to the flag.

Do all this; and yet remember that it is all of little avail unless we also show by the valor of our fighting men at the front that there is in us the great quality which makes us willing and eager to do and dare and die at need for the things we hold sacred.

I make my appeal to all Americans without distinction of creed or of national origin, of birthplace, or of the section in which they live. In time of war like this all party distinctions vanish, and I know only those who are for America and those who are against America.

I make my appeal to northerner and southerner, to easterner and westerner. I appeal equally to the Protestant and the Catholic, to the Gentile and the Jew, and to the men whose fealty to the great laws of righteousness is given outside the limits of any recognized creed.

I care not a rap whether the man was born here or abroad. I care not a rap whether his forefathers came from England, Ireland, Scotland, from Germany, France, or Scandinavia.

But I demand that this single-hearted loyalty be given to the one flag that floats over all of us, the flag which we are bound to reverence and hold dear to the exclusion of every other.

We are a new nation, by blood and culture akin to, but different from, every nation of Europe. We are in honor bound in every crisis to judge every other nation by its conduct in that crisis. We are bound to pay heed only to our own national honor and need and to the just interests of mankind as a whole—the interests of the men and women now existing and of the generations yet unborn. We are in honor bound to be swerved from our duty neither by improper friendship for nor unworthy antipathy toward any other nation.

I speak as a man who himself has German blood in his veins. The American of the future will have in his veins the blood of many different nationalities, and he will not be American at all unless he is loyal to the principle of the American of the past, who opposed any nationality, if that nationality was a foe to his country and to humanity.

The Americans who followed Washington in his first campaign fought against Frenchmen. The Americans who followed him at Trenton fought against Germans. The Americans who followed him at Princeton and Yorktown fought against Englishmen. His followers included men of English descent, like Lighthorse Harry Lee and Greene; of German descent, like Muhlenberg; of Irish descent, like Sullivan. But they were all Americans and nothing more! They treated one another each on his worth as a man without regard to that man's creed or blood. When they were pitted against an enemy they did not ask as to his national origin, but only as to whether he was an enemy of their common country and of that country's flag. Twice we have fought Great Britain; and in each case the immense majority of our citizens of British origin were undividedly loyal to the United States. And now, when we fight Germany, I know I utter the sentiments of the immense majority of my fellow citizens of German origin when I say that their undivided allegiance is given to the Stars and Stripes and to the nation for which the banner stands.

I appeal especially to the descendants of those heroes of liberty, the Germans of '48 who so valiantly stood against tyranny. If I am allowed to raise the division for which I have asked I most earnestly hope that it will have as large a proportion as possible of Americans who are in whole or, like myself, in part, of German blood. The other day I was with the head of the War College at Washington, General Kuhn. He is of pure German blood, his father and his mother being born in Germany. But he is an American, and nothing else! I would welcome the chance, if I am allowed to raise a division, to serve with that division under him at the front; and I would ask no favor of any kind save thus to serve with him and to be judged on my merits by him for my service.

In similar fashion I would gladly serve under General Barry, who is with you here in Chicago, and who is of Irish parentage; or under General Pershing, or, of course, with deep enthusiasm under my old friend and commander, General Leonard Wood, who like Pershing is of revolutionary stock; or under any other man of the same type.

Each of the men I have named has held my commission when I was president; and I would wish nothing more at the close of my active career than the chance to serve under one of them or under any other officer of their type. They differ in blood and in creed among themselves and from me. But they and I are Americans and nothing else. Our lives are actuated by the same principles of honor, and our undivided loyalty is given to the same flag.

This is the appeal I make especially to the men and women of the west. I do not merely ask you to go to the front, you men of the west; or to cheer your men when they go, you women. I also ask you to see that I am given the high privilege of making my words good by my deeds and going to the front with you.

I have asked leave to be allowed to raise a division to take to the front in the first expeditionary force, under the commander of that force; a division which, after two or three months' preliminary training here, can be taken for intensive training to France, and then put into the trenches at the earliest possible moment that the allied generals deem it fit to render service. I ask that I be allowed to join others who feel as I do in making good the President's message.

I ask that I and those dearest to me and closest to me by blood shall be given the chance to prove the truth of our endeavor and be sent at the earliest possible moment under the flag to the firing line.

I have led a regiment in battle and commanded a brigade on active service, and since then I have been the commander-in-chief of the army and navy of the United States. Let me raise a division to serve in an army corps under its chief, or to serve in command of a brigade under the division chief.

Let me be given the authority to help raise the division or the army corps and to serve under whoever is appointed over me, but let me be put in the position where I can say to the men I address that I do not merely ask them to go to the front, but to come with me to the front; that I am to be allowed the great privilege of sharing with them the hardship and the hazard.

Remember, friends, that what I am asking is not in any way a substitute for, but as a supplement to, the plan for a great army to be raised on the principle of universal obligatory military service, a plan which I favor with all my heart. I do not ask for men in the classes which would be taken under the administration's plan for any army raised under the obligatory system. I ask for men who would not otherwise be allowed to go.

The force I propose to raise would represent an absolute addition to the nation's military strength, an addition which could be used at once, which would serve to put the flag and keep the flag on the firing line during the time that the great army itself was being raised, and while our flag would otherwise not be on the firing line.

The favor I ask is the great favor of being allowed to render a service which I believe that my record entitles me to say that I am able to render.

I ask to be allowed effectively to do my part in showing that the

Americans of today are worthy of the great heritage bequeathed to them by their fathers who lived in the days of Lincoln, and their forefathers who lived in the days of Washington; that we are loyal to the spirit of the mighty men of the past; and that we, too, as freemen who prize beyond measure our freedom and who feel that the enjoyment of rights and the observance of duties go hand in hand, are eager, in our turn, to prove that those who are fit to live are not afraid to die.

AN ADDRESS BY SHAILER MATHEWS, DEAN OF THE DIVINITY SCHOOL, UNIVERSITY OF CHICAGO[14]

Given before the Chicago Association of Commerce, Chicago, July 18, 1917.

The United States has entered the war in self-defense. Two chief elements of its history and its position as a nation are in danger. We have been assailed in our citizenship, and that international law on which our national integrity rests and to which we have contributed new elements and moral worth has been denied and rejected.

First, let us see how our conception of citizenship has been assailed.

If you go back to 1776, you will see a world without written constitutions, yet a world that had been struggling for the rights of subjects to have a share in government. In Great Britain there had been a continuous struggle with varying success between monarchy by divine right and the conception of a state in which government is responsible to people possessed of rights. But nowhere else on the face of the earth, except in little Switzerland, will you see any such institution such as even the unwritten British constitution in the middle of the eighteenth century.

The American colonies continued that phase of English constitutional development represented by the Whig party. In the eighteenth century the government of England had fallen into the hands of a German family, and into the hands of a king, George III, by whom the effort was made to bring England under the control of a government regardless of the existing constitutional rights of Englishmen. When George III ascended the throne, his mother said to him,

[14] *Chicago Commerce* (Chicago Association of Commerce), July 20, 1917.

"George, be a king"; and between fits of insanity providentially given him for the constitutional rights of his subjects, he tried to be a king. In one of his fits of insanity he undertook to enforce upon the American colonies those theories of government which were being combatted by statesmen like Edmund Burke, and compel the Englishmen on this side of the water to yield to his new and anti-English conception of royal prerogatives. Englishmen in the American colonies refused to submit, and there ensued on the soil of America a struggle which saved liberalism not only on this side of the Atlantic, but in England itself.

When England thus made its contribution to the history of democracy, it little thought that there would appear on American soil a conception of citizenship more extensive and more ideal than that which obtained at home. But when the American colonies organized themselves into a federation and later into the United States of America, they made the rights of Englishmen give way to the rights of men, and the United States then made its own contribution to the development of the theory of the state and to the development of democracy with the state.

This political adventure which was expressed in successive bills of rights was something more even than its founders themselves imagined. In the establishment of the new nation, the fathers not only made the rights of men paramount in government, but they made the people exercising those rights the state. Thereby they instituted a new conception of the state. On the continent of Europe the government—the *Regierung*—was the state, and the state was not responsible to those it governed. In the United States of America there appeared the conception of a statehood in which the government and the governed were the same. Nor were Americans even then content. Those two political steps would have marked an epoch; but we did more than that. We offered citizenship, which involved the rights of being the governor of oneself, to all the world.

Other nations had offered to the oppressed of other peoples the rights and privileges of asylum. England had done this for the Huguenots. Prussia had done it for the Jews. But rights of asylum are by no means identical with citizenship, much less with government itself. In offering this citizenship to the world, the United States took a step of which men had hardly dreamed, and I fancy the foremost of our people could not imagine it would carry America to its present political situation. For thereby came political democracy. Not a fully developed democracy, but a germinal conception which made government identical with the governed, and opened government and the office of governor through citizenship to every man. Now we may say to every woman also, but we have advanced since 1787.

No sooner had this great conception been realized on our shores than it became contagious. The history of the world since 1776 has been the record of slow infiltration of all peoples with the American conception of the state as consisting of the governed as a free citizenship electing their governors. It passed into France. Many of the Frenchmen had fought in the American revolution. In the success of the American colonies they saw the possibility of establishing a French state in which the rights of men should be the basis of government. And they brought to France our gift, the assurance of the success of the democracy. From this emerged the French Revolution. At first it was a movement almost without bloodshed, and culminated in the constitution of 1791, which was prefaced with a declaration of the rights of the man and the citizen—an ideal taken from the old bills of rights which the colonies of America had shaped, and which had inspired the political thinking of men interested in a citizen state. Now, at last, France became the present splendid republic.

England followed, and in the course of forty years Englishmen with characteristic caution, with their inability to readjust privileges, slowly developed the English reform bills, and at last developed a democracy with essentially the same basis as that of the United States; that is, a citizenship electing a responsible government. Of course, the British have a king—a very interesting person when the cornerstone of an orphan asylum is to be laid or a cabinet is to be changed. But a king without political power. There are two Georges in England at the present time — George V, who is a figurehead government, and the son of a Welsh schoolmaster, Lloyd George. It is this second George who is the real governor of the kingdom.

This conception of a state based upon the rights of men, in

which the administrators are responsible to the people, gradually colored the hopes of Europe during the first half of the nineteenth century, but was everywhere pressed back except in Great Britain and in France. But you know its extension in the second half of the century; how nation after nation adopted written constitutions, and how in those constitutions, with ever-increasing emphasis, the government was made responsible to the citizens. You can see this development in the Scandinavian countries, in Belgium, and Spain, and Italy—Portugal became a republic—until the only great states that had not yielded to the impulses in 1914 were Prussia, Austria, Turkey, and Russia.

In the latter part of the nineteenth and the first quarter of the twentieth [centuries] this tremendous tide of democracy continued to rise. It worked its way over into China — the last place on earth in which you would expect to see a republic fifteen years ago. Yet, if the reports that come to us are indicative, the present attempt to replace the Manchus is a complete failure, and the poor little Manchu emperor, who was dragged from the security where he had been carefully deposited by the Chinese republicans, into some sort of puppet-like imperial position, we are told, has resigned. That is the way emperors do nowadays—they resign by request.

Democracy spread into Russia. Four years ago you would hardly have said that Russia was a state that was likely to adopt democracy. In 1815, at the Congress of Vienna, when the kings of Europe were gathered to dismember the Napoleonic conquests, the little republic of Genoa was tossed off to some king. Its representatives came to the czar and protested that a republic should not be so treated. The czar said, "Republics are no longer fashionable." A hundred and two years later Russia said to the czar, "Czars are no longer fashionable." The difference between those two statements is the measure of the influence of the American conception of the state as coextensive with citizenship and of a government as responsible to this citizenship.

But there was another conception of the state. In the midst of this great development there are two of the nations that have remained all but untouched—the kingdom of Prussia, and the kingdom of Austria. These two kingdoms early set themselves against the constitution. That sweep of idealism that had given rights to the French republic and the new democracy of England was repressed. The Prussians had pled for a constitution, but they had had a king who claimed to derive his power from God. He still claims to derive it from God, but we have a good many doubts about it unless he may get it from the *Deutscher Gott.*

In Prussia the conception of a state that spread itself over human lives, recognizing in those human lives no power and right to express themselves in their own government, was enforced by every type of censorship and proscription and military power. The sinister influence in Europe after Napoleon for thirty-five years was Metternich of Austria, and he looked at the government of England as a type of government to be avoided by all the monarchs of Europe. Frederick William III of Prussia followed in the wake of Austria. His people wanted a constitution, and they were promised it again and again.

The people of southern Europe wanted constitutions, and they got them; Bavaria and Baden in 1818, Württemberg in 1819, Hesse-Darmstadt in 1819. Saxony gained a constitution so liberal that it became almost a "red kingdom," until Prussia stepped in and forced Saxony to adopt a constitution of the Prussian sort. For, while this process was on in other states of Germany, Prussia stood like Gibraltar against constitutional government. When Frederick William III died, and his son, Frederick William IV, a very affable gentleman, came to the throne, he refused to give a constitution, uttering words which sound strangely like some recently given, "Never will I let a sheet of written paper come like a second Providence between our Lord God in heaven and the land to govern us by its paragraphs."

In 1848 a new sweep of democracy came over Europe. It was the democracy of the grandchildren of the earlier agitators, and it was stronger than that of the grandfathers. The revolution of 1848 in France expressed the undercurrent of the democracy that was working through all Europe. France has ever manfully sought to maintain its republic. Governments have been pushed aside time and again by some *coup d'état*; but in 1848 this persistent loyalty to democracy expressed itself anew and with great power; the king was thrust out and the new republic of France was established. A short-lived republic, to be sure, soon to go down into the hands of Napoleon III, but nevertheless an illustration of the new democracy. And this movement swept across Europe to Austria and it dislodged Metternich, and he took himself away to England and safety.

England has a wonderful collection of ex-autocrats. For you will notice that ex-kings do not go to autocracies when they resign—they go to democracies. One of these days it may be there will be added to England's colony of royal refugees Mr. Romanoff and Mrs. Romanoff and all the family of Romanoffs. Constantine of Greece has got as far as Switzerland.

But Prussia would not yield. Eighteen hundred and forty-eight was the year in which Prussia undertook to crush all the rising democracy of the liberal Prussians. It was the year in which Carl Schurz tried with men of like liberal mind to bring in constitutionalism. But revolution itself was in vain. The succeeding years saw the migration from Prussia and other sections of Germany of some of the finest idealists and democrats that ever came to the United States.

As we judge this war we can say to the descendants of Germans who struggled so bravely for privileges and rights in Germany that their attitude as American citizens is like that of Englishmen who in 1776 fought for the rights of Englishmen here, and gave assured liberty in England. The American of German descent who today enters into the war for democracy may do for his Fatherland what those Americans of English descent did for England—assure the victory of democracy.

In 1851 a constitution was finally given to Prussia, and a cleverly devised constitution it was. While it permitted suffrage, it had absolutely no conception of responsible government, and gave no power to the people to express themselves as a people in the making of the law. Citizenship was not in the slightest identical with government. For the divine right of the Hohenzollerns still remained, and the people had such a confused system of election that even to this day a large proportion of the members of the Landtag is elected by individuals who pay a certain amount of taxes. And this irresponsible government is today engaged in a herculean effort to make the whole world subject to itself.

Contrast these two conceptions. You will see that sooner or later there was bound to be a conflict—on the one side in [is] a nation where the government is coextensive with citizenship; on the other is a nation where the people have no control of the government. Those two conceptions have now come into conflict through the unrestrained ambition of Prussian autocracy. In the history of the last three years, you can see that Prussia has come to believe that the citizenship of the United States does not possess sovereign powers to be respected. A friend of mine in 1903 went to Germany to engage a number of distinguished scholars to take part in the congresses of the St. Louis exposition. He was told all over Germany that Germany was going to fight the United States. They said that we were not a nation, that we were interfering with their foreign trade, and they would have to fight us. "You are not a nation!"

I take it, that expresses the precise opinion of Prussians today of dors of Germany and of Austria plotting to interfere with our na- accorded us by the German government. We have seen the ambassa- dors of Germany and of Austria plotting to interfere with our national life. We have convicted their official representatives in open court of organizing within our own shores armed forces against Great Britain and Canada. We have seen them organizing strikes to interfere with our business. We have seen them putting bombs in the vessels that are to sail the seas. We have seen them using money in enormous quantities to establish and subsidize publications and to establish an anti-American spirit in the United States and in Mexico.

We have seen them deliberately undertake to foster loyalty of German-born citizens in the United States to Germany and all over the United States to establish societies to maintain the German language and traditions. We have heard Americans who have refused to become Germans in this sense, but who have remained loyal to their true citizenship, called outlaws and ingrates. We have seen the effort made through the visit of Prince Henry and all sorts of flattery to make us feel that the German nation was superior to the American nation. We have seen this anti-American propaganda pushed by representatives of the German government, and we have actually seen a law passed by the German Reichstag which makes possible two things: first, the naturalization of Germans without their living in Germany; and, second, that a German who takes the oath of allegiance to another nation may retain his citizenship in Germany.

We have seen our entire conception of national power assailed and denied the sea. It was the German ambassador who sent forth the notice that our citizens should not sail on the Lusitania except at their own peril. It was the Germans, if not the German government, who issued a medal celebrating the sinking of the Lusitania; a medal fit to be preserved in hell with the medal celebrating the massacre of Saint Bartholomew. We have seen mines and submarines sent to sea so that no nation can send a vessel to Europe without the danger of having it blown up.

It is true that Germany said she would leave a little crack through which American ships might go once a week if they sent notice beforehand and became subject to German regulations. We have seen our ships sunk and our citizens drowned. We have seen promises broken and our nation threatened with foreign war stirred up by German officials and official letters.

It is this flouting of our sovereignty as a nation which has brought war upon us. For over two years we turned one cheek and then another cheek, writing a note each time, until after these last assaults we came to realize that war had indeed been waged against us despite our over-sensitive neutrality. We did not enter into the war. War was thrust upon us in bloody and arrogant denial of our right as a nation of citizens to govern our own affairs.

And yet there are some people who are still arguing whether we ought to go to war. Few persons have belonged to more peace societies than have I, and I do not take back a word I ever said as to the unchristian character of war. But there is something that is worse than war—the destruction of those institutions and that nationality which embody our conception of a state that is composed of free, self-governing citizens.

When a man questions whether we ought to protect democracy by war, I reply to that whoever cannot see a duty to repel this assault upon our national life, our conception of a nation with sovereignty expressing and based upon a universal citizenship is either a myopic idealist, a fanatic or a pro-German.

But it is not merely our sovereignty at home that is assailed. We are threatened with the destruction of the very basis of our international relations. Such relations are the finest test of morality. International law is a product of long experiments of nations to live together righteously without the sanction of force. It is the finest expression yet known of the ethical sense of human nature. From the days of Grotius there has been a steady movement of the codification of international law. We have seen the growth of treaties. We have come to feel, at least, three years ago we had come to feel, that there actually was a body of international law. We had The Hague tribunal where nations could get together and agree at least as to how they should act in times of war. We believed we should see the day in which the relations of nations were expressed in moral terms, when the nations would recognize that their relations with each other must be governed by law.

Whence came this splendid idealism? From a long pedigree, of course. But within recent years a new conception of international law has appeared. International law has come to include the duties as well as the rights of states. And the conception in no small way has come from American democracy.

Compare the conceptions of our democracy and the relation of nations, and you can see the growing emphasis upon the rights of other nations, particularly of weaker nations.

We have by no means been sinless. The United States has been guilty of things undoubtedly which we would do well to repent. I cannot easily justify the war with Mexico, although I met a man in Texas the other day, just as intelligent as I, who took exactly the opposite view. But let us not fear that. After we conquered Mexico we paid her $15,000,000 for the land we took. We annexed, but we also indemnified. The Prussian has annexed, and his victims have indemnified. The basis of this difference in policy lies in the different international attitudes of Prussianism and democracy.

We have undertaken to recognize the rights of other peoples. You see the difference of policy sharply drawn in Russia. Her history is a mass of secret treaties looking toward the absorption of neighboring peoples. But when the czar went, the people of Russia declared, "We will have no indemnities and no annexations, and we call upon our allies to tell us what they want from the war."

Democracies nowadays are not in the business of looting their neighbors. Yet democracy itself has had to be educated in this nobler internationalism. Take our attitude toward Cuba. The first fifty years of our national history saw many statesmen determined to take Cuba. Twice presidents of the United States said that we ought to take Cuba. But Congress refused. Therein democracy rather than "manifest destiny" spoke. We sometimes grow impatient with Congress, you know; we say that our representatives take too much time in passing laws. But it is the cost of being democratic, and on the whole, it is a blessing.

Talk is the salvation of democracy. We sometimes get a surfeit of salvation, it is true, but the laws that are passed after long discussion generally better represent public opinion. Contrast the Ostend manifesto concerning Cuba with our present attitude. Twice we had Cuba in our hands, and twice we gave her back to herself. That is the way democracies should and do act. And it is a splendid piece of poetic justice that when the militaristic power that denies that the state should consist of its citizenship and denies there is an international law to be respected brought war upon us, the first nation to step forward to be our helper was brave little Cuba. A democracy again understood international law to mean duties as well as rights.

Similarly with the Philippines. When we got the Philippines or the Philippines got us, twenty years ago, what did we do? We paid an indemnity of $20,000,000 to Spain and then we undertook to educate the Philippines into a capacity for self-government. If you have any doubt about our sincerity in this undertaking, you have only to consult any American in business in Manila at the present time.

That is a part of our treatment of weaker nations. Our democracy feels an obligation to the Philippines, to Cuba, to Haiti, to San Domingo. We refuse to loot them or to bind them into a world-state over which we rule.

And then there is Mexico. I do not know what your feeling towards Mexico and its affairs may be. But I know this: Our refusal to intervene in Mexico was only a continuation of our policy that a democracy shall not be made the catspaw of any commercial interests. President Wilson has done something vastly bigger than to keep America merely out of war with Mexico. He has been showing the South American continent that the United States in applying its democracy to international affairs is not what they have been told it is, a big bully seeking to aggrandize itself at the expense of other nations. South America is at the present time practically as a unit with us in the war—a situation that would never have been possible if once we had shown our attitude toward other nations capable of self-government to be that of intervention in their internal affairs.

Our action illustrates and furthers the new international law that democracy is evolving. We champion the Monroe doctrine in self-defense it is true, but we have never made it an excuse for exploiting the nations to the south of us. In our maintenance of the political integrity of the nations on the American continent we have evolved a new law of nations—a law of helpfulness as well as of self-defense. And the democracy of Great Britain has been one fellow worker. To English statesmen belongs no small share of the credit for this progressive conception of international relations.

The Monroe doctrine would have been difficult if not impossible without British coöperation. Not only have we been able to leave common frontier across the continent unguarded by fort or battleship, but in the affairs of South America, Great Britain and the United States have worked in political harmony. Democracies respect because they rest upon international law.

One chief expression of this growing morality among nations is arbitration. Germany refused to recognize arbitration in the second Hague conference, and of all the two hundred and fifty-five arbitration treaties, drawn before 1915, not including the "bide-a-wee" treaties with Bryan, the Central Powers had made but seven, of which Germany had made but one—with Great Britain—which expired July 12, 1914. Indeed, the one time in which Kaiser Wilhelm II got recognition as favoring arbitration was when President Roosevelt gave him the choice between such reputation and fighting Dewey's fleet.

The United States has not gone so far in relying upon arbitration as some of us would like, but its sympathies and influences have been consistently more pronounced in this regard. For we have seen the inevitable choice in international affairs lies between coercion,

won, there would no longer have been a balance of power in Europe, or a British fleet to support the Monroe doctrine and protect America.

Does any one indulge in the foolish assumption that Germany would not then have extended her lust for power by conquest to the American continent? Let him consider what it is for which the nations of Europe have been chiefly contending for centuries past. It has been for colonies. It has been to bring the unoccupied or weakly-held spaces of the earth under their flags and their political control, in order to increase their trade and their power. Spain, Holland, Portugal, England, France, have all had their turn, and have covered the earth with their possessions. For thirty years Germany, the last comer, has been pressing forward with feverish activity the acquisition of stations for her power on every coast and every sea, restive and resentful because she has been obliged to take what others have left. Europe, Asia, and Africa have been taken up. The Americas alone remain. Here in the vast and undefended spaces of the New World, fraught with potential wealth incalculable, Germany could "find her place in the sun," to use her Emperor's phrase; Germany could find her "liberty of national evolution," to use his phrase again. Every traditional policy, every instinct of predatory Prussia would urge her into this new field of aggrandizement. What would prevent? The Monroe doctrine? Yes. But what is the Monroe doctrine as against a nation which respects only force, unless it can be maintained by force? We already know how the German government feels about the Monroe doctrine. Bismarck declared it to be a piece of colossal impudence; and when President Roosevelt interfered to assert the doctrine for the protection of Venezuela, the present Kaiser declared that if he had then had a larger navy he would have taken America by the scruff of the neck. If we had stayed out of the war, and Germany had won, we should have had to defend the Monroe doctrine by force, or abandon it; and if we abandoned it, there would have been a German naval base in the Caribbean commanding the Panama Canal, depriving us of that strategic line which unites our eastern and western coasts, and depriving us of the protection which the expanse of ocean once gave. And an America unable or unwilling to protect herself against the establishment of a German naval base in the Caribbean would lie at the mercy of Germany, and subject to Ger-

(7)

many's orders. America's independence would be gone unless she was ready to fight for it, and her security would thenceforth be, not the security of freedom, but only a security purchased by submission.

But if America had stayed out of the war and Germany had won, could we have defended the Monroe doctrine? Could we have maintained our independence? For an answer to this question, consider what we have been doing since the second of April last, when war was declared. Congress has been in continuous session, passing with unprecedented rapidity laws containing grants of power and of money unexampled in our history. The executive establishment has been straining every nerve to prepare for war. The ablest and strongest leaders of industrial activity have been called from all parts of the country to aid the government. The people of the country have generously responded with noble loyalty and enthusiasm to the call for the surrender of money and of customary rights, and the supply of men, to the service of the country. Nearly half a year has passed, and still we are not ready to fight. I am not blaming the government. It was inevitable. Preparation for modern war cannot be made briefly or speedily. It requires time, long periods of time; and the more peaceful and unprepared for war a democracy is, the longer is the time required.

It would have required just as long for America to prepare for war if we had stayed out of this war, and Germany had won, and we had undertaken then to defend the Monroe doctrine, or to defend our coasts when we had lost the protection of the Monroe doctrine. Month after month would have passed with no adequate army ready to fight, just as these recent months have passed. But what would Germany have been doing to us in the meantime? How long would it have been before our attempts at preparation would have been stopped by German arms? A country that is forced to defend itself against the aggression of a military autocracy, always prepared for war, must itself be prepared for war beforehand, or it never will have the opportunity to prepare.

The history, the character, the avowed principles of action, the manifest and undisguised purposes of the German autocracy, made it clear and certain that if America stayed out of the great war, and Germany won, America would forthwith be required to defend herself, and would be unable to defend herself against the same lust for conquest, the same will to dominate the world, which has made Europe a bloody shambles.

When Germany did actually apply her principles of action to us; when by the invasion of Belgium she had violated the solemn covenant she had made with us to observe the law of neutrality established for the protection of peaceful states; when she had arrogantly demanded that American commerce should surrender its lawful right of passage upon the high seas under penalty of destruction; when she had sunk American ships and sent to their death hundreds of American citizens, peaceful men, women and children, when the *Gulflight* and the *Falaba* and the *Persia* and the *Arabic* and the *Sussex* and the *Lusitania* had been torpedoed without warning in contempt of law and of humanity; when the German Embassy at Washington had been found to be the headquarters of a vast conspiracy of corruption within our country, inciting sedition and concealing infernal machines in the cargoes of our ships, and blowing up our factories with the workmen laboring in them; and when the government of Germany had been discovered attempting to incite Mexico and Japan to form a league with her to attack us, and to bring about a dismemberment of our territory; then the question presented to the American people was not what shall be done regarding each of the specific aggressions taken by itself, but what shall be done by America to defend her commerce, her territory, her citizens, her independence, her liberty, her life as a nation, against the continuance of assaults already begun by that mighty and conscienceless power which has swept aside every restraint and every principle of Christian civilization, and is seeking to force upon a subjugated world the dark and cruel rule of a barbarous past. The question was, how shall peaceful and unprepared and liberty-loving America save herself from subjection to the military power of German.

There was but one possible answer. There was but one chance for rescue, and that was to act at once, while the other democracies of the world were still maintaining their liberty against the oppressor; to prepare at once while the armies and the navies of England and France and Italy and Russia and Rumania were holding down Germany so that she could not attack us while our preparation was but half accomplished, to strike while there were allies loving freedom like ourselves to strike with us, to do our share to prevent the German Kaiser from acquiring that domination over the world which would have left us without friends to aid us, without preparation, and without the possibility of successful defense.

The instinct of the American democracy which led it to act when it did, arose from a long-delayed and reluctant consciousness still vague and half-expressed, that this is no ordinary war which the world is waging. It is no contest for petty policies and profits. It is a mighty and all-embracing struggle between two conflicting principles of human right and human duty. It is a conflict between the divine right of kings to govern mankind through armies and nobles, and the right of the peoples of the earth who toil and endure and aspire, to govern themselves by law under justice, and in the freedom of individual manhood. It is the climax of the supreme struggle between autocracy and democracy. No nation can stand aside and be free from its effects. The two systems cannot endure together in the same world. If autocracy triumphs, military power, lustful of dominion, supreme in strength, intolerant of human rights, holding itself above the reach of law, superior to morals, to faith, to compassion, will crush out the free democracies of the world. If autocracy is defeated and nations are compelled to recognize the rule of law and of morals, then and then only will democracy be safe.

To this great conflict for human rights and human liberty, America has committed herself. There can be no backward step. There must be either humiliating and degrading submission, or terrible defeat, or glorious victory. It was no human will that brought us to this pass. It was not the President. It was not Congress. It was not the press. It was not any political party. It was not any section or part of our people. It was the fact that in the providence of God the mighty forces that determine the destinies of mankind beyond the control of human purpose, have brought to us the time, the occasion, the necessity, that this peaceful people so long enjoying the blessings of liberty and justice for which their fathers fought and sacrificed, shall again gird themselves for conflict, and with all the forces of manhood nurtured and strengthened by liberty, offer again the sacrifice of possessions and of life itself, that this nation may still be free, that the mission of American democracy shall not have failed, that the world shall be free.

VICTORY DEMANDS UNITY, AN ADDRESS BY SAMUEL GOMPERS[18]

Delivered at a patriotic mass meeting held under the auspices of the National Security League, Chicago, September 14, 1917.

There is such a thing as humility. There is such a thing as patience. But when some bully undertakes to make an assault upon an innocent, peace-loving man or woman, patience ceases to be a virtue and humility brings the brand of cowardice. That was the position in which the United States found itself as a nation by the repeated insults and assaults upon the character and upon the lives of our people, our men, our women and our innocent children.

There is one thought in connection with the atrocious murder of our people in the case of our torpedoed boats. I ask you, my friends, to consider for a moment the fact that the German ambassador, Count von Bernstorff, a few days before the sailing of the *Lusitania,* had an advertisement in the newspapers of our country, warning the people of the United States against taking passage on the *Lusitania,* and advising them that there was danger in their taking passage on that vessel. The impudence of the whole transaction caused a smile to spread over the countenances of the people of the United States. They thought it a hoax, a jest of a very, very somber character, and many of them took passage, and then within a few days the great ship went on her way, where she had a perfect right to go.

Nearly two thousand souls boarded that vessel before her departure. More than one hundred and fifty American men and women and children were on that vessel when she sailed; she was torpedoed without a moment's warning, and all of them sent to the waters, and more than fifteen hundred human souls, of which more than one hundred were American men and women and children, were sent to a watery grave.

[18] This address is reprinted from Samuel Gompers, *American Labor in the World War,* George H. Doran Company (New York, 1919), by permission of the author and the publisher.

I ask you, my friends, to reverse the position for a moment. Suppose our ambassador at Berlin, Mr. Gerard, had placed an advertisement in the newspapers of Germany advising the German people against taking passage on a steamer to go to any port that that steamer and her master had a right to go, and suppose further that some American U-boat had sent a torpedo into that merchant ship, and suppose that there had been one hundred or more German men, women and children sent to an untimely grave, what do you think the treatment of Gerard would have been at the hands of the Kaiser? Do you think for a moment that there would have been any further parley with Gerard or the government of the United States? Is it possible to imagine that with Germany's mental attitude Gerard would have been given his passports? Or is it not in keeping with the whole policy of *Kultur* that Gerard would have paid the penalty with his life?

Surely, it would be untimely and inappropriate did I attempt or did anyone attempt to interject any political issue in this campaign of education and Americanism in our country. But I ask you, my friends, whether it is not true that considerable of the opposition to the reëlection of Mr. Wilson to the presidency was based on the accusation that he had too long kept us out of war? It is doubtful if there has been in history a more patient yet courageous man to meet a great emergency than Woodrow Wilson. It was for more than two years that President Wilson pursued his policy, basing his position upon the belief that there was some honor at the core, possibly to be discovered, of the German imperial government. He was misled into the belief that there was some honor in German diplomacy. He finally discovered that there comes a time, and that the time had come, when men would be too proud not to fight.

To me it seemed that the entrance of our republic into this conflict had been too long delayed, but as a loyal citizen I yielded to the judgment of the Commander-in-chief of the army and navy of the United States. I felt that the time was near at hand when the outrages would increase in such numbers and in such horror that in self-respect we would take advantage of the current as it served or we would lose our ventures.

We have entered into this struggle, and there can be no let-up from the time of our declaration of war until either imperial Germany, with her militarism, shall surrender to the democracies of the world or the democracies shall crush Germany.

We have heard the cries of a few of our people echoing the wishes and the hope of defeated Germany today. I say defeated Germany, although she is not conquered by any means. But Germany is defeated in the objects for which she entered into the war. We have heard an element here and there crying out in the wilderness, for it finds no lodgment in the conscience or the hearts of red-blooded men, "Peace! Peace!" Yes, I have seen it printed in newspapers, taken up by other pacifists, so-called, masking under the name of pacifists; but through ignorance or pro-Germanism, I do not know which, they have declared: "Why not now?"

Let us bear this fact in mind, that Germany and Austria are still fighting on land invaded by them. If we were to consent to peace to-day, without the surrender of Kaiserism, in all history written in the future the Teutonic forces would be given the credit and the prestige of being the conqueror in this war. There can be no peace, not while there is a Teuton on the soil of glorious France. There can be no peace, and there must not be any peace, until the Teutons are driven back, back, from outraged Belgium.

There cannot be any peace until the people of the world who love peace and liberty more than their own lives are assured that never again shall it be possible for Germany or Austria, or any other country for that matter, to make such a bloody war upon the freedom of the people. To me it is a subject of much obscurity how it is physically or mentally possible for any man who loves liberty, who is a native or a naturalized citizen of the United States, to make even the slightest manifestation of objection to the prosecution of this war until the final end.

I grieve that many of our poor boys may fall, and God grant that but few shall fall or be hurt, but I ask you, my friends, to think back whether there is anyone among you who can trace some distant ancestor who fought in the Revolution to establish this republic and give to the world not only a new nation but a new meaning of the rights of man. Is there any one among you who begrudges the sacrifice of any man who gave his life in order that that great privilege should be established? Who among our men, who among our women, regrets even the sacrifices that were made during the Civil War to abolish human slavery and to maintain the Union? Who among us regrets the sacrifices that were made to rescue Cuba from the domination of Spain and make her an independent republic? Why, all our hearts throb and our whole beings thrill when we can trace one who gave some contributory effort or sacrifice in order that these great achievements should lie as the successes of our country.

That which we call freedom, that which we call liberty, are not tangible things. They are not handed to any people on a silver platter. They are principles, they are questions of the spirit, and people must have a consciousness that they not only have the term liberty and freedom, but they must have the power and the right to exercise these great attributes of life.

And if liberty, freedom, justice and democracy are not meaningless terms, they are worth something to us. They are too priceless to surrender without a struggle, and he who is unwilling to fight for freedom is undeserving to enjoy that freedom.

May I suggest this: It is proposed as a result of a great conference which closed in Minneapolis a week ago tonight,[19] so far as possible to let every controversial question be laid on the table until after the war is closed. Of course, my friends, I would not have you or anyone else interpret that statement to mean that the human aspiration for a better life can be or will be suppressed; that ought to be encouraged; but shall we array church against church, party against party, religion against religion, politics against politics, nationality against nationality, aye, even the question of raising funds to carry on the war, the bonds that are to be issued? Let us do

[19] A conference of the American Alliance for Labor and Democracy, held in Minneapolis, September 5-7, 1917. The object of this organization, local units of which were formed in a large number of cities during the summer and autumn of 1917, was to develop among American workingmen a sense of their responsibilities in the prosecution of the war. Declarations embodying pledges of loyal support were adopted at the Minneapolis conference, and the proceedings were endorsed by the American Federation of Labor at its convention in November, 1917. John H. Walker, president of the Illinois State Federation of Labor, was chairman of the permanent organization committee of the American Alliance for Labor and Democracy.

our share to see to it that Uncle Sam has the fighting men and the men to produce at home and the money with which to carry on the war. Let us defer questions which can be deferred, questions that are likely to divide any appreciable element of our people in this war; let us remain united and fight it out, no matter how long we fight, until America and America's allies shall have proved victorious in the struggle.

To me the term America is more than a name. It is more than a country. It is more than a continent. To me America is a symbol of the ideas and the ideals for human betterment and human justice among the peoples of the world. Perhaps it may be strengthened by hope, but somehow there is a subconsciousness in me that tells me that when for the first time in the history of the world a Teutonic army shall face the soldiers of the United States with the flag, the Star Spangled Banner waving above them, it will penetrate the very souls of the men in the German uniform. In all their fights they have met men carrying the standards that Germany hated. They have never yet come in contact with Old Glory.

I ought to say, my friends, that the policy pursued by the government of the United States in this war, in matters of development and growth and preparation, amazes those who are permitted to know the truth. Some day, my friends, you and I, who may be kept from all the information just now, will know what marvels America has wrought within these past few months. And then, too, we have started out on a different line of action from that followed in any previous wars in which we or any of the other countries on the globe had entered. It is to the honor of the committee of which I am chairman,[20] that, as a member of the Advisory Commission of the Council of National Defense, the bill was drafted that provides not only for compensation for injured soldiers and sailors and for their dependents, but also an opportunity of insurance, so that if any of the men come back injured they at least shall have the insurance to give them and their dependents an opportunity to live in some degree of comfort, the opportunity of increasing their pay so that they can afford to lay something away, so that when they return they shall have something as a nest-egg to give for themselves

[20]Committee on Labor, Council of National Defense.

or to give to their families.[21] We have tried to formulate a measure that shall relieve for all time the people of our country from the scandals and the injustice of the old pension system, but at the same time taking into consideration our experience of the difference of the industrial and employers' liability acts, and the substitution of compensation for workmen so as to apply it to the soldiers and the sailors of Uncle Sam. We hope that the boys who are already in France and the boys who are going over to France shall have their minds free from the worry that their families might possibly go down in the standard of life in our communities. We want the boys of Uncle Sam fighting for us to feel that America, great America, will stand by them or those they may possibly leave behind them. And I am proud to say that that measure passed the House of Representatives yesterday by an almost unanimous vote.

We do not know now just exactly what sacrifices we may be called upon to make. Let us pray and hope and work that they may be few, if any at all; but this we feel assured of, from the President down to every one aiding him in the great work of carrying on the war, it is the purpose that the home shall be maintained, that the standard of American life shall not go down, but shall be maintained throughout the war.

We must make it possible that our fighting force shall be provided with every necessity to fight and every means contributing to their subsistence and comfort, and that the American people shall go on in their economic, industrial, social and spiritual life just as well as it is possible to do. And so, when it is necessary to make additional sacrifices, we shall—you, and you, and you, the people of Chicago, the people of Illinois, the people of the United States—stand as one solid phalanx of the manhood and the womanhood of the people of our country, of our republic, united, determined to stand by our cause and our gallant Allies until the world has been made safe for freedom, for justice, for democracy, for humanity.

[21] The War Risk Insurance Act, approved October 6, 1917.

RESOLUTIONS ADOPTED AT MASS MEETING, MEDINAH TEMPLE, NOVEMBER 28, 1917[22]

America is at war to defend the lives and liberties of her people, to perpetuate her principles of self-government, to destroy the malign power of the German government, whose imperial ambitions have plunged the world into war.

We were patient and slow to wrath. We endured German crimes against us, within our borders, and on the high seas, until it became clear beyond all doubting that our liberties, no less than those of European nations, must be defended by force of arms or be held subject to the German will for power. Any nation worthy to be free must be ready and willing to fight for freedom.

In declaring war upon Germany our country, by reason of its vast man and money power, has become the final arbiter in the world-wide and world-old struggle between democratic right and autocratic might. Between these two principles there can be no compromise. An inconclusive peace would be only a truce. We must win. We must win a victory of democratic advance worthy of the terrible sacrifices that have been and will be made. Peoples are fighting this war, not merely armies. And those free peoples who are sowing their blood and treasure must reap a peace which shall lift from their shoulders the burdens of great armaments and lift from their hearts the menace of future wars.

We citizens of Illinois, meeting with our senators and representatives, make with them a joint and mutual pledge of whole-hearted support of our government in the prosecution of this war. Its vast consequences demand unprecedented sacrifice and unstinted devotion. They demand that we lay aside domestic differences and labor together regardless of politics, race, or creed; that we forgo petty

[22] *Chicago Tribune*, November 29, 1917. This mass meeting was a part of the program of the Congressional Conference, held under the auspices of the State Council of Defense of Illinois in Chicago, November 28, 1917, for the purpose of discussing Illinois' part in the war. To the conference were invited the two Illinois senators, the members of Congress from Illinois, and state officials. The speakers at the public meeting which closed the conference were Senator L. Y. Sherman, Senator James Hamilton Lewis, Henry T. Rainey, member of Congress from the twentieth district, and Samuel Insull, chairman of the State Council of Defense.

jealousies and ambitions; that we renounce private and personal advantage in order that we may overthrow the great power of an army that has made itself a nation by the greater power of a nation that has made itself an army.   Shoulder to shoulder, with unwearying pace and unrelenting purpose the men and women of Illinois and their representatives in Congress will march behind the President in the battle array of the United States, fighting the good fight until we win national security and enduring peace and reëstablish the supremacy of Christian civilization throughout the world.

COALITION TICKET FOR JUDICIAL ELECTIONS

Resolutions adopted by Republican and Democratic conventions of Cook County, October 1, 1917.[23]

Fourteen judges of the circuit and superior courts are to be elected in November.   Obviously the purpose of the statutes governing judicial elections here is to remove these elections, as far as practicable, from the distractions of other issues and from the high tension partisanship which accompanies general elections.

While no other public officials are to be chosen in November, the abnormal times in which we are utterly preclude the possibility of focusing public attention upon this election, as contemplated by the statutes.

Our country is engaged in the greatest war of all time.   Prosecution of the war to a victorious conclusion is the nation's paramount purpose—a purpose to be achieved only by complete concentration of national effort of every kind.   It thus becomes the paramount duty of each citizen to contribute his utmost to that purpose in thought, word, and act.   All else in our affairs, individual or collective, is subordinate.

It is time for coöperative citizenship, for a drawing together, for the elimination of the differences which ordinarily divide us, for complete harmony of purpose and of action in our social, commercial, industrial, and political life, to the end that winning the war speedily and decisively be not impeded a hair's breadth by controversy over

[23] *Chicago Tribune*, October 2, 1917.   The coalition ticket was elected on November 6, 1917, by a majority of approximately 70,000.

questions which, no matter how important in normal times, are now dwarfed by the gigantic issues at stake in the world war.

In these circumstances it is practical wisdom and good citizenship to insure, if possible, the election of fourteen good judges without arousing partisan feeling and without risking the consequences of public inattention. This can be achieved most certainly by a nonpartisan election, returning to office the sitting judges who have earned retention in office and electing along with them carefully selected men of undoubted character and approved legal ability.

Therefore, be it resolved, by the Democratic [Republican] convention of Cook County that we recommend to the voters of Cook County the election of the seven judicial candidates nominated today by this convention and the seven Republican [Democratic] judicial candidates nominated today by the Republican [Democratic] convention of Cook County.

RESOLUTIONS ADOPTED BY ILLINOIS STATE TEACHERS' ASSOCIATION, SPRINGFIELD, DECEMBER 27, 1917[24]

The Illinois State Teachers' Association assembles this year with a solemn consciousness of the tremendous significance of the issues of this world war, realizing that the outcome of this mighty conflict will determine the destiny of our own country and the future civilization of the world. Democracy, whose authority is the will of the people and whose supreme purpose is to promote the welfare of the people, has come into deadly conflict with autocracy, whose authority is the will of a monarch and whose purpose is to carry out his plans of conquest and dominion. Autocracy, relying on brutal force, and savage might, is trying desperately to destroy free government from the earth. If democracy survives, it will be through heroic sacrifices of liberty-loving people of every land.

We realize that these two forms of government are so antagonistic in purpose that the world cannot continue partly under the one and partly under the other. Either all peoples and all nations shall be free, or all shall bow to the will of the Kaiser, who has al-

[24] *Illinois State Journal*, December 28, 1917.

ready been heralded by his war lords as Emperor of the world. Liberty, ravished and wounded, looks to America for help. Our brave sons will defend and protect her at any cost; therefore,

Resolved that we, of this association, representing more than thirty thousand teachers of Illinois, in this serious hour when our country is offering its treasure and its choicest young manhood on the altar of freedom in support of the same sacred principles for which our fathers offered their lives, solemnly pledge allegiance to our country, and whole-hearted support to the cause for which we and our allies are fighting. We will endeavor at all times to teach the youth committed to our charge loyalty to our government, reverence for our flag, and devotion to the principles of liberty, justice and humanity for which our nation stands. We will do all in our power to uphold our President and our Governor and to assist by our efforts and our influence in winning this war and securing a just and lasting peace.

AN ADDRESS BY WILLIAM HOWARD TAFT[25]

Delivered before the Illinois State Teachers' Association, Springfield, December 28, 1917.

One can not come before an intelligent audience like this and fail to talk about the war. I have talked about the war a good deal in various parts of the country and I have been impressed with the feeling that the war could be talked about a good deal more about the country, throughout the country, to the people of the country, with very great advantage. There are so many who are doubtful—they are for the government and they are for the war, but they are walking interrogation marks as to whether we did not make a mistake here, or did not make a mistake there, or whether we are fully and rightfully in the war, that I think an evangel ought to be preached on the subject to demonstrate that we are rightfully in the war, that we never have done anything that was not justified, and that the cause now presented to us is so righteous that if we are the people we claim to be we must win it if it costs the last man and the last dollar that we have.

[25] From a manuscript copy furnished by Chief Justice William Howard Taft.

You meet men who are now, after we have decided to go into the war, and after we are in it, who are now "judicially minded"—that is to say, they do not say they are neutral, but they are judicially minded. While I am in favor of being judicially minded, I am not in favor of masquerading under a judicial mind a lack of that fine edge of loyal patriotism that we need to carry this country through the war. I am opposed to apathy; I am in favor of team work, and of knowing why we are in, and what we are going to do, and in favor of being determined to do it.

You will find this judicially minded person suggest that we were unneutral during the three years that we were not in the war because we furnished ammunition and other supplies to the Allies. Well, we had a right to do that under international law. Germany herself had agreed to that rule of international law with respect to the powers and duties of neutrals—not that neutral governments could furnish such supplies, but that neutral governments could permit their citizens to do so, the citizens taking the risk of confiscation of those articles as contraband if found upon the high seas. And there were those who sympathized with Germany after the German commercial marine had been driven from the seas, and they said it was unneutral for us to furnish one side.

The fortune of war was not our fault. The President was right in insisting that we should stand by the rule of international law in that regard, because if by our acquiescence the rule of international law was to be changed, requiring every neutral government to suppress its citizens from carrying on such a trade, it would only make overwhelming the advantages of a military nation that devoted itself, as Germany has done for fifty years, to getting ready for this war, a nation which has piled up the ammunition and supplies needed to carry her through years of war. We, if subjected to a war, are never likely to be ready. We would always be unprepared, and as a consequence when forced into war, we would have to look about to prepare suddenly, and then find denied to us the right to get our material and supplies from the citizens of neutral nations, under the new rule suggested. Therefore, it would have been the wildest lunacy for us to consent to a change of international law in that regard, and the merits were wholly with the President in taking that position.

But, notwithstanding the fact that we pursued the path of neutrality as laid down by the law, Germany sank an English commercial liner having three thousand persons on board, and sent to their death one hundred fourteen American citizens by the murderous torpedo which her submarines hurled at this vessel. Then for a year we continued a discussion, arising from Germany's unfounded claim that the sunken vessel was armed; then she sank another vessel under similar circumstances; then we said that we would sever our relations with Germany; then she said that she would discontinue that method of warfare until further notice; then on the 31st of January last Germany notified us, as she notified the world, that she intended to resume the ruthless submarine warfare; then shortly afterwards we severed our diplomatic relations with Germany; then she sank four or five American vessels, returning to this country in ballast, and sent to their death some twenty-five or thirty American sailors; and then we declared that a state of war existed.

Now, my friends, is there anything else that we could do but that? That is where your judicially minded person would come in. The answer to my question depends, first, on the proposition of what were our rights, and what were the rights of our citizens. And secondly, what was our duty as a government with respect to those rights? International law is indefinite in certain respects, but it is as definite as is the law on promissory notes, with reference to the rule of the capture of commercial vessels at sea. A belligerent may capture the commercial vessels of its enemy and sink that vessel. It may capture, under certain circumstances, a neutral vessel violating a blockade, and possibly may sink it, but an incontestible rule for a hundred years has been that that right of capture and right of destruction is subject to one limitation, namely, that the ship's company of the captured vessel shall always be put in a place of safety before the vessel is sunk.

Admiral Semmes in the Civil War sank perhaps four hundred vessels of the United States commercial marine, but he prided himself that in all that destruction not one single human life was lost. He was an international lawyer of repute; he was also a naval commander, and his course in that regard is the strongest evidence of what international law is on that point. Therefore, Germany violated the rights of those citizens whom she exposed to death and whom she sent to death. When a man kills another deliberately, without right, it is murder, and there is no other word nor any other term in international law that can be applied to a case where a nation kills men and women and children without right.

Ah, but it is said these people had notice. That distinguished and eminent Christian statesman, Count von Bernstorff, had whispered over the telephone and had intimated very enigmatically that anyone who went aboard the *Lusitania* would run the risk of being torpedoed, and it is stated that those who went down in ships sunk afterwards knew that Germany was on the sea with these murderous instruments. Well, that is a fine plea. Suppose a man in New York should warn a neighbor that he could not go down into the street upon which [his] house abutted, because if he did he would kill him; and suppose this man who was warned was a courageous American citizen, who knew what his rights were and he went down into the street, and the threatener did kill him. Suppose that man was indicted and haled into court and called upon to plead, and he pleaded "Not guilty" on the ground that he had notified this man that if he would come down into the street he would kill him, and therefore he was not guilty because the man himself was guilty of contributory negligence in running into a bullet whose presence he ought to have anticipated on the street.

. . . .

We will now assume, therefore, that this was murder of our citizens. What was our duty? The Constitution as interpreted by the Supreme Court, indeed our general knowledge of government, would teach us that while we owe service, military and civil, to the government, the government owes us a primary consideration, protection. Government is nothing but a partnership in which we are all members, and we all agree to contribute to the objects of a partnership by service; and then the partnership is to help us in enabling us to enjoy our rights. Therefore, when these citizens were actually deprived of their rights, it is very plain that it was the business of the government to call for reparation in respect to those whose rights had been taken away, and security and an announcement of the policy which would prevent subsequent interference with similar

(8)

rights of our citizens. Otherwise, if not, then we ought to go out of the government business, because such protection is the object of government.

Now, Germany announced that she not only justified what she had done, but intended to continue to murder our citizens on the high seas. Our citizens are entitled to the protection of the government at home and on the high seas, and abroad. Abroad there is some qualification, because they voluntarily submit to another jurisdiction, but on the high seas, on an American vessel, and under an American flag, on that great road of the nations, they are just as much within the jurisdiction and within the protection of the government at home as if they stood on the shores of New York, or Massachusetts, or New Jersey, and an invasion of their rights on the high seas by a foreign government is just as much an invasion as if Germany had landed a Uhlan regiment on our shores and shot into the homes of American citizens and killed them.

Therefore, if we were to continue business as a government, there was nothing else for us to do—Germany did not leave it open— except to measure swords with her in protection of those rights. If this act had been committed by Venezuela or Costa Rica, if either of those countries had sunk an American ship with a loss of one hundred lives, the President would have promptly sent a message demanding reparation and security against further invasion, and might have sent a warship down to convey the message, just by way of suggestion, and every man, woman and child, . . . and every pacifist, would have said, "Well done." Well, now, what is the difference between that case and the one we are considering? There is not any in principle, but there is this real difference, that Germany is the greatest military power in the world, and Venezuela is not, and therefore we are very urgently and strongly in favor of the protection of the rights of American citizens when invaded by a foreign country, provided the country is little enough, but when it is a great power— the greatest military power—then the rights are "technical."

Oh, my friends, there was not anything for us to do except to declare war, and a pacifist or anyone else who says otherwise or intimates otherwise does not understand. The President has set a precedent by calling them stupid, and, after such an authority, I am willing to say I agree.

Now that brought us into the war, but when we got into the war we found what possibly we ought to have known before—some did know—that the particular cause which brought us into it was only a phase of the far greater cause which the Allies were engaged in fighting. We found ourselves in the beginning ranged with democracies against autocracies. I know that our judicially minded friend will suggest that England is a monarchy and so is Italy. Yes, that is true, but a democracy is a country in which the people rule, in which the policies of the government are determined by the popular will. The proof of the pudding is in the eating of it. Any one who knows anything about England and Italy cannot say otherwise than that the people rule in these countries; and where that is the case, they are democracies. Where that is the case, the question of kings is only a question of taste. As a matter of fact, the King of Italy and the King of Great Britain have not any more to do in determining acute questions of the policies of their respective countries than an ex-president of the United States.

Now, the President has said that we are fighting this war to make the world safe for democracy. That is a truly exact statement. But it has been misconstrued. It does not mean that we are to force democracy on other countries, that we claim to have a patent for our form of government that we are going to drive down the throats of other people. That is not what it means. It only means that the power of a people with a military and foreign policy such as that of the Imperial German Empire is dangerous to the continued and safe existence of smaller and less powerful countries that desire to have democracies and to work out the happiness of their people through that kind of government. That is what it means.

We cannot understand the issues at stake without understanding the character of the German people. We cannot understand their character without following their training in the last fifty or sixty years. We all have known Germans. We have liked them. When in Germany we have enjoyed seeing them. They are a kindly people; at least they were some years ago when I visited Germany. They are a kindly people, who love their homes; they love their families, they love music and they love poetry, of which they have some of the greatest exponents in the world. They conform to authority with a kind of pleasure. They are an intellectual people, they are an earnest people, a little lacking in a sense of humor, but a great people, people capable of great effort.

The truth is, while I have a profound admiration for the English people and the history of England, because having been educated as a lawyer I believe she laid the foundations of true constitutional liberty, nevertheless I am bound to say that when I went to Europe and traveled in Europe, I would a great deal rather be closed up in a railway carriage with a German than with an Englishman; because the Englishman—I mean the regular Englishman—was constantly engaged in an affirmative effort to convince me that he did not know I was in the carriage, whereas the German was always courteous and friendly and anxious to engage in conversation.

The Germans for a long time were divided into twenty-eight different states, Austria the greatest of them, Prussia the next, and twenty-six others, and every one who longed for an improvement in the world, and an improvement among the Germans, wished for unity among them. There were liberty-loving Germans, and in '48 they rebelled against the divine right of kings, and they had revolutions. They were not successful. They did get a constitutional monarchy for a little while in Prussia, and offered the crown to Frederick William, the great-uncle of the present Emperor, and he said he would not take it, because he got it from God, and did not purpose to take it back again out of the mud, showing that the divine right of kings came honestly down that line to its present exponent.

A large number of these liberty-loving Germans were driven out of Germany and came to this country, and made one of the most valuable elements of our citizenship here; and when the Civil War came on, loving liberty as they did and hating slavery, they went into the war, enlisted in great numbers and on every battle field in that war the blood of our German citizens was shed.

Their descendants and others who have come here since have continued to make a valuable part of our citizenship, and during these three years when we were neutral they have naturally, because of their pride in the success and prosperity of their brethren at home, had a sympathy with Germany and listened to the arguments in her behalf which have been put forth in this war. And now the war between America and Germany has come on, and their allegiance requires them to be loyal, and they are put in a sad position, and one in respect to which we should be considerate of them. But they are loyal, they have enlisted; they have gone into the draft, and contributed to the great patriotic funds; and while they are not vociferous— we could hardly expect them to be so—that they are going to be loyal I have not the slightest doubt, and one of the things we ought to be most thankful for is that very thing. The reason why Germany treated us as she did was because she counted on dissension among our people, growing out of the disloyalty of that very element, and she has been disappointed in that regard as she has been disappointed in so many of those instances where she has attempted to read the motives of other people.

Instead of founding a constitutional monarchy, with representative institutions, and bringing about unity, as those leaders of German thought, Carl Schurz and others, hoped for, there came into the history of Germany a very different individual, Prince von Bismarck, who was the premier of Prussia in 1862. His theory was that he would conquer and unite the German nation by blood and iron, and he developed the army, always a well-controlled body in Prussia, and he made the nation into an army, and an army into the nation, and then he planned the wars upon which he founded the unity of Germany. He became involved in a quarrel with Denmark, and induced Austria to go in with him, and took away Schleswig-Holstein from Denmark; and then when he got it, he found it was so easy that he annexed it forcibly to Prussia; and when Austria asked, in a diplomatic way, just what there had been in that war for her, he said there was not anything. And then he got into war with Austria, as he had intended, and in six weeks he wiped her off the map of Germany. Then in that war he annexed forcibly Hanover and Frankfort, and made an offensive and defensive alliance with Württemburg and Baden, and several other German countries; and then he sat down to wait until that faker, Napoleon III, in his pirouetting, would bring about an appearance of a war of aggression against Germany, which was exactly what Bismarck was waiting for, and he only had to wait four years for that; and if you will read his memoirs you will see how he brought that about. You will be interested in reading, I am sure, that interview between himself and von Roon and von Moltke. They received a telegram from the Emperor, outlining an interview between him and Beneditti, Napoleon's ambassador, and they were thrown into gloom, because the interview was one which seemed so pacific to them that they thought its publication would prevent war; and Bismarck sat down and without changing the body of the message, changed a few words in it and published it; and then von Moltke said, "Now we will have war." He said, "That telegram, when it came, sounded like a parley. As you have changed it, it sounds like the rattle of a drum." This was stated by Bismarck himself. So, true to his plan, Napoleon declared war, and then, in a short time, Bismarck defeated France and took Alsace-Lorraine and an indemnity of a billion dollars, which the Germans put into the army, and Bismarck crowned a Prussian king Emperor of Germany at Versailles, and he went back to Berlin and sat down as the head of the Empire to digest the pieces of territory he had bitten off in the last three years.

He was not in favor of world dominion. He wanted to raise Germany to a great power in Europe, and he succeeded. He made fun of the idea of world dominion, but there was held out to the German people the idea that all the rest of the world would try to get back from them this territory which had been taken, and therefore they must defend themselves, and so they went on and provided greater and greater armies.

They also adapted in their wonderful way, as you gentlemen of science know, the principles of science to the manufacture of everything, and to every field of industry and business. They introduced a system which they called *Kultur,* and which brought about a prosperity in competition with the world that attracted the admiration of the world. Their population increased and pressed upon their borders, and with their marvelous successes in the three wars, with their wonderful administration and the demonstration of their efficiency in their prosperity, and with their increase of population, they acquired megalomania, and they learned to think that they were supermen. They believed they had invented *Kultur,* and it was their

duty to spread it over the world and enlarge their borders and conquer the world for the purpose of spreading that *Kultur*.

And they soon, by reason of their elevation as a people, associated
themselves with God. They regarded themselves as the agents of
God. They are a people of an inexorable logic. If they begin with
a false premise, as they often do, their confidence in logic is such
that they wipe out any fact that is inconsistent with the conclusion
reached by that logic. You remember the story of the old German
who was in the California gold diggings and met a man out there
whom he had seen only recently in New York; and, anxious to find
out how he had gotten there, he asked: "You came the plains across?"
The man replied, "No." "Then you have come the Isthmus over?"
"No." "Oh, then you come the Straits of Magellan through?" "No."
"No?" and then the German's eyes opened and he looked at the man
for a minute and he said: "Well, then, you have not arrived."

Having established that *Kultur* was necessary for the world and
that they had invented it, they believed that they were the people to
spread it, and then, with that inexorable logic, all of these other
conclusions followed. The state, the German state, was to spread
Kultur. It was to do God's work. Therefore, every consideration
must yield to the doing of that work. The state was above everything. The state, engaged in this work, could do no wrong. Therefore, these considerations of honor and decency, and the performance
of obligation, could play no part. International morality was eliminated. The only sin of a state was weakness, its virtue was power.
And that doctrine, or its elements, the idea that Germany was over
all, was preached in the schools, in the academies, in the universities,
by the great lecturers, by the military writers; and the conviction
grew with the people, first, that they must protect and defend themselves and give everything to their state of force and maintain that
force in order that they should spread *Kultur* to the world by domination and conquest. They eliminated, as I say, international morality.

Now, that is the nation and that is the people that we are engaged in fighting. They are obsessed, as with insanity, otherwise you
cannot explain what you see and read and know. "Why is it," you
ask, "we did not know this before we got into the war?" Well, we
read excerpts from the lectures and military writings, but we have

cranks of our own—I need not mention them—and certainly we do not want to be held responsible for their writings and their statements and their actions, and we assumed that these people thus speaking among the Germans belonged to that necessary and conspicuous, but we hope with us unimportant, element. But it was not so in the case of Germany, and you can read the books that now have been printed impartially showing these sermons and lectures, and showing that these lectures spoke for all the people. Consider, for a moment, that there was a writer who in one of his writings incorporated a prayer like this: "Oh, Thou, who presides over all, up above, high in the skies, up above the Cherubim and Seraphim—and Zeppelins—"

Now, that association, if it did not shock your feelings as irreverent would suggest a humorous view; but to the German mind, with the idea of what the Zeppelin was to do in spreading *Kultur*, it was the agency of God; the association between the cherubim and seraphim which are supposed to be God's agents, with the Zeppelins, was entirely proper. They preached sermons on the German God.

It is the people of Germany we are fighting, with the characteristics they have of subordination to the authority of the Prussian military regime and the Kaiser, and we must not assume they are compelled against their will to do this fighting. They have made too many heroic sacrifices in loyalty to this false idea, and in loyalty to the leadership of the Kaiser and therefore what the President says must not be misconstrued. What we are trying to do is to separate the people of Germany from the rulers of Germany, but the only way we can separate them from their rulers is by hitting them on the head with a club so that the psychology of the situation will be brought home to them.

If you look for proof of this position of Germany with reference to the abolition of international morality, you can find it in their method of warfare. I do not think it necessary to go into a detailed recital of the awful atrocities that have been proven before you can arrive at a general conclusion as to their violation of every rule of warfare. They bombarded unfortified towns, an act which is forbidden by international law, and the men who bombarded these unfortified towns on the east coast of England were rewarded by being decorated with the Iron Cross.

The Hague Conference provided certain rules with respect to carrying on the war by means of aircraft, one of which was that belligerents were not to drop explosives from aircrafts on undefended towns; and the Germans promptly sent their Zeppelins, that were assembled for the purpose of carrying on war, and to which they turned for the purpose of carrying on the war, and they sent these Zeppelins to England and slaughtered innocent [non]combatants. Of the thousands of victims of the Zeppelin raids, possibly not more than fifty soldiers and sailors were hit, and only one or two arsenals, but the great body of the victims is composed of women and children and old men. The men who navigated the Zeppelins in these raids were also rewarded with Iron Crosses.

When the Germans entered Belgium they violated their treaties through which they had given their plighted faith for sixty years with the other nations. You would think when they went into Belgium under those circumstances, they would treat the people with some consideration, even in spite of their obsession. Did they? No. What they did was to take a district in Belgium, and direct their soldiers to pursue the policy of *Schrecklichkeit,* that is, to stand up against a wall the leading citizens and shoot them, as well as the women and children. You ask for proof? Well, read the report of Lord Bryce. He is a lawyer, an able lawyer, and an historian, and he was on the committee with other lawyers and judges, and they ignored the evidence as to the sporadic brutalities by soldiery which you encounter in every war, and took only the evidence of cases that could not have been committed except by the order of officers, and they showed that this was part of the military policy of Germany in terrorizing the rest of the innocent Belgians by such cruel atrocities in respect to the families of this particular little district.

But the worst thing they have done has been with respect to Armenia. When England brought over the Indian troops to help that small regular army of hers, and they came and made good soldiers, showing they had been well treated, the Germans held up their hands in holy horror and said, "They are sending Mohammedans to fight Christians," all the time having the eminently Christian monarch, the Sultan of Turkey, in alliance with them. And after the alliance was secure, then Turkey proceeded to carry out a purpose that she had partially attempted to carry out years before in ridding herself of Armenian Christians in her empire. She proceeded, with Germany looking on and with officers of the German army at hand, through her regular soldiery and her irregular soldiery, to murder eight hundred thousand Armenians because they were Christians. Now that is the effect of the false philosophy, the horrid philosophy, that there is no international morality, and that nothing should stand in the way of military success and the advance of the state in the spread of *Kultur*.

That is the kind of enemy we have to fight. That is the psychological state of the German people, and the only way in which we can change it, as I say, is by defeating them. If we defeat them, then they will appreciate the falseness of a philosophy which can only be justified by victory, and then when they are defeated, as we must defeat them, then they will relegate the Kaiser—it will not need any action on our part—they well relegate the Kaiser and the Prussian military regime to the place where they ought to go.

It is a very satisfactory thing to see that the sin of the Germans in this regard has found them out. When the war began, good Christians hesitated about believing in a good God, when they saw that so many innocent men could be hurled into a vortex of destruction, agony, suffering and death like this. Now the thing is cleared away, and what we see is that the world has been suffering from a cancer of militarism, and Germany has been responsible for it, and she had led the world on to these great armies, and on her hands is the blood of this awful war—this war with fifteen or twenty times the number of men engaged in it, and with an equally interested amount of suffering and agony, compared with any other war—with 40,000,-000 men engaged, 7,000,000 men dead, 6,000,000 men in the hospitals, and 6,000,000 men in prison camps. That is due to Germany. The causes cannot be cut out but by suffering. God works by inexorable laws, and the penalty of sin must be paid.

This is a German war of aggression as any schoolboy can now see. The White Paper did not show any communications between Germany and Austria during that anxious time, and they have never been disclosed, but we know that Russia was not prepared, and England not any more prepared than we are today, and France was very lacking in her preparation, and yet we are to believe that these three countries conspired to attack Germany who was ready to the last cannon and the last reservist. Why, that is enough to make a horse laugh. It is true that Germany did not advise the killing of the Crown Prince and his Consort. That is not the way Germany has begun her wars. She gets ready. She plans a war. She gets ready and then she waits for the opportunity so that it shall seem to be a war of aggression by other powers. That is true in every war she has waged since Prussia has been in power.

So to go back to this sin of Germany finding her out. She has been perfect in military preparation; she has been perfect in military strategy, but where has she made her blunders? She has made her blunders, and her great blunders, in misreading other peoples, in her diplomacy, and she has made these blunders because she has eliminated from her own soul considerations of morality and motives of good, motives of service and allegiance and unselfishness, and she has fallen into the error of ignoring those motives in others when she attempts to judge of what other people will do. So she made a mistake about Great Britain, and her conscience in respect to Belgium. She made a mistake as to the British possessions—I mean those independent dominions. She said, "The tie which binds the dominions to the mother country is very light. There is no reason why they should go in, there is nothing in it for them," and she was indignant and exasperated when she found that her judgment in that regard was wrong. That is because she could not appreciate the filial relation between those countries and Great Britain. She could not appreciate the daughter's loyalty to her mother that had protected her. Is there anything more noble in this world war than the way in which Canada and Australia have responded to the call of the mother country? Canada has sent 420,000 men, and Australia 400,000 men, Australia having a population of five millions and Canada six or seven millions. In proportion we would have to send an army of seven millions. And then France. Germany said France was decadent, permeated with socialism, [had] no patriotism, and [was] deeply affected with frivolity. France was not prepared, but she rallied her legions—and is it not inspiring to think of the fight that she made, knowing that Germany's military staff was attempting to crush

France?—France stood up, and with the aid of that thin line of the British regular army, she hurled back the German hordes at the Marne and saved the world.

The biggest mistake Germany has made has been with respect to this country. I remember some of the things the papers said—they said we were a tangoing nation. They said we were too fat to go into the trenches. They had a contempt for us because we had not prepared for war. They assumed our citizenship of German origin would prevent the war, and political considerations would divide the people in that regard. They were also obsessed with the idea that they could end the war with this murderous weapon, this weapon they could not use except by accompanying its use with the murder of neutral people. So they used it.

Now, ten, fifteen or twenty years hence, when our grandchildren go to their fathers, after having read a history of this war, they will say, "Papa, why in the name of common sense did Germany force the United States into this war?" And papa will have a hard time to tell, unless he goes into all of the circumstances and treats the subject from a psychological standpoint, because the boy will say, any child would say, "Why, they had been fighting this war for three years, exhausting as no other war has been before, so that they were all not exhausted, but nearly so; and at that time they deliberately forced into the war against them that gigantic young nation that could furnish what is absolutely necessary, and what must determine the victory in the war, more food, more money, more fighting men than any nation in the world."

Now, that is what they have done, and nothing can explain it except that obsession that I have referred to—their failure to see things in other people, because they have eliminated from their own consideration those moral motives. Now what are we going to do about it? I have said potentially we are the greatest power in the world. We are a potential military power, and we have got to make that thing which is potential actual, and that is no mean job. We have before us a war of two, three or four years. We have got to raise an army of five million or seven million, or possibly more. It is man power that is going to win this war. Russia has become a pulpy mass, and it has got to work out its own salvation. There is one feature about that situation, and that is that the Germans will not know any more about what is going to happen in Russia than we do, but it is going to enable the Germans to bring back, doubtless, many of her divisons to the western front. We must fight the war out on the western front, and it may be that the western front will reach from the North Sea to the Adriatic. We have got to furnish to our Allies not only food, not only money, but we have got to furnish them the man power that will give a predominance that will win this war. We have got to wear them out, it may be by attrition, as Grant wore Lee out, but we have got to do it, because civilization depends upon it, because our own independence depends upon it. The war is not in our souls yet, not as it will be when our boys are shot down, and when we consult the casualty lists to see whether those dear to us have suffered. One of the great satisfactions is that when we are in it, when we meet disaster through blunders—for there will be blunders—the American people are so constituted, with their inherited traits, that those disasters and blunders and defeats and humiliations will only make us stronger to carry out the struggle that is essential to liberty and Christian civilization.

AN ADDRESS BY GOVERNOR FRANK O. LOWDEN[26]

Delivered at the Congress of National Service held under the auspices of the National Security League, Chicago, February 21, 1918.

Mr. Chairman and Delegates of the Congress of National Service, Ladies and Gentlemen:

Illinois appreciates the great honor this Congress does her in holding this session at the supreme crisis of our national life within our borders. Illinois, in common with the other states of the nation, hopes much from the deliberations of this Congress. You are met here to consider how best and how most speedily we can win this war. The outstanding achievement of America to this time in the war, I think all will agree, has been our selective draft law and its administration. Our enemy did not dream when the gauge of battle was flung down that America would adopt this law, enforce it thoroughly, without fear or favor and without internal disturbance. Our

[26] From a manuscript copy in the possession of Governor Lowden.

enemy now, however, affects to believe that this law is but a temporary expedient, that America will soon grow war weary, and therefore
she renews her hope for a continuance of the war, until America shall
become too fatigued to fight. The answer to this belief on the other
side, which undoubtedly is stimulating them to hold out against us and
our allies, can best be given, can most effectively be sent by writing a
permanent law in our statute books for universal military training.

The time has come when not only in its bearing upon this war,
but in its bearing upon the permanent welfare of America, we must
recognize that with manhood's suffrage must go manhood's service.
To those who profess to believe that this means our entering upon a
military career as a nation, I answer that this is the alternative, and
the only alternative to our becoming a military nation. We must
elect whether we will have universal military training, so at all times
to be ready to defend our honor and our shores, or whether we shall
indefinitely maintain a large standing army, an army that in itself
is a part of our common citizenship. All history teaches us that the
danger of militarism is not a danger that comes to nations whose citizenship is also that nation's defenders; but the only country to which
militarism has come as a curse in the past has been that nation which
employed a professional army to defend its liberty.

Not only because of this war, but because of the necessity which
has been revealed to us of elevating our nation to the value of American citizenship, is this subject one which is imperative now. Years
before the war our people had been indifferent to the duties of citizenship. They regarded their country as a fairy godmother from
whom all gifts were to be received, but for which no return was made.
We complained of our public officials and then declined to go to the
polls to change them unless someone provided for us an easy and free
conveyance. Citizenship is like everything else in this world in this
respect. Human nature is such that it prizes nothing that it is not
compelled to pay some price for. Our citizenship, according to the
views of our fathers, was our highest and most sacred possession. Of
late years, however, it has been neither a matter of pride nor a matter of prizing to the average man that he had citizenship. Now, if
our young men at the age of nineteen, if you please, could complete
the education which our schools bestow by a year in their country's

service, during which time they could be instructed upon the duties of citizenship, that year educationally would be worth more to them than any other year in their school course, and it would give us a citizenship that appreciated its high privileges.

Another thing I have no doubt that you gentlemen will consider—whether the time has not come to write down a definite and concrete financial program. We not only have the men we need, if we can mobilize them, as I have pointed out, but we have the money if that can be mobilized. With the experiences that these months have brought, isn't it essential that now we should write out a definite financial program contemplating not that the war will end this spring, or this summer, but providing for a budget for an indefinite continuance of the war, if need be, for us?

We ought to know now how much money we should be able to raise through thrift stamps and war savings certificates. I want to take occasion to say that in my opinion this is one of the most promising features of our financial program so far announced. The treasury officials hope to raise in this way two billion dollars a year. That would be less than twenty dollars for each of our people, and that amount should readily be forthcoming. The beauty of that method of financing is if we raise two billion dollars this year, it will be easier to raise two billion dollars next year, because the money that comes in this way is from income, not capital. Having determined that, it ought to be possible—and I have no doubt that this is being considered by the treasury officials at Washington—to have the financial interests of America come together and work out how many billions may be raised each year without unduly checking industry. When that is determined, then with the experience we have had, it ought to be possible to determine how much money can be raised by taxation. In the light of the last few months there must be some point which we can readily discover beyond which you cannot safely tax incomes or excess profit. Equally certain is it that there is some point up to which you could raise taxation in this way without permanently injuring the business of the country; and when that has been done, we will know the maximum of money we can raise each year for the prosecution of this war. In other words, we will have a budget, at least so far as revenues are concerned, and who shall doubt if we will do this but that we will have abundant governmental income to prosecute this war at least as long as any other nation on the face of the globe can prosecute it.

Let me remind you of another fact: If we shall know definitely, concretely, just what our governmental revenues may be forced to, then we shall know how much money can be expended for the war. I want to remind you that human nature is such that if a man knows that he has got to limit his expenditures to a certain sum, he will find some way to do it, and accomplish all the results that would have been accomplished if he had had no definite maximum figure in his mind. I have no doubt but that if we have the courage to face the facts we shall have abundant revenue for an indefinite continuance of this war. That does not mean that I want an indefinite continuance of the war, but I regard the issues involved so mighty that I think the part of prudence is to so marshal our men and so marshal our resources that we can continue to conduct this war until victory and a permanent peace may come.

There is nothing to be gained by shrinking from the facts. There is no advantage in disregarding the plain situation before us. The sooner we face the facts the sooner we will meet those facts. I want to suggest that with universal military training, with a definite financial program contemplating a series of years, the last and dearest hope of the Central Empires will quickly vanish. Each of these methods is not a method for prolonging the war, but for shortening the war.

There is one other thing about which I am going to speak very briefly. We have the men; we have the means, if we will only use them wisely as I have pointed out. We have the cause if our people can only be made to understand how precious that cause is, and how far-reaching the results of this war are. I haven't the slightest doubt in the world but with a unanimity never witnessed before in this or any other land, our people will resolve to use their men and the means to the winning of a complete victory.

When the war broke out there were a lot of people out in this part of the country, and I have no doubt that was true elsewhere, who believed that it was the ordinary war between two nations that were jealous of each other's commercial prestige, or which coveted each other's territory. It is true that way back in the last century we had heard the great German professor of history declare the doctrine that nations are above the moral law, that there was no sacredness in a treaty and that any nation was at liberty to disregard its treaty provided only that this violation was of advantage to that nation.[27] We had heard that doctrine, but we thought it was simply the vagary of some university professor somewhere. It was only when the German army crossed the frontier of Belgium, it was only when the German chancellor declared a treaty but a scrap of paper, that we realized for the first time that this doctrine that had been preached for half a century before was not simply the fugitive thought of a college professor, but we knew that it was an act in pursuance of a deep imperial design for world conquest. Then we began to open our eyes, and yet we did not realize to the full extent what it meant. But as we have painfully traced the acts of the central powers from week to week since this war began, we find that every deed they have done and every word they have said was in pursuance of a conspiracy of the military autocracy of Germany which the military autocracy of Germany had entered into fifty years ago to enslave the world; that at least has become clear to us. If anyone is deluded by any of the talk by some of their statesmen of no indemnities and no annexations, let him pick up his morning paper and read this last sad chapter in their relations with Russia. Whenever that talk was indulged in, in Germany, it was but a form of diplomatic camouflage, and the German statesmen who happen to be at the present time the men in control of the German army have never committed themselves to anything else. Then think of what they are doing today in that great unhappy country to their east.

A great many people feel that this war is a long way off. They are getting over it now, I think. Every once in a while someone intimates that it is three thousand miles away. My friends, there never was a war in the history of America that was as near your heart and hearthstones, whether you live in Illinois or on the Atlantic seaboard, as this war that is raging today. In all the wars of the past, even in the darkest hour, the people who were waging those wars could see something of the future even in the event of their defeat;

[27] Heinrich von Treitschke.

(9)

but if this war goes against us, all is lost. As I have frequently said, even in the dark hours preceding our war of the rebellion, overcast and gloomy as were the skies, there never was a minute when on either one side or the other the people did not know that if they lost they still would have some kind of a country left. It might be fragmentary, it might be inglorious, it might fall far short of its glorious mission as our forefathers dreamed of that mission, but still there would be some portion of a country left to north and south, some place where the defeated of either side might find a home. If this war goes against us, it involves us just as much as though our soil were within the confines of Holland or Denmark or Switzerland. If we lose, the results of this war will follow alike upon every spot of earth and sea, the wide world around.

This is the final battle, skirmishes of which have been fought since the dawn of time. It is the final conflict to determine whether men, just plain men, are worth striving for and building for, or whether in all the centuries that lie before us men must delve and toil and sweat in order that a few thousand of favored supermen somewhere shall enjoy all the fruits of the earth.

It is the final battle not only between the rights of men and the so-called divine right of kings, but it is the final battle between the spiritual forces of the universe and the cold, grasping material forces of the universe.

If our people realize our cause, who shall doubt the result? We have the men, we have the means, we have the cause, and now will democracy show to the world that it too can use these men and means with efficiency? Let democracy show to the world that it knows what its liberties are worth.

I thank you, my friends.

AN ADDRESS BY GOVERNOR FRANK O. LOWDEN[28]

Delivered before a gathering of members of the Grand Army of the
Republic, State Fair Grounds, Springfield, August 14, 1918.

*Mr. Chairman, Members of the Grand Army of the Republic, and
Ladies and Gentlemen:*

A year ago I had the privilege of appearing before you, almost
on this very spot. At that time we had hardly entered the war. Then
we were wondering, some of us, what our boys would do when they
reached the battle front. It is human nature for one generation to
suspect that the generation which follows it has not quite the same
iron in its composition that it has had. Those of my generation knew
that the soldiers of today, if they lived up to the traditions which you
had made for them in the greatest war the world up to that time had
known, would be the wonder and the admiration of Europe. They
had not then had a chance to appear in the battle line. All that has
changed within the twelve months that have gone by and the American soldiers at Chateau Thierry, or on the Marne, or at the fiercely
contested battle of Cierges, showed that they were worthy of the
glorious traditions of the Grand Army of the Republic.

I recall very well, how, in the early weeks and months of the
war, the posts of the Grand Army of the Republic were the centers
of patriotic propaganda and effort. I recall, when some of our people
could not understand the magnitude of the issues involved, it was the
soldiers of the Grand Army of the Republic who said, "What matter whether we understand or not, our country is at war, our flag is in
peril, and that is enough to know, to rally around that flag." Although the Civil War had been over for more than half a century,
the influence of the survivors of that great war was never more potent
though their numbers had been much larger than it was at that time.
When the history of this present war is written, it will be recorded
that this great spirit of patriotism which is now sweeping over the
land had its earliest origin and encouragement in the posts of the
Grand Army of the Republic.

. . . .

As I look into your faces I marvel how you can bear your

[28] From a manuscript copy in the possession of Governor Lowden.

years so easily and so gracefully. But let none of you think that your work is done. Perhaps the most important of all the years since you were mustered out lie before you. There will come times now when some people, weary of the war, will cry for peace. There are many people today who feel, because of the victories the allied armies have won, that peace is near. You old soldiers know better. You went through Gettysburg, some of you, and many of you went through the siege of Vicksburg. I know that because I see some of you before me who did. Every student of military affairs knows that when Vicksburg fell and Lee's army was driven across the Potomac after Gettysburg, that the war ought to have stopped, that we had won; yet you know, my friends, that two years of bitter warfare endured after both of those events.

I am putting this to you, because, when you go back to your homes, whatever you say to your people will have influence with them. So, today, if our victorious pursuit of the German armies continues until they are driven to the Hindenburg line, if we are wise and profit by the history of the past, we shall still go on preparing on the theory that the war has just commenced. Nothing in the world will postpone victory so much as for us, as a people, to get it into our minds that the war is practically won. We should assume, and, if we are wise, we will assume, that the war has years yet to run before the Central Empires will acknowledge defeat. That being true, we should go on making preparations as fast as we can. We will extend the draft ages; we will proceed with the greatest speed of which we know in the manufacture of munitions of war. We will multiply airplanes until we think we have enough to darken the very heavens above Berlin. Then there can be no doubt about the result, and that result will come quicker that way than it otherwise would.

So, members of the Grand Army of the Republic, as I said a moment ago, the most important work you have ever done may lie ahead of you. Your people will listen to you when you talk to them of the probable duration of the war, because of what you have seen and what you have endured. Let us, then, proceed with even greater speed with each victory we win and assume that we have only reached Vicksburg and Gettysburg in this war, and that years of fighting lie ahead of us. We will save the lives of many American boys by that course.

When peace comes and these magnificent boys who survive come back, what a sight it will be when they, the veterans of this new war, shall meet you, the veterans of this old war, who have helped keep the morale of the American people so high while they, your sons and your grandsons, are fighting at the front. . . .

I thank you heartily for the privilege that I have had this morning of meeting you. I should like to discuss in a larger and more adequate way this war, but I leave that to General Dickson, who will do it with his usual ability and charm. I want you to have the best time possible while you are here. If there is anything that I can do to add to your good time, let me know, and I will do it. I thank you.

AN ADDRESS BY GOVERNOR FRANK O. LOWDEN[29]

Delivered before the American Life Convention, Chicago, September 18, 1918.

Mr. President and Gentlemen of the American Life Convention:

It is a great pleasure for me to be with you a few minutes this morning. I have come in contact with representatives of your profession, more or less, all my life. I have been engaged in many debates with representatives of this great industry in America and have usually been vanquished in those debates.

I see before me representatives of two at least, yes three that I now recall, of the oldest life insurance companies of this state. I had the honor of being counsel for one of them at one time when I was practicing law at this bar, and the opportunity of speaking to this great representative body, coming from all parts of the country, is greatly appreciated by me. I desire to devote my attention to one phase of this great war which grips the world and which must appeal pecularily to the life insurance fraternity. I have reference, when I say that, to what you gentlemen call the "moral risk." In the first place, society has long recognized the very great part which you play in any civilized state. We business men know that in order successfully to conduct business it is necessary to lay aside something at the

[29] From a manuscript copy in the possession of Governor Lowden.

end of the year to meet depreciation of the implements of business. If we are farmers (I am a farmer myself, and have been for a good many years), at the end of the year we find ourselves safe only if we charge off depreciation upon the implements of our farm work, upon our horses and mules. If we farm in Texas, it is upon our mules that we charge off depreciation. And yet the biggest asset in business, namely the genius of the American business men, we neglected altogether to provide for, until the insurance man came along and enabled us to take something out of our profits of the year and insure against debt or illness or old age. Therefore, you have preserved the solvency of the business of America by virtue of the work which you have been doing. We are going to carry this idea of insurance further. It has been developing very rapidly. We insure now against accidents of all kinds and we are adding some new lines to the field of insurance every day, and I think I can say that the progress of insurance is the measure of the progress of a civilization.

Now, a moment ago I said something about what you call, I believe, the "moral risk." That plays a very important part in the question of whether in a given case you shall write a policy or not; because it isn't simply the robustness of a man's health, it isn't simply his physical resources, it isn't even a question alone of his ancestry as to whether he is a good risk, but you go further, you insure a man more readily who acknowledges obligations wherever they are found. You insure a man more readily because of his mode of life, if it is a proper one. In other words, one of the most important considerations which you take into account in the exercise of your occupation is the moral risk of the applicant, and you are wise.

We are engaged in a war in which the material resources of our enemy were marshalled more effectively and in larger force than had happened before in the history of the world. Their philosophy had taught them simply to inventory the material things of the world. They made just one mistake when they went into this war. They left out of account the moral risk, so although their enemies had not been dreaming of wars then, and were ill prepared and had not these great stores of munitions that had been accumulating for a quarter of a century, and were without the material resources of war, as compared with the Central Empires, yet because of the superior ideals, of the superior moral forces which actuated the Allies, we find that the tide of battle has turned and that again the principle of your profession, that the moral risk is the most important one, is being vindicated upon the greatest battle fields of the world.

The fact is, that if you eliminate all consideration of spiritual things, you eliminate the most powerful forces that operate in this universe. Let me give you an illustration of what I mean. When this war began, the Central Empires, which stood by the doctrine that might is right and that this world belongs to the strong and to the strong alone, and that there is no other law except the law of force in the relations of either individuals or nations, they made great progress at first. But what has happened? We read now in the papers from day to day that when misfortune comes, when disaster threatens, their morale gives way. You can keep up the morale of a materialistic army when victories come, but you have to reinforce your courage with your spiritual resources to keep up your morale when disaster comes. And the Germans calculating, and calculating rightly from their standpoint, that they would, this summer, break through the lines of the Allies before America could come, made this mistake: That the morale of the Christian soldier is sustained by the faith that right in the end must prevail and that the soldier who is fighting for his land and who is fighting for his ideals and is fighting for civilization, that soldier fights the hardest when his back is to the wall.

Early in the war, the German military autocracy, believing honestly in the doctrine of might, bombarded open cities and killed helpless women and children, against all rules of civilized warfare. There was no revolt in the German mind against this atrocity, no protest was raised either—and we must face this fact—by the ruling powers themselves or by the people. It was only recently, I think within the last week, that I noted in the papers that when a few of our airplanes had flown above some of the Rhenish cities, they held a great meeting of eleven of those cities and protested to their government against this sort of warfare and asked that a convention of the warring nations might be called to agree to spare the open cities of the belligerent lands. It took the German people a little over four years to come to the view that the bombardment of defenseless cities was wrong, and they only came to that view when bombs fell from American and French and English and Italian airplanes upon some of their cities. That is another result of simply considering the material things of the universe, the things that you can touch and handle, the things that are visible, the things that the senses can grapple. If they had had anything of spiritual light within their hearts, they would have protested more than four years ago, but it was only when the bombs fell above their cities that they saw the crime of this method of warfare.

.   .   .   .

As I view it, the greatest gain we are going to make when peace shall come, because it is going to be a peace through victory, will be that such peace will also mark the final triumph of the moral and spiritual forces of the universe over the mere brazen, cruel material resources of the universe.

I want to say just one word about the last peace offensive. I am going to read you something that I saw the other day in a soldier's letter, but before I read that, I wish to call your attention to this fact: In nearly all the letters that we are receiving from our Illinois soldiers, and I am sure that the same thing is true from the soldiers of other states, we find a good deal, not of hatred—the American soldier is too big to hate, he is too big to be cruel, he is too big to emulate the methods of our enemy—you will find in all these letters a growing indignation and contempt, in a way, for the character of their enemies. Such phrases as this are very frequent. You have seen it. I have, a score of times in the last few weeks: "As long as they can kill their enemy, they are very brave, very ferocious, but the moment that the fortune of war goes against them, they lose all their courage and raise their hands, crying 'Kamerad!' and while 'Kamerad' is the word upon their lips, there is only a malignant hate and treachery in their hearts."

So today, the governments of Austria and Germany are showing exactly the same quality in their suggestion of peace. It is only when the fortunes of war are going against them, it is only when they have seen the civilized world arise in its might, as it had never arisen before, to vindicate all of the principles of civilization which had been held sacred, it is only then that they cry out for peace; but in their hearts, there is nothing but hate and treachery toward the Allies.

I want to say that, gloomy as were the weeks which followed March 21st and when the furious drives of our enemy met with great success, in none of these drives was there more danger to ourselves and our allies than in this treacherous peace offensive that Austria-Hungary, with the consent of Germany, launched the other day.

I am going to read from a statement made by Doctor Rosemeyer, a very distinguished and brilliant journalist and publicist of Germany, who was asked why he did not write something to move the German people, and this is what he said: "Nonsense, haven't I been writing my fingers off for thirty years? What those fellows need is not ideas for their brains, they need bombs on their skulls. Help can only come from one place, from Bethlehem—Bethlehem, Pennsylvania. They will cheat you yet, those junkers. Having won half of the world by bloody murder, they are going to win the other half with tears in their eyes, crying for mercy." They are like those soldiers upon the battle fronts who win the contempt of the American soldier, who is also a sportsman, by their appeal to mercy the moment they are helpless in the hands of their foe. This German publicist's words ring true. There is a warning for us. So I say that the President of the United States never made a better answer in his life to any proposition than the one he made promptly to Austria.

Let us follow the advice of Lieutenant Lee, of Detroit, who wrote a letter home the other day in which he said: "I want to tell you this, Bill, tell the people over there to forget this peace talk for a while. The time to talk peace is when the Boche is so badly whipped that he will crawl to us and ask us to stop. We can do it and we will do it if the people at home only keep their mouths shut about something of which they know nothing. Let them devote as much time to getting tobacco and magazines over here. What we want is to see the enemy scattered so far that he will never be able to come back."

I think this young soldier's advice is sound, and whenever you hear of a peace meeting in your section, just say to them that you have heard from the battle fronts of Europe, and the boys over there say that if the peace meeting would get busy and raise funds for tobacco and magazines for the boys, they would be of some use in this world-wide conflict. It is a tragedy which grips the world as it was never gripped before, but out of it is emerging the finest body of young manhood this country or any other country ever had. We won't have as many boys, as many young men, when this war is over as we would have had without it, but, my friends, we will have the finest lot of young men that America ever held in all its past. These letters that come from our forces abroad, you have read them, all of you, and you know that it would have been impossible for those same boys to have written those letters a year before they went. The spiritual forces which had been yielding, in the years that preceded the war, to materialism, are reviving in the hearts of these young heroes, and with us also; and when they return, no man of your profession need have any fear about the moral risk of guaranteeing the future of those young men.

I welcome you to the second city of the continent, the fourth city of the world, the commercial capital of Illinois. I need not say anything about Chicago, Illinois, because your president, in very generous words, gave recognition to us. I am glad that you have come. I hope that you will have a profitable session. I know it is a great work in which you are engaged and humanity is the better for it. When this war is over, the test of any business is going to be "Does it improve, does it help the condition in life of just the plain average man?" Your profession can stand that test.

I thank you.

MEMORIAL TO CONGRESS—FREEDOM OF POLAND AND IRELAND

House Joint Resolution Number 19, Fiftieth General Assembly, State of Illinois.

WHEREAS, A war between the powers of Europe and their dependencies has been waging for almost three full years. Millions of men, the flower of the manhood of the Old World, have given up their lives that their countries might continue to be reckoned among the nations of the earth. The blood of every race and every creed has intermingled in drenching the soil of Europe. Millions of lives have been lost and billions of treasure have been spend [spent]. When the end of the conflict shall come, no one can foretell, but when it shall come it is the earnest desire of all lovers of liberty that this conflict shall not have been waged in vain; and

WHEREAS, Much difference of opinion exists as to the causes of this conflict between the statesmen of the contending powers, but whether the causes of this war are commercial or racial, the President of the United States, the spokesman for our nation, has proclaimed upon the occasion of our country's entry therein, that this is a war for the preservation of democracy and for the abolition of autocracy; that each race and each nation, whether a small principality or a vast empire, has the right to exist and grow in usefulness to a world according to its hopes and aspirations; and

WHEREAS, The people who inhabit Europe sprang from one common ancestral stock, but before each left its ancestral home in Asia, this common stock had divided into four great families, viz: The Celts, the Greeco- [Graeco] Romans, the Teutons and Slavonian, and each in the order named emigrated westward over the continent of Europe and founded the great nations of Europe that have existed in the past and those that exist at the present day. Each of these great families was endowed with individual characteristics and temperament and each had a different language and literature. The forcible imposition of foreign ideas, ideals, language and literature upon a people can do nothing less than stunt the mind and intellect of such a people and hinder or prevent its progress; and

WHEREAS, The ancient kingdoms of Ireland and Poland were among the first great nations of Europe. Each established a language, literature and government of its own long before any of the present nations of Europe came into being. The people of Poland belong to the Slavonian race, and their nation stretched from the Black to the Baltic Seas, across the continent of Europe. But by force, its government was destroyed and its territory absorbed by less enlightened and less scrupulous adjoining nations and its people brought into subjection without their consent. But the brave Pole has never willingly submitted to foreign domination and his country has nothing in common with the governments and peoples of the nations who dominate over him. The people of Ireland belong to the Celtic race and have maintained their distinction from all other peoples for more than sixteen hundred years. When this distinct race established itself no historian has presumed to relate for its beginning is buried in the shades of the centuries long past. The people of Ireland worked out their own salvation independent of all the other people of Europe. They were pioneers in elevating man from the savage state to as great a degree as were the Greeks and Romans. They worked out a language and literature of their own, which bears no resemblance to any other language and literature of Europe, and we have it from the great modern scholars of Europe that the language, and literature of these people sprang from the oldest world language, the Sanscrit. They founded a government of their own and their government was not the government of one man, but was a representative government. The assembly, made up of representatives of the people that met at Tara every three years to make laws for the government of the people, was the first representative government in western Europe; and

WHEREAS, Although Ireland and Poland have been by might and without their consent deprived of their right of self-government, yet the spirit of independence is still fondly cherished and will live forever in the hearts of their people. A foreign power can never subdue a people that has established a language, literature and government and maintained them through succeeding centuries. Peace and tranquility [sic] can be maintained amongst such a people only by restoring to them their rights; therefore be it

Resolved, by the House of Representatives of the State of Illinois, the State Senate concurring herein, That Ireland and Poland are of right entitled to self-government and to the restoration of all the rights of which they have been deprived, and that it is the duty of the political powers dominating those countries to concede self-government and the restoration of such rights without further delay; and be it further

Resolved, That the President of the United States and the Federal Congress be and they hereby are urged to exert all legitimate influence at their command to effect the granting of self-government and the restoration of their rights to Ireland and Poland; and be it further

Resolved, That the members of the United States Senate and of the House of Representatives of the United States from the State of Illinois, be and they are hereby urged to exercise every legitimate effort for the purpose of securing action on the part of the United States with the end in view of assuring to Ireland and Poland self-government and the restoration of their rights; and be it further

Resolved, That the Secretary of the State of Illinois be, and he hereby is, instructed to forward authenticated copies of these resolutions to the President of the United States and the United States Senators and members of the House of Representatives from the State of Illinois.

Adopted by the House May 8, 1917.

Concurred in by the Senate, May 16, 1917.

RIGHTS OF IRISH PEOPLE AT THE PEACE CONFERENCE

House Joint Resolution Number 2, Fifty-first General Assembly, State of Illinois.

WHEREAS, The Allied powers associated with the United States about to assemble in conference for the purpose of drafting terms of peace affecting the settlements of various questions arising out of the World War, and for the purpose of drafting agreements affecting the rights of the nations involved in said war, and for the purpose of readjusting conditions brought about by said war relative to those nations whose people are either subject to or whose National integrity has been endangered by the autocratic powers responsible for said war; and

WHEREAS, The Allied powers associated with the United States have subscribed to the fourteen principles enunciated by President Wilson as a basis for a just peace, one of which principle is that the people of all nations forming a separate and distinct race in a particular country have the right of self determination in the creation of the administering power of government within their borders to the end that the power of government may conform to their ideas of justice and freedom, thereby preventing their subjection by governments or peoples foreign to their race and ideals; and

WHEREAS, The Allied powers associated within [with] the United States have given assurances to many of the smaller nations that they will guarantee that such rights of self determination will be provided for in the final treaties or agreements which shall be presented by the Peace Commissioners to the various powers for signature and ratification by said powers; and

WHEREAS, The people of the State of Illinois believe that the right of self determination or self rule ought to and does apply to all nations no matter under whose rule such people are subject, and believing further that the people of Ireland come within the classification of such nations, and believing further that consistent with justice and humanity the Irish people are entitled to the same rights as other subject nations. Therefore, be it

Resolved, by the House of Representatives of the State of Illinois, the Senate concurring herein, That the Representatives of the people of the United States at the Peace Conference be requested to present to said conference the claims of the Irish people to the right of self government, and that they further be requested to exercise their influence to bring about a just consideration of the Peace Conference of the rights of the Irish people to govern themselves, and that said representatives of the United States at the Peace Conference further exercise their influence so that the Irish people may receive such measure of self determination as is consistent with justice and humanity towards the Irish people. Be it further

Resolved, That these resolutions be spread on record in the Journal of the General Assembly of the State of Illinois, and a copy of same properly attested with the Great Seal of State and signed by the Speaker of the House of Representatives and the President of the Senate, the Secretary of State and the Governor of Illinois, be forwarded to the President of the United States and to the representatives of the United States at the Peace Conference.

Adopted by the House January 14, 1919.

Concurred in by the Senate April 22, 1919.

RIGHTS OF JEWISH PEOPLE IN PALESTINE

Senate Joint Resolution Number 27, Fifty-first General Assembly, State of Illinois.

WHEREAS, The future prosperity and peace of the world depends upon a just and equitable settlement of the European war whereby each and every nationality, however small, be granted the liberty to determine its own destiny and the opportunity of living its own life; and

WHEREAS, The government of the United States of America is recognized as an ardent exponent of the rights of the small nations; therefore, be it

Resolved, By the Senate of the State of Illinois, the House of Representatives concurring therein, that the national aspirations and historic claims of the Jewish people with regard to Palestine be recognized at the peace conference, in accordance with the British government's declaration of November second, nineteen hundred and seventeen, that there shall be established such political, administrative and economic conditions in Palestine as will assure the development of Palestine into a Jewish commonwealth, and that the American representatives at the peace conference shall use their best endeavors to facilitate the achievement of this object; be it further

Resolved, By the Senate of the State of Illinois, the House of Representatives concurring therein, that express provisions be made at the peace conference for the purpose of granting the Jewish people in every land the complete enjoyment of life, liberty, and the opportunities for national development to the end that justice may be done to one of the most suffering people on earth—the Jewish people; and be it further

Resolved, That a copy of these resolutions be transmitted by the Secretary of the State of Illinois to the President of the United States.

Adopted by the Senate, April 22, 1919.

Concurred in by the House of Representatives May 7, 1919.

CLAIMS OF ITALIAN GOVERNMENT BEFORE THE PEACE CONFERENCE

House Joint Resolution Number 5, Fifty-first General Assembly, State of Illinois.

WHEREAS, The Allied Powers associated with the United States are assembled in conference for the purpose of drafting terms of peace affecting the settlements of various questions arising out of the World War; and for the purpose of drafting agreements affecting the rights of the nations involved in said war; and for the purpose of readjusting conditions brought about by said war, relative to those nations whose people are either subject to or whose national integrity has been endangered by the autocratic powers responsible for said war; and

WHEREAS, In addition to the sympathy and interest which the people of the United States of America have for Italy as an ally, there is a sentimental interest in Italy because Italy was the mother of modern civilization, and because Italy is the birthplace of Christopher Columbus, who discovered America; and

WHEREAS, Italy has fought with heroism and great sacrifice since its entry into the war, and has done its share in bringing about the great victory of the Allies; and

WHEREAS, Italy is making claims at the Peace Conference for the restoration to it of certain lands and territory formerly belonging to it, and for lands and territory which it is alleged are necessary for its economic needs, and for its national security and preservation; now, therefore, be it

Resolved, by the House of Representatives of the State of Illinois, and Senate concurring herein, That the Representatives of the People of the United States at the Peace Conference be requested to exercise their influence to bring about a just consideration of the claims of the Italian Government for the restoration to it of its lands and territory and of its claim for lands and territory which it is alleged are necessary for its economic needs and for its national security and preservation; and be it further

Resolved, That these resolutions shall be spread on record in the Journal of the General Assembly of the State of Illinois, and that a copy of the same properly attested with the Great Seal of State and signed by the President of the Senate and the Speaker of the House of Representatives, the Secretary of State and the Governor of Illinois, be forwarded to the President of the United States and to the Representatives of the United States at the Peace Conference.

Adopted by the House February 5, 1919.

Concurred in by the Senate June 5, 1919.

PERSECUTION OF JEWISH PEOPLE IN POLAND AND ROUMANIA

Senate Joint Resolution Number 38, Fifty-first General Assembly, State of Illinois.

WHEREAS: It has been charged by persons, worthy of belief, that many people of the Jewish faith, including men, women and children, have recently in different parts of Poland and Roumania been murdered, tortured and otherwise ill treated and subjected to pillage; and

WHEREAS: The existence of such a situation, if in fact it does exist is, in this day of enlightened civilization, deplorable in the extreme; and

WHEREAS: The conditions which are alleged to exist in Poland and Roumania should be investigated so that proper steps may be taken, if need be, to remedy the situation; now therefore be it

Resolved, by the Senate, the House of Representatives of the State of Illinois concurring therein: That the Government of the United States of America, through its proper officials, investigate said charges and that the United States of America use its good offices and influences to end the persecution, if any there be, of the people of the Jewish faith in Poland and Roumania; and be it further

Resolved: That a copy of this resolution, under the seal of State, be sent by the Secretary of State, to each member of Congress from this State.

Adopted by the Senate June 19, 1919.

Concurred [in] by the House of Representatives, July 20, 1919.

(10)

II. MOBILIZING THE STATE'S RE-
SOURCES FOR THE WAR

INCREASING FOOD PRODUCTION IN ILLINOIS—
A PROCLAMATION

We are in the midst of war. We must mobilize our forces for the production of food. The Mississippi valley is the granary of the continent; Illinois, the greatest of all of the food-producing States, is its center. Illinois must do her part in feeding the armies of democracy, for let us not forget that this war has become, not a war against Germany but a war of democracy against absolutism.

I feel certain in this crisis that the farmers of Illinois will employ the utmost endeavors to farm as large an acreage as possible and to raise the maximum yield of crops.

As a result of industrial changes it has been increasingly difficult for more than a decade to employ sufficient labor for the farms. That condition now has become acute. The State of Illinois, through its superintendent of public instruction, has advised all school superintendents and school officers in Illinois to provide a plan whereby any school-boy above the age of fourteen years may be released from school to devote himself to work in the garden or upon the farm, receiving the same school credits as though he had remained at school. This should help greatly to recruit the army of agricultural workers. I suggest that farmers in the vicinity of public schools, who may need additional help, offer to share upon an equitable basis the profits from their crops with school-boys who may be willing to help in producing such crops.

Mr. B. M. Davison, the secretary of the State Board of Agriculture at Springfield, Illinois, has converted his office into an employment agency, and will seek to bring together men who desire to find work upon the farm and those who require their services. The new Department of Agriculture of the State, now being organized, will coöperate to the fullest extent with the agricultural interests of the State to promote the largest possible production.

Let us all remember that at this time we cannot serve our country better than by devoting our energies to the increased production of food. This war is likely to be finally won, not upon the world's battle-fields but in America's grain fields.

I know the difficulty of either extensive or intensive farming at the present time because of the difficulty of securing adequate labor. There are, however, many ways by which we can increase the yield of crops without additional labor. If our farmers would all test and screen their seed corn, they would doubtless increase the total yield by twenty per cent. And twenty per cent might be the margin of safety before another crop is raised. The winter wheat crop in the southwest has largely failed. Something may be done through spring wheat, but relief this year will come largely from the corn crop, and I propose to the State of Illinois the slogan "A Hundred Per Cent Stand of Corn".

Two litters of pigs should be produced where one is now produced, and this might save us from meatless days. Poultry should be produced as it never was produced before.

Measures for increasing food should be confined to those crops and practices that have proved successful in the locality. This is no time for the experimentation with new crops.

The term "Municipal Farming" ought to come into public thought. In the small towns and villages, where much idle land can be had, small fruits and vegetables should be grown under the supervision of those who are skilled in the cultivation of the soil. In order to secure proper results, I earnestly urge upon city and village councils, upon commercial clubs and women's clubs, to exert themselves to provide at once competent supervision for this cultivation. I suggest that retired farmers living in these cities and towns would be available for this service.

Above all we must avoid waste and extravagance. These are our national sins. It often has been said that the average family in America wastes enough to support a family in Europe.

We must reflect that the labor employed to satisfy our demands for luxury might otherwise be used to supply food indispensable to the armies fighting our battles.

If we are to win this war, the labor of the country must be bestowed upon only needful things, and I call upon the people everywhere to practice universally those reasonable economies without which we shall not do our part in this great struggle.

The issue is closed. We did not desire war, but, in spite of our wishes, war is upon us. Our independence as a nation, our liberties, are at stake. If we are worthy of our forebears, we will shrink from no effort and from no sacrifice which may be needed to win an enduring peace.

(SEAL)

GIVEN UNDER MY HAND AND THE GREAT SEAL OF STATE AT THE CAPITOL IN SPRINGFIELD, THIS FOURTEENTH DAY OF APRIL, IN THE YEAR OF OUR LORD ONE THOUSAND NINE HUNDRED AND SEVENTEEN, AND OF THE INDEPENDENCE OF THE UNITED STATES THE ONE HUNDRED AND FORTY-FIRST.

FRANK O. LOWDEN

LOUIS L. EMMERSON
    By the Governor:
        Secretary of State.

DUTIES OF THE PROPOSED STATE COUNCIL OF DEFENSE

Remarks by Governor Frank O. Lowden at a luncheon given in honor of Theodore Roosevelt, Chicago, April 28, 1917.[1]

All classes of society must coöperate, if we are to win this war. We are fighting for the principle of democracy. Democracy must find expression in all the numerous organizations forming to help our country in this time of stress. All over the land societies are being

[1] From a manuscript copy in the possession of Governor Lowden.

formed to help on the great work which has been thrust upon us. If the energies of these voluntary organizations are not to be wasted, they must be coördinated. They may be made the decisive influence which shall win the war. Unless properly coördinated, they will result only in confusion.

I shall appoint a State Council of Defense for Illinois, consisting of fifteen members, whose business it will be to coöperate with the National Council of Defense, and to coördinate the thousands of patriotic agencies formed, or in process of formation, in Illinois. I expect that council to be the clearing house of all the patriotic activities in the state. I suggest that where civic organizations, relief and other societies, are formed, they put themselves into relations with our State Council of Defense, so that all may work together without duplication of effort, without confusion, and with effectiveness.

The committees appointed by these various bodies should contain representatives of all classes of society. This is especially true of what we sometimes call Capital and Labor. This is not a war of capital; it is not a war of labor; it is a war of all the people against autocracy in government. Surely, when our very future as a nation is at stake, there must be hearty coöperation between those who employ, on the one hand, and those who are employed, on the other. If, at this grave time, democracy cannot show solidarity, the future is dark indeed.

We are all involved in a common danger. If we do not stand together now, we all go down in common ruin. Employers and employees alike must will to live together in amity. This is the lesson which the Old World has taught us in the last three years; this is the lesson we must practice now.

The word brotherhood is a word which is seen emerging now from out the smoke of battle with a new radiance. If we, in the great democracy, cannot show that our hearts respond to that lofty sentiment, our fathers builded in vain.

I urge, with all the earnestness of which I am capable, that the people of this state, in organizing to meet the multitudinous needs of war, shall make their organizations as broad as is our common citizenship.

AN ACT AUTHORIZING THE ORGANIZATION OF THE STATE COUNCIL OF DEFENSE OF ILLINOIS

Senate Bill Number 488, Fiftieth General Assembly, State of Illinois.

AN ACT *to establish a State Council of Defense, and making an appropriation therefor.*

SECTION 1. *Be it enacted by the People of the State of Illinois, represented in the General Assembly*: There is hereby established a State Council of Defense.

§ 2. The State Council of Defense shall consist of fifteen persons who shall be appointed by the Governor by and with the advice and consent of the Senate.[2] Their term of office shall be for the duration of the war in which the United States is now engaged, and no longer. The Governor shall designate the member who shall act as chairman.

§ 3. The members of the State Council of Defense shall be appointed with reference to their special knowledge of labor, industries, public utilities, the development of natural resources, sanitation, finance, transportation, or some other subject matter relating to National or State defense.

§ 4. It shall be the duty of the State Council of Defense:

[2]The Governor named the fifteen members of the State Council of Defense on May 1 as follows: Samuel Insull, president, Commonwealth-Edison Company, Chicago, chairman; J. Ogden Armour, president, Armour and Company, Packers, Chicago; Dr. Frank Billings, Chicago, representing the medical profession; Mrs. Joseph T. Bowen, Chicago, chairman of the Woman's Committee; B. F. Harris, banker and farmer, Champaign; John H. Harrison, newspaper editor, Danville; John P. Hopkins, former mayor of Chicago; Levy Mayer, Chicago, representing the legal profession; John G. Oglesby, lieutenant governor, Elkhart; Victor A. Olander, secretary, Illinois State Federation of Labor, Chicago; David E. Shanahan, speaker of the House of Representatives, Fiftieth General Assembly, Chicago; John A. Spoor, chairman, Union Stock Yard and Transit Company, Chicago; Fred W. Upham, president, Consumers' Company, Chicago; Charles H. Wacker, chairman, Chicago Plan Commission; John H. Walker, president, Illinois State Federation of Labor, Chicago.

John P. Hopkins, died on October 13, 1918, and Roger C. Sullivan, of Chicago, was appointed to fill the vacancy in the membership of the State Council of Defense.

(1) To cooperate with and assist the Council of National Defense in the execution of the duties prescribed by an Act of the Congress of the United States approved August 29, 1916, entitled, "An Act making appropriations for the support of the army for the fiscal year ending June thirtieth, nineteen hundred and seventeen and for other purposes," or any Act amendatory thereof or supplemental or additional thereto;

(2) To cooperate with councils of defense in other states in so far as such cooperation is in harmony with the policies of the Council of National Defense;

(3) To carry out within the State of Illinois such plans of national defense as are mutually agreed upon between it and the Council of National Defense;

(4) To recommend to the Governor and to the General Assembly the enactment of such laws as are, in its judgment, necessary, in time of war, to the common defense or the public welfare.

§ 5. The State Council of Defense shall have power:

(1) To adopt rules for its internal government and procedure;

(2) To form advisory and other committees outside of its membership;

(3) To organize subordinate bodies for its assistance in special investigations;

(4) To appoint, without reference to the State Civil Service Law, experts, stenographers and clerks and to fix their compensation;

(5) To make full investigation as to all questions directly or indirectly relating to or bearing upon the powers or duties vested in it by this Act, and to subpoena witnesses and to require their testimony and to compel the production of account books and files and all papers and documents relevant to any investigation or matter which may be under consideration by it.

§ 6. The members of the State Council of Defense shall serve without compensation, but the actual and necessary expenses of the members thereof, incurred in the discharge of duties under this Act, shall be a proper and legitimate charge against the appropriation hereinafter made.

§ 7. All officers, departments, institutions and agencies of the

State Government, and all local and municipal officers, shall cooperate with and render such aid and assistance as the State Council of Defense may require.

§ 8. The Secretary of State shall provide the State Council of Defense with suitably furnished rooms in the capitol. The Superintendent of Printing or the Department of Public Works and Buildings, after July 1, 1917, shall furnish it with all necessary printing, binding, stationery and office supplies.

§ 9. In case of the refusal of any person to comply with any subpoena issued hereunder or to testify to any matter regarding which he may be interrogated or to produce account books, files, papers and documents relative to any investigation being conducted by the State Council of Defense, any Circuit Court of this State, or any judge thereof, either in term time or in vacation, upon the application of the State Council of Defense, or any member thereof, shall issue an order requiring such person to comply with such subpoena, or to testify, or to produce account books, files, papers and documents, or either, and any failure to obey such order of the court, or judge thereof, may be punished by the court as a contempt of court.

§ 10. The sum of fifty thousand dollars is hereby appropriated for the purpose of carrying out the provisions of this Act. The Auditor of Public Accounts shall draw his warrant for the sum hereby appropriated upon the presentation of vouchers certified to by the chairman of the State Council of Defense and approved by the Governor.

§ 11. WHEREAS, an emergency exists, therefore this Act shall take effect from and after its passage.

APPROVED May 2, 1917.

PROMOTION OF PATRIOTIC MEETINGS

Resolutions adopted at a meeting of the State Council of Defense of Illinois, August 16, 1917.[3]

WHEREAS the maintenance of good will and whole-hearted cooperation in the National interests between all classes of citizens on the basis of a thorough public recognition of mutual responsibilities

[3] Minutes of the meeting of the State Council of Defense, August 16, 1917.

and duties, as well as rights, will inspire to the utmost the unselfish spirit of devoted patriotism essential to a thoroughly vigorous and successful prosecution of the war into which we have entered to safeguard the democracy of the world,

THEREFORE BE IT RESOLVED that the publicity committee of the Illinois State Council of Defense be requested to develop and put into execution a plan under which volunteers among patriotic citizens in every community in Illinois shall be called upon to organize and address patriotic neighborhood meetings, for the purpose of arousing the people of our State to the greatest possible understanding and appreciation of the ideals of true patriotism and love of country from which will come certain and triumphant victory for our flag—for the People of America. Such meetings shall, wherever possible, be held in school houses and other public buildings and under the supervision of local neighborhood committees reporting to and acting under the guidance and control of central city or county committees which shall be appointed by The State Council of Defense of Illinois, and shall be representative of all classes of citizens in such city or county.

FORMATION OF NEIGHBORHOOD COMMITTEES

Resolutions passed at a state conference held under the auspices of the State Council of Defense of Illinois, Chicago, August 28, 1917.[4]

RESOLVED: That, we citizens of the United States of America and of the State of Illinois assembled at the call of the State Council of Defense, favor the union of the loyal people of Illinois into one general, patriotic campaign under the State Council of Defense, in order to help our country win the war in which we are now engaged for human rights and secure a just and lasting peace for all nations. It should be participated in by all men and women who are willing to pledge their whole hearted support to our Government. We believe that this meeting may properly nominate a large general or advisory committee to be selected from the entire state and to be recommended to the State Council of Defense for appointment by the State Council with such changes and additions

[4] Minutes of the meeting of the State Council of Defense of Illinois, August 28, 1917.

as it may think desirable, and that the State Council should designate from this general committee a smaller Executive Committee of about nine members to be charged with the general management of the organization.

USE OF PUBLIC BUILDINGS FOR PATRIOTIC MEETINGS

Resolutions passed at a meeting of the State Council of Defense, November 9, 1917.[5]

RESOLVED that in the opinion of the State Council of Defense of Illinois, it is most important that all public school buildings, court houses and other public buildings throughout the State shall be made and kept available at all times during appropriate hours (so long as the present war continues) for public gatherings whose purpose is the dissemination of views and the development of action to support this country, its army, its navy and its people, in all steps deemed necessary to win the War.

RESOLVED FURTHER, that this Council has heard with regret that in a few localities in this State some public officials have denied the use of public buildings to public meetings called for patriotic purposes.

RESOLVED FURTHER, that under and pursuant to the law creating this State Council, and in accordance with the authority in it vested by said law, all officers, departments, institutions and agencies of the State of Illinois and all local and municipal officers are hereby requested to comply with these resolutions and to render all necessary aid and assistance in carrying them out.

RESOLVED FURTHER, that these resolutions be at once given the widest publicity.

[5] Minutes of the State Council of Defense, November 9, 1917.

FIRST REGISTRATION OF ILLINOIS WOMEN

Statement issued by Governor Frank O. Lowden in behalf of the registration of Illinois women for war service which took place under the auspices of the Woman's Committee, State Council of Defense, during the week November 5-10, 1917.[6]

To the Women of Illinois:

The week beginning November 5, 1917, has been set aside for the registration of the women of Illinois. I urge upon all women to go to the place designated in their communities and to register their names. This applies as well to those who feel that they will not have time for other duties than they now discharge as to those who have the time and are willing to help directly in the work which the war has brought. There are some who will be able and willing to take the places of men who have been called to the colors. There are others who will help in the work of caring for the families of those who have gone to the front. There are still others who will be glad, through the Red Cross and other like organizations, to help to minister to the comfort and welfare of our soldiers in the field. There are a thousand activities for which women are peculiarly fitted, and which will help greatly to maintain our morale in the field, and what is equally important, to maintain our morale at home. The registration cards which will be provided at the places of registration will enable each woman easily and fully to indicate where her chief usefulness to our country will be in this crisis.

A general registration of our women will bring cheer to our soldiers in the field, strength to our government, and will give notice to the world that the spiritual resources of Illinois are mobilized in the prosecution of this most righteous war.

FRANK O. LOWDEN.

September, 1917.

[6] *Final Report of the Woman's Committee, State Council of Defense of Illinois, and Woman's Committee, Council of National Defense, Illinois Division, April 1917-July 1919*, p. 81.

SECOND REGISTRATION OF ILLINOIS WOMEN

Statement issued by Governor Frank O. Lowden in anticipation of the second period for the registration of Illinois women, April, 1918.[7]

To the Women of Illinois:

As the war goes on, the difference between the Prussian ideal of womanhood and the American ideal of womanhood becomes clearer day by day. In the view of the military caste of Prussia, woman's function is to bear soldiers and to be the slave of men. Under the "Kultur" which proclaims force the controlling factor in the universe, woman, of course, must become subordinate to man.

The American ideal, looking to the finer and spiritual qualities of woman, gives her a higher place in our scheme of life. America believes that moral force must, in the end, control mere brute force. Therefore, the future of women depends upon the utter overthrow of the Prussian ideal of womanhood.

The women of Illinois cannot better show their appreciation of what this war means than by a general registration. More than half a million women of our state, by registering, already have been mobilized for wartime service. This is a great accomplishment, indeed. We should not rest, however, until every woman who cares for the future of her sex and her children shall have registered her willingness to serve in this cause.

FRANK O. LOWDEN.

April, 1918.

FIRST RED CROSS DRIVE FOR WAR FUNDS, ADDRESS BY GOVERNOR FRANK O. LOWDEN[8]

Delivered at a meeting held for the purpose of inaugurating Red Cross Week, State Arsenal, Springfield, May 18, 1917.

Ladies and Gentlemen:

War is a horrible thing. It is exactly what General Sherman called it. And, therefore, there is all the more reason why the Red Cross movement of this country should have the earnest and sym-

[7] *Final Report of the Woman's Committee*, pages 85-86.
[8] From a manuscript copy in the possession of Governor Lowden.

pathetic support of the people of this country. Their banner is the only banner upon the red field of war which speaks of beautiful things. Their banner is the one under whose folds the devoted men and women of the Red Cross heal up the wounds that war has made, whisper into the ears of the stricken soldiers words of sympathy and hope. That is the banner which seems to carry beneath it, even to the dread carnage of war, the teachings of the lowly and gentle Nazarene. It is the Red Cross, when this war is over, around which civilization again must rally and take up its new work.

I hope with all my heart that the people of Springfield and Illinois, who have shown their patriotism in these troubled times, who have furnished more men as volunteers to serve their country at this time, in proportion to their population, than any other state in the Union, I hope that Illinois, that has stood every test of patriotism, will in this matter of the Red Cross work show to the world that we out here know the sacredness and the importance of the cause in which we fight, that we are resolved, in so far as within us lies, to make easy the lot of our soldier boys who again are entering into the war for human rights and human liberties.

For we must not forget that we have entered into the greatest war of time. We cannot forget, if we would, that the principle for which our Revolutionary fathers fought and died, the principle for which our fathers fought in the Civil War, is the same principle that is involved today. The only difference is that our Revolutionary fathers were fighting for the liberty of men on a narrow country along our eastern coast, and that the men of the Civil War were fighting for union and thereby to demonstrate to the world that men could successfully govern themselves. But this present war involves the liberty of all the world. It is not a war against men—it is a war for men everywhere, and for the right of men to rule themselves, as against the right of an autocracy to rule them.

We opened the battle away back at Lexington. That battle has now communicated itself around the world, and everywhere men, on the one hand, are fighting for exactly the principle that our Revolutionary fathers fought at Lexington, and upon the other hand are fighting for the divine right of kings. That is the issue which has been joined and which tonight encircles the globe. We cannot show our devotion to our common country any better than by helping to swell, to the largest limit, the funds that are being raised by the Red Cross, because its funds will show the world that we know that the principles for which we are battling now are so sacred that we will battle to the end for them.

AN ACT TO REGULATE THE SOLICITATION OF FUNDS FOR WAR AID AND WAR CHARITY

House Bill Number 1028, Fiftieth General Assembly.

An Act. *To regulate the solicitation of funds and other property for purposes of war aid and war charity during the duration of the war in which the United States is now engaged.*

Section 1. *Be it enacted by the people of the State of Illinois, represented in the General Assembly:* That the State Council of Defense be and it is hereby given full power and authority to issue licenses from time to time, and to revoke the same from time to time, authorizing the solicitation during the duration of the war in which the United States is now engaged, by individuals, societies, clubs, associations or corporations, of funds and other property for the following purposes:

(a) Aid and relief in the prosecution of said war or for the use or benefit of any hospital or relief service exclusively connected with the prosecution of said war.

(b) Aid and relief to the soldiers and sailors who are or have been in the service of the United States in said war, for their individual benefit and comfort.

(c) Aid and relief to the families and dependants of soldiers and sailors who are or have been in the service of the United States in said war.

(d) Aid and relief to the families and dependents of soldiers and sailors killed in the service of the United States during said war.

§ 2. It shall be unlawful for any individual, society, club, association or corporation to engage in any solicitation for any war aid or war charities of the character enumerated in section 1 aforesaid, without having first obtained a license to make such solicitation, issued by the said State Council of Defense.

§ 3. All applications for licenses to solicit for war aid or war charities as aforesaid, shall be in writing, addressed to said State Council of Defense, and shall state the particular war aid or war charity for which the applicant desires to solicit, together with the amount desired to be raised and the method and channel of disbursing or distributing the same, and whether or not compensation or a commission is to be paid for the subscriptions, funds or other property obtained by such applicant, and the amount of such compensation or commission. If such application shall be on behalf of an individual, it shall state the name, age, sex, residence, business and occupation of the applicant. If such application shall be on behalf of a society, club, association or corporation, then said application shall state the name, office or place of business, whether incorporated or unincorporated, and if incorporated, when and where incorporated, and the objects and purposes of such applicant, and the names and residences of its officers. Every such application if made on behalf of an individual, shall be signed and sworn to by such applicant, and if made on behalf of any society, club, association or corporation, shall be signed in the name of such society, club, association or corporation by the president or secretary thereof, and shall be sworn to by such president or secretary.

§ 4. All individuals, societies, clubs, associations and corporations to whom licenses as aforesaid shall have been issued by said State Council of Defense, shall obey and comply with all the rules, requirements, regulations and directions that may be issued from time to time by said State Council of Defense, and the said State Council of Defense shall have power to revoke any license that may have been issued by it upon failure of the licensee to comply with the rules, requirements, regulations and directions prescribed by said State Council of Defense, or whenever in its judgment the purposes of said license have been accomplished or have ceased to be useful or necessary.

§ 5. Any individual, society, club, association or corporation, or any officer, director or member of any society, club, association or corporation, who shall knowingly violate any of the provisions of this Act, shall be deemed guilty of of [sic] a misdemeanor, and upon conviction thereof shall be fined in a sum of not exceeding one thousand dollars ($1,000) for each offense.

§ 6. Nothing contained in this Act shall be construed as prohibiting,

(a) The family or friends of any soldier or sailor who is or has been in the service of the United States during said war, from supplying such soldier or sailor or the family and dependents of such soldier or sailor with any moneys, goods, articles or property of use or of comfort at any time.

(b) Any society, club, association, corporation, congregation or religious association or corporation from soliciting any war aid or war charity as aforesaid, among its own members, unless such solicitation shall be prohibited by the regulations of the military or naval authorities of the United States.

(c) The solicitation by any individual, society, club, association or corporation, for any war aid or war charity authorized by or under any law or resolution passed by the Congress of the United States or by or under any act or proclamation of the President of the United States.

APPROVED June 25, 1917.

NEED OF FOOD, FUEL AND COMMODITY LEGISLATION

Resolutions adopted at a meeting of the State Council of Defense of Illinois, May 12, 1917.[9]

RESOLVED, that it is vitally necessary to our country and people, that there be immediate conservation by the United States of food-stuffs, grains, fuel and other basic commodities, and that upon the prompt enactment of proper legislation of this kind will depend the safety and preservation of our nation and our success in the War; and that delay in adopting such a law will be fraught with dangerous consequences.

RESOLVED FURTHER, that the Congress of the United States be urged to enact at once a rigid and comprehensive Food,

[9] From the minutes of a meeting of the State Council of Defense for May 12, 1917.

Fuel and Commodity Act that will vest in a Commission to be appointed by the President, full power (subject to appropriate safeguards) to regulate and control the production, distribution, transportation and price of food-stuffs, grains, fuel and other basic commodities.

RESOLVED FURTHER, that these resolutions be signed by the individual members of this Council and that a copy thereof be at once telegraphed to the President, to Vice-President Marshall, as presiding officer of the Senate, and to Hon. Champ Clark as Speaker of the House, and that a copy thereof be forthwith furnished to the Press.

FIRE PREVENTION AS A CONSERVATION MEASURE

Letter from Governor Frank O. Lowden to the State Fire Marshal, April 23, 1917.[10]

The importance of conservation of all property in this state is exceedingly necessary. Especially is this true with reference to the conservation of all grains in storage and in transit, and all foodstuffs in elevators, warehouses and storehouses throughout the state.

It is my desire that the state fire marshal department shall at once direct special attention to the inspection of all elevators, mills, warehouses and other buildings containing foodstuffs, with the idea of removing as quickly and effectively as possible all approximate occasion to fire.

To bring about the greatest safeguard and protection in these matters, I trust that you will at once cause to be organized a campaign of inspection looking to the conservation of these foodstuffs, and that every available employee of your department will be directed to report to you in Chicago at the earliest practical date to carry on as rapidly as possible the work of cleaning up and protection against fire which may be occasioned by the accumulation of debris and other unsafe conditions in and around these depositories.

It is my idea that a campaign of protection in this respect can best be effected through the hearty and patriotic coöperation of the owners and proprietors of these mills, elevators and warehouses with

[10] *Illinois State Journal*, April 24, 1917.

the department, and I hope that the coöperation may be brought about.

I shall be pleased to have your advice as to how soon this work can be inaugurated, and from time to time such information as you may deem necessary for me to possess with reference to the progress and effectiveness of this campaign.

AN ADDRESS BY DEAN EUGENE DAVENPORT, COLLEGE OF AGRICULTURE, UNIVERSITY OF ILLINOIS[11]

Delivered before the Chicago Association of Commerce, Chicago, April 4, 1917.

I may say that the University of Illinois, or at least the agricultural part of it, has had gooseflesh ever since the prospect of war looked keen. And one of the reasons why we have had gooseflesh is because nobody else seems to think much about the thing that is troubling us most. We are constantly thinking about the fact that Europe is destroying its own power to produce food. We remember that a half million men have gone from Canada, many of them never to return, and when you kill a Canadian you stop a tractor from raising wheat. We remember that we are at the end of the line; if we fail to produce food for ourselves and western Europe, there is no place we can import it from in sufficient quantities.

We are at the last ditch in food. We are concerned for the further reason that we know we have two lean years behind us, that the production of food under normal conditions is not keeping pace with the increase in population, that there has been a steady drift of labor from the land for many years, and that for the last two years thousands of farmers have given up all expectation of farming their lands to the best advantage, and are going back to the self-sufficing system, which means, "we will take care of ourselves," which the farmer can very well do, and the public will have to do the best it can.

And because that is true, and because those are the conditions, I will say that the University has been working upon a definite plan, which I want to present to you in the few moments at my disposal.

[11] *Chicago Commerce*, April 6, 1917.

You must take for granted some things, some facts which I must rapidly recite, and give your attention then to what seems to be, so far as we can discover, a workable plan.

I may say that they are now enlisting off the fields, from the plows and from the ditch, to go to the service of this country now. I see girls on the streets enlisting men, and in our own estimation these days we very rapidly divide them into two classes—heroes and cowards—and those who stay at home are the cowards.

If we are to fight this thing out, and it looks as though we will have to, it is to be a war of exhaustion; and if it is a war of exhaustion, the food supply must not fail. Therefore, I invite your attention to this definite plan. I say definite, because I have seen a number of plans, very few of which have recognized the magnitude of the situation and very few of which prescribed a remedy that could be used.

This plan is necessary if we are to supply ourselves with food. This plan has been worked out by the faculty of the agricultural college and the department of economics, represented by Dr. Kinley,[12] who has been our good friend in this whole matter, because of so many things that the agricultural faculty does not know. This is presented as the plan of the University of your state. This plan is based upon the following facts:

1. The present production of food in the United States is not increasing in proportion to the increase in population.

2. In going to war, the production of food is our strongest asset, particularly in view of the reduced food production in Canada and in western Europe.

3. The experience of all time indicates that every nation, in going to war puts men into active military service without regard to the disturbance of basic industrial conditions, even the production of the food of the people.

4. Indiscriminate enlistment from the farms with no plan for labor replacement is certain to reduce food production below the level of positive need, for we already have two lean years behind us, and under present conditions of a hungry world continued shortage may mean disaster.

[12]Dr. David Kinley, then vice president and dean of the Graduate School, University of Illinois; president, University of Illinois, 1920—.

5. If an adequate food supply is to be assured, the military plan must include an enlistment for food production as definite as for service at the front. From the first the Department of War should as rigorously protect the food production as it does any other means of national defense.

6. Anything like limiting the food of the people is wholly unnecessary if reasonable attention be given to the business of production. America has land enough, if it is properly handled, to feed both herself and western Europe; besides, more men would be required to enforce a police restriction of food than would be required to turn a scarcity into an abundance.

7. For years labor has been deserting the land and building up conditions of employment that the farmer cannot meet, for it is impossible to conduct a farm upon the eight-hour plan and according to union rules. The typical family of five cannot work to the best advantage the typical farm of one hundred and twenty to two hundred and forty acres, and the farmer has reached the limit in the use of machinery and in the employment of his children to replace the hired help that has gone to the city. Any plan to be safe, therefore, must not only make good the enlistment from the country, but must actually add to the present labor supply of the farmer.

I. Registration. Register every farm operator, whether owner, tenant or manager, together with the number of acres of tillable land, pasture and timber; the number of men he usually employs and the number of men he would need to employ in order to insure maximum crops.

II. Enlistment. Enlist in the civil-military service and under military pay the following classes:

1. Men of military age or older, of good health, either permanently or temporarily unfit for war service at the front.

2. Boys from 14 to 18 years of age, whether from the country or from the city.

III. Training camp farms. 1. Establish at convenient points on land rented by the government and suitable for intensive farming, military camps where the enlisted men not otherwise employed may be gathered and housed, such farms to be devoted to the raising of crops requiring a maximum amount of hand labor, such as vegetables, small fruits, cotton and tobacco.

2. Erect at these centers facilities for drying and canning such food products for preservation and for transportation.

IV. Employment. 1. On farms: The largest asset for food production is the thousands of farms already organized under the management of experienced farmers, each with an independent business operating through established channels of trade. Here should go the maximum of the enlisted men, and the camps should be ready at all times to furnish lists of available help, it being understood that men under employment by the farmer are on furlough and off government pay, receiving from the farmer the "going wage" of the locality, dependent upon the work the man or the boy is able to do. All such enlisted men should be reported from time to time as may be required by the military authorities.

It should be understood as a part of the plan that an enlisted man having taken service with a farmer and becoming dissatisfied may return to the camp, and the lower wage; or if he is unable to give satisfaction, he may be discharged, in which case he must return at once to camp.

2. Enlisted men not employed on private farms should be at the camp farms under military discipline, but under agricultural leadership, such men to devote their first attention to the production of food under the direction of an agricultural leader, chosen in each case for his ability in the particular kind of farming followed at this special camp.

The plan of farming should be such as to afford time for regular military drill for those of military age and below; not only for the welfare of the camp, but in order to afford preparation for such as are going to the front as soon as their age limitations or physical disabilities are removed. In general, men of military age and above, without farm experience, should be quartered in regions engaged in intensive farming where oversight is possible.

As the camp is depleted by members entering the active military service, its numbers should be systematically replenished by new enlistments.

Enlistment for civil-military service should not only be considered as a patriotic service, but it should be made attractive through formal recognition, as by uniforms, by use of special organizations, ranks and degrees of efficiency, even promotion and commissions. Especially is this true for the younger men and boys.

AN ADDRESS BY CARL VROOMAN, ASSISTANT SECRETARY OF AGRICULTURE[13]

Delivered before the Chicago Association of Commerce, Chicago, May 9, 1917.

My chief topic is a world need so great that none of us will be able to grasp its full significance, and yet all of us must try. We are going to be asked during the coming year to supply food for our one hundred million people; for our armies; for the armies of our allies, which today on a half dozen battle fields in Europe are dying by the thousands, fighting your battles and mine, and we are going to be asked to feed the neutral countries who but for our food will starve within a few weeks. After the war is over, and victory is ours, we are going to be asked also to feed the starving millions of the Central Powers. This is a herculean task, a task so great that the mind cannot seize it at once. It would be impossible for me to overstate the seriousness of the European food shortage.

Can we meet this demand; is it possible? Our natural resources are great enough to meet it. There is no doubt about that. But we are faced with the disconcerting fact that the wheat prospect today is the worst in the memory of anyone here present. Wheat has gone above three dollars today, and yet Congress has not given anyone authority to meet the crisis. If Congress does not give such authority soon to the Department of Agriculture, or to the President of the United States, there is no telling to what prices wheat, or the other foodstuffs of the country, will go.

The majority of the business men of this country, the overwhelming majority of them, have shown more disinterestedness, more patriotism, more loyalty to their government, more of the spirit of

[13] The account of this speech published in *Chicago Commerce* on May 11, 1917, was revised by Mr. Vrooman for publication in this volume.

sacrifice, than any body of business men have ever shown in any country in any other war in human history.

Business men by the hundreds, by the thousands, are coming to the government, not stealthily, as in the past, to see how much they can get for themselves, but practically to see how much they can do to help the government. It is the most splendid exhibition of patriotism among the business element that any nation has shown in a time of national peril.

However, I regret to say that this attitude is not universal. There is a small minority of business men, both rich and poor, who look upon this crisis as an opportunity to exploit their fellows, and to exploit the necessities of the nation. Those people today are speculating in the nation's food, and in the other necessaries of life. They are filling their pockets with what is nothing less than blood money. Any man who takes advantage of this world tragedy to enrich himself at the expense of his fellows in an illegitimate fashion, is not only lacking in patriotism, but is disloyal, is fighting on the side of the Kaiser.

When I left Washington, a number of these men were gathered together there like so many vultures—lobbying to prevent Congress, if possible, from granting to the federal administration the necessary war powers.

The Department of Agriculture, at the request of Congress, drew up some bills. These bills were not drawn up without consultation. A meeting was held in St. Louis not long ago to which were invited all of the state secretaries of agriculture, and the commissioners of agriculture of all the states east of the Rocky Mountains. A similar meeting was held on the Pacific coast, and other meetings were held in Boston and in Atlanta. Those bills were drawn up as a result of these conferences and these conferences were unanimously in favor of all the measures that were incorporated into these bills. Furthermore, we discussed the experience of England and the other countries in the war zone in dealing with the same gigantic problems that now confront us. We learned that every country in the war zone has granted its government powers similar to those asked for in these bills.

The prices of food are going up every day. Yet there are at

Washington men fighting these bills on theoretical grounds, or imaginary grounds, on sordid grounds—appealing to prejudice, appealing to selfishness, appealing to everything except a rational recognition of the fact that we are in the midst of the greatest crisis this nation ever encountered, and that all the antiquated methods of the past must be scrapped and power to employ the most successful known methods conferred upon our various executive governmental departments.

The Department of Agriculture should have been the first department to be put upon a war basis. For most of our staple crops, the planting season is now nearly over. Still the Department of Agriculture has not yet been put on a war basis. We are making bricks without straw. We have not the necessary men, we have not the necessary funds, we have not the necessary authority, and Congress or the committees of Congress are too busy to give our need much attention. They are struggling night and day over the problem of our military establishment. And just as they thought they had it nearly solved, there was injected into it the fortunes of an individual, and Congress today, or that part of it which handles military matters, is focusing its attention upon the fortunes of that individual. Not until his fortunes are taken care of will the business of the nation and the needs of the nation, and of the world, again get the right of way.

A MEMBER: Let us raise a protest.

MR. VROOMAN, continuing:

The proposition that a division, or an army of untrained men headed by a man untrained in the science of modern warfare, should be sent over into the trenches, means nothing more or less than wholesale murder.

A MEMBER: Not necessarily.

CHAIRMAN MOSS: Gentlemen, the spirit of thousands of men of Chicago is here; our government that we profess to love and serve is speaking through its representative. I am sure that from this time each individual of us will realize where we are, who is speaking, and what is our relation.

(This pronouncement secured round after round of applause, the audience rising.)

Mr. Vrooman, continuing:

I wish to say that no one honors more than I do the courage that is willing to go and face the hell of European trenches without flinching. But England made the fatal mistake, at the start, of relying on courage unbacked by scientific principles and training, and unbacked by the necessary supplies of big guns and munitions of war. Courage alone does not win wars. To send untrained soldiers, led by untrained generals, against the most perfect military machine the world ever saw, to face clouds of poison gas, lakes of liquid fire and the hell of shrapnel and machine gun fire, is on a par with that almost miraculous courage manifested in the Children's Crusade in the middle ages. Hundreds of thousands of children said: "The men have failed, God will take care of the children. Trusting in God, we cannot fail." They swept down through France, down into the Orient, and they never came back. Their bleaching bones were left to rot along that long pathway of death, a monument to courage badly directed.

No man admires courage more than I do. But English officers in the Boer War, and in the present war, made the cruel, costly mistake of exposing themselves unnecessarily, with the result that thousands of the best and bravest of them were shot down by the enemy sharpshooters, when England needed their services most. I hope that not a single American boy will be sent to the trenches until he is well trained, well supplied with munitions, and led by our ablest, most experienced and most highly trained officers.

This situation today is more serious than any of us realize. We are going to need every heart throb of courage and devotion; we are going to need every ray of intelligence; we are going to need every dollar of our great wealth; we are going to need all of our industrial efficiency; we are going to need all of our latent agricultural productivity. For this war is not won yet. So far as we are concerned, it has just begun.

When the war started, England thought that all that she needed was to create an army. They said: "We already have a navy." They called volunteers and the flower of the youth of England responded. They rallied to the British flag, and were drilled and trained, and were sent into the trenches. There they were mowed down like the grass. After a few months of this ghastly and needless slaughter, England awoke to the fact that something more than an army was needed—that where they had ounces of powder and munitions, they should have had tons and shiploads. Moreover, they had no cannon that would shoot anywhere near as far as the German cannon. So for months the British army stood and was shot to pieces by German cannon which they could not see and which they could not reach with their antiquated artillery.

Then England awoke. She called upon Lloyd George to become director of munitions. He at once declared that they must establish more and more munitions factories—that they must dot the landscape with them until they could exceed the output of the Central Powers. This program has been carried out so successfully that they are turning out more munitions every week than they turned out during an entire year at the beginning of the war.

Just as they got this matter taken care of, they were confronted with another problem that they had not foreseen. There was a strike, a strike in the mines and factories. The English workmen said: "Our families have not wherewith to live. We toil all day and the price of food goes up steadily; we must have higher wages." They were called disloyal; they were called unpatriotic, but they replied: "Hold on, we will see who is disloyal. We will not only work for the same low wages, but we will work for no wages at all *on condition that our masters in like manner* put their mines and their factories into the service of the government, without any remuneration at all."

Then the government called the representatives of capital and labor together with government officials and all other interested persons at a round table. They discussed the problem from every angle and decided to give to capital a fair profit and no more, to labor a living wage and no more, to the farmer a reasonable price for his products and no more. Upon this basis of simple justice, all classes got together. Old animosities were forgotten. The latent energies of the nation were released and harnessed in a mighty common endeavor. From that time England has been like a powerful automobile, suddenly thrown into high; she has been leaping forward with a power which nobody had ever suspected she possessed.

After she had solved these three great problems, she suddenly came face to face with another problem, the problem that the Germans had been exhausting all their ingenuity to solve, the problem that France, Italy and the other countries had been struggling with from the first, the world-old problem of food supply. They discovered late in the game that this war is going to be won not by the nation with the most soldiers in the field, not by the nation with the greatest quantities of munitions piled up behind their armies, not by the nation with the most gold and other financial resources, not by the nation with the most courage, but by the nation which is able to feed itself the longest.

Famine is stalking right over the horizon of every country in Europe. The only hope of the world is the American farmer. If we cannot feed the hungry millions of Europe, more people will starve during the next year than will be slaughtered in battle. We cannot send many troops to the trenches during the next three months; I hope we will send at least one division. I hope we will send enough men there to take over a mile or two of trenches. I hope we will be able to run up Old Glory there alongside the flags of our allies just to show them over there that we are there in the flesh as well as in the spirit; just to show them that America never forgets what was done for her by LaFayette and Rochambeau, and those other great Frenchmen who came to us in the time of our need to help fight our battles and help us win independence. But as for putting enough soldiers there to amount to anything in a military way, that is impossible within nine months at least.

And, during that time, what are we going to do? Are we going to sit around here on the side lines as idle spectators, watching brave Frenchmen, Italians, Russians and Englishmen fighting our battles and dying for us? That is not the American spirit. That was demonstrated when Congress passed the bill appropriating seven billion dollars for war purposes. Seven billion dollars is probably the largest sum ever appropriated by any nation at any one time in the history of mankind. Do you know what that appropriation meant, what it means to us, and what it means to every intelligent man in every country in Europe? It meant that America by that act declared to the world that we have underwritten victory.

But there is one thing they need over there even worse than money, worse than men, and that is food, more food, and still more food, every week and month as long as the war shall last. That is our chief, our supreme responsibility during the next year, to see to it that Europe is fed. Can we do it? We have been sadly and unnecessarily delayed, but I believe we still can do it.

The government today has two things it is going to do. One is to stimulate production as much as is humanly possible, and the second is to conserve our food products as much as is physically possible. Anybody who wastes food in ordinary times is doing something reprehensible, no matter who he is. But anybody who wastes an ounce of food in these times, not only is doing something that is reprehensible and despicable but that is also disloyal.

There are a number of measures proposed in the matter of food conservation that have been objected to. But we had better stop right now objecting to little discomforts. We are not going to win this war without doing some things that will be disagreeable. It has been suggested that we eat too much meat. A lot of people like to eat meat three times a day. It is not necessary, it is not hygienic, and in times of war it is not loyal to eat meat three times a day. Let's pass the meat to the soldiers first, and we'll eat what is left.

It is up to us to cut down our rations. Other nations say that we eat too much. But it is what we waste that is the worst. Our experts tell us that we waste seven hundred million dollars' worth of foodstuffs every year. In our hotels and in our clubs we are accustomed to have served to us portions larger than we need. Those huge portions ought to be cut down. We should have half size "war portions" from this time on. When a man buys a large portion of lamb or beef, if he is of an economical turn of mind, he feels that he has to eat it all up. If he does not, it is wasted; and if he does, it is worse than wasted. And when it comes to bread, we all like plenty of white bread and hot rolls. But this nation will probably have to be put on a "war bread" basis, and that soon.

Now, there are a number of practical problems to be worked out to safeguard the legitimate interests of the millions of people in this country. This government can safeguard the legitimate interests of every industry. We are rich enough and strong enough not to call for any undue sacrifice on the part of any particular interest. There is no reason for making millers the goat or making farmers the goat.

The farmers have said that they do not know what grain to plant, because fertilizer is so high, and the prices of farm crops uncertain. The federal government must meet that situation. If this nations wants, as it does, to stimulate production as much as possible, *then the nation as a whole, and not the farmers as a class, should be made to incur the necessary risks of such a policy.* The farmer should be assured a minimum price for his wheat, corn, rye and other crops. We have asked Congress for power to guarantee such prices. Congress is considering the proposition, but by the time it can give us the power, the small grain will all be planted and perhaps the corn as well.

Congress is working day and night on these problems. I am not criticising Congress. I never saw men work harder. But they need your help. They need your longer perspective and your advice on these problems. You see the big issues. Write to your congressmen, your senators, your members of the cabinet and give them your viewpoint. Help us in Washington to rise above the masses of details that threaten to swamp us. In that way you can help us to solve these problems upon which the salvation of this country depends.

The victory we are fighting for is no common victory. We not only are fighting for victory for our flag and our allies, we are fighting for the triumph of democracy and civilization—for a victory that will mean the establishment, at last, of permanent peace upon this tear-stained, blood-drenched, war-scarred old world. We are engaged in the greatest crusade that human beings have ever been engaged in. We tried to keep out of war. We did keep out of war as long as it was possible to do so and keep our self-respect. And when the time came that we had to choose between helping democracy on the one side and despotism on the other side, we could not stay out any longer.

We have gone into this war with hands clean and hearts as pure as any knight in the middle ages ever went out in quest of the Holy Grail. This is a war of liberation, the liberation of the masses, not only of Belgium and Russia and France, but a war of liberation for the masses of every nation, including the masses of the German people. As the President said, we are not at war with the German people, we are at war with the imperial German government. Today one hope of the world is that the German people may follow the example of the Russian people, that they will do with the Hohenzollerns what the Russians did with the Romanoffs, that they will make Germany a great democracy. And when they have done that America and her allies will be willing to reach forth their hands, covered though they may be with German blood, to shake hands with Germans whose hands, perhaps, may be covered with the blood of our brothers. Why? Because, upon the basis of democracy, all these nightmares of war can be forgotten, and we can look forward to a peace which will be enjoyed by all the peoples of the earth, including the German people—peace builded upon democracy, peace builded upon international law, peace builded upon the recognition of the sacredness of treaties, peace builded upon the recognition of the fact that nations as well as individuals have the right to life, liberty, and the pursuit of happiness.

The federal government expects every man, woman and child in this country to get into this crusade. There is a place for all. It is a priceless privilege that we are offering to every American, young and old. We need soldiers in the furrows just as much as we need soldiers in the trenches. It is my hope that the soldiers in the furrows may win this war before the soldiers in the trenches have had a chance to fire a shot. Here in this great middle west, the heart of the food-producing regions, a great responsibility is upon us. From what I hear from official sources and from the press of the country, I know that you are meeting your responsibilities. I have recently made a tour through the south, bearing the message that the federal government expects the south to feed itself. The south is responding magnificently. It is plowing up its cotton fields where necessary and putting them into corn, sweet potatoes, beans and other food crops.

If this government is going to help bring this war to a successful termination, it means that every atom of industrial ability, financial ability, military ability and agricultural ability must be mobilized and placed at the disposal of the federal government. That means that we must have a united nation, just as England is a united nation, and France is a united nation, and Germany is a united nation. England at the start lost tens of thousands of lives and billions of dollars because of the lack of that coördination of the efforts of all the inhabitants of the empire into one supreme endeavor.

If the business men will continue in the future as they have in the past to place their trained intelligence, their business organizations, their wealth and their influence throughout the country at the disposal of the federal government, this great task will be achieved. And remember this, when this is done temporarily for war it can be done also later for peace. Thus this nation, for the first time in her history, will have become a nation with a national consciousness, a national ideal and a national spirit. When we have accomplished this, and we will accomplish it in the next two years, it will mean that we have made more progress in two years than we have made in the twenty years preceding.

This is the greatest hour in history. You and I now have a chance to realize some of our youthful ambitions and dreams. Every man, woman and child, has a chance to do something heroic, to do something unselfish, to make some sacrifice for the ideal. In the past we have lived, more or less, in a complacent and commonplace way. We have lived in what the French have called a bourgeois way. The time has come to awake to a conception akin to that which the crusaders had in the middle ages; a conception like that which has inspired the choice spirits in the world in all ages to realize that each one of us has the opportunity in this historic crisis to dedicate our moral powers, our intellectual powers, our emotional powers, and our business powers to the highest ends, by utilizing them in the service of our country, of human freedom and of civilization.

RESOLUTIONS ADOPTED BY ILLINOIS GRAIN DEALERS' ASSOCIATION, SPRINGFIELD, MAY 12, 1917[14]

WHEREAS, The United States of America faces a crisis, the greatest since the Civil War; and

[14] *Illinois State Register, Illinois State Journal,* May 13, 1917.

WHEREAS, All the resources of the nation, of every kind, will be needed that the nation may wage a successful warfare; and

WHEREAS, The members of the Illinois Grain Dealers' Association, in 24th Annual Convention assembled, appreciate the problems involved, and desire to express their unswerving loyalty to the nation and its cause. Therefore be it

Resolved, That the secretary is directed to convey to the President of the United States, to the Secretary of War, to the Secretary of Agriculture, to the Council of National Defense, and to the Governor of the State of Illinois and the proper agencies our wholehearted support. And be it further

Resolved, That the secretary is further directed to offer to the above-named the facilities of this association, and its headquarters office, and the services of the secretary of this association to be used by the government, state and national, in any way that may be deemed for the good of the cause. And be it finally

Resolved, by the Illinois Grain Dealers' Association meeting in regular convention that we pledge our individual and collective support to the government without reservation, and pledge ourselves to give our most efficient services to the government in the handling and marketing of grain.

DAYLIGHT MEMORIAL TO CONGRESS

House Joint Resolution Number 20, Fiftieth General Assembly.

WHEREAS, Great economy will result from the plan of beginning each active day earlier during the spring and summer of each year; and

WHEREAS, Such an earlier day for active work will save very greatly not only in health but also in the cost of fuel and light; and

WHEREAS, Substantially all of the great nations of Europe have for these reasons adopted the policy of setting forward by one hour the standard time employed in the spring and summer months; now, therefore, be it

Resolved, by the House of Representatives of the State of Illinois, the Senate of this State concurring herein, That the plan commonly known as daylight saving, should be adopted in this State and that the two Houses of the Illinois General Assembly place themselves upon record as in favor of the adoption of such a plan for this State; and, be it further

Resolved, That we approve of the proposed legislation now before the Congress of the United States for the accomplishment of the same purpose, and urge the United States Senators and members of the House of Representatives from this State to support such proposed legislation; and, be it further

Resolved, That the Secretary of State of this State be requested to send copies of this resolution to the Representatives of this State in the Senate and House of Representatives of the United States.

Adopted by the House May 24, 1917.

Concurred in by the Senate May 29, 1917.

NON-USE OF ALCOHOLIC BEVERAGES

Resolutions adopted by the Executive Committee of the Woman's Committee, State Council of Defense of Illinois, June 3, 1917.[15]

WHEREAS:

This nation is facing a period wherein it must feed not only its own people but the larger portion of the world, and

WHEREAS:

We are being urged by those in authority to conserve all foods, particularly grains, and

WHEREAS:

A large amount of grain so needed for food is consumed in the manufacture of alcoholic liquors, and

WHEREAS:

By the terms of the conscription act men in uniform who must bear the heaviest burden of the war may not be served with alcoholic beverages;

THEREFORE BE IT RESOLVED

That we, the Executive Committee of the Woman's Committee, Council of National Defense of Illinois Division, request all clubs, on the grounds of economy and justice, not to serve alcoholic beverages during the war times, and

[15] Minutes of the Executive Committee, Woman's Committee, State Council of Defense, June 3, 1917.

(12)

BE IT FURTHER RESOLVED

That a copy of these resolutions be sent to the Presidents and Secretaries of all clubs in Chicago.

AN ADDRESS BY DR. C. G. HOPKINS, COLLEGE OF AGRICULTURE, UNIVERSITY OF ILLINOIS

Delivered at a State Conference of the Woman's Committee, State Council of Defense of Illinois, Chicago, June 26, 1917.[16]

Ladies and Gentlemen:

I deeply appreciate the honor of being invited to address this gathering of Illinois ladies. I know that you have left your own work at your own homes in order to come here, possibly to get something that you may take home and use to exert influence for the good of your communities in the state.

If, in the 'nineties, anybody had suggested a meeting like this for the discussion of food production, I imagine there would have been a great deal of wonderment. In the 'nineties, when corn was selling at 20 cents a bushel, wheat at 50 cents, beef cattle at 4 cents a pound, hogs at from 2 to 3 cents, who would have thought that within twenty to twenty-five years there would have been gathered in this great city such a body of people to consider the subject of food production?

There are a few broad facts which, it seems to me, we may well consider, which bear upon this question. It is now more than three hundred years since the first settlement at Jamestown, but until within the last decade or so there was in the United States always a farm of rich, well-watered land for anyone who desired it, and for the first time in the history of this country we are now beyond that possibility. If you will look up the records of increase in farm lands and population of the United States, you will discover, for example, that from 1870-1900, the last thirty years in the third century since white men began to settle in the United States, you will note that the population

---

[16] From a stenographic report of the conference. Dr. Cyril G. Hopkins was head of the Department of Agronomy, College of Agriculture, University of Illinois. During the war Dr. Hopkins held a major's commission and served as chief of the Agricultural Section of the American Red Cross Commission to Greece. He died at Gibraltar on October 6, 1919, while on his way home.

increased by 98 per cent during that generation, that the farm lands increased by 104 per cent, from 1870 to 1900. The area of land in farms in the United States during the last generation of the century just closed, I say, increased by 104 per cent, while the population increased only 98 per cent. In other words, the area of land in farms until the close of the last century increased more rapidly than our population.

Then, during the last ten years of the old century the area of land in farms increased by 34 per cent and the increase in population was only 21 per cent, and that, friends, is the great explanation for the abundance of foodstuffs in the 'nineties.

You can remember when they sang, "Uncle Sam is Rich Enough to Give Us All a Farm," and so he was until about the year 1900. But almost coincident with the closing of the old century we came to the end of the free government land in the United States, well watered and at once suited to agriculture. And during the first ten years of this century, according to the census reports, our population increased again by 21 per cent, but the farm land did not increase by 34 nor by 21, but by less than 5 per cent.

In an address before the National Conservation Congress at Kansas City in 1911, I heard the President of the United States report that according to the best information the federal government had, the total possible increase in area of farm land in the United States was only 9 per cent; that the population increased 21 per cent every decade, as we have been doing for a considerable length of time. And that means, keep in mind, that an increase of 21 per cent means more decade after decade in the absolute. That is, an increase of 21 per cent the last time meant 16,000,000 new people in the United States. But what will the next increase of 21 per cent mean? Twenty-one per cent of the hundred million that we have now would mean not 16,000,000, but 21,000,000 more mouths to feed. We have a different situation, I think you can readily see, existing in the United States, because we have no longer the free government land. Now, you may call it a crisis if you will, but we must recognize the fact and those who studied the statistics saw this before there was any European war at all. If we study the records of food production and of our increase in population, it could be seen some years ago that food shortage was coming in the United States unless we changed our practices, and we have not done it yet to any appreciable extent.

During the last decade, although our population increased by 21 per cent, the increase in food grains produced in this country was less than 2 per cent. You might ask how we fed our increased population. If we had more than 21 per cent increase in population and less than 2 per cent increase in corn, oats, wheat, barley, rye, rice, buckwheat, all of these crops that we know as food grains, then how did we feed the increased population? One might think at first we did it by increasing our food-producing animals and became more and more a meat-eating people, but let us see what the census tells us. During the last census decade the number of cattle in the United States decreased from 68 to 58 per head. The number of swine decreased. The number of sheep decreased. Those three great classes of food-producing animals decreased by 10 per cent in numbers. In other words, we made no increase whatever in food-producing animals.

So then, we ask again, how did we feed our increased population, because we have not had famine or starvation in the United States? It so happens that the statistics which bear upon that question are also available, and I can tell you at once that we fed our increased population, not by increasing production, but by decreasing our exportations. I have taken the records of five years centered upon 1900—1898, 1899, 1900, 1901 and 1902—and made an average of those five years on exportation of foodstuffs for the United States, and then I have made a similar average at the end of the next decade, ending in 1910, and what do we find? A comparison of those two five-year averages shows that we decreased our exportation of wheat from 215,000,000 bushels a year to 103,000,000 bushels a year. How long can we continue to feed an increasing population by decreasing our exports? You can see at once that another decade like that would absolutely wipe out our exports of wheat unless we increased our production.

A similar comparison shows that during the decade exports of corn decreased from 163,000,000 bushels a year to only 48,000,000 bushels. If you project a curve, based upon those two points, 163 and 48, you will see that in about 1914 the United States should have discontinued the exportation of corn. I watched with a great deal of interest for the year 1914 to come and some of you will perhaps remember that for the first time in the history of the United States, in 1914, this country imported corn from Argentine to the extent of millions of bushels. It came into Baltimore, into New York, into Philadelphia, into Portsmouth, into Mobile, into Galveston, the importations of corn.

Our exportation of meats during the last census decade decreased from 2,500,000,000 pounds to 1,500,000,000 pounds; 40 per cent of our exports were cut off, which indicates that along about '24 or '25 we would have no meats to export.

Food production means primarily crop production, because animal foods are produced from crops. Wheat is our great breadstuff in America, the great breadstuff of the Caucasian race, and corn is the great foodstuff out of which we make our beef and pork. The primary basis of increased food production then is increasing the crop production.

You know the Romans had the same problem that we have, and without any war, in which we were not engaged until very recently, and in which we are now engaged, without any war the same situation was coming upon us just as it came upon the Roman civilization. History tells us that Roman agriculture declined until a bushel of seed brought only four bushels in the harvest, as an average, and Roman civilization declined, Roman education declined, as must always be the case because an impoverished people cannot afford general education of its people, cannot afford schools for the masses.

If a child must begin to earn its bread at the age of eight or ten, as is the case in many countries, then I say it is impossible to have a well-educated people, when the masses are considered. Let me illustrate that. A friend of mine was traveling in China. He found where they were dumping water from a canal onto a field to irrigate it. The pump was made of a long pole with what might be called spokes at a dozen different points, resembling wheels upon the pole. On the ends of the poles were sticks one could step upon. At one place on this pole was a pulley-wheel and on that was a belt which ran into another belt and this belt ran down into the water and came over with the water and emptied down on the field in which the irrigation was needed. And the power supplied was man power, and the men were women. And my friend asked one man who was in charge, "Why don't you use a gasoline engine at the pump?" He said, "Well, what would it cost me?" And he gave him the information. "What would the gasoline cost, fuel cost?" and so on. And he figured it out and in a moment he said, "This is cheaper. This costs five cents a day and rice"—not cooked rice, just cook it themselves.

If we are going to have conditions improved, either with or without a war, we must have food production increase at least as rapidly as our population. The basis of increased food production was not known to the Romans. They knew the art of agriculture, how to plow and how to plant, and how to select the seed and how to cultivate the crop and how to harvest and care for it, but, friends, they did not know what the soil contained nor what the crop required. And now almost for the first time in the history of the world the people have the scientific information in regard to soil fertility and crop yields, the power of the soil and the food which it needs to produce plants.

All of you, I have no doubt, have studied the importance of balance of rations sometime in studying food subjects, in preparing food for the family, but how many of you have studied the balance of rations for the production of the crop out of which foodstuff is made. And yet you see that is most important because it lies under the food supplies which we need.

If I had the time which I devote to a class in soil fertility at the University every year, I think I could make those points pretty plain to you, but I would have to keep you here eighteen weeks, as I do that class.

We have normal and abnormal soils and I cannot take the time to discuss the abnormal soil. It so happens that the soil of Illinois in the main is normal soil. That is, it relates in composition to the average of the earth's crust. It bears direct relationship, because the soil of Illinois was made by the glacial action which came from the north and ground up all sorts and classes of material, the rocks and stones of the earth, and spread it out over Illinois as the ice melted away, leaving this glacial drift. And that is a general mixture of the earth's crust, you might say, and that gives us a normal soil, and I am only going to talk for a few minutes more, and in regard to that normal soil. I am not going to take the time to discuss with you all the different elements required to produce crops. There are ten of them and I think the time is coming when any man and any woman, whether they live on a farm or live in the city of Chicago, will not be satisfied with his or her education if it does not include a study of materials out of which wheat is made.

There are three materials which must go back into our normal soil in order to make it more productive than it was in the virgin state, and that, friends, is the greatest problem before us. You have heard of the power behind the throne. I think there is a great deal of power represented in this audience this afternoon, behind the farmers of Illinois, in one manner or another. Some of you or your relatives or friends own lands. Some of you perhaps are on school boards and you are going to encourage the establishment of the consolidated schools, to which Mrs. Dunlap referred. You will encourage the teaching of agriculture in the schools; and as you study the subject somewhat yourself, you will easily see that there is just as much of culture and more of utility in a study of some of these fundamental scientific principles underlying agriculture than there is in studying dead languages, to which some of you gave four years.

And I should like to emphasize that there is just as much of culture in a study of the bacteria that have to do with gathering nitrogen from the air to feed the plants. It is not only information but there is a cultural value in it as there is in studying many of the things that we think are high class. There is mental development.

The three materials which we need to put back into our normal soil are vegetable matter—to be grown upon the farm, not to be purchased ordinarily, except where they purchase it in the city from the stables—the vegetable matter that is to be turned back to maintain the supply of nitrogen, which can be gotten from the air by those who know how to do it, and to maintain the supply of humus in order to give the soil power to absorb the rain which falls upon it and resist drought. That is one of the materials that is required by the soil, that vegetable matter. Another one is limestone, just pulverized limestone, of which Illinois has an inexhaustible supply. Perhaps one-half of the state is underlain with limestone. You can hardly come out of Chicago, I think, on any railroad but what you see it used for ballast on the roads, and you pass the great quarries around this city and in many parts of the state, especially along the Mississippi River, reaching almost from Cairo to Galena. It needs only to be pulverized and put upon the land, and there is no danger in using too much. In fact, when you advise anybody to apply limestone to his soil you had better advise him to put on too much, or, at least, do as they taught us in *The Hoosier Schoolmaster,* to get a plenty while you are getting. The limestone makes the soil sweet. It cures the acid in the soil, just as in the human system you destroy the sour by the use of baking soda. Then the clovers and the alfalfa, that have this power to get nitrogen, and make the most valuable food for our growing stock and our dairy cows, get this nitrogen from the air.

The third material is phosphorus. Phosphorus is an element of plant food that is deficient in normal soil. Even these rich fertile prairies of Illinois were not at the maximum producing power without this element.

Now, our farmers in the west have been following the practice of the farmers in the east. There was now and then a progressive farmer who adopted a permanent agricultural method of making the land richer instead of poorer, but in the main, friends, the farm lands of Illinois are still growing poorer and poorer as they are farmed, just as the lands further east are growing poorer and poorer.

I said to you a little time ago that there is no more free government land, but there is plenty of land yet that can be had almost for the asking, but it is not in the west now. It is in the east. You know, friends, during the last thirty years in New England, New York, New Jersey and Pennsylvania there were 9,800,000 acres of improved farm lands agriculturally abandoned. In other words, there were practically 10,000,000 acres of lands that were farmed in 1880 that in 1910 were agriculturally abandoned, and you who have ridden through the New England states and part of New York, who have ridden from Washington south down to the Gulf, have passed through thousands and thousands of acres that were once farmed that are not now farmed.

If we are going to turn from that tendency in Illinois, then in all soils we must use those three materials.

In conclusion, I am going to give you just a few of the facts that have been gathered where this preaching has been practiced, where the matter has been put to the test. Thirty-nine years ago, Professor George E. Morrow began these experiments at the University of Illinois and, friends, that institution was not located in the city of Chicago but was located out on the prairie, in the corn belt, where the experiment took application to the soil there is in the state. There he began crop rotation and later on we began the application, on a part of these old fields, of these materials required for the improvement of the soil.

This morning, before I left on the train, I went out to those old fields and I just got samples of crops that I thought you would be interested in seeing. I have here two stalks of corn. Friends, the seed of that corn was planted the same day. It was the same kind of seed. It was planted in the same kind of soil. Originally, I mean, the soil was the same. It had been watered by the same rains and warmed by the same sun. The cultivation has been the same. There are just two facts which bring about this enormous difference. Of course, you get just a little idea of what this will be at harvest time, but I might state to you as an average of the last ten years, the land which grows that kind of corn now has produced twenty-six and eight-tenths bushels of corn per acre. And the land which produced this kind of corn, we will find has produced seventy-nine and five-tenths bushels of corn per acre. The difference is vegetable matter, limestone and phosphates and a good crop rotation.

Then I have samples here of our great breadstuff, wheat. In this case the rotation is the same. We have exactly the same rotation where it is wheat as where it is corn. The two bunches of wheat came from the same sized area of land. It was seeded at the same time, the same variety of wheat, the land prepared alike, and there the only difference is that where this [indicating] grows, we have applied vegetable matter and ground limestone and phosphate. I would call your attention to the fact that in producing this wheat we use only natural materials in the increasing of the fertility of the soil. We use no manufactured fertilizers. We use no stimulants. We use vegetable matter that grows upon that land and is returned to the soil, the waste materials from the barns or the valueless part of the crop, such as the straw and chaff materials—all that sort of thing goes back; and then we apply ground natural limestone and we also apply ground natural phosphate. The phosphate comes from great natural deposits in Tennessee, corresponding to our limestone deposits in Illinois. You know some states have the coal and some have the gold and some have the phosphates and some have the limestone, and so forth.

As an average for the last six years—that is, since we have grown wheat in rotation—the land had been producing twenty-two and one-tenth bushels an acre. The difference between the two is getting greater and greater. The average for the six years has been forty-one and one-tenth bushels, a difference of nineteen bushels of wheat. Now, friends, when you consider that the average yield of wheat in the United States is fourteen bushels per acre, then you see the possibilities of producing foodstuffs if we apply this great basic information to the problem.

FOOD CONSERVATION—A PROCLAMATION

We shall have men enough to win the war. We shall have money enough to win the war. The question that remains is, Shall we have food enough? In addition to our own needs at home, we must feed our armies in the field and assist our allies as well. Military autocracy has staked its all upon world empire. Democracy can win only if it marshals all its resources against Democracy's common foe. This means that every person must help—women as well as men. It may be reserved to the women of America to be the decisive factor in winning this war.

The housewife who saves enough in the kitchen to subsist a soldier in the field will be doing as great a service to her country as the soldier himself. The Federal Food Administrator will help the housewife to accomplish this. I earnestly urge that the women of the state sign the pledge card prepared by him and thus do their "bit" in the winning of this war. The directions of the Food Administrator will permit sufficient food for the family and yet will make it possible to supply our armies at the front. For the self-denial it enjoins, there will be full compensation in the thought that the things we deny ourselves go to comfort and strengthen the brave men who are fighting our battles for us.

> GIVEN UNDER MY HAND AND THE GREAT SEAL OF STATE AT THE CAPITOL IN SPRING-FIELD, THIS THIRTIETH DAY OF OCTOBER, IN THE YEAR OF OUR LORD ONE THOUSAND NINE HUNDRED AND SEVEN-TEEN, AND OF THE INDE-PENDENCE OF THE UNITED STATES THE ONE HUNDRED AND FORTY-SECOND.

(SEAL)

FRANK O. LOWDEN

By the Governor:
  LOUIS L. EMMERSON.
      Secretary of State.

MEMORIAL DAY, MAY 30, 1917—PROCLAMATION

The day we devote to the memory of our patriot dead will have a new significance this year. We are engaged in a war which challenges the principle for which they fought. From Lexington to the battle of Santiago Bay, Liberty has been the watchword of America's fighting men. This is a war in which the supreme issue is the liberty of the world. Again we have been compelled to draw the sword in the defense of human rights.

If our enemies should prevail, our heroic dead will have died in vain. Our forefathers who bought with their blood our priceless heritage of liberty, and their brave sons who have given their lives in its defense upon a thousand battle-fields, have been mustered out on earth. But the principle for which they fought still lives. If, in this crisis, we are to be worthy of those whose graves we shall garland on Memorial Day, that principle will prevail throughout the world. This is the last battle between human freedom and the "divine right" of kings. Hereafter the world will be ruled entirely by the one principle or the other. Therefore I urge that our men and women and children especially observe Memorial Day this year. Let us observe it by reconsecrating ourselves to the cause of liberty which is in great peril at this time!

(SEAL)

GIVEN UNDER MY HAND AND THE GREAT SEAL OF STATE AT THE CAPITOL IN SPRING-FIELD, THIS TWENTY-FIRST DAY OF MAY IN THE YEAR OF OUR LORD ONE THOUSAND NINE HUNDRED AND SEVEN-TEEN AND OF THE INDE-PENDENCE OF THE UNITED STATES THE ONE HUNDRED AND FORTY-FIRST.

FRANK O. LOWDEN

By the Governor:
    LOUIS L. EMMERSON
        Secretary of State.

FLAG DAY, JUNE 14, 1917—A PROCLAMATION

In compliance with custom, I hereby set apart Thursday, June 14, 1917, as

FLAG DAY.

There has been no Flag Day in our history so significant as this. Our flag, and the principles for which it stands, are now assailed by the mighty forces of autocracy. Let us show in this crucial year that we are heart and soul for that flag, and that there is no price too high to pay to keep it floating in the sky. Let it fly on Flag Day from our public buildings, our school-houses, our places of business, and our homes. Let us all—men, and women, and children—wear a small flag in honor of the day.

> GIVEN UNDER MY HAND AND THE GREAT SEAL OF STATE AT THE CAPITOL IN SPRING-FIELD, THIS TWENTY-FOURTH DAY OF MAY IN THE YEAR OF OUR LORD ONE THOUSAND NINE HUNDRED AND SEVEN-TEEN, AND OF THE INDE-PENDENCE OF THE UNITED STATES THE ONE HUNDRED AND FORTY-FIRST.

(SEAL)

FRANK O. LOWDEN

By the Governor:
LOUIS L. EMMERSON
    Secretary of State.

RESOLUTIONS ADOPTED BY THE CHICAGO CITY COUNCIL, JULY 6, 1917[17]

WHEREAS, Since July 14, 1917 is the one hundred and twenty-eighth anniversary of the independence of the French republic, and

WHEREAS, Our army is now fighting in France, and

WHEREAS, The President has called for volunteers to join our army, and

WHEREAS, We, as a nation, owe a debt of gratitude to the French for their aid in helping us secure our independence;

Be it therefore resolved, that the city council, in regular session assembled, hereby call upon all citizens to display the tri-color of France, our ally, on July 14, and to otherwise materially assist by urging all who can do so to go to the front; and

Be it further resolved, that patriotic organizations and community centers celebrate the day in befitting manner.

[17] *Chicago Tribune,* July 7, 1917.

AN ADDRESS BY ARTHUR REYNOLDS[18]

Delivered before the Chicago Association of Commerce, April 18, 1917.

With a country of vast extent, blessed with resources of untold value, and animated by a spirit of determination and accomplishment that knows no fear of results, Americans have the notion that no task is too big for them. It is a national trait, or conceit, it might be termed by some who do not understand us; it is a quality born of optimism and manly courage of which we are proud. In the gigantic undertaking upon which we have just embarked, I fancy this characteristic will prove both a help and a hindrance. It will cause us to attempt big things with full confidence, but it may also produce a feeling of present security and sufficiency that will hold preparation in check.

Let us not deceive ourselves. Now that we are in the war, it is vitally important that we not underestimate its magnitude, but that we weigh in the balance with analytical precision each problem and development as it is brought to issue. We are confronted by the most serious problem with which we have had to deal in our entire history as a nation. The world is in an upheaval and we have been plunged into the vortex.

Unless by some great good fortune there should be an early termination of the conflict, every possible resource of the United States must be utilized, every citizen might as well decide now that individual sacrifices will be required of him, sacrifices that may cut deep into his methods of living, make unexpected changes in his hours of labor and place burdens upon his shoulders that will weigh him down with grief and sorrow, but I have faith to believe that we shall all acquit ourselves like men; that we shall consider no sacrifice too great when made for the common cause.

Not the least of our troubles will be the financing of this incomparable effort. To what extent we shall have to go in this direction no man dare predict. All we can say is that the financial load

---

[18] *Chicago Commerce*, April 20, 1917. Arthur Reynolds is president of the Continental and Commercial National Bank of Chicago, and is the author of a number of monographs on banking and finance.

will be heavy during hostilities and for years thereafter. The expenditures, necessary expenditures, will be enormous.

For a comprehensive estimate of our ability to raise the needed funds, a brief review of certain events will be helpful. Up to the beginning of 1915 we were in reality a debtor nation; though export and import figures usually showed a comfortable balance in our favor, this visible balance was more than absorbed by the invisible. The economic status of this country changed quickly and to an astonishing degree. Europe had urgent need for everything we could spare from farm, mine and factory and we sold at constantly rising prices.

From a condition of perturbation as to how we could settle even our emergency obligations abroad, almost instantly we became purveyor and banker to the world. Foreign countries sent us streams of gold and we bought back millions of our own securities held across the water and absorbed other millions of bonds issued by Great Britain, France, Russia and other governments. It is important to remember that the interest and dividends on these securities now remain here and swell our investible assets. We have added considerably over one billion dollars of gold to our holdings since the close of 1914. Today we have more of the yellow metal, the basis of money transactions, than any other country. Before the war we had about two billion dollars of gold; today we hold over three billion; or about one-third of the gold of the world. Any sordidly selfish persons who think the hoarding of gold during this war will bring them a paltry soul-searing premium will be doomed to disappointment. There will be no lack of gold in America.

Acquisitions of gold and securities do not tell the whole story of our strength. Under date of March 5 the Comptroller of the Currency issued a call for statements of all the national banks. The response exhibits a remarkable ease as to reserve money held by the 7,500 odd national banks, the excess above legal requirements being $1,100,000,000. In making up our statement of assets, we should not overlook the excess reserves carried by the 17,000 or 18,000 state banks. The figures of the latter are not available down to as recent a date, nor in as complete form, but I watch them in a general way and know that the state banks also carry considerable excess reserves.

During the period under review every laborer willing to work has been employed full time or better at wages higher than ever before known, the mines have increased their output tremendously, manufacturers have been crowded to the limit of capacity in their endeavors to fill orders, and both wholesalers and retailers have faced an insistent and increasing demand for all kinds of goods. The agricultural community has prospered very greatly in all sections. Deposits in commercial and savings banks have increased month by month.

Practically everybody save the banker has made money on an unprecedented scale. The very nature of our unusual and unparalleled activity has prevented the banks from sharing in the profits harvested in all other lines. The inflow of gold has kept interest rates down to a point where bank earnings, in the main, have been less than normal, but the bankers are not complaining. They are eager to serve their country in the hour of peril.

A few days ago wonderfully interesting figures were published in the daily papers. They showed the relative wealth and indebtedness of different countries at the commencement of the war, as follows:

Great Britain and her possessions—
    Debt ....$ 7,436,000,000
    Wealth 130,000,000,000
France and her colonies—
    Debt ....$ 6,071,000,000
    Wealth 55,000,000,000
Germany—
    Debt ....$ 1,174,000,000
    Wealth 85,000,000,000
Austria-Hungary—
    Debt ....$ 3,975,000,000
    Wealth 25,000,000,000

Other countries were named, but these will suffice. They had a combined debt of $18,656,000,000 and aggregate wealth of $295,000,000,000, while the debt of the United States the first of the present month was $1,223,773,000 and our wealth was recorded at the astounding figure of $250,000,000,000, within forty-five billions of dollars of the combined wealth of all of the great nations which I have just mentioned. These countries, engaged in a great and destructive struggle covering nearly three years since the date for which their figures were compiled, could not have increased their wealth, while their indebtedness is larger by many times.

With the foregoing in mind, can any one doubt the formidableness of our financial strength or our ability to raise funds with which to conduct a long and costly war, if, unfortunately, it should come to that? History tells us some of the ancient states were immeasurably rich, but we have no authentic records by which satisfactory comparison can be made. We do know that no modern nation approaches the United States in wealth. By no means is this said in a spirit of boastfulness, for we also know that mere riches and their resultant indulgences have caused the downfall of powerful nations. Pride in our wealth should rest rather upon the fact that it gives us the strength to stand out boldly for the right and to aid others who are battling for the freedom of the world.

I do not believe that a government loan will seriously affect the banking, industrial, or commercial interests of the country. In fact, it seems to me that most all lines of business endeavor will be quickened by the requirements of the war, and in view of the splendid financial condition of the banks and the country, I am confident that we shall be able to take care of any reasonable government financing.

While the resources of the United States are simply marvelous, we have not the ready facilities for making our resources available that exist in England and other countries, for we do not have centralized banking power, like that of the Bank of England. We have twelve federal reserve banks, of which all of the national and a few of the state institutions are members, but there are 18,000 of the latter still outside the system not subject to its control, and not adding to its prestige. With us it is a case of unprecedented power without the means of quickly and effectively coördinating and using that power.

I have unbounded faith in the American people, and am confident that they will patriotically and unitedly rise to meet any situation, but they must first get a clear understanding of that situation. They must realize that the marketing of a government loan of $7,000,000,000, an amount of which we talk as glibly as though we could reach up and pick it out of the clouds, is a herculean undertaking, and one that requires far more patriotic coöperation than would be necessary, under similar conditions, to place an equal amount of bonds abroad.

It is imperative that you men here today, and your personal and business friends and associates, get a comprehensive conception of what must be done to accomplish this unusual piece of financing. The men in Iowa, Colorado and other states, will need to know the scope of what we are about. Even here in the metropolitan city of Chicago, we do not appreciate the gravity of the situation as do the people on the Atlantic seaboard, where the dangers of war and the task of raising men, supplies and funds is getting to be more real than with us or with the people farther west.

Stop to consider that $7,000,000,000 exceeds the savings bank deposits of the country by $2,000,000,000, that the money of all kinds in the United States is only $5,000,000,000, and you get an idea of what is meant. Therefore, much educational work lies before us and a note of caution should be sounded lest we overreach in our efforts to place too much of this loan at one time.

It would not be the part of wisdom to try to raise $5,000,000,000 at one stroke, nor without due consideration of what is involved. It seems to me that all the banks, state and national, should be invited to participate as distributing agencies, and that in order to make all these agencies more effective, legislation should be enacted that would encourage all the state banks to join the federal reserve system. With some changes in the law these institutions could probably be induced to set an example in patriotism by becoming members and thus give the country the full benefit of a unified banking system. The state banks would gain the valuable rediscount privileges accorded by the federal reserve banks, and would naturally add to their supply of gold.

I fully believe these changes in the law should be made as speedily as possible, and that, as a further inducement, a provision should be inserted permitting state banks to withdraw automatically from the system six months after the war is over.

It is my opinion that war financing should be by means of popular loans as far as possible, in amounts of, say, $1,000,000,000 to $2,000,000,000 at a time, and that bonds of small denomination should be offered the public. Of course the banks will gladly stand back of the country and buy the bonds in large amounts for investment if necessary; but this course would tie up their funds in long-time investments. The situation will remain stronger if the financial institutions are used principally as agencies for the distribution of government bond issues, leaving the banks free to employ their loanable funds in sustaining the business of the country by making short-time commercial loans as at present, and in doing such refinancing of government issues as may be needed from time to time.

Every citizen should come forward promptly with his subscription when the issue is announced. If those who have investible funds wait for the federal reserve, national, state and savings banks to buy and carry these securities, they will penalize business, for this method would clog the banking system at the source and all the way down. Ultimately this would result in enforced contraction of loans and at a time when such action would prove most detrimental to the government, to industry and to labor. The operation will be much more simple and less liable to disturb general business, if as sales of bonds are made, the proceeds are deposited in banks, state and national, in the community, to be checked out by the Treasury Department, either direct or through the federal reserve banks. Yesterday's dispatches indicated this to be the intention of the administration.

This would not involve a harmful degree of unsettlement of financial conditions, or take an undue quantity of cash out of any one community at one time. The funds would be raised as fast as the government needed to make disbursements, and by this method each transaction would be handled largely through book entries, or the transference of credits. Remember, this is not a cash transaction, but an operation in credits, with the banks merely acting as the medium of transferring those credits so that they can be drawn against by the treasury.

Failure to redeposit the proceeds of bond sales in state and national banks alike would be fruitful of undue contraction of credits of the state institutions and inflation of the credits of national banks. The money, or credit possibility, is in the banks, the difficulty is to make it serve the best interests of the whole country with the least disturbance, and it does not take a profound knowledge of finance to see that purchases of bonds in a community will be paid for by checks on savings and state banks quite as freely as by checks on national banks. This being true, if the proceeds of these checks were all placed with national or federal reserve banks, the credit machinery of the country would be thrown badly out of gear, thus multiplying our difficulties. If the proper course is pursued, the deposits will remain almost wholly with the banks now holding them until such time as the government makes disbursements, and we shall have a gradual shifting of these credit balances that will be largely offset by redeposits growing out of these very government payments.

The proceeds of bond sales will be spent in our own country. It will not be a case of sending money out of the United States. Even that portion used in granting credits to the Allies will not call for the exportation of gold. They will use the credits to settle obligations here. In fact, I look for a cessation in the international movement of gold for the present.

I regard the interest rate proposed, 3½ per cent, as fair. In justification of it, let me call attention to the fact that our 2 per cent bonds which sold at par or better for so long a time, carried the circulating privilege which made a market for them among the national banks. The banks could buy them at par, and, using them to secure circulation, at a small margin of profit, make a little money out of them; but these bonds are not to carry that privilege and therefore will have to sell on a purely investment basis. Being tax exempt, the rate is attractive. In fairness to purchasers, it is my opinion that the bonds of each issue should provide that the rate of interest will be increased automatically to as high a rate as that stipulated in any future issues to be put out during the war.

Very naturally there will be some shifting of deposits and reserves under any plan. While it is true and eminently proper that many saving depositors will invest in government bonds if the rate of interest is sufficiently attractive, and while savings accounts will probably temporarily decline somewhat on this account, yet I have no doubt that the withdrawals will very soon be made up by additional deposits, in accordance with the experience in Russia, where savings banks' deposits have very largely increased during the war, and information which has come to me indicates that savings deposits have grown quite large in banks of the other countries at war.

Formerly it was thought by many savings banks that it was not good policy to furnish their customers with investments, on the theory that it caused a reduction in deposits, but in recent years, I believe savings deposits have grown more rapidly in those banks which have made it a practice to coöperate with their depositors in securing desirable investments, and it has been found that the deposits withdrawn for investment not only have not had the tendency to lower the deposits permanently in savings banks, but, in fact, the deposits of such banks have greatly increased.

I cannot see anything in the situation which should in any way disturb savings depositors or cause them to cease depositing their money in banks. In fact, the banks never were on a more sound or substantial basis, or so strong as to reserves.

It must be remembered that money withdrawn from savings banks and invested in government bonds will be disbursed through the treasury in the purchase of materials and supplies, and through this channel these funds will be paid to the various manufacturers and jobbers of the country, who, in turn, will keep the money in circulation; much of it will go to their employees and laborers. These latter will continue to deposit in savings banks as formerly. Put in another way, a great and rich nation at war, through its enormous expenditures at home, increases the circulation of money, takes up or absorbs any possible slack in the labor market and stimulates industry to a point where money naturally flows into the banks more freely than in ordinary times.

I do not believe there will be an acute disturbance in the money market. Rates may harden slightly, but everybody will admit a moderate change in this respect would be extremely beneficial in that it would tend to curb speculation. Cheap money may become a dangerous element in our national life.

The entire subject of financing the war is closely connected with the agitation regarding taxation and the curtailment of excess profits. It is proper that taxes should be increased and that the government should not be compelled to pay exorbitant prices, but at the same time we are operating on a high price basis, brought about partly by speculation, possibly, but more largely by that inexorable law of supply and demand; and if prices are suddenly and arbitrarily forced to a low level, or taxation becomes excessively burdensome, all industries will be crippled, confidence will be shattered and government financing greatly hampered.

A disturbed industrial situation, which would carry with it an unsettlement in the labor world, would curtail the investment possibilities of millions of people and thousands of institutions. We are at a critical period, and it would be a grave mistake to upset industrial conditions by falling into such an economic error as that advocated by radical agitators who want the entire cost of our participation in the war levied and collected as expenditures are made. It simply cannot be done without destroying values to the extent of bringing a wave of bankruptcy and depression that would defeat the aims of our government. The best we can hope to do through taxation is to provide a small percentage of the funds as needed.

In its effect upon our entire citizenship, it makes no difference whether we resort to undue direct taxation or force a too severe cut in selling prices. Either would destroy that individual initiative and incentive to go about our duties with that quality of American vigor upon which success in this unparalleled struggle depends. Unquestionably the administration and the Congress are fully alive to the great importance of this phase of the situation and its relation to the confidence of the people in the soundness of our economic position.

Our taxes will be heavy. We cannot expect anything else, but in all fairness the burden should be divided between this and future generations. Following the Civil War we had to share the expense of that mighty and devasting conflict. That fight was not only for liberty in those troublous days, but for the national life of the future, and we now go to war to secure for posterity, as well as for ourselves, the rights to which all are entitled under the law of nations and the dictates of humanity, and there is no good reason why coming generations should not help bear the financial burden of guaranteeing that they shall be free in the exercise of their inalienable rights.

High taxes, which are not compatible with democratic principles, should not be regarded as permanent. When the war is over, public expenditures should be cut to the minimum and taxes lowered as far as possible. The war should never be made the excuse for future extravagance; economy in governmental affairs should ever be the aim of our public officials. Members of Congress should avoid making the mistake that popular approval of a grant of seven billion dollars, or any other amount, for war, gives them license to levy taxes for any kind of wasteful purposes, either during or after the war. Such an error upon their part will insure merited retirement when the voter next exercises the privileges of the ballot.

This war will be won through the hearty and self-sacrificing coöperation of the American people. It is now time to realize very clearly that every man's labor, if well and patriotically performed, will be a contribution towards the accomplishment of that which we have set out to do. The mines, lumber camps, factories, railroads, all must be operated on the highest standard of efficiency; production must not lag anywhere, for we shall need materials as never before.

The farmer is the essential element in the whole scheme. His acres should be made to bring forth produce in abundance. Even then there will be no surplus until long after peace is declared. He will reap handsome profits. Sacrifice does not mean the giving of life or possessions alone, but he who surrenders ease and leisure heroically to labor for the increase of materials and food and feed with which to support our government and its fighting forces will be doing his part along with the patriot who shoulders the rifle and goes to the front.

All these forces, by contributing effort without stint, will be making easier the financing of the war. This process is usually pictured in terms of dollars and cents and as a banking function; but the men who grow crops and those engaged in thousands of useful and necessary occupations, to whom a large portion of the proceeds of bond sales will be paid for the products of their toil, will be helping to finance the war quite as much as will the investors who buy the bonds or the bankers who use their cash to finance commercial and industrial enterprises. All are necessary; all can assist in one way or another.

With the loyal, the intelligent coöperation of every citizen, with unselfish service upon the part of all, with proper regard for duty and with a high purpose to meet the obligations of citizenship in all that term implies, we shall face the hardships of war with traditional American courage; but let us not for one moment forget that economy is fundamental. Every wasteful act should be scorned. Especially does this apply to food; though our mines break all records of production, our factories turn every wheel and our laborers receive more wages, yet all of these will not add one iota to the food value of a bushel of wheat, a pound of meat or a peck of potatoes. Gentlemen, practice economy yourselves and preach it to your neighbors.

I believe President Wilson very properly stated that our fight is against Prussian militarism and its methods, rather than against the German people.

We did not seek to take part in this world-wide conflict. We did not enter the war through any selfish greed of our people. But when humanity approached us with outstretched and pleading arms, we responded to the call and are proud to take our place at the side of that great sister republic which answered the pleas of Franklin and so fully and freely rendered us every aid, not only in money and supplies, but gave of the very blood of its people in our struggle for freedom. And we are happy to coöperate with that great mother country who gave us the tongue with which we speak, and it is a pleasure to aid all those other peoples engaged in so righteous a cause.

Where will the bankers be found in this great struggle? At your side, shoulder to shoulder with every good American citizen, ready and willing to make any sacrifice. We will all, laborers and business men, bankers and farmers, stand as a unit, working for the common cause of this wonderful land of liberty, the United States of America!

LIBERTY LOAN WEEK, MAY 28–JUNE 2, 1917— A PROCLAMATION

We are entering upon a war of such magnitude as we have never known before. The result of this war will determine for all time, as far as man can see, whether or not men shall have the right to govern themselves. If we win, we can look forward to countless years of happiness for our children, and our children's children. If we are conquered, it matters not if we shall have lost everything in this world-wide strife.

War in modern times means enormous cost in money, as well as in men. I, therefore, urge upon all citizens to subscribe to the limit of their financial ability to the Liberty War Loan. In no other way can we show the world so well that we know what this war means, and that we are resolved, at whatever cost, to win.

(SEAL)

GIVEN UNDER MY HAND AND THE GREAT SEAL OF STATE AT THE CAPITOL IN SPRING-FIELD, THIS TWENTY-FIRST DAY OF MAY, IN THE YEAR OF OUR LORD ONE THOUSAND NINE HUNDRED AND SEVEN-TEEN, AND OF THE INDE-PENDENCE OF THE UNITED STATES THE ONE HUNDRED AND FORTY-FIRST.

FRANK O. LOWDEN

By the Governor:
LOUIS L. EMMERSON
Secretary of State.

REPORT OF THE COMMITTEE ON LAW AND LEGIS-LATION OF THE STATE COUNCIL OF DEFENSE REGARDING THE FUEL SITUATION[19]

Submitted at a meeting of the State Council of Defense of Illinois, August 7, 1917.

CHICAGO, ILLINOIS, August 7th, 1917.

TO THE STATE COUNCIL OF DEFENSE OF ILLINOIS:

Your Committee on Law and Legislation submits this report as supplemental to that heretofore made by the Special Committee on Coal;

Under the law giving it creation, the State Council exists for the

[19] Minutes of the State Council of Defense, August 7, 1917.

purpose of adopting, during the war in which this country is now engaged, plans and methods deemed by the council appropriate to the common defense or the public welfare of the State. All State and local officers, departments, institutions and agencies are required by that law to cooperate with and render such aid and assistance as the Council requires.

The coal situation in this State is most critical and requires immediate and decisive action. Though not heretofore invoked, there are available, fundamental principles of law that furnish means for relief.

We recommend for the consideration of the Council the following methods, any one or more or all of which can be concurrently adopted:

1. Seizure by the State, and operation by it during the period of the War, of the coal mines in this state.[20] Illinois is one of the leading coal-producing states in the United States. The annual output of the State is about 70,000,000 tons. The powers of the State to meet present conditions exist in their full measure. *Salus populi suprema lex* is a principle as old as government itself. There is an implied agreement on the part of every member of society that his own individual welfare and property shall, in cases of necessity, yield to that of the state. Houses may be pulled down and bulwarks raised on private property for the preservation of the State and its people. Property may be destroyed to prevent the spread of fire or pestilential diseases. The safety of the State and of its people overtowers private interests. The seizure of the coal mines can be effected without the institution of judicial proceedings, and thus court delays be avoided. The right of the state in cases of this kind has for its foundation the security of sovereignty itself, and the doctrine of eminent domain and the police power support the right. The constitution of Illinois (Article II, Section 13) furnishes warrant for the plan of seizure of the mines. This article provides that—

[20] In answer to a letter of inquiry from the Governor dated August 17, 1917, the Attorney General replied upholding the right of the State of Illinois to seize and operate the mines. See Opinions and Summaries, No. 5012, August 30, 1917; *Illinois Attorney General Biennial Report 1917-1918* (Springfield, 1918), pages 606-617.

"Private property shall not be taken or damaged for public use without just compensation. Such compensation, *when not made by the State,* shall be ascertained by a jury as shall be prescribed by law."

It will be observed that *when the compensation is made by the State,* a preliminary court proceeding is unnecessary. The Constitutional Debates of 1870 (pp. 1580-1) show that the language just quoted was inserted in the constitution in order to preserve the vital energies of the State and to enable it to preserve its own existence. The necessities that confront a State in the exercise of its sovereign powers, whether for military purposes or for the safety and protection of the people, inherently require that the State shall have the power to take property for public use and to make just compensation therefor *thereafter.* The courts have held that where the State undertakes the payment of just compensation, it is not necessary that payment should precede the use of the property by the State.

The State of Illinois can not be sued. The Court of Claims has been created for the purpose of passing on claims against the State. If the State operates the coal mines during the war, a scale of prices for the coal mined can be established by the State and changed from time to time to meet varying conditions. The existing wage scale can, if conditions require, be increased by the State. The coal can be sold at such prices above the cost of production, as will (after allowing all proper charges and deductions) leave a fair and reasonable margin of profit with which to pay such just compensation as the Court of Claims may allow the operators.

The course here indicated, if pursued, will, in our opinion, not violate the State or Federal Constitution, nor constitute an interference with Interstate Commerce.

2. Call an immediate meeting of representatives of the State Councils of the neighboring coal-producing states so that an adequate and uniform measure of relief can be at once contemporaneously adopted and enforced in all these states.

3. Either separately or in conjunction with the State Councils of the neighboring coal-producing states, take immediate steps to bring about the adoption of a Federal law which will give full and sweeping Federal powers of control over prices and distribution to an

administrative body possessing the machinery to render complete and instant relief.

Respectfully submitted,

COMMITTEE ON LAW AND LEGISLATION

By Levy Mayer, Chairman
John G. Oglesby,
David E. Shanahan.

RESOLUTIONS ADOPTED BY THE STATE COUNCIL OF DEFENSE OF ILLINOIS, AUGUST 7, 1917[21]

RESOLVED: That the Report of the Committee on Law and Legislation just adopted and approved in the Coal matter be at once sent to the Governor of Illinois and to the President and various officials at Washington, and to United States Senators and the members of Congress from Illinois and to the Governors and members of the State Councils of

Indiana	Nebraska
Iowa	North Dakota
Kansas	Ohio
Kentucky	Pennsylvania
Michigan	South Dakota
Minnesota	Tennessee
Missouri	West Virginia
	Wisconsin

RESOLVED FURTHER: That the Chairman call a prompt meeting to be held in Chicago of the Chairman and a representative Committtee of the State Councils of the above named States for the purpose of meeting this Council and taking appropriate action on the matters included in paragraphs two and three of said report of the Committee on Law and Legislation.

[21] Minutes of a meeting of the State Council of Defense, August 7, 1917.

AGREEMENT ENTERED INTO BY GOVERNOR FRANK O. LOWDEN AND REPRESENTATIVES OF THE ILLINOIS COAL OPERATORS, SPRINGFIELD, AUGUST 10, 1917[22]

The operators agree to reserve the amount of coal necessary for consumption by the people of the State of Illinois and to sell same at prices to be determined as hereinafter provided.

The Governor is to appoint a representative to be known as Director of Coal, to act in the Governor's behalf upon all questions arising as to the production, prices, distribution and transportation of coal to be consumed by the people of Illinois during the remainder of the coal year expiring on March 31, 1918.

The State Council of Defense is to appoint a committee of three of its members to act hereunder.

The Illinois coal operators are to appoint a committee of three who are to be granted full power to act upon behalf of all the coal operators in the State of Illinois with respect to all such questions.

The mine workers of Illinois are to appoint a committee of three members who are to be granted full power to act upon behalf of their organization upon all such questions.

The Director of Coal shall have the power from time to time to determine the price of coal at the mine month in the various districts of the state, to be sold as above set forth to consumers in the State of Illinois; such price, however, in no case to exceed the maximum price as fixed from time to time by the Federal Government. Such Director of Coal, before determining any price of coal, shall in respect of such price give to all the above named committees an opportunity to be heard.

[22] *Final Report of the State Council of Defense of Illinois, 1917-1919* (Chicago, 1919), pages 46-47. In accordance with this agreement the Governor appointed as fuel director the Chief Justice of the Supreme Court, Orrin N. Carter, who on August 17 began hearings preliminary to price fixing. Representatives of the operators, claiming that before the agreement could become effective it had first to be submitted to the Illinois operators for ratification, and that the Food and Fuel Control Act, which became a law on August 10, expressly prohibited measures embodied in the agreement, appeared before Judge Carter and repudiated it. Hearings were continued, however, until the President appointed Dr. Harry A. Garfield United States fuel administrator.

The Director of Coal and the three above named committees are immediately to take up the subject of distribution and retail prices with the coal retailers of the state, to the end that the retailers join with the operators in the powers herein conferred and to be conferred upon the Director of Coal so far as retail prices may be concerned.

The Director of Coal and the three above named committees are immediately to take up the subject with the railroads, to the end that the railroads join with the committees herein provided for in the powers herein conferred and to be conferred upon the Director of Coal, so far as the question of transportation may be concerned.

It is the substantial essence and spirit of the arrangement provided for by this instrument that all action of every kind taken or to be taken under this arrangement shall be had and taken with the utmost possible dispatch.

RESOLUTIONS ADOPTED AT THE COAL CONFERENCE CALLED BY THE STATE COUNCIL OF DEFENSE, CHICAGO, AUGUST 16, 1917[23]

The Governors and State Councils of Defense representing the States of Indiana, Iowa, Kansas, Kentucky, Michigan, Minnesota, Missouri, Nebraska, North Dakota, Ohio, South Dakota, Wisconsin and Illinois, have met at Chicago in conference today, for the purpose of devising the best ways and means for meeting the critical coal situation that prevails in this country, and which, if not immediately regulated and controlled, threatens certain disaster to the successful conduct of the War, and to the people and industries of this country. Realizing that situation, the Conference agrees upon the following:

(1) The production, transportation, distribution and price of coal require immediate and drastic supervision, regulation and control, both on the part of the Federal Government and of the States. We recognize that, in order to effect appropriate and instant relief, it is necessary that there should be concurrent, co-ordinate, harmonious and immediate action on the part of the Federal Government and of the different States. The States, in their individual capacity, have

[23] Minutes of the meeting of the State Council of Defense of Illinois, August 16, 1917.

the power to effect such control and regulation within their respective States. Under the legislation just passed, the Federal Government has the power to make such regulation and control decisive, complete and effective.

(2) The production of coal must be stimulated, encouraged and increased to the utmost capacity of the mines, so that the needs of the people and industries of this country and of our Allies may be fully and promptly met. Therefore, every possible agency within the power of the Federal and State Governments should be immediately brought into requisition so that the necessary production of coal can be promptly effected; and in bringing about this result there must be no interference with the earnings and wages of laborers.

(3) There is an urgent necessity for a complete reorganization of the methods and machinery of transportation and distribution. These facilities should be at once enlarged and increased to the utmost. The elimination of delays in transportation, the non-despatch of coal from the mines to the nearest markets by the shortest routes, the shipping of coal into coal producing States, the abuse of reconsignment privileges, delays in unloading—these and other practices which interfere with the production, despatch and handling of coal should be at once corrected. We urge that the nine gateways of Lake Erie be utilized to the fullest extent. At present only two are so used.

(4) The price of coal is unreasonably excessive, and in many cases extortionate. Therefore, it is recommended that the Governors and State Councils in the coal producing States should immediately proceed, if they have not already done so, with the ascertainment of the approximate cost of producing, handling and distributing coal to the ultimate consumer; and we recommend that this be done, so that a report can be made to an adjourned meeting of this Conference, to be held in Chicago on next Thursday, the 23d inst.

(5) We recommend that in those States where proceedings are already on foot to fix the price of coal to the ultimate consumer, such proceedings shall continue to their final conclusion. Whatever action is so had shall be taken and co-ordinated with such steps as the Federal Government may take, it being the purpose of this report to make it plain to the people of this country that there is no desire, and that

no attempt should be made, to bring about a conflict between Federal and State authorities. The purpose of this conference is to accomplish a general and uniform result, for the best good of all the people, with the use of all National and State instrumentalities which can possibly be made available.

(6) These resolutions are adopted with the single end in view of protecting, not merely the people of the coal producing States, but equally the consumers of coal in all other States, it being the design and intention of this Conference to avoid all possible discrimination, and to take steps for the common good of the entire nation.

(7) We recognize the far-reaching provisions of the Food, Feed and Fuel Control Bill, which became a law on the 10th inst., and also of the Preferential Shipments Bill, otherwise known as the Newlands Bill. Under both those enactments the Federal Government is equipped with the authority and machinery to effect instant relief, in connection with such action as may be found proper and necessary on the part of the different State Governments; and we must earnestly but respectfully urge immediately action on the part of the Federal Government. The States here represented pledge their heartiest support to and co-operation with all action which the Federal Government and the various States may take to relieve the most critical emergency, which now exists in the coal situation throughout this country.

(8) We recommend that a copy of these resolutions be forthwith telegraphed to the President of the United States; and that copies be sent to the Governors and State Councils of Defense of the different States.

> Samuel Insull, Chairman,
> J. H. Hammill, Secretary.

and the names of all those who attended the Conference.

RESOLUTIONS ADOPTED AT THE ADJOURNED SESSION OF THE COAL CONFERENCE OF MIDWESTERN STATES, AUGUST 23, 1917[24]

The Governors and State Councils of Defense representing the States of Illinois, Indiana, Iowa, Kansas, Kentucky, Michigan, Minnesota, Missouri, Nebraska, North Dakota, Ohio, South Dakota and Wisconsin, have met this 23rd day of August, 1917, in conference, at an adjourned meeting, for the purpose of taking further action on the coal situation. The conference unanimously agreed upon the following:

(1) We express our great appreciation of the promptness, dispatch and thoroughness with which the President of the United States has acted.[25] We convey to the President our deepest recognition of the splendid work he has already accomplished for the benefit of the nation and all its people, in fixing a schedule of maximum prices at which bituminous coal shall be sold, F. O. B. mine, and in this way he has taken the initial step to avert a calamity which threatened the country with dire results in the prosecution of the war, and also would certainly have brought disaster to the American people and their industries. The prices fixed by the President are, as his proclamation announces, provisional only. Those prices are very generous to the operators and allow them a wide and liberal margin of profit, but as the prices are "provisional only," adequate and just changes can be made from time to time to meet circumstances and conditions.

The President further announced in his proclamation that subsequent measures would be adopted to govern supply and distribution of coal, and the prices to be made by the middlemen and the retailers. In order to further convey to the President the views of this conference, and to assist him in properly adopting further needed measures,

[24] Verbatim report of the conference.

[25] Following the enactment of the Food and Fuel Control Act, approved August 10, 1917, the President on August 21 designated the prices to be charged for bituminous coal at the mine mouth. In Illinois these prices were as follows: run of mine, $1.95, prepared sizes, $2.20, slack or screenings, $1.70; third vein—run of mine, $2.40, prepared sizes, $2.65, slack or screenings, $2.15. On August 23 the President appointed Dr. Harry A. Garfield U. S. fuel administrator.

and in supplement to the resolutions adopted by this conference on the 16th inst., a copy of which was, on the same date, wired to him, we further resolve as follows:

(2) That every possible means be employed to stimulate the production of coal to the maximum capacity of the mines, and increase transportation facilities afforded for the carriage of the coal to destination, by making an allotment of coal cars to the coal fields, which will be adequate.

A number of the northwestern states, notably Wisconsin, Minnesota, Nebraska, and the two Dakotas, are sure to experience a coal famine unless the transportation facilities, during the period of lake navigation, be immediately increased, so as to meet the existing emergency. Those northwestern states, unless supplied with their coal needs within the next ninety days, when such navigation closes, will be unable to produce and distribute for the benefit of the nation at large and our allies, the necessary food products which they are capable of producing. In these named northwestern states, the supply of coal now on hand is a very small fraction of what will be needed to carry these states through the winter. In this connection, the adoption of an appropriate method for the requisite territorial distribution of the coal supply, will be found of incalculable value.

We recommend that the price to the ultimate consumer be immediately fixed, in order that distribution may be made equitably in all parts of the country.

(3) We recommend that the priority order heretofore issued by the government be amended so as to include a provision that mines, now or hereafter having coal sold for delivery or consignment, to Lake Michigan and Lake Superior ports, shall be furnished with a car supply sufficient to promptly move such coal to Lake Erie ports.

(4) We recommend to the states that they use their power to the utmost to compel the prompt unloading of all carloads of coal received within their borders, and to prevent, so far as it is possible during the present emergency, the use of coal cars for other purposes than the transportation of coal.

(5) We recommend the immediate appointment of a permanent committee of thirteen, composed of one from each of the states represented at this conference, the duties of which committee shall

embrace the investigation and consideration of the production, transportation, distribution and price of coal, and that that committee shall tender aid to and co-operate with the appropriate federal government agencies.

In view of the fact that the coal operators have national and state organizations, whose purpose it is to have coal prices fixed with the view of benefiting the operators, therefore we further recommend that said committee be particularly authorized and directed, in order to protect the consumers of coal, to keep constantly in touch with the federal agencies, so that the latter may be promptly and fully advised in the premises.

(6) All of the recommendations made in these resolutions, and in those adopted during the last conference held a week ago, with reference to bituminous coal, apply with equal force to anthracite coal.

(7) RESOLVED, further, that a copy of these resolutions be forthwith telegraphed to the President of the United States, and that copies be sent to the Governors and State Councils of Defense of the different states.

Samuel Insull, Chairman.
F. H. Hammill, Secretary.

LABOR DAY, 1917—A PROCLAMATION

The Laws of the State have designated the First Monday in September as Labor Day. In accordance with this provision of our laws and established custom, I, Frank O. Lowden, Governor of the State of Illinois, do hereby proclaim Monday the Third Day of September, Nineteen Hundred and Seventeen, as Labor Day.

This is a day of significance not to working men alone, but to society as a whole. For it must not be forgotten that the final test of a civilization is the lot in life of the average man and woman. Whatever tends to improve that lot helps society as a whole.

Never in our history has it been so important that labor and capital should sympathetically cooperate, as it is in this crisis which the war has brought upon us. I think I see a better understanding between capital and labor coming out of the common sufferings and

sacrifices of this war. Then let our people generally join in the celebration of Labor Day. I urge that all business be suspended in order
that all men and women, whether they employ others or are themselves employed, may participate in the exercises of the day.

GIVEN UNDER MY HAND AND
THE GREAT SEAL OF STATE
AT THE CAPITOL IN SPRING-
FIELD, THIS TWENTY-FOURTH
DAY OF AUGUST IN THE YEAR
OF OUR LORD, ONE THOU-
SAND NINE HUNDRED AND
SEVENTEEN, AND OF THE IN-
DEPENDENCE OF THE UNITED
STATES, THE ONE HUNDRED
AND FORTY-SECOND

FRANK O. LOWDEN

(SEAL)

By the Governor.
    LOUIS L. EMMERSON.
        Secretary of State.

MEDIATION FUNCTIONS OF LABOR COMMITTEE, STATE COUNCIL OF DEFENSE

Resolutions adopted at a meeting of the State Council of Defense
of Illinois, August 28, 1917.[26]

RESOLVED: That the Committee on Labor of the State
Council of Defense be authorized to assist and co-operate with the
Industrial Board of Illinois in the adjustment of labor difficulties
whenever in the judgment of the committee such assistance and co-
operation is necessary or wise.

[26] Minutes of the State Council of Defense, August 28, 1917.

AN ADDRESS BY WILLIAM G. McADOO, SECRETARY OF THE TREASURY[27]

Delivered during the second liberty loan campaign, Chicago, October 2, 1917.

I have come to you today to discuss one of the greatest tasks the American nation has ever faced—a task upon which depends the success of America in this war, a task upon which depends the safety of democracy in the world; a task upon which depends the security of our beloved America.

I do not exaggerate when I say that, because it would be difficult to express even in superlatives the disastrous consequences which would follow the failure of America in this war. That prospect is so appalling that we cannot consider it for a moment, and we shall not have to consider it if the patriotic men and women of this country do their full duty. The patriotic men alone cannot do the task and the patriotic women alone cannot do the task—but together they can accomplish it and save America, as well as the rest of the world, from further infamies and further suffering.

This is the task that confronts the American people today. It is a task which we have not chosen for ourselves because we tried with all our might to escape this horrible maelstrom that has thrown civilization into chaos and has brought suffering upon mankind unequally in the history of the world. But because America has prospered, because America has been made great by her own ideals and her own achievements, because America is self-governing, because her institutions are founded upon the immutable rock of democracy, which means that the voice of the people shall control, there has come to America the heavy responsibility of rescuing suffering humanity, of restoring peace to a war-torn world. It is a God-given mission to which we have all been called, a mission which we could not have avoided if we would, and a mission that a brave and noble people could not avoid because they would not avoid it when the path of duty was pointed out.

We are not fighting this battle, we are not taking the transcendently important part which has come to America in this war

[27] *Chicago Tribune*, October 3, 1917.

merely because we have an altruistic end in view. Of course we fight
for our ideals, but the call would not have come so immutably if there
had not been in addition aggressions upon American rights of such a
character that we could not have endured them and survived as a
self-respecting nation of free people unless American blood had run
yellow.

I am not going deeply into the causes of this war, but I do wish
to call your attention to this fact. Every civilized nation, until this
war broke out, recognized and observed the principle that a merchant
vessel containing noncombatants, particularly a passenger vessel containing noncombatant men, women, and children, should never be
sunk unless the lives of all the passengers as well as of the crew should
first be made safe.

What was the reason for that rule? You can understand it
more quickly if I illustrate it in this way: If a German division,
after capturing a French town, and while marching through the
streets crowded with the terrified and captured population, with their
hearts torn with the agony and distress which would come from such
a situation, had suddenly halted and, under the orders of their commander, had fired a volley into defenseless, unarmed, and helpless old
men, women and children, and had murdered many of them, we
could not express the horror that would have shocked civilization.
That would have been an unspeakable crime and nothing could have
been said in defense of it. In such a contingency as that some people
would have been killed outright, others would have been horribly
wounded, others might have fled and escaped with their lives, because
they were on the land. Those who were wounded might have been
taken to hospitals and nursed back to health again. Others would
have recovered, but would have been maimed for life.

But do you realize what it means to sink a passenger vessel
containing a similar number of noncombatants upon the high seas
without notice—a sudden explosion, every one thrown into the water,
no chance for escape, every vestige of human life swept away without
a trace?

Therefore it is that civilization has exacted of every civilized
country upon the face of the earth, until this war broke out, the immutable principle of international law that no passenger ship and no

unarmed freight-carrying ship, even one of a belligerent power, should be sunk by an enemy vessel until the passengers and crew had been given an opportunity to escape with their lives.

American citizens, since the outbreak of this war, have been murdered repeatedly on the high seas under the conditions I have described to you. Germany repeatedly had been called to account and repeatedly had assured this government she would desist, and just as repeatedly she violated that promise and proceeded to kill other American citizens upon the high seas.

That of itself was enough to have driven any self-respecting nation into war. But finally we were ordered by the Kaiser to take our ships off a part of the high seas. He said: "You must not send American ships and American citizens must not travel anywhere in the five hundred miles of water surrounding Great Britain, France, and Italy. If you do, we shall sink your ships on sight, we shall kill your people without warning."

If we had submitted to that order, the German Emperor would have been able to accomplish by the stroke of a pen what all the might of the German armies and navies could not have achieved.

If we had submitted to it what would have been the next step? It might have suited his purpose to order us off the entire Atlantic ocean and say: "Confine yourself to the three-mile limit around America."

And so if we had submitted to that order the surplus products of our farms, our forests, our mines, and our factories would have piled up, and that which was perishable would have rotted and disaster would have come upon the American people.

The only difference between that situation and the actual war would be that property would be destroyed while life would not be imperiled. But what would life be to a nation of freemen with the red blood of our ancestors in our veins if we had said: "We tamely and cravenly submit to the violation and destruction of our vital rights." Rights without which the prosperity and the safety of this nation should not survive.

Therefore, we are in this war, both because we intend to defend and vindicate the vital rights of America, and, while doing that, to achieve the altruistic ideals for which we contend. If we can make democracy universal, if we can translate present despotic governments into free governing nations you will not have wars any more. That will be the best guarantee for peace because self-governing nations are pacific, as we know by our own experience. It is very difficult to bring them into war. As long as we can accomplish that, and at the same time preserve our own rights, we have a double mission in this war.

The thing that is underneath every war and without which war cannot progress, without which national security cannot be achieved, without which the wheels of government stop, without which business and all the affairs of American life could not live, is money. It is of paramount, primary, elemental importance in time of war.

Do you realize that there is not a soldier in a training camp in this country, nor one of our gallant sons upon the battle fields of France, the shock of whose bullet or the explosion of whose blank cartridge in gun practice is not translated to the treasury building in Washington?

Do you realize that there is not a dollar paid to a gallant son of American mother or father who is in the army or the navy of the United States that is not felt in the Treasury Department?

Do you realize that there is not a cent expended upon any activity of the government that is not drawn from the treasury of the United States, and that your army and your navy and your air fleets and your merchant marine and every single activity in which this great nation is engaged is transmuted from money in the treasury of the United States?

I want to impress upon you the magnitude of the problem now confronting the American people and the vital necessity of keeping the gold pile in the treasury sufficiently large to take up the shocks of those demands and make America constantly safe. If one single loan offered to the American people should fail, it would be a more fateful disaster than the loss of a great battle.

I know that every man and woman in this country had to suffer when they saw one of their boys go to the front, because I have three sons myself who are in the navy of the United States. I expect nothing more of them and nothing less of them than what every gallant boy intends to do in this conflict—die, if need be, that liberty may be safe, that democracy may be secured, that the lives of all the women and men of this country who cannot go out to fight may be safeguarded and their property preserved and their liberties eternally secured.

What is the least you can do for them? The least you can do for them is to give them the means of defending themselves so that when they meet a German soldier in the deadly grapple of war, when the battle is raging and life is hanging in the balance, every brave boy at that front will know that in his hands, put there by American love and American skill, is a weapon, the best that can be devised, that will give him a possible superiority over his foe, so that he may strike sufficiently well to save his own life and be able to strike again for America and for liberty.

I want them to know, too, that the line of communication between them and home will be protected. It is 3,000 miles wide, imperiled by the deadly submarine and the tempests and storms of the waters.

I want them to know that you women of America and you men of America are going to put back of them the entire resources of this country; that if need be, we will surrender every dollar of property we have got to the government.

We must be just as willing to sacrifice all our money for them as we know they are willing to sacrifice their lives for us.

We can achieve these stupendous and colossal operations if we go at them in the right spirit, with full determination and with knowledge of the problems that confront us. There is not an American soldier or American sailor who cannot have everything that glorious America has got if we will only organize our resources and concentrate them for the benefit of our brave defenders.

The government does not ask you to give it a dollar. It does not ask for any gifts so far as money is concerned. The bulk of the necessary money must be raised by bond issues since taxation represents only a small part of this colossal task.

And what does the government offer? A superlatively safe and desirable investment—the greatest ever offered to any people. There is nothing so good as a government bond; there is nothing so near cash as a government bond; there is nothing the principal of which is so absolutely safe as a government bond; there is nothing which is so available as collateral in a bank as a government bond; and there is nothing upon which your interest will be paid so certainly as upon a government bond.

And while you are buying that bond which is the best investment in the world for yourselves, you are helping every soldier and sailor who wears the uniform of his country, and you are helping moreover to keep the flag of America, the Stars and Stripes, in the skies. Never shall it be trailed in the dust while there is a drop of blood in the veins of an American freeman.

We want it always on high as a hope for humanity; we want it to be maintained there in order that the rights of our people at home may always have protection, that democracy here may be secured, because we know that so long as the Stars and Stripes wave, democracy is safe in America.

And if we can bring a glimpse of its glory to those people in Europe who have suffered the tortures of the night for these three long black years, if we can imbue them with the splendid ideals for which it stands, if we can make them enjoy once more the inestimable blessings of peace and restore to their stricken hearts the joy of knowing that the light which shone in the east when Christ came upon the earth has been restored again in all of its effulgence and beauty, we shall have done something of which we as a nation may feel proud, and we can then transmit to posterity unimpaired that beautiful thing which our ancestors gave to us—a free country and a democratic government.

SECOND LIBERTY LOAN—A PROCLAMATION

This is a war to establish the right of people to govern themselves. It is therefore a people's war. But a people cannot govern itself successfully, unless it is willing to finance a war waged upon it by military autocracy. Democracy is doomed, unless it has the vitality to put forth its resources in support of a war, in which its very right to exist is challenged. The people, therefore, owe it to their country to subscribe as liberally to Liberty Bonds as their means permit.

In addition, let the owners of factories and farms, and of all other forms of property, reflect that if we prevail in this war, the Liberty Bonds which they shall have bought will be the best investment that they have made during this time. If we should fail in this war, it doesn't matter much how we invest our money now.

(SEAL)

GIVEN UNDER MY HAND AND THE GREAT SEAL OF STATE AT THE CAPITOL IN SPRINGFIELD, THIS SECOND DAY OF OCTOBER, IN THE YEAR OF OUR LORD ONE THOUSAND NINE HUNDRED AND SEVENTEEN, AND OF THE INDEPENDENCE OF THE UNITED STATES THE ONE HUNDRED AND FORTY-SECOND.

FRANK O. LOWDEN

By the Governor:
LOUIS L. EMMERSON.
Secretary of State.

LIBERTY DAY, OCTOBER 24, 1917—A PROCLAMATION

The President has proclaimed Wednesday, October 24, as Liberty Day. In accordance therewith, I urge the people of Illinois to devote the afternoon of that day to the Liberty Loan. I urge that all places of business, and all Public offices, so far as possible, be closed at that time. I urge that the Mayors of our cities take every measure within their power to direct the attention of our people to the significance of an over-subscription to this Loan.

This is an event of supreme importance at this stage of the war. The day may be made as potent in helping to win the war, as a great victory of our troops abroad.

Our enemy has frequently said that we, as a Nation, care for money alone. More than a million of our young men already have given the lie to this charge by offering the supreme sacrifice—the sacrifice of life itself—that their country might endure. Shall it now be said of the other millions—the millions who remain at home—that this charge is true? Will not our people at home—for whose security and future our soldiers have already gone to the colors—will not they merely *loan* their dollars to the Government in the support of a cause, for which these men gladly offer to *give* their lives?

Remember, that money is as needful as men, if we are to prevail. Remember further, that if we do prevail, these bonds will be the best investment we shall have made during the period of the war. If we fail, even then they will be worth more than our cattle and lands, our factories and stores, or any other property we may own.

Our wage earners, our business-men, and our capitalists alike, are vitally interested in the triumph of our arms. Let all subscribe in proportion to their means. The number who shall partake of this Loan, is as important as the total amount subscribed. If our people generally are united in absorbing this issue of Liberty Bonds, it will prove to the world that Democracy knows what its liberties are worth, and is willing to defend them at any cost.

(SEAL)

GIVEN UNDER MY HAND AND THE GREAT SEAL OF STATE AT THE CAPITOL IN SPRINGFIELD, THIS EIGHTEENTH DAY OF OCTOBER, IN THE YEAR OF OUR LORD ONE THOUSAND NINE HUNDRED AND SEVENTEEN, AND OF THE INDEPENDENCE OF THE UNITED STATES THE ONE HUNDRED AND FORTY-SECOND.

FRANK O. LOWDEN

By the Governor:
    LOUIS L. EMMERSON.
        Secretary of State.

FIRE AND ACCIDENT PREVENTION DAY, OCTOBER 9, 1917—A PROCLAMATION

Our country is engaged in a world war.

Next to the care of those who are offering their lives on the front line of battle, the conservation of all our energies and resources is our most important problem. The conservation of human life takes the first rank in this secondary line of defense. The saving of human life and the prevention of loss of property through needless destruction by fire is an aid which every one must give willingly to his government and to his community.

In addition to the death and devastation directly traceable to preventable fires in normal times, there is now the need of combatting the secret attacks of our enemies. There is no more insidious weapon that can be wielded by the hidden agents of our enemy than fire.

The annual fire loss directly due to carelessness and negligence is entirely too high. It constitutes a total waste and destruction of property that is a tremendous drain on the resources of the state. The loss can be minimized only by awakening in the public mind a universal watchfulness against heedlessness, ignorance, arson, and the treachery of those who, living and prospering in this land, would strike secretly at its government for the aid of a government with which it is at war.

Because of this great need and in order to arouse a sense of watchfulness in the public mind and to create a greater personal responsibility in reducing the destruction by preventable fires, I hereby proclaim that Tuesday, the

NINTH DAY OF OCTOBER, 1917

the forty-sixth anniversary of the great Chicago fire be known as

FIRE AND ACCIDENT PREVENTION DAY

and urge that on this day attention be called to the need for care and special exercises be held to impress on the public mind lessons of fire and accident prevention. It is desirable:

That the people generally be directed to the need of refraining from exposing themselves to unnecessary risks which are liable to cause injury and death.

That there be a general cleaning up of rubbish and waste about all property, public and private, in order to reduce fire hazards and promote health.

That general educational exercises be held to emphasize the need for protection of life and property against loss by fire and accident.

That all heating apparatus and electric wiring and chimneys be inspected and repaired for use in the coming winter.

That hotels, factories, theaters and all public and private institutions where a large number of persons are housed be carefully examined for improvements that will safeguard further the lives of their occupants.

That wherever necessary, watchmen be engaged to guard against fire and other destructive agents that might be employed by a secret enemy.

That local legislative bodies give attention to the need of building regulations, fire prevention ordinances and importance of adequate apparatus everywhere for fire fighting.

That the press lend impetus to the lesson in carefulness by giving proper publicity to the purposes for which this day is set aside.

That fire drills be held on that day and frequently thereafter in schools, factories and all public buildings where a greater degree of safety can thus be insured by acquainting the occupants with the best and quickest methods of exit in time of danger.

(SEAL)

GIVEN UNDER MY HAND AND THE GREAT SEAL OF STATE AT THE CAPITOL IN SPRINGFIELD, THIS EIGHTEENTH DAY OF SEPTEMBER, IN THE YEAR OF OUR LORD ONE THOUSAND NINE HUNDRED AND SEVENTEEN, AND OF THE INDEPENDENCE OF THE UNITED STATES THE ONE HUNDRED AND FORTY-SECOND.

FRANK O. LOWDEN

BY THE GOVERNOR.

LOUIS L. EMMERSON.

SECRETARY OF STATE.

RESOLUTIONS ADOPTED BY SPRINGFIELD DISTRICT MINERS[28]

Formulated and telegraphed to the United States Fuel Administrator, Dr. Harry A. Garfield, October 21, 1917.

WHEREAS, It has been falsely represented that the membership of the miners' union are in favor of a coal price raise of 50 cents a ton, under which arrangement the coal profiteers would further burgle the coal consuming public; and

WHEREAS, Permanent peace and continuous production is apparently impossible in the coal industry so long as exploitation and unparalleled excess profits are the watch words of a large element of the operators of the coal mines.

Therefore be it resolved, That this convention of delegates elected by 8,000 members of local unions in the Springfield district hereby demand government control and operation of the mines as a measure for permanent peace, continuous production, and more equitable prices to the coal consuming public and miners.

Resolved, That once the coal properties of the nation are conscripted for war necessity, the mine workers stand ready to be conscripted for individual service if that measure is required for the winning of the war against Germany.

WAGE INCREASES TO MINERS

A letter sent by Frank Farrington, president of the Illinois Mine Workers, to officers of all mine locals in the state, October, 1917.[29]

[28] *Illinois State Journal,* October 22, 1917.

[29] *Illinois State Journal,* October 25, 1917. A demand for an increase in wages on the part of the miners in Kentucky, Illinois and Indiana in the early fall of 1917 had been followed on October 6, 1917, by a joint conference of operators and miners in Washington under the auspices of the Fuel Administration. An agreement was made whereby operators agreed to grant the mine workers an increase in wages if the price of coal was raised to cover the amount. No increase in the price of coal was authorized immediately, however; and when it appeared that there was to be no increase in wages, the miners went on a strike. The combined efforts of the officials of the United Mine Workers and of the U. S. Fuel Administrator brought the strike to an end; and on October 26, at the recommendation of the U. S. Fuel Administrator, the President authorized an increase in the price of coal at the mine mouth of thirty-five cents a ton in order that the wage increase might be granted.

Convinced that the time is here when our members must do some sober thinking this circular is addressed to you with the hope that the things herein said will receive your thoughtful consideration and perhaps be the means of influencing you to know your obligations as citizens and as members of the United Mine Workers of America.

Judging from the conduct of some of our members the value of our union is being discounted, if not forgotten; reason has fled and men are acting with a thoughtless abandon that threatens to overwhelm us with discredit and destruction. So that those who seem to have forgotten the value of our union may be reminded of its worth a few facts are cited.

In 1898 the United Mine Workers of America entered into an agreement providing that the maximum rate to be paid for inside day labor in the mines throughout the central competitive field—Illinois, Indiana, Ohio and western Pennsylvania—should be $1.90 a day. Due to the power of our union this rate was advanced from time to time until in the agreement effective April 1, 1916, and expiring March 31, 1918, it was agreed that this class of labor should receive $3 a day, or in other words, during a lapse of eighteen years, extending from April 1, 1898 to April 1, 1916, this class of labor secured an aggregate increase in wages of 94 cents a day. During the years it took to accomplish this the great majority of our members viewed our progress with pride and satisfaction.

April 1, 1916, we entered into an agreement which does not expire until March 31, 1918. This agreement was ratified by a referendum vote of our membership and specifies that the maximum rate to be paid inside day labor shall be $3 a day and under every precedent and policy of our union our members were honor bound to continue to work for that rate until the expiration of the agreement.

However, notwithstanding this fact, through the influence of our union this class of labor was advanced 60 cents a day beginning April 15, 1917, and through the medium of the interstate joint conference recently held in Washington it was agreed that an additional advance of $1.40 a day should be paid, which brings the rate up to $5 a day, or in other words, this class of labor has advanced $2.16 a day during the last nineteen months, where previously it took eighteen years to secure an aggregate advance of 94 cents a day for the same class of labor and $2 of this increase was secured in face of an agreement that denied us the right to claim any advance whatever during that time. The maximum inside day wage rate is used merely as an illustration to show the progress we have made during the last nineteen months. Other rates have been advanced at practically the same ratio and yet our union is now torn with dissension. Men who have no official responsibility nor vested right and who are not accountable to the membership for their acts have assumed to issue calls for delegate meetings to dictate policies for your future guidance, and incited by propaganda of these irresponsible malcontents thousands of our members have suspended work in defiance of every fundamental of our union.

True, the Washington increase cannot become effective until the federal government, as represented by Dr. Garfield, says it shall. His position is not an easy one. Upon him devolves the duty of protecting the public against unwarranted coal prices. When he allows the increase, which we have no reason to believe he will not do, unless our members refuse to continue at work, it will be upon the condition that the prices paid for coal by the public will be increased enough to absorb the wage increase. This fact gives the public the right to demand service of you. If the public is to pay an increased price for coal so as to allow you to have an increased wage, then the public has the right to insist that you shall mine the coal to supply its needs.

Then, too, this nation is at war. War means sacrifices and we cannot escape our share and by no means can we hope to escape our duty. Our acts must be founded on reason. The nation's sons are going to war. As time goes on, thousands of homes in this nation will be stricken with poignant grief and our people will be in no frame of mind to temporize with those who do not do their duty. The government needs coal and the public must have it. We may hamper the military operations of the government by refusing to supply coal but we cannot hope to prevent the final accomplishment of its objectives.

The government will follow its course without hesitation and without weakness, taking no account of persons, and they who stand in the way of its success will be regarded as enemies of the government. If we do our duty by the government and by the public, we shall retain the good will of both. If we do not, we shall be treated as enemies of the government and be condemned at the bar of public opinion and we cannot hope to stand out against two such powerful forces. We should not forget that there will be another day. The war will not last always, but the miners' union must. We must look to the future. If we do our duty throughout the war, no one can deny us just consideration after it is over. If we do not, then surely we will not be able to overcome our enemies and the miners' union will surely perish by reason of the discredit brought upon us by our failure to do our duty in this great crisis.

But war or no war, we must not forget that we still have a miners' union in this state with well-defined rules for the government of its membership and that the membership must obey those rules, respect constituted authority and maintain discipline in the ranks if our union is to be saved from disintegration.

Then, too, we should not think that a joint agreement entered into in good faith by our union is a mere "scrap of paper" to be torn up and cast to the wind as may suit the whim of those who do not seem to understand their responsibilities. Remember that we have a joint agreement which does not expire until March 31, 1918. Any improvement in any of its clauses that we may be able to secure through the medium of orderly joint conference should be regarded as so much gained and not as a license to, at this time, demand the correction of all the objectionable working conditions in the state nor as a license to transgress our constitution, defy officers and to strike in defiance of every fundamental of the United Mine Workers of America.

Organization means solidarity and united action taken as ordered by the rules we have devised for our own government. If we keep this fact in mind and act accordingly, we shall come through this crisis with credit and success. But, if we are to act without regard to our obligations to the nation, the public and our own union, it is inevitable that we shall be crushed with the burden of our opposition.

The old axiom, "United We Stand, Divided We Fall," is as true today as it was the day the axiom was coined.

RESOLUTIONS ADOPTED BY EXECUTIVE BOARD OF ILLINOIS MINE WORKERS, NOVEMBER, 1917[30]

WHEREAS, the recent advance granted to the miners in the Washington conference, for the purpose of stimulating production and enabling our members to purposely provide for themselves and their families, is being systematically filched from them by the merchants in the mining towns, who, after the advance was granted, immediately increased the selling prices of their commodities to such an extent that the raise in wages was more than absorbed, thereby rendering the advance ineffective as a means of accomplishing the purpose for which it was designed. Be it further

Resolved, That as long as individuals or groups of individuals permitted to exploit the people by charging exorbitant prices for the necessaries of life, just that long will it be impossible for us to guarantee to the government the results which are so necessary in this the hour of our nation's need.

We, therefore, urge upon you the immediate necessity of taking such action as will effectually curb the activities of the unscrupulous merchants and speculators who place self interest and private gain above the public weal.

THANKSGIVING DAY, 1917—A PROCLAMATION

The President of the United States has designated Thursday, November 29, 1917, as Thanksgiving Day.

In pursuance of the proclamation of the President, I, Frank O. Lowden, Governor of Illinois, do hereby urge our citizens to observe that day as a day of thanksgiving and prayer. I ask that our people assemble in places of public worship, and there render thanks to Almighty God for the preservation of our liberties in all our past, and invoke His guidance through the great perils which now beset us.

There are many things for which we should give thanks even though we are in the grip of a world-wide war.

We should give thanks that our people have come to realize, while yet there is time, the calamity that threatens our civilization.

[30] *Illinois State Journal,* November 14, 1917.

Our young manhood has shown its loyalty and worth. Our training camps, north and south and east and west, proclaim that we know what our liberties are worth and are willing to fight for them—aye, to die for them if need be.

Our people are giving generously of their wealth to that government of equal opportunity under which their wealth was won, in order that equal opportunity may be preserved for those who shall come after them. Our people are united as they never were before. Class distinctions are breaking down. New spiritual forces are coming into our lives. In the death grapple of two ideas for the mastery of the world, littleness and selfishness are falling away.

(SEAL)

GIVEN UNDER MY HAND AND THE GREAT SEAL OF STATE AT THE CAPITOL IN SPRINGFIELD, THIS FOURTEENTH DAY OF NOVEMBER, IN THE YEAR OF OUR LORD ONE THOUSAND NINE HUNDRED AND SEVENTEEN, AND OF THE INDEPENDENCE OF THE UNITED STATES THE ONE HUNDRED AND FORTY-SECOND.

FRANK O. LOWDEN

By the Governor:
LOUIS L. EMMERSON.
Secretary of State.

RED CROSS MEMBERSHIP CAMPAIGN—
A PROCLAMATION

The Christmas season is upon us. The question that comes to all is, How shall we best observe it? It usually is a time of mingled joy and reverence, of tender thought and kindly deed. The joy this year will be chastened and subdued by the great tragedy which enfolds the world. All the more reason why the reverence, the tenderness, the generosity which have marked other Christmases should find full expression in this. How can this now be better done than by a mighty enlistment in the army of the Red Cross? For the Red Cross affirms the reality of mercy and gentleness and compassion, and the triumph of the spirit, just as did that other Cross in Palestine long centuries since.

The Allies have captured the sacred spot where that Cross stood. And if we now shall only recapture the spirit which went out from Calvary, all will be well.

Our soldier boys in the camps and at the front, with stout hearts and serene faith, go to meet our enemy. They anxiously ask, How about our people at home? Do they realize the magnitude of our task? Do we have their sympathies, their support and their prayers? If so, we shall surely win.

Let us, in this Christmas week, make answer by rallying all our patriotic men and women and boys and girls under the banner of the Red Cross.

(SEAL)

GIVEN UNDER MY HAND AND THE GREAT SEAL OF STATE AT THE CAPITOL IN SPRING-FIELD, THIS FIFTEENTH DAY OF DECEMBER, IN THE YEAR OF OUR LORD ONE THOU-SAND NINE HUNDRED AND SEVENTEEN, AND OF THE IN-DEPENDENCE OF THE UNITED STATES THE ONE HUNDRED AND FORTY-SECOND.

FRANK O. LOWDEN

BY THE GOVERNOR:
LOUIS L. EMMERSON.
SECRETARY OF STATE.

U. S. BOYS' WORKING RESERVE—A PROCLAMATION

Illinois is the greatest food-producing state in the Nation. Her farmers fully realize the duty resting upon them during the continuance of the war, to strain every energy in order to produce the maximum of food. What they most need to accomplish this is additional labor. There are in our schools, and in occupations not essential to the conduct of the war, many thousands of active, vigorous and patriotic boys, between the ages of sixteen and twenty years. They are not subject to the Selective Draft. Most of them desire to do their bit, if only the way be pointed out to them. The problem is to fit them in some way for the farm, and to bring them into practical relations with the farmers who need their help. The Educational Committee of our State Council of Defense, cooperating with our Department of Agriculture and State College of Agriculture of the University of Illinois, has arranged a special three months' farm course, together with some practical training, by which these boys may be fitted, by the end of April, to undertake work upon our farms. These boys are to be enrolled in the United States Boys' Working Reserve, with the consent of their parents, but in no event are they to be employed in military service. The boy will receive full credit in his school work, and his moral and physical welfare will be conserved by volunteer visitors. Instead of detracting from their education, this service, in my opinion, will greatly aid it.

Agriculture, as an occupation, is becoming more and more attractive. The drudgery and isolation which drove those of a generation ago from the farms to the cities are rapidly giving way. Science has laid its hand upon the soil, and the farmer of today finds full scope for the exercise of his mind. Many, very many, of the boys who shall go from the school-room this spring to the farm will find the farmer's life so attractive that it will determine their permanent occupation.

I earnestly urge upon the able-bodied youth of our State, of from sixteen to twenty years of age, to enroll themselves in the Boys' Working Reserve, and for this purpose I hereby designate the week of January 21-26, inclusive, as Special Registration Week.

GIVEN UNDER MY HAND AND
THE GREAT SEAL OF STATE AT
THE CAPITOL IN SPRINGFIELD
THIS FOURTEENTH DAY OF
(SEAL) JANUARY, IN THE YEAR OF OUR
LORD ONE THOUSAND NINE
HUNDRED AND EIGHTEEN, AND
OF THE INDEPENDENCE OF
THE UNITED STATES THE ONE
HUNDRED AND FORTY-SECOND.

FRANK O. LOWDEN

By the Governor:
  LOUIS L. EMMERSON.
    Secretary of State.

RESOLUTIONS, ILLINOIS FARMERS' INSTITUTE

Adopted at twenty-third annual meeting, Bloomington, Illinois,
February 21, 1918.[31]

. BLOOMINGTON, ILL., *February 21, 1918.*

*To the Hon. Woodrow Wilson, President of the United States,
Washington, D. C.:*

Members of the Illinois Farmers' Institute, representing more
than two hundred thousand farmers in Illinois, at its Twenty-third
Annual Meeting held at Bloomington, Illinois, to-day adopted the
following resolutions and respectfully ask your earnest consideration
of same:

WHEREAS, The food situation is so serious as to threaten a national crisis; and,

WHEREAS, Unless the Government adopts at once a strong and
unequivocal agricultural policy, nothing but a season much more favorable than normal can prevent a food shortage bordering on famine;
therefore be it

Resolved, That we call the attention of the President of the
United States to the following facts:

[31] *The Twenty-third Annual Report of the Illinois Farmers' Institute* (Springfield, 1918), pages 221-223.

1. The attitude of the Food Administration is tending to shake the confidence of farmers in its good faith, and is seriously affecting the morale of our agricultural population.

2. The Food Administrator of Illinois signed a written agreement to fix a price for milk, through a commission, which would give producers cost of production plus a reasonable profit. The commission appointed by the Food Administration did not consider cost of production in fixing the price. It set a price for the producers that is sending thousands of good dairy cows to the stockyards and threatening the dairy industry of Northern Illinois with ruin. The State Food Administrator has refused to overrule this action of the Commission, thus repudiating his agreement to fix a price that would give the producers cost of production plus a reasonable profit. The National Food Administration has so far failed to overrule the action of the Illinois Food Administrator.

3. The National Food Administration last fall announced that it would do everything possible to maintain a minimum price of $15.50 for this winter's run of hogs and urged farmers as a patriotic duty to increase the meat supply by feeding hogs to heavier weights. The Food Administration announced that there was a crying need for fats. Yet, now that these heavy hogs are coming onto the market, the packers are discounting them heavily. The packers are under Government control, and farmers can not help but question the action of the Food Administration in allowing them to take this advantage of the man who put surplus weight on his hogs at heavy expense.

4. About a week ago Joseph P. Cotton, chief of the meat division of the Food Administration, sent a letter to a number of hog men and others in which he stated that there was a demand of the withdrawal of the minimum price of $15.50 for hogs and that he felt that it would be "perfectly fair" to withdraw such minimum if he thought wise. Mr. Cotton has since decided not to withdraw this minimum price, but the very suggestion that he could dismiss the obligation of the Food Administration to maintain this price with the statement that such action would be "perfectly fair," has appalled farmers and tended still further to shake their faith in the good intentions of the Food Administration.

Farmers have added greatly to their number of brood sows in

response to the appeal of the Food Administration. We now wonder if the Food Administration will consider it "perfectly fair" to withdraw its minimum ratio of 13 to 1 when the pigs begin to come onto the market next fall. The fear that this agreement may be repudiated is already sending many breed sows to the stockyards.

5. Including mutton in the meatless day regulations has brought loss to a large number of sheep feeders and we understand that the Government has bought little or no mutton for the army and navy, or for export.

6. The meatless days have so reduced the demand for prime beef that feeders of such beef have been forced to take heavy losses. The result of this is bound to be felt in greatly curtailed feeding operations next winter with a consequent meat shortage.

7. In a telegram addressed to this meeting, Mr. Cotton says, "The price of corn is at a fictitious level," and adds, "I hope the price of corn will fall." Such statements do not add to the confidence of the farmer. Mr. Cotton evidently bases his conclusion on the greatly over-estimated corn report of the U. S. Department of Agriculture. The truth is that the greater part of our corn did not mature and that corn that will keep through the summer is so scarce that the problem of the summer's feed supply is serious one. The price of good corn bids fair to be much higher before the new crop is harvested. Farmers did not make an excessive profit from their corn crop last year in spite of high prices for good corn, since few of them had any corn of the better grades to sell. On many farms the 1917 crop of corn was almost a total loss.

8. The most serious obstacle in the way of producing large crops this year is a lack of skilled labor. The Classified Draft Rules provide a splendid means for raising armies with as little interference as possible with agriculture and the essential industries. When these regulations were adopted we were given to understand that they meant what they said and that they would be administered impartially. We do not ask for exemption from military service, but we did welcome this assurance, that skilled farmers would not be taken from their vitally necessary work until such time as the need for men in the army is so great as to make such action imperative.

We now find that some of our district boards are not taking

these regulations at their face value, but are placing the majority of single farmers of draft age in Class 1. Many of these men are farm managers and the production of their farms will suffer materially from their absence.

We are not asking for any special favors, but we do believe that our close association with food production gives us a clear insight into the seriousness of this problem. We realize our full responsibility in the war and are willing to give our strength, our money, and our lives, if necessary, to our country, but a discouraged agriculture can not supply food in quantity needed to win the war.

Most serious of all is the loss of confidence in the good faith of the Food Administration and the Exemption Boards. Morale is as important in the army of food producers as among the fighting forces. Morale can not be maintained in the fact [face] of vacillating policies that keep food producers in a state of uncertainty. We take the liberty, therefore, to make the following recommendations and to ask that the President of the United States give them his immediate and careful consideration:

(a) That the War Department issue immediate instructions to the District Boards to review all agricultural claims for deferred classification and decide them in accordance with the plain intention of the draft classification rules.

(b) That the Food Administration issue immediately a plain and unequivocal statement of its policy toward agriculture; that it show its good faith by fixing a milk price for the Chicago District in accordance with Mr. Wheeler's signed promise; that it give assurance that the minimum ratio of 13 to 1 for the 1918 crop of hogs will be maintained; and that meatless days be enforced with more consideration for their effect on future production.

We feel that the Food Administration is over-emphasizing the importance of food saving and overlooking the much greater importance of food production. No amount of saving can make up for a partial failure of the work of production.

We hereby reaffirm our loyalty to our Government in this crisis and pledge the fullest measure of effort to food production during the period of the war. It is only because of the sincerity of our desire to make our efforts fully effective that we ask for the removal, so far as possible, of the obstacles in the way of increased production.

Respectfully submitted,

ILLINOIS FARMERS' INSTITUTE,

H. E. Young, *Secretary.*

Springfield, Illinois.

AN ADDRESS BY FRANK A. VANDERLIP, CHAIRMAN NATIONAL WAR SAVINGS COMMITTEE[32]

Delivered before the Illinois Manufacturers' Association, Chicago, December 12, 1917.

. . . .

You may say this country is worth $250,000,000,000 and that $19,000,000,000 [to be raised from loans and war savings certificates] does not look so big in the light of that. But to fight this war the government does not want farms and houses, stores, banks— all those things that all this $250,000,000,000 of wealth is composed of. It wants current effort; it wants something new to be produced for this particular purpose.

It cannot draw on this stock of wealth, this great accumulation of past savings. It must draw on current efforts, and upon future savings in order to equip this army. You cannot shell a German out of a trench with a stock certificate. You cannot bring down an armored aeroplane with a guaranteed bond. No landlord's rent roll will be a protection against a submarine torpedo.

Everything that is to be done is to be done with new muscle, new material, new work. It is to be measured by man power, exerted from the time that war was declared.

And everything that we want we have got to produce. We had nothing; we are as totally unprepared as it was possible to be. We had to begin at the bottom to make all this marvelous preparation for a war such as never was before—a war of men, it is true, first; men who must offer their lives and whose valor will count tremendously at the right time. But those men must be equipped, and we must produce a great part of $19,000,000,000 worth of things.

[32] *Chicago Tribune*, December 13, 1917.

Let us see how large a task that is. The census department measured three years ago the output of all the workshops in the country, that is, the total of every manufactured thing that we produce, and they gave the value at $24,300,000,000.

We have expanded our workshops, we have increased our labor. Prices have gone up, and so the output today would be a much higher figure—$30,000,000,000, $35,000,000,000, put it where you choose; but compare with it this demand for a substantial part of $19,000,000,000 and you will see that the thing that we are calling on the workshops to produce has a relation so great to the total capacity of the workshops that the workshops cannot produce what the government wants unless you and I and this whole country forego our usual demands upon the workshops, forego our command of things, our command of labor, and get on with fewer of the non-essentials.

That is not a theory; it is an inexorable fact, a fact you cannot get away from, that if we are to equip an army, if we are to play our part in this struggle for liberty, if we are to do our duty, if we are to come to the rescue of Europe, then we have got to forego our usual demands upon the workshops and give the government a free and clear way.

That, it seems to me, is the most important thing that we have got to learn at the moment—that we all have a personal direct responsibility for winning this war.

The question is, will you go into the workshops and compete with the government for the things the shop has been making for your pleasure, for your comfort, for your luxuries? If you wanted a chauffeur would you stop a man driving an ambulance on an errand of mercy and say to him, "I want you. Get down from there. I will pay you more than the government is paying"?

If you saw a man at a lathe turning a shell, you would not tell him to stop and make your boy a bicycle or a pair of roller skates, to make some article of pleasure, or of comfort. If your wife saw a woman making a gas mask and knew that mask was likely to save the life of an American soldier, she wouldn't say, "Stop. I want a new garment. I want a new hat. Make that for me."

We are not saying that, but we are all doing it when we thoughtlessly exercise our command of labor with the dollar that we have in our hand.

We must make people see that it is not the money they give, but the money they refrain from spending otherwise that is the great help. We must make the boy see, for example, that if he buys a baseball he is using rubber that might go into an ambulance tire. He is using leather that might go into a soldier's boot. He is using labor, he is using shop room. He is directly taking away from the government the means to quickly and thoroughly equip the army. He will consider whether he cannot wait for that baseball.

I am not proposing anything that is going to wreck business. I am not proposing receivers for the manufacture of nonessentials. Labor was never so fully employed, never paid such wages as it is paid today. The amount of wages was never so great.

Now, you don't think that we are going to preach this doctrine of economy with 100 per cent efficiency to men who never before had such money. Let us raise our voices as high as we can. Let us make this war lesson as clear as possible, and we will still have a great business in luxuries, a disturbingly great business in luxuries.

No man needs to fear that by clearly recognizing the economies of the situation, we shall make people suddenly turn economical to the extent that we shall derange business or bring to a standstill the business of nonessentials. We have had a crop this year valued at $21,000,000,000 as compared with $14,000,000,000 last year.

The government wanted to spend on its domestic production $1,000,000,000 in October, $1,000,000,000 in November, and $1,000,-000,000 this month. The fact is that it spent $462,000,000 in October and $526,000,000 in November. It spent half what it had contracted to spend—not because it didn't have the money, but because there was not labor and shop room and material—there was not an industrial organization that could produce it.

We got in the way of the government. We competed. We hired men the government wanted. We used material the government needed. We occupied workshops. That was the reason, and it will continue to be the reason why the government will not succeed in doing this great work in the time it should be done.

Here at the moment we have this railroad problem. If there

were a body of opinion that was clear, if men like you had thought upon the problem instead of "grouched" about it, if you had a plan in your mind of what should be done, I believe it would be done.

If there were as clear a body of opinion on the railroad situation, as there was on the banking situation when the Federal Reserve Act was passed, that body of opinion would be respected by Congress. Today nobody knows quite what to do. The railroads must have money. It is said, and I have no doubt it is well within the truth, that they must have $1,000,000,000 a year. They cannot get it from the free money that is in the pocket of the investor, while conditions remain as they are. The railroads must be rehabilitated in the minds of investors, or they must go into the hands of the government. There is no alternative. They must have the money, they must have the credit; and if investors have not the confidence to give it to them, the government must give it to them.

Take the matter of the government bond issue. You are quite as interested in the subject as the treasury. There must be another soon. The measure of success with which these war savings certificates are sold may delay a little or advance a little the date. That cannot be much.

There will have to be another issue. What rate shall it be? With the last issue selling well below par must we go to a higher rate with all the bad effect that that will have upon other securities? Now, here is a chance for you to think of the treasury's problem. Give the treasury some advice.

I believe there is some way of doing this thing so that we can continue on a 4 per cent basis. I don't know just what it is. I have no doubt if this group of men were giving some thought to that subject, along with the great deal of thought they are giving to their own affairs, that somebody here would evolve a suggestion for the next bond issue that would permit it to be made on a 4 per cent basis and would save us from what would seem to be some pretty serious consequences of a high rate.

There is nothing in the war news that is very encouraging, nothing to make us look for an early day of settlement, but there is certainly much in it to give us incentive, much in it to wake us up, and to make us begin to comprehend, and we as a nation are just beginning to comprehend what the true significance of this war is, how it is going to reach out and test our characters, and see whether we are ready to make the sacrifices we are called upon to make.

We have got to have a waking up. We have to be brought to this realization, so that we feel it in our souls, so that it governs our lives, so that it leads us cheerfully to make the sacrifices that we must make.

THRIFT WEEK, FEBRUARY 3-8, 1918— A PROCLAMATION

We should meet the extraordinary expenditures of our Government at this time, so far as possible, from individual savings. This is the old-fashioned way — it is the safest way. To accomplish this, the Government has worked out a plan for the sale of War Saving Stamps and Certificates. That plan is admirable.

Under it, even the day-laborer can become the holder of Government securities, on terms more favorable than the richest in the land. Under it, there is opportunity to teach even the school-children habits of thrift such as never existed before. Our people have been noted for their extravagance and wastefulness. If we shall succeed in cutting out that waste and extravagance, we shall easily be able to finance the war. What is equally important, we shall form such habits of saving as to be able to meet all of the cost of reconstruction at the close of the war. If these habits shall become fixed, we shall have acquired our greatest national asset, and shall be permanent gainers financially because of the war. If our people generally shall become owners of Government securities, they will be better citizens, and we shall have a better country.

I, therefore, designate the week beginning February 3, 1918, as Thrift Week, and urge upon all the men and women, and boys and girls, of Illinois, to begin to save in proportion to their means, through the safe and generous medium thus afforded by the Government.

(SEAL)

GIVEN UNDER MY HAND AND
THE GREAT SEAL OF STATE AT
THE CAPITOL IN SPRINGFIELD,
THIS TWENTY-FOURTH DAY OF
JANUARY, IN THE YEAR OF OUR
LORD ONE THOUSAND NINE
HUNDRED AND EIGHTEEN, AND
OF THE INDEPENDENCE OF
THE UNITED STATES THE ONE
HUNDRED AND FORTY-SECOND.

FRANK O. LOWDEN

By the Governor:
    LOUIS L. EMMERSON.
        Secretary of State.

CAMPAIGN FOR SALE OF THRIFT AND WAR SAVINGS STAMPS

Statement issued by Governor Frank O. Lowden, May 9, 1918.[33]

Illinois has now gone "over the top" in its drive for the Third
Liberty Loan. The energy given to this has detracted from interest
in the campaign for the sale of war savings stamps and certificates.
This enterprise, in my opinion, is one of the most promising and
useful of all the methods employed for financing the war. It is of
utmost importance to raise the largest sum of money possible in this
way, for the amount of war savings certificates sold for the first
year will probably fix the minimum thus to be raised during each year
of the war. Therefore, when we sell a war savings certificate the
government can count upon receiving annually at least the same
amount.

It follows that if we can raise the two billion dollars proposed
to be raised in this way this year, the government can count indefinitely upon a similar amount during the continuance of the war.

What is equally important, habits of thrift are formed by our
people. Illinois can easily save in this way her quota, which is one

[33] *Illinois State Journal*, May 10, 1918.

hundred and twenty-five million dollars, this year. That would mean that each year thereafter her people would save in this [manner] at least one hundred and twenty-five million dollars. What this would be worth to the future of the state it is hardly possible to estimate.

These savings would be invested in the best possible security on earth. In the past in our country, our government securities have usually gone in the first instance to the bankers. Under the plan now presented the man of the least means can invest in government securities on even more favorable terms than the largest banking syndicate in the land. Our liberty bonds have been more widely distributed among our people than any bonds that have ever been issued. There are, however, many millions of our people who have not subscribed for liberty bonds. Every one of these, man, woman or child, should own some of these thrift and war savings stamps.

This is a war in which the humblest and the greatest are equally interested. It is the people's war. Democracy can give no finer exhibition of its might than by a general participation in the purchase of these thrift stamps and war savings certificates. Nothing will so nerve our soldiers on the European battle fronts as the knowledge by them that the men and the women, the boys and the girls of America are giving them the largest measure of support. Such support means the purchase by all our people of these stamps and certificates.

LIBERTY DAY, APRIL 6, 1918 — A PROCLAMATION

On April 6, 1917, the United States of America entered the great war, with the sole object of guaranteeing national liberty to those people of the earth then threatened by the harsh hand of autocracy. No greater sacrifice on the Altar of Freedom ever was or ever could be made by any nation. That day truly was LIBERTY DAY in the highest sense.

Our National Congress has been asked to set aside this day each year hereafter as a National Holiday. If such action be taken, LIBERTY DAY will be our only National Holiday, taking precedence over every other day we celebrate.

(16)

NOW, THEREFORE, I, JOHN G. OGLESBY, Acting Governor of the State of Illinois, in recognition of this proud day and the patriotic fervor and universal loyalty of the citizens of Illinois, hereby recommend and urge that throughout the length and breadth of our great State, SATURDAY, APRIL 6, 1918, be observed and commemorated as LIBERTY DAY; that on that day the American Flag be flown from every home and other building; that the flags of our allies also be conspicuously displayed; that fitting exercises mark the occasion; and that our people in convocation wherever possible dedicate themselves anew to the spirit of liberty and the cause of Democracy.

I also recommend that appropriate programs be arranged in the schools, to the end that the lesson of liberty may be more deeply instilled in the minds of our children.

Attention is especially directed to the fact that our country's Third Liberty Loan campaign is to be launched on LIBERTY DAY, and I appeal to our people for such an overwhelming response as will impress the world that the citizens of Illinois stand ready to back with their last dollar the cause for which they are already making such heroic sacrifices in their flesh and blood.

GIVEN UNDER MY HAND AND THE GREAT SEAL OF STATE AT THE CAPITOL IN SPRINGFIELD, THIS TWENTY-FIFTH DAY OF MARCH IN THE YEAR OF OUR LORD ONE THOUSAND NINE HUNDRED AND EIGHTEEN, AND OF THE INDEPENDENCE OF THE UNITED STATES THE ONE HUNDRED AND FORTY-SECOND.

(SEAL)

JOHN G. OGLESBY
Acting Governor

By the Acting Governor:
LOUIS L. EMMERSON.
Secretary of State.

LABOR'S LIBERTY LOAN PARADE, APRIL 20, 1918— A PROCLAMATION

Saturday, the 20th of April, has been selected by Labor for a Liberty Loan Parade. It is proposed by the movers of this patriotic demonstration to show to the country, and to the world, that Labor in Illinois knows that all it holds dear is involved in this mighty contest.

There was never a war in the history of the world which so directly involved the rights of man—the common man—as this. Labor realizes full well that every step it has taken in its slow march to better conditions would have been impossible under a military autocracy. If we should lose this war, every one of these steps would have to be retraced. This is the people's war, and when the people realize this to the full, there can be no doubt of the result.

I urge that our people generally cooperate whole-heartedly in this crisis with the representatives of Labor, who have undertaken to show the world where Illinois Labor stands and that Illinois Labor is prepared to defend its rights against military autocracy, at whatever cost.

GIVEN UNDER MY HAND AND THE GREAT SEAL OF STATE AT THE CAPITOL IN SPRINGFIELD, THIS EIGHTEENTH DAY OF APRIL, IN THE YEAR OF OUR LORD ONE THOUSAND NINE HUNDRED AND EIGHTEEN, AND OF THE INDEPENDENCE OF THE UNITED STATES THE ONE HUNDRED AND FORTY-SECOND.

(SEAL)

FRANK O. LOWDEN

By the Governor:
   LOUIS L. EMMERSON.
      Secretary of State.

THIRD LIBERTY LOAN — A PROCLAMATION

The President, by proclamation, has made Friday, April 26, Liberty Day. We are in the most crucial period of the war. We are rapidly augmenting our forces on the western battle front. Many thousands of our soldiers are there, offering heroic resistance to the enemy. We at home can send them no message so heartening as that we have largely over-subscribed the Third Liberty Loan. In every appeal which the Government hitherto has made, Illinois has responded promptly and generously. I am sure that our people will not fail in this instance if they shall only realize the significance of this loan.

While I have not the power to declare Friday, April 26, a legal holiday, I strongly urge that all places of business and all public places, so far as possible, be closed upon the afternoon of Liberty Day. I also urge that the mayors and chief executives of the various municipalities within the State use their influence to make the Liberty Loan the chief business of Liberty Day. Let the Liberty Loan take the place of business on that day!

(SEAL) Given under my hand and the Great Seal of State at the Capitol in Springfield this twenty-fifth day of April in the year of our Lord one thousand nine hundred and eighteen and of the independence of the United States the one hundred and forty-second.

FRANK O. LOWDEN

By the Governor:
    LOUIS L. EMMERSON.
        Secretary of State.

MEMORIAL DAY, MAY 30, 1918—A PROCLAMATION

Memorial Day has come to be the most beautiful of all our patriotic holidays. On that day, in every part of America, loving hands bear blossoms to the graves of our patriot dead. This year, the significance of the day will have crossed the seas, and equally devoted hands will strew the new-made graves of our soldiers in Flanders and France. However far from home these graves may be, they mean the same sacrifice for the same sacred cause as do the graves which we shall decorate at home.

It may be that in future ages our own Memorial Day shall be extended to every land which now is fighting for its liberties and independence in this war. It may become the day when all nations, now united in our great cause, shall resolve anew that their common sacrifices shall not have been in vain, but that they owe it to the memory of the uncounted dead to preserve peace forevermore among themselves, and for all the world. But first we must win.

Memorial Day this year will also mean that whatever the cost, whatever disasters may come, we shall forfeit the right for all the future to garland these graves, whether old or new, on Memorial Day, unless we shall prosecute this war to a successful end.

Therefore, I urge that our people specially observe Memorial Day this year.

GIVEN UNDER MY HAND AND THE GREAT SEAL OF STATE AT THE CAPITOL IN SPRINGFIELD, THIS FOURTH DAY OF MAY, IN THE YEAR OF OUR LORD ONE THOUSAND NINE HUNDRED AND EIGHTEEN, AND OF THE INDEPENDENCE OF THE UNITED STATES THE ONE HUNDRED AND FORTY-SECOND.

(SEAL)

FRANK O. LOWDEN

By the Governor:
LOUIS L. EMMERSON.
Secretary of State.

FLAG DAY, JUNE 14, 1918 — A PROCLAMATION

One of the gains that has come to us out of the great war is a rebirth of passion for the flag. Our soldiers salute it, our civilians uncover before it, with new reverence. We now see its symbolism. We now know that though we may not have appreciated it in the long years of peace, it was the protector all the time of everything that was dear to us. Human nature is such that we do not appreciate our richest possession unless there is danger that we may lose it. And so, only now, when the armies of autocracy and brute force seek to drive it from the sky, do we realize that our flag is the sacred guaranty of all we cherish most. Only now do we know that if it shall not lead us to victory, all is lost. At this moment, men go gladly to their death that it may continue to be to all Americans the fairest object in the sky.

We are again about to celebrate Flag Day. Upon that day, let all our people—men and women, boys and girls, even little children—devote some part of the day to the special honoring of the flag. Let them recall to their minds and hearts the things for which it stands. Let them feel that the future of our country and all mankind would be dark indeed if it should go down before our brutal foe. We will then resolve anew that our flag shall retain its place in the firmament at whatever cost.

(SEAL)   GIVEN UNDER MY HAND AND THE GREAT SEAL OF STATE, AT THE CAPITOL IN SPRINGFIELD, THIS TWENTY-SEVENTH DAY OF MAY, IN THE YEAR OF OUR LORD ONE THOUSAND NINE HUNDRED AND EIGHTEEN, AND OF THE INDEPENDENCE OF THE UNITED STATES THE ONE HUNDRED AND FORTY-SECOND.

FRANK O. LOWDEN

By the Governor:
LOUIS L. EMMERSON.
    Secretary of State.

INDEPENDENCE DAY, JULY 4, 1918—
A PROCLAMATION

Every nation has its birthday festival. In an autocracy it is the birthday of emperor or king. That day changes with each succeeding sovereign. In America we celebrate the same birthday in the twentieth century that our fathers did in the eighteenth, for we celebrate not the day upon which some king or emperor was born, but the day of a nation's birth. Our national holiday signifies, not the birth of a single man, but the rights of all men.

Of late years its real significance has been largely lost in smoke and noise and ill-timed sports. Formerly, the reading of the Declaration of Independence was the chief event—an impressive one—of our natal day. As our independence became more firmly established, we ceased to recall the principles upon which it was founded. The Declaration of Independence was taken for granted, not read. We had seen France and Italy transformed under the influence of its high ideals. We had even seen the party in England which made war against the colonies driven from power. Those great British statesmen, Pitt and Fox and Burke, who had been the champions of our cause during the Revolutionary War, now became the real rulers of England. The last vestige of the divine right of kings in England was buried with George the Third, and now England joins with us in celebrating our Fourth of July. The world seemed following after us towards democracy. But now, every principle of government which the Declaration of Independence enunciated is challenged by the most powerful and the most ruthless armies of all time. Again the ringing sentences of that Declaration have their message for us, as they had for our forefathers in Independence Hall. The swiftly moving events of the last four years have put in peril again the hopes and aspirations of mankind which still find their best expression in that historic document. The challenge to autocracy which it boldly flung out has again been taken up.

Our citizens of foreign birth plan a special celebration for our next Fourth of July. They have earned the right to participate in all the ceremonies of the day. On every battle field above which flies our flag, our citizens of foreign birth are found fighting for it with as much zeal and courage as if their fathers had helped place it in the sky. Let all our people unite on Independence Day in doing honor to the flag and its brave defenders everywhere! Let us ponder deeply on that day upon the things for which we fight! Wherever our people are gathered together, whether in church or school-house, or in the home or in the open air, let the Declaration of Independence be read with a solemnity befitting the time! And let us make our own, the words with which the great charter of our liberty closes: "And for the support of this declaration, with a firm reliance on the protection of Divine Providence, we mutually pledge to each other our lives, our fortunes, and our sacred honor".

(SEAL)

GIVEN UNDER MY HAND AND THE GREAT SEAL OF STATE AT THE CAPITOL IN SPRING-FIELD, THIS FOURTEENTH DAY OF JUNE IN THE YEAR OF OUR LORD ONE THOUSAND NINE HUNDRED AND EIGHT-EEN, AND OF THE INDEPEND-ENCE OF THE UNITED STATES THE ONE HUNDRED AND FOR-TY-SECOND.

FRANK O. LOWDEN

By the Governor:
LOUIS L. EMMERSON.
Secretary of State.

FUNCTIONS OF COMMUNITY LABOR BOARDS

Statement issued by Governor Frank O. Lowden, August 3, 1918.[34]

From now on, the supplying of war industries with common labor will be centralized in the United States Employment Service, of the Department of Labor, and all independent recruiting of common labor by manufacturers having a payroll of more than one hundred men will be handled by the United States Employment

[34] *Illinois State Journal*, August 4, 1918.

Service. This is in accordance with the decision of the War Labor Policies Board, approved by the President on June 17. This action has been taken to overcome a perilous shortage of unskilled labor in war industries. In Illinois, this work will be under the direction of Charles A. Munroe, director of Public Service Reserve, Mark L. Crawford, state director for the United States Employment Service, and John Fitzpatrick, president of the Chicago Federation of Labor. It will be the duty of the board composed of these men to appoint community boards for the different sections of Illinois. The community board will consist of three members: an employer of labor, an employee, and one other who is to act as chairman. The duties of the community boards will be to determine what are essential and what are nonessential industries, and to determine what and how many laborers are necessary in each industry, and to apportion these men.

There is a dangerous scarcity of labor at the present time, particularly of unskilled labor. This scarcity has been accentuated by the constant shift of labor from one community to another. Extraordinary efforts have been put forth to induce the workmen of one community to emigrate to another. In many cases, agents, often acting upon little or no authority, have gone into a community and made attractive offers in order to induce workmen to emigrate to some other community. On arriving there, they sometimes find that they have not materially benefitted themselves by the move. This results not only in uncertainty and confusion, but in a very great loss in the actual amount of labor available on any day because of the loss of time in traveling and making changes.

It is very necessary at the present time that both employer and workman submit as loyally to the rulings of the labor boards as the military recruit to the rulings of the war boards. To win this war, labor is as much of a necessity as the soldier in the trenches. Employers are urged to get into immediate communication with their own community boards, find out what regulations are to be enforced, as early as possible, and prepare themselves as far in advance as they can to coöperate in every way with these community boards.

THE NATIONAL WAR LABOR BOARD

Message from Frank P. Walsh, joint chairman with William Howard Taft, of the National War Labor Board, read at the Labor Day meeting, Springfield, September 2, 1918.[35]

This world war has provided the beginning of a splendid education in democracy. Democracy has been our great fighting slogan, and we have—some of us—begun to analyze democracy and to find out, in the concrete and in detail, what our slogan means.

In this reëxamination the country has discovered one thing, at least, about democracy—that it must mean more than old-fashioned political democracy. The old idea that when everybody votes you have a democracy—that is pretty well exploded. When one man or two men, assisted by a Wall Street bank or two, can silently and secretly corner the steel supply of the world and obtain control, one after another, of the basic materials of industry, as well as hundreds of thousands of workers in the factories, raising prices and manipulating markets at will, anyone who is honest knows that that is not what people mean when they talk about American democracy and volunteer to die for it.

When a labor man, convicted of a heinous crime, by the use of the blackest perjury can be blocked for two years in a nation-wide demand, voiced by the President of the United States himself, for a fair trial on honest evidence, the thinking citizen knows that this is not what the American people mean by democracy.

Democracy surely means that people shall control the condition of their lives. And no one knows better than the trade unionist that the average wage-earner has very little control over the conditions of his life, especially over the part of his life which is the core of all the rest—his job.

The wage-earner sees the purchasing power of his dollar diminishing. (It is now worth about 65 cents compared with its value at the beginning of 1916.) In other words, he sees his wage decreasing steadily and relentlessly, month after month, while his wife and children sink lower and lower in the scale of living. He asks his employer, let us say, to receive [a] committee representing himself and

[35] *Illinois State Journal*, September 3, 1918.

his fellow-workmen, to discuss the matter. He is told that the firm "doesn't employ committees" and won't deal with them. He suggests arbitration. He is told there "is nothing to arbitrate." And the suspicion begins to take root in his mind that this is exactly the way he would be treated if he were a German subject appealing to the Kaiser for some political reform. He begins to understand that he is in relation to his job, up against the very thing that makes Germany hideous—autocracy.

The country, I promise you, is beginning to understand that we may have 100 per cent democracy in the form of our political government and yet have autocracy of the most despotic type in industry. It is a fine thing to elect our representatives to legislative halls, but it is a more practical and useful thing to elect our own representatives in industry. It is a necessary thing to have full share in the varied political activities of the community, state and nation; but it is infinitely more vital to have a compelling voice in the industrial policies under which we work every day in the year.

It is now clear to all understanding men, and especially to those who work for their living, that to attempt to control the conditions of one's life through the roundabout way of political oratory and legislative action is futile, and that this old-fashioned attempted substitute for a direct and common-sense control through the workshop must be put into the scrap heap of pre-war absurdities.

Now, just as the people of the country, under the searching criticism of war conditions, are becoming familiar with the idea of industrial democracy, so the industries of the country are becoming increasingly familiar with the new industrial dispensation. Under the National War Labor Board scores of industrial disputes have been settled in the last four months, involving in the aggregate hundreds of thousands of wage-earning men and women. And in every case where collective bargaining has been denied the workers heretofore, it has been installed by order of the board.

In the Pittsfield, Mass., plant of the General Electric Company, for example, no form of group representation of the employees had ever been permitted by the company, and men were hired under an individual contract which in effect prohibited union membership. The board ordered these contracts abolished, at the same time protecting the employees in their right to join the union of their trade. Further, the board itself installed, through a representative, the machinery for collective bargaining in a form acceptable to the men, a form which they will make their own and improve upon in the future as their experience suggests. The system introduced provides not only for collective bargaining in the restricted sense, but also (what is still more important) for securing to the men a voice in the technical operation and day-to-day routine of the shop.

The board ordered that "the election by the workers of their representative department committee" to present grievances and mediate with the company shall be held, during the life of this award, in some convenient public building in the neighborhood of the plant, to be selected by the examiner of this board assigned to supervise the execution of this award, or, in the case of his absence, by some impartial person, resident of Pittsfield, to be selected by such examiner. Such examiner or his substitute shall preside over the first and all subsequent elections during the life of this award, and have the power to make the usual regulations to secure absolute fairness.

The duties of the department committees shall be confined to the adjustment of disputes which the shop foreman and the division superintendents and the employees have been unable to adjust.

And this scheme of democratic coöperation has been introduced by the War Labor Board in plant after plant, where an autocrat has heretofore reigned supreme.

These department committees, together with the representative of the employer with whom they meet, might well be called the two houses of the local or state legislature of this new industrial democracy.

Here is the provision for the "Federal Congress":

The department committees shall meet annually and shall select from among their number three employees who shall be known as the committee on appeals. This committee shall meet with the management for the purpose of adjusting disputes which the department committees have failed to adjust.

In practice this committee on appeals will deal with many of the broader questions of policy which affect the shop as a whole. Perhaps this federal legislature might be better likened to the English parliament, with its House of Commons representing the citizenry and the House of Lords representing vested privilege, than to our American forums of legislation. But it is well here to remember that the English House of Lords recently lost its veto power over those measures most vitally affecting the welfare of the people.

The War Labor Board, by proclamation of the President, must institute collective bargaining in every case which comes under its jurisdiction, for its first principle reads:

"The right of workers to organize in trade unions and to bargain collectively through chosen representatives is recognized and affirmed. This right shall not be denied, abridged or interfered with by the employers in any manner whatsoever."

Moreover, the government does not wish the workers to be unrepresented; it realizes that the national welfare demands the common sense and economy, the collective loyalty and collective responsibility which free collective bargaining insures. It does not wish to have industrial autocrats in this country who can say, kaiser-like, to their employees, "What you wish does not concern me. I do not will it."

With your aggressive assistance I believe the process of democratization will continue until there remains not one wage-earner in the country deprived of full voice in determining the conditions of his job and consequently of his life.

AN ADDRESS BY BARNEY COHEN, DIRECTOR OF THE DEPARTMENT OF LABOR, STATE OF ILLINOIS[36]

Delivered at the Labor Day meeting, Springfield, September 2, 1918.

Every once in a while the results of past thought, past planning and past work begin to mature and we have the actual results before us in a form that eye can see, ear can hear and mind can comprehend.

We see the work planned in a great factory—the draftsmen working upon the specifications—the groups of toilers busy at bench

[36] *Illinois State Journal*, September 3, 1918.

and forge and lathe—working, it may be, apparently without plan. Then, after a few days have gone by, the various parts of an intricate machine are brought together in the assembly room, and, as if by magic, under the skilled workmanship of the assemblers, the plan of the designer comes to completeness, and we have a finished machine ready for its lifetime of labor. Past causes have come to completeness in the finished product.

We have lately seen our men taken from civil life, leaving their homes and communities—perhaps marching in a more or less orderly manner down the street on their way to training camp. Then, after a period of steady routine work and careful drill, we have seen the same men in perfect formation march on the parade ground in a final review before embarking for France. Past work shows itself, as the men move with routine-like precision, obeying the commands of their superior officers as one man. In our shipyards we have seen the giant ships grow steadily from day to day under the workers' labors, as the monarchs of the forest were changed to monarchs of the seas. The plan of the designer, worked out in wood or steel or concrete, finally manifests itself in a ship that will do its part in getting to our brave men "over there" the supplies which will help win the war.

The student of history knows that events which take place now commonly are brought about by a long series of preparation. Events do not merely happen—they come about because previous events, apparently having no relation to each other, shape themselves into a given form, so that the mighty event which will go down in history comes before us completed, a result of many minor events which have gone before.

Labor—and here I wish to say that I believe labor to be the greatest power there is or any that will be in the world—is now so shaping itself as to present a finished condition to view just as the locomotive gradually assumes shape in the shop, the ship on the ways, the completed army that makes it possible to win a world war.

The great importance that labor now occupies in the scheme of things along with the world war, is due, in great part, to the fact that the same love of liberty that is at the root of our war against Germany is and always has been the basic factor of unionism. We fight and have always fought for the recognition and acceptance of the same principles in industry as our armies are fighting for in France, as they wage war for the recognition of a great governmental idea.

Meeting secretly and alone in some secluded place, and scanning every member in the small group to determine his unswerving loyalty and whether he had the persistence to continue fighting for the cause, no matter what the results were to himself, these secret meetings and exchange of opinions were the tiny acorn from which has grown the great oak of unionism as it is today, spreading its broad branches over the land, offering its shelter to every worker of every class and creed.

The workers making up these groups know from their own bitter experience that the conditions under which they were obliged to work were wrong, but many of them could do no more than voice their protest as they named the wrongs that were done them. The worker who toils long hours in surroundings which sap his vitality, for a wage which does not permit his family the decencies—to say nothing of the necessities—of life, who never knows what it is to feel the rest and comfort which comes from short hours spent at pleasant work, such a worker may know from daily, lifelong experience that industrial conditions are wrong and yet not be able to propose constructive measures that will right them.

And while we are considering the radical and the benefits he brings to the world, I wish to remind you that here in Illinois we have one of the best and most beneficial examples of constructive legislation that has ever been enacted—the Civil Administrative Code.

When our present governor, Frank O. Lowden, proposed that a consolidated, unified code bill be actually put through, and it was learned that this was not mere political camouflage, but was a sincere and earnest effort to have such a bill passed, Governor Lowden was denounced by political parties and other interests as an advocate of too radical a change in our administrative law.

Prior to the passage of the Civil Administrative Code, over one hundred boards and commissions reported directly to the governor. In many cases their duties overlapped and two boards or commissions were doing practically the same work in the enforcement of certain laws. In other cases, there was no one department to which a laboring man, a business man, a teacher or professional man could go and from which procure complete and related information. He was obliged to take a simple matter up before several boards or commissions before he could get complete information on the subject. Even then, the heads of different boards might have different ideas about how these laws were to be interpreted and enforced with the result that ordinary citizens often became disgusted with an attempt to transact business with the state, and it was no uncommon thing to hear someone say, who had tried to get complete information on the subject, that, "If I ran my business as the state is being conducted, I would be bankrupt in no time."

All this has been changed, and what was then called the radicalism of Governor Lowden, was supported by the legislators of the state when they found that the governor was really in earnest, and has since been stamped with the seal of approval by the citizens of the state.

Now there are nine departments having jurisdiction over all sub-departments (called "divisions" in the Code) which are in any way related.

For instance, in the Department of Labor, all the six free employment agencies are grouped together. Besides this, there are other divisions not so closely related—the Industrial Commission which attends to the awarding of compensation when a workman meets with an accident and his employer has elected to come within the jurisdiction of the Compensation Act. This commission also includes the Board of Arbitration, which acts in strike matters. [There are also in the department] the Division of Factory Inspection, in which thirty inspectors are maintained as a traveling force to see that the laws protecting the life, limb and health of the working men and women are protected, and that there are no violations of the child labor law, [and] the Division of Chief Inspector of Private Employment Agencies, which attends to the enforcement of the law affecting the licensing of employment agencies which ask a fee for their services.

Besides these principal divisions of the Department of Labor, there are two other divisions: the General Advisory Board of Free Employment Agencies, of which our good brother, J. H. Walker, is an important member, and the Division of Labor Statistics, in which account is kept of the various figures having to do in any way with labor conditions throughout the state.

What I wish to particularly emphasize in connection with the code is the fact that any workman or employer or citizen of the state can secure from the Department of Labor, through its director, any information concerning law, labor conditions, employment matters or, in fact, any matter which has to do in any way with labor or the cause of labor.

He does not have to make a call on half a dozen boards or commissions. There is one centralized head which governs the policy for all of the divisions, unifies it and sees that there is harmonious and complete unity in all the divisions relating to labor.

This legislation, I believe, marks one of the greatest steps ahead that has ever been taken by any state or any nation in the world. Even Australia and New Zealand, which long have been held up as having ideal legislative conditions, have no legislative methods which compare with the idea of bringing all boards and commissions into a number of centralized departments, as is now in successful practice in the State of Illinois.

And, mark you well, when Governor Lowden proposed doing the very thing that has been done and has proved by a year's test to be successful in every way, he was called a radical by men who did not have the foresight to see that the proposed civil administrative code, as it is now in operation, was to be one of the greatest feats of constructive legislation ever accomplished.

After the radical has thrown his whole life and being into his idea, and demonstrated it can be made a success, the more conservative follow in behind him, taking up his work when it ceased to be radicalism and became an accepted, successful fact. The conservative often lives to help work out the very ideas of the men he denounced as radicals. Both have their time, their place—the radical to dare, the conservative to do after the other man has shown it can be done.

Unionism has long passed the radical stage. The union man is no longer looked upon as a wild-eyed reformer—a sort of cross between a poet and a Russian bolshevikist—but is now known and acknowledged to be a man who uses business methods in marketing

(17)

the labor of his hands, and who, when he does not work as an individual, delegates his authority to contract to someone authorized to represent him and his fellows, an able representative, who is able to look out for his client's legal, financial and protective interests.

The union card is no longer a ticket for dismissal; it is a certificate of confidence, and a diploma entitling the bearer to participate in a fair and just wage. Unionism is no different than it used to be; the essential principles are the same as when the first union was founded. The difference is in how it is regarded—that is all.

The cause of unionism no longer demands apologies, when such men as ex-President Taft, Charles M. Schwab, and the great ship-builder, Early, announce themselves in favor of union principles, treat with union workers and themselves become advocates of collective bargaining. The rank and file of good union men have always felt that men of the type of Taft, Schwab and Early eventually would come to a state of enlightenment, when they would know —if not acknowledge—that the principles of unionism are right. It's one thing to know a thing—and quite another to admit it.

When the great Lincoln—himself one of the greatest examples of the common people—pronounced the immortal words "that government of the people, by the people, and for the people shall not perish from the earth," he stated the fact which has lately been reiterated in the form that the "world shall be made safe for democracy." For the general definition of democracy is "government by the people." Democracy therefore is merely government by the people instead of by a certain favored few.

When working men unite, their representative, in bargaining for them, is merely following out what has been found to be a good custom on the part of the firm with whom they seek to bargain. It is by no means just and right to look upon the act of workmen who seek to unite for collective bargaining as a conspiracy, when the same act on the part of the individual stockholder of the corporation is looked upon as sound business and good sense. If it savors of conspiracy for the workingman to delegate his right of sale to an agent, then it must be wrong for the stockholders of a corporation or the citizen of a state, similarly to delegate their powers to their agents.

No! Collective bargaining is fair and right, and has come to

stay. Labor will make its contracts by collective bargaining and
each worker so delegating his power will live up to the agreement as
made by those who represent him.

For a long time, our higher institutions of learning practically
taught that this distribution was best to be made by taking over
entire, or by modifying some of the forms of insurance or profit-
sharing in vogue in Germany. The earnest student of labor economics was always puzzled by the fact that the trail of all proposed
plans for the benefit of the working man seemed to lead to Germany.
Pensioning systems, as an instance, at one time were hailed by the
university authorities as a solution for shortage in the pay envelope.
Opposed to this was the insistence from the practical, hard-headed
worker who said, "I neither want a pension when I am 60 or 75
years of age nor do I want a subsidy in the form of a compulsory
insurance, to which I must subscribe. What I want is a fair wage—
one that shares with me the profit which is made from the work
which I do."

The workman has never wanted to be treated as though he
lacked all discretion in money matters. Give him today's rights and,
I firmly believe, he can be trusted to provide for tomorrow's needs.

We must resist, as a single man, any attempt to saddle the Ger-
manic system of labor economics upon free and enlightened America.
Now, as we meet in council with the employer, is the time to lay the
foundation for equitable wage adjustment for a scale of wages which
will permit every worker to secure his profit, not when he is disabled or has arrived at an age when he can no longer either work
or enjoy, but here and now, as the workers themselves have always
insisted upon in the face of much learned propaganda supposed to
be for our benefit, but really designed to make the worker content
with something in the future, perhaps, instead of his rightful due
surety on pay-day.

FOURTH LIBERTY LOAN — A PROCLAMATION

The 4th Liberty Loan opens on Saturday, the 28th of September.

I urge that our people give proper recognition to the day; that they fly flags from their residences and their places of business, and in every other way, show their hearty participation in this important event.

When our Boys first appeared on the Battle Front, our first feeling was of pride, and then we asked ourselves what we could do to show our appreciation.

Since then, as they have appeared in ever-increasing number in the Lines of Battle, our pride and our gratitude have increased.

Many thousands of them have already given their lives that we may continue to enjoy the blessings of free Government and of civilization. Many thousands of others are lying wounded in hospitals. Not so many—Thank God!—are in Prison Camps. As we read of our soldiers' exploits, we ask, again and again, what we can do to prove ourselves worthy of them.

As I write, more than a million and a half of Americans in uniform are "Somewhere in France", as willing to give their all, as their comrades who have already fallen upon the Battle Field. And now, our opportunity has come to show that we appreciate, even if Fortune does not permit us to imitate, these heroes, living and dead! Words, even emotions, do not really count at a time like this, but only deeds! If we are grateful to our soldiers in the field, we will show it by subscribing to the new issue of Liberty Bonds. If we appreciate what they do, and are, we shall subscribe to more Liberty Bonds. If we would match, so far as we may, their deeds upon a score of Battle Fields they have made immortal, we shall subscribe to still more Liberty Bonds. Now is our opportunity!

We would have been content, if, for the present, our Allies and our Soldiers had simply held their lines. Instead, they have swept forward, mile upon mile.

Our Soldiers in the Field have over-subscribed and overpaid *their* undertaking!

Shall we now fail to oversubscribe *our's?*

GIVEN UNDER MY HAND AND
THE GREAT SEAL OF STATE
AT THE CAPITOL IN SPRING-
FIELD THIS *TWENTY-SIXTH*
DAY OF *SEPTEMBER* IN THE
(SEAL)   YEAR OF OUR LORD ONE
THOUSAND N I N E HUNDRED
AND EIGHTEEN, AND OF THE
I N D E P·E N D E N C E OF THE
UNITED STATES, THE ONE
HUNDRED AND FORTY THIRD.

FRANK O. LOWDEN

BY THE GOVERNOR:
    LOUIS L. EMMERSON.
    SECRETARY OF STATE:

WEALTH ENLISTED IN THE NATION'S SERVICE—
AN ADDRESS BY JOSEPHUS DANIELS,
SECRETARY OF THE NAVY[37]

Given before the American Bankers' Association, Chicago, September 27, 1918.

You have, all of you, as individuals, as members of associations and patriotic bodies, expressed your pride and appreciation of the magnificent achievements of our armies and our soldiers; our navy and its sailors; our manufacturers and their factories; our workmen and their industry. You have all given unstinted and unselfish praise for the splendid way they have met the tremendous problems of this fearful war.

I am here to express to you, speaking for our government, speaking for the citizens of our country, and, I can add, speaking for the allied world at large, to tell you of our appreciation of the splendid achievements and unselfish patriotism, of the efficient efforts shown by the bankers of America; to let you feel that we realize

[37] Reprinted from Josephus Daniels, *The Navy and the Nation*, George H. Doran Company (New York, 1919), by permission of the author and the publishers.

what you have done, what you are doing, and what you will do towards the winning of this war; that we feel that you, by your abundant labors and generous contributions to provide the funds for fighting men and to benevolent objects, have given the lie to the sneers and taunts of our adversaries that we are a mere nation of money-makers, interested only in profits. We have proved that so obviously, so absurdly and patently false as to cause the most rabid of Prussians to drop as an useless and obviously absurd libel their whole campaign of belittlement of our national aims and motives.

The country is proud of you. You have shown the world that when your country calls, our bankers, like our soldiers and our sailors, have forgotten all selfish interests, all class interests, all interests of every kind, and with no thought of personal advantage or disadvantage, have set out to help win this war as best they can. And if we are proud of the spirit in which you have done this, we are no less proud of the splendid intelligence and the magnificent business efficiency with which you have translated your willingness to serve into actual efficient service, the magnitude of which cannot be overstated.

We are now well into the second year of our participation in this war. We are spending more money in a day than we spent at one time in a year. We are asking you and our people for billions, many billions, at a time. We have diverted to war work much of our national industry, by which money is normally accumulated by our people, and yet you are able, today, to attend this convention with no fear of panics at home; with no anxious inquiries after possible telegrams of financial troubles at the hotel desk; with balance sheets of actual profits more satisfactory than they have ever been before; as undisturbed, as unafraid as if we were in the middle of the "piping" times of peace. Think of it. You have paid out over your counters already over six billion dollars for Liberty Bonds, out of the total of nine billion nine hundred and seventy-five millions allotted, and yet your resources, instead of shrinking, have grown in the year preceding last May, from sixteen billion, one hundred forty-four thousand, to eighteen billion, two hundred forty-nine, an actual increase of more than two billion dollars; and the Comptroller of the Currency reports that the total resources of the national banks of our country at this date exceed more than one billion dollars the whole world's production of gold from the discovery of America in 1492 up to the year 1917.

More wonderful than all, perhaps, is the fact that during the year 1918 not a single national bank has failed—a record equalled only in 1881, since 1870—and during the past year one hundred and six new charters for national banks have been asked for, representing a capital of nine billion [sic] dollars more.

Figures are tiresome things. They are popularly supposed to be utterly incompatible with romance or imagination, but surely these figures stand out clothed with as vivid picturesqueness as any word picture of the struggle at the front. While our soldiers and our sailors have carried forward our colors and kept us magnificently at war at the front, you gentlemen, with equal patriotism, have kept us, financially, magnificently at peace at home. For this we thank you.

None know better than we at Washington the value of your services or how impossible our achievements abroad would have been but for your help here. If we have given to the world a new conception of democracy, a democracy that is real and virile and sincere and not a mere hypocritical cant of politicians and diplomats, but a democracy that believes in democracy, you have on your part enabled America to give the world a new conception of finance, as unselfish, as patriotic, as broad and far-seeing, as pledged to the common cause of humanity as any of our other beliefs or actions, as perfectly fitting into the general example we have set of the same spirit which inspired our forefathers in the creation of this republic as any other things we have done or said since this conflict began. You have taught the other nations that the American's idea of his money, like his idea of his life, is something which is to be freely and ungrudgingly given for his ideals and his country whenever his country calls.

I have spoken, incidentally, of your own prosperous condition. It is pleasant to think that virtue is not always its only reward, that in helping your country, I think, perhaps, you help yourselves. It is the silver lining to our present clouds, just as our boys will come back stronger, better, more efficient men than they went forth, just as our manufacturers have learned many things which will make them far more efficient as manufacturers than before the war began, just as the whole country will be a stronger, more efficient country than it ever was before, so have you bankers learned by actual experience that in sacrificing much to your country, you have found increased ways of efficiency by which you may also help yourselves.

We are now starting another liberty loan. We are relying with the absolute confidence which comes from past experience upon you bankers to make it an even greater success than those which have preceded. Splendidly have you met our calls for aid in the past, even more splendidly will you meet our call of the present. It is through you that our greatest subscriptions have come; it is through your efforts that our greatest subscriptions must come. We have no fear, nor do we even feel that we are obliged to use any special efforts to arouse you to even greater efforts in the future. I do not intend to attempt to spur you on in this coming campaign because I know you need no spurring. I am trying merely to let you feel that what you have done has been appreciated and will be appreciated; to express to you so far as I can the feeling of pride, the feeling of gratitude which the whole country shares with me in regard to the bankers of America.

Back of all the pride and pomp of war, behind the roar of guns and the shouting armies, with no Legions of Honor, or Victoria Crosses dangling in front of their eyes as glittering awards, must sit in their quiet counting houses the controllers of the world's finances, and through anxious hours and sleepless nights must they provide ways and means by which the guns and armies may move forward to the front. In this silent, unpicturesque, unheroic struggle, which is really our first line of defense, we are now preparing a forward movement in force; we are at the beginning of this loan campaign going over our accouterments, testing our ammunition, preparing, as it were, a sort of general charge. I have not the slightest doubt but what at the very head of all the soldiers in this assault, we will see, as heretofore, our bankers, the first "over the top."

Fortunately, before the strain upon our resources in financing this expensive war, the Federal Reserve Act had become a law and was in successful operation. If this system had not been created prior to our entrance into the war, the first duty of government would have been to provide the facilities for buttressing our financial buildings by its prompt enactment. It is the outstanding creative constructive act of this generation, the perfect product of the study of the needs of a sound American financial policy. Before that measure stabilized our financial and banking system, periodical panics wrought destruction when there was a heavy drain upon our resources, but since the Federal Reserve Act made national wealth instantly available to protect national credit, there has been no hint of panic or financial disturbance to give apprehension to business men. Instead, it has given confidence, promoted enterprise and expansion, and been a foundation of rock upon which we have builded trade and manufacturing expansion unprecedented in history. It has enabled, without a jar or creaking of the splendid machines, the financing of this war, which calls for many billions. For years, before the federal reserve law was devised, the wisest men among us had pointed out the defects of our outgrown financial system to afford elasticity and confidence necessary to business, but differences of opinion had delayed action. All honor to the wise men who drafted the federal reserve law; all honor to the men who had the wisdom to put it on the statute books; all honor to those charged with its operation and success! From the day the President signed that epoch-making measure and the Secretary of the Treasury successfully launched it, the coöperation and assistance and wise counsel of the bankers of America have been hearty, sincere and complete.

Without such wise and helpful coöperation by the financial leaders in every part of the country the system would not have translated the statute into the living fountain from which confidence and assurance have sprung to safeguard American prosperity. Financial disturbances of other days, which hung so often like a pall upon the enterprise and expansion of American industry, were dissipated by this measure and its wise operation.

The whole world recognizes the soundness of our system. A typical expression of approval was voiced by Sir Edward H. Holden of the London City and Midland Bank of London, England, who said: "The United States has built up a banking system which surpasses in strength and excellence any other banking system in the world."

Democracy in financing this war has illustrated its firm hold upon our country. In other wars, when large loans were to be placed, a few great bankers were relied upon by the government to act as its fiduciary agents. Sometimes a single great banker floated loans, securing, of course, the coöperation of others. In this day, when billions rather than millions were needed, the government looked with confidence to all the banks to take the laboring oar; and in metropolis and hamlet, they have safely navigated three liberty loans, and tonight have launched the ship that they will steer safely into harbor, carrying with it six billion dollars and the pledge of as much more as may be needed to win the war.

AN ADDRESS BY WILLIAM G. McADOO, SECRETARY OF THE TREASURY[38]

Delivered at a massmeeting held in the Auditorium Theater, Chicago, October 12, 1918.

When the third liberty loan was offered, the Germans had pushed their line in a great circle westward, so that they were in shelling distance of the city of Paris. Never were the liberties of the world in such peril as at that time. But as soon as we transformed those liberty bonds into fighting Americans on the front and into the munitions and supplies those fighting men needed, we began to make dents in the German circle, and now we are pushing it eastward towards Berlin instead of the Germans pushing it westward towards Paris.

I said in the third liberty loan campaign that we would push that circle eastward as soon as America could get her strength upon the battle front, until its perimeter included Berlin. We are doing it. America's soldiers have answered the Kaiser. With American bayonets they have already written upon the soil of Germany this notice to the Kaiser, "The jig's up." If our home army fails to put the fourth liberty loan over, it will be notice to the Kaiser that the jig is not up. It will contradict everything our soldiers are doing. It will be new incentive to Germany to keep on fighting, and it will be a confession in America of humiliating and disastrous failure.

[38] *Chicago Tribune*, October 13, 1918.

Our soldiers are winning victories with their blood and heroism. Shall we at home turn their victories into defeats? No! Pershing has the Germans on the run and we are going to lash the backs of the fleeing enemy until the victory is complete.

Pershing needs locomotives and rails to follow up our victories, and a part of the money of the fourth liberty loan will be used to send them to him. It takes American locomotives now to keep up with the fleeing Germans! Let us see to it at home that the necessary locomotives and rails are provided for the chase. We may as well send our American soldiers in first class trains to Berlin instead of leaving them to march that long distance on foot.

We are approaching the Christmas season. What more beautiful present can you give than liberty bonds or war savings stamps? They represent what no other conceivable gift can represent. Liberty bonds represent the vital aid we at home are giving to our gallant sons upon the field of battle, and everyone who makes a Christmas gift of a liberty bond can have the satisfaction of knowing that he is not only bringing joy and gladness to the recipient of that gift, but he is giving aid and comfort to the soldier in the trenches whose Christmas cannot be gladdened in any other way.

Let us start here tonight a movement to buy a Christmas bond for the boy in France, for the boy on the high seas, or for the boy in the cantonments.

Everyone who buys a bond as a Christmas present for a loved one or a friend at home is buying a bond for our gallant soldiers and sailors, even though he himself has no sons in the service, because the proceeds of those bonds will bring help and comfort and strength to the American heroes who are fighting for loved ones at home and their country's honor.

Italy made a transcendent contribution to the cause of civilization when she produced Christopher Columbus; and Columbus laid the foundation for world liberty when he discovered America four hundred and twenty-six years ago. In America has arisen the mighty republic which, when liberty and democracy in Europe were about to be extinguished by the Kaiser, sprang to arms, determined to make the world safe everywhere for democracy. All honor to the genius of Columbus and to the great nation which produced him.

All America recognizes the patriotic duty of supporting our soldiers in the field and of helping them fight until a conclusive victory is won; but patriotism is of little value if it is professed only with the lips and is not backed by actual deeds. We must do the necessary things at home just as our soldiers must do the necessary things on the battle field. They cannot fight, they cannot win, unless the great home army provides the means for victory. The question before us is intensely practical. We must be performers as well as patriots. The $6,000,000,000 the government now requires must be subscribed by the people. It is the practical evidence of our patriotism to do it and it is notice to the Kaiser of our unshaken determination to do the job thoroughly and conclusively.

The fact that only one week remains to subscribe the fourth liberty loan and that we are still short $3,500,000,000 makes it necessary for us to consider some of the specific things that must be done to win success. Many families, for instance, think they have done their full duty when the head of the family subscribes for bonds, but the head of the family has not done his full duty unless he has bought all of the bonds he can pay for immediately and in the near future. If the wife is able to buy bonds and has not done so, she should buy them immediately; if the children are able to buy bonds and have not done so, they should buy immediately. Wives and children have as much interest in liberty and in security of life and property as the husband. In every family the question should be immediately reviewed and additional subscriptions made to liberty bonds as far as it is possible to do so.

A word particularly to the farmers: They did splendid work in the third liberty loan, but they must do more for the fourth liberty loan. Farmers have not yet sold their crops and may not have the ready money to pay for bonds immediately. But they are selling their crops right along and will soon have the money to invest in liberty bonds. Each and every farmer in the United States should subscribe for liberty bonds now and pay for them when he has sold his crops. He can buy bonds on the installment plan and the bank ought to carry the farmers and every other class of our people on their subscriptions until they can pay them. The banks owe it to the country still further to demonstrate their patriotism by lending money to all subscribers to liberty bonds at the same rate of interest the bonds bear, namely, 4¼ per cent.

The banks can afford to do this and it is their duty to do this. We must not penalize the patriotism of subscribers to liberty bonds by charging them higher rates of interest than the government pays them. There are thousands of patriotic bankers throughout the United States who are carrying liberty loan subscriptions at the government rate of interest, but there are many who do not. I hope that all the bankers of the United States, national and state alike, will realize how important it is to them and to the government to assist subscribers for liberty bonds by lending them the necessary money at the government rate of interest until they can pay for them on the installment plan.

What I have said about the duty of farmers to buy on the installment plan applies to every class of people, rich and poor and of moderate means alike. In the third liberty loan there were 18,000,000 subscribers to $4,000,000,000 of bonds. Of this vast army only 22,500 individuals and corporations bought bonds in excess of $10,000. This shows that the third liberty loan was subscribed more largely by people of small than of moderate and large means. This time, well-to-do and rich people and corporations must improve their record. They can do more than they did in the third liberty loan, and the country expects them to do more. They are just as patriotic as any other class of our people, but they must give a practical demonstration of it in the fourth liberty loan. Why should the well-to-do and rich men and corporations hesitate to buy bonds on the installment plan if they have not the ready cash, when people of small means are doing so?

A few days ago I took the subscription of the President of the United States for $20,000 of liberty bonds on the installment plan. The President, the commander-in-chief of the army and navy, does not feel demeaned by buying liberty bonds on the installment plan. He knows the importance of doing it, and he knows that this war cannot be financed unless people use their credit as well as their savings. The President is going to pay for his liberty bonds out of his salary as it comes to him monthly, and every other man and woman and every corporation in the United States should buy all the liberty bonds they can, just as the President has done, and pay for them out of their salaries or their incomes on the installment plan.

I know that the patriotic bankers of America will be glad to extend credit on reasonable terms to every purchaser of liberty bonds on the installment plan, no matter whether the purchaser is big or little or of moderate means.

Counties, cities and school districts throughout the country must realize that it is in the highest degree a duty of patriotism, as well as a matter of intelligent self-interest to invest their funds in liberty bonds. Great sums of money are accumulated in this country for sinking fund purposes. All such sinking funds should be invested in liberty bonds. There can be no safer or more desirable investment for such funds. As long as they are idle in sinking funds or invested in other classes of securities than government bonds, they have no vital fighting power. The minute they are invested in liberty bonds they are a contribution to the strength of our armies at the front.

The same thing may be said of estates and trust funds generally. We must understand that our task is so great that every resource of the nation must be employed if we are to gain success. Government bonds are peculiarly attractive investments for estate and trust funds. Let every trustee of such funds awaken to his duty and promptly invest the funds under his control in the bonds of the fourth liberty loan.

This loan must be widely diffused. We had 18,000,000 subscribers for the third liberty loan, and we ought to have 36,000,000 subscribers for the fourth liberty loan. I earnestly hope that we may get such a wide distribution because it adds to the strength of the financial situation and imposes no strain upon the country's resources and ability to go forward with the commercial and industrial enterprises and to continue the production of the materials required for the successful operations of the army in the field.

FIRE AND ACCIDENT PREVENTION DAY, NOVEMBER 2, 1918—A PROCLAMATION

In times of peace, our losses by fire have been excessive through lack of proper precaution. The hazard by fire is increased because of the war. This is due to the speeding up of industry, and the possible presence of enemy incendiaries. It thus becomes necessary to exercise extraordinary care to prevent loss of property and life, by fire.

Therefore, I hereby proclaim that Wednesday, the

SECOND DAY OF NOVEMBER, 1918

be known as

FIRE AND ACCIDENT PREVENTION DAY,

urging that on this day especial attention be invited to the need for watchfulness and care that our people may cooperate in the effort to prevent fires and accidents so wasteful of life and property. On this day it is desirable:

That the attention of our people be directed to the need for care and of refraining from exposure to unnecessary risks which may cause injury and death.

That in public and private places there be a cleaning and disposal of waste and rubbish in order that the hazard of fire may be reduced and health promoted.

That heating apparatus, chimneys, electric wiring and ventilating devices be inspected and repaired that they may be safely operated during the coming Winter.

That all places where large numbers of people congregate— hotels, factories, theatres, churches and all public and private places— be adequately examined and safeguarded that the lives of occupants may be protected.

That watchmen be engaged where there is danger of incendiarism on the part of the enemy; that fire drills be held and thereafter continued with frequency in schools, factories and public buildings and every effort be made to acquaint occupants with the best and safest means of exit in times of danger.

That general educational exercises be held that our people may be impressed with the necessity for this important work of conservation and that local legislative bodies give exacting attention to the need of building regulations, fire prevention ordinances and the importance of ample protection against fire.

And it is especially desirable that the press lend its support and give all possible publicity to the purposes for which this day is named.

(SEAL)

GIVEN UNDER MY HAND AND THE GREAT SEAL OF STATE AT THE CAPITOL IN SPRINGFIELD, THIS TWENTY-NINTH DAY OF AUGUST, IN THE YEAR OF OUR LORD ONE THOUSAND NINE HUNDRED AND EIGHTEEN, AND OF THE INDEPENDENCE OF THE UNITED STATES THE ONE HUNDRED AND FORTY-THIRD.

FRANK O. LOWDEN

By the Governor:
    LOUIS L. EMMERSON.
        Secretary of State.

AN ADDRESS BY GOVERNOR FRANK O. LOWDEN[39]

Delivered before the United War Work Campaign Committee of Illinois, Chicago, September 24, 1918.

Mr. Chairman and Ladies and Gentlemen:

As I listened to the great address which you have just heard, it seemed to me that it was not necessary for me or anyone else to give additional reasons why the full quota demanded from Illinois should be met and met promptly.

When we reflect that no matter how much we do, nor how much we give, that our offer is insignificant compared with the supreme offerings of our boys on the battle fronts, the question is not how much shall we give, but how much can we possibly give.

As Mr. Eddy spoke to you about the great sacrifices that our

[39] From a manuscript copy in the possession of Governor Lowden.

Allies had made before we got into the war, I reviewed in my mind the events of the last six fateful months. I recall those depressing days late in March, which Mr. Eddy described for you, when the Germans seemed to have broken through our western front. I recall the events which followed when it looked as though Paris and the channel ports would fall; I remember that, sad and depressing as those days were, the thing which came nearest my heart was this: Suppose that Paris should fall; suppose that the channel ports should be captured by our enemy; suppose France should fall a prey to the Central Empires and that those cruel powers should win this war, notwithstanding the heroic sacrifices of England and France, how happy their fate would have been compared with ours, who had stood by while civilization was fighting its battle, and who had not yet gotten into the battle line. Because in that event, France and England, fighting with their backs to the wall, if they had been vanquished, would have gone down in honor, and while history would have spoken with sorrow of their misfortunes, it also would have spoken with pride of their heroism.

But what would history have said of us, if in the supreme battle, not only for democracy, but for civilization, for righteousness, for decency, aye, for religion itself, this great, rich, powerful nation had stood to one side while the destiny of all the world for all time was being determined upon those battle fronts. We not only would have lost ultimately all that France and England would have lost, but we would have lost something more than that, and that is honor and self-respect. So today I rejoice not so much because the tide of battle has turned, not so much because the future beckons with rosier fingers than it has in the past, but because at last our boys are in the lines and helping fight the battles for freedom.

When we stop to think that this is not England's war, nor France's war, nor Italy's war, nor America's war, but that it is the final battle between the forces of evil and the forces of right that have been contending since the dawn of time, and that this great struggle has become at last world wide, and that the result of this war will determine all the future of the world, we then may know that there is no sacrifice so great, no price too high to pay for the triumph of our armies.

(18)

There was a time when faith seemed to yield before the hard, metallic facts which confronted us on the battle front. We knew that Germany had eschewed the old ideas in the name of which our own country was established, had eschewed the old notions of morals and ethics which we were taught at our mother's knee, but had announced this new, strange doctrine of *Kultur* under which force, and force alone, was to rule the world, and we wondered for a time if, after all, their doctrine might not be right. We knew that the spiritual forces were ever the finest forces in all the universe. We did not yield our faith in that, but we wondered whether those finer spiritual forces could conquer in a war of the magnitude of this. But, thank God, any doubts that came to our depressed hearts have vanished in the last few months, and we know now that not only are the spiritual forces of the universe the finest forces in all the world, but we know, too, that they are more powerful than all the forces of evil.

I could not but recall the old fable that we used to read in our schoolboy days of the contest between the wind and the sun. I think most of you are familiar with this, whether or not the wind was stronger and more powerful than the sun to compel the traveler to remove his cloak. The wind blew with all its might, but the traveler only wrapped his cloak more tightly about him, and finally the wind gave up in despair. Then it was the turn of the sun to show its power. The sun emerged from the clouds and its rays beat upon the shoulders of the traveler until he threw his cloak aside; and so the sun had won in the old fable, in this great contest. Today, in the contest between physical might, between brutal strength on the one hand and the qualities of the human soul on the other, I see a semblance to that old contest between the wind and the sun. The wind has poured forth its blasts in vain. Now, the sun of justice is emerging from the clouds and the sun of righteousness is in the skies, and this world-wide contest between these two forces is ending as it ended in the old fable of our school days.

I am not going to make an extended speech today, because I know that you have much important business to do at your business sessions. I want, however, to say that our boys at the front form our first line of defense, and that the brave and devoted officers of these seven organizations which are represented here today in a real sense form the second line of our armies of defense. It is upon them that we must depend to bring comfort and solace to our soldiers. It is upon them we must depend to carry the sweet things of home across the sea to those battle lines. It is upon them we must rely to carry the spiritual blessings which we breathe at home. So this second battle line of defense must have our hearty and unfaltering support.

Then there is the third and last line. That is composed of us who remain at home. It is just as important that our morale be maintained to its utmost limits as it is that the morale of our boys at the front should be maintained, and the best way in all the world to maintain our morale is for each man and woman and child within our borders to think, and think unceasingly, of what he can do to perform his part in this greatest war of all the world.

Letters have come to me from our soldier boys (and they are coming in increasing numbers), all asking, "How about the folks at home? Are they supporting us to the limit of their ability? Are they thinking of us as we fight their battles for them?" I can send them no better message than when I say "each day our people know more and more the sacrifices that you are making, and realize more and more thoroughly the mighty issues of this war." When I go from this meeting I want to say, as I shall write the boys in the days and weeks to come, that there was held in the city of Chicago the greatest meeting for this combined war program that was ever held within the borders of Illinois. I want to say to them that every section of the state was represented at that great meeting, and that the only rivalry between the different sections of the state was as to which would first fill its quota.

One word more and I am done. It seems to me that we of Illinois are peculiarly under obligation in this war. We are celebrating, as you know, the hundredth anniversary of our statehood. We have been recounting all over the state the achievements of our fathers and their fathers before them, and we have been inspired by those heroic achievements, by the great names which our history has produced, better to meet our obligations in this war. It was out of Illinois that the leader of all the armies of freedom in our civil strife came. Before the war, there was a simple, obscure citizen who lived out on the banks of the Mississippi River, but in four years that simple citizen had emerged to the heights of immortal fame, and there held aloft the American flag redeemed.

We owe it to the memory of that greatest captain of the century to respond to every demand of the war. I shall not have time to enumerate the other great sons of our state. At this time, when the world everywhere has its eyes raised to the rainbow hope of democracy wherever democracy's name is mentioned, and wherever men dream of throwing off the chains they have worn for centuries, to breathe the pure air of liberty, those men breathe the name of Abraham Lincoln of Illinois. I, myself, have seen missions of distinguished visitors from other lands make their pilgrimage to Lincoln's tomb. I drove out to that sacred spot with Marshal Joffre and his party from France upon their visit here a year ago last spring. I saw that old hero of the Marne with tear-dimmed eyes lay his wreath of blossoms upon the casket which contained Lincoln's immortal dust, and I fancied that I saw that the old hero, war worn though he was, had gathered new inspiration at that tomb and had formed in his heroic old heart a new and firm resolve that "They shall not pass."

So, we of Illinois owe a great obligation to the world if we would be worthy of our illustrious past. Let us put ourselves in a position where, when we go to sleep at night, we may have the sweet consciousness of knowing that nothing that we should have done on that day to bring comfort and joy to the hearts of our heroic soldier boys has been left undone by us.

Mr. Chairman, I think I know Illinois well enough to say that she will respond and respond fully and generously to the appeal you are making here today. I thank you.

UNITED WAR WORK CAMPAIGN SUNDAY—
A PROCLAMATION

Sunday, November tenth, has been set aside by National Headquarters as United War Work Campaign Sunday. A combined budget has been prepared for the war activities of the Young Men's Christian Association, the Young Women's Christian Association, the National Catholic War Council, the Jewish Welfare Board, the

War Camp Community Service, the American Library Association, and the Salvation Army. Upon that day, subscriptions will be received for this common fund.

The Fourth Liberty Loan, which has just been successfully closed, was to provide for the material things needed in war. The United War Work Campaign aims to provide funds for those great agencies which minister to the moral and spiritual needs of our soldiers in the field. It is, therefore, a true complement to the Liberty Loan. Liberty Loans provide the means by which our soldiers can successfully meet with the enemy in actual battle. But there is much of the time when our boys are not in combat with the foe. At such times, the men need a thousand things which the Army regulations cannot provide. They need those influences which go to make up a wholesome home; they need recreation; they need the presence of spiritual influences. These can only be supplied through the great agencies named above.

Our armies are fighting the battles of civilization. Surely, then, we should muster in full force, as near the battle lines as possible, all civilizing influences. This is being done through the agencies which you will be asked to help on November tenth, United War Work Campaign Sunday.

Proof constantly comes from the battle fronts of the effective and beneficent influence of these organizations. There never was a cleaner Army, morally, in the history of the world, than the American Army of today. There never was an Army, as is abundantly shown, more deeply moved by spiritual influences. This is due, in a large measure, to the influence of the organizations you are now asked to help. And let it not be forgotten that the morale of our soldiers— the admiration of the world—is greatly strengthened by the activities of those organizations.

Our people, through the Liberty Loans, have generously supplied, the materials for war. Let them now, in this United War Work Campaign, make equal contribution to the moral and spiritual welfare of our men at the front.

(SEAL)

GIVEN UNDER MY HAND AND
THE GREAT SEAL OF STATE
AT THE CAPITOL IN SPRING-
FIELD, THIS TWENTY-SECOND
DAY OF OCTOBER, IN THE
YEAR OF OUR LORD ONE
THOUSAND NINE HUNDRED
AND EIGHTEEN, AND OF THE
INDEPENDENCE OF THE
UNITED STATES THE ONE
HUNDRED AND FORTY-THIRD.

FRANK O. LOWDEN

By the Governor:
LOUIS L. EMMERSON.
Secretary of State

EXTENSION OF UNITED WAR WORK CAMPAIGN— A PROCLAMATION

WHEREAS, The Honorable John R. Mott, Director General of the United War Work Campaign has today officially advised the Governor of Illinois that the National United War Work Campaign has been extended until the night of Wednesday, November 20, 1918, and has requested that official notice of this action be given to the people of Illinois; and

WHEREAS, An erroneous impression has gained circulation as to the time necessary for the return from Over-seas and demobilization of our great American Army; and,

WHEREAS, Many problems resulting from the war are and will be vividly before us for a long time to come; and,

WHEREAS, Especially must we all carry on for the preservation of our ideals for the young womanhood and manhood of America; and,

WHEREAS, With the stimulus of fighting ended and consequent tendency to relaxation until demobilization has been completed ministration to the physical and spiritual wants of our soldiers will be more essential than ever before, now,

THEREFORE, I, John G. Oglesby, Acting Governor of the State of Illinois, appeal to the people of the State of Illinois to continue their splendid efforts in behalf of the United War Work Campaign until the very last moment in order that the allotment originally asked may not only be met but very generously oversubscribed, so that the patriotic women and men who have so unselfishly given of their services to the various welfare agencies represented in this campaign may not be handicapped in their future activities in behalf of our men under arms.

GIVEN UNDER MY HAND AND THE GREAT SEAL OF STATE AT THE CAPITOL IN SPRINGFIELD, THIS SEVENTEENTH DAY OF NOVEMBER IN THE YEAR OF OUR LORD ONE THOUSAND NINE HUNDRED HUNDRED AND EIGHTEEN, AND OF THE INDEPENDENCE OF THE UNITED STATES THE ONE HUNDRED AND FORTY-THIRD.

(SEAL)

JOHN G. OGLESBY

BY THE ACTING GOVERNOR:
LOUIS L. EMMERSON.
SECRETARY OF STATE.

III. MOBILIZING ILLINOIS MEN FOR SERVICE

NATIONAL GUARD AND NAVAL MILITIA MOBILIZATION EXPENSES

Senate Bill Number 587, Fiftieth General Assembly, State of Illinois.

An Act *to appropriate the sum of seven hundred fifty thousand dollars for the supply, clothing, equipment, pay, transportation, preparation of camp sites and cantonments, mobilization, subsistence and incidental expenses for the National Guard and Naval Militia, Volunteers or other organizations of Illinois authorized, organized or furnished by the state on a call, order, request or requisition made or hereafter made or issued by the President of the United States or organized, authorized or ordered for duty by the Governor.*

Section 1. *Be it enacted by the People of the State of Illinois, represented in the General Assembly:* That the sum of seven hundred fifty thousand dollars or so much thereof as may be necessary is hereby appropriated for the supply, clothing, equipment, pay, transportation, preparation of camp sites and cantonments, mobilization, subsistence and incidental expenses of the National Guard and Naval Militia, Volunteers or other organizations of this State, authorized, organized or furnished by the State on a call, orders, request or requisition made or hereafter made or issued by the President of the United States, or organized, authorized or ordered for duty by the Governor.

§ 2. The Auditor of Public Accounts is hereby authorized and directed to draw his warrant for the sum herein specified upon the presentation of proper vouchers certified to by the Adjutant General and approved by the Governor, and the Treasurer shall pay the same out of any money in the State Treasury not otherwise appropriated.

[252]

§ 3. Whereas an emergency exists, this law shall take effect from and after its passage and approval.

APPROVED June 21, 1917.

ORGANIZATION OF LOCAL DRAFT BOARDS

Message from Governor Frank O. Lowden to Fiftieth General Assembly, June 1, 1918.[1]

STATE OF ILLINOIS,
EXECUTIVE DEPARTMENT,
SPRINGFIELD, *June 1, 1917.*

Gentlemen of the Fiftieth General Assembly:

Under the operation of the Selective Service Law, recently passed by Congress, it becomes my duty to recommend to the President an exemption board of three in each county whose population is under forty-five thousand. In counties containing a population of more than forty-five thousand, the county is to be divided into districts containing thirty thousand each, as near as may be practicable, and for each of such districts a like board is to be appointed. One of the members of each board must be a physician, and I have decided to recommend the appointment of the physician member after advising with the medical societies of the State. In the selection of the other two members, I desire the assistance of members of the General Assembly. These boards will have very important and responsible duties to discharge during the continuance of the war. I desire that they may be made up of the most representative men in each county and district. I think that the responsibility of this selection should be shared with me by members of the General Assembly from the several senatorial districts. They know, better than anyone else, who are best qualified in their several districts and who enjoy to the largest degree the confidence of the community. I desire a conference with the members, without reference to party, from all districts, and ask that the members meet me in the House of Representatives at the hour of noon, on Tuesday, June 5, for a conference. I shall ask, at such conference, that all the members from each

[1] *Journal of the House of Representatives of the Fiftieth General Assembly of the State of Illinois,* June 1, 1917, pages 1203-4.

district, without reference to party, unite in recommending to me two names for the two above named places for each county or district within their senatorial district. I wish to call the attention of the members from the several districts to the fact that they are equally interested with me in having these boards composed of the best men to be had in the several counties and districts. The President hopes that men may be found willing to perform this patriotic work in this crisis without compensation. I feel confident that each county and each district in the State of Illinois will furnish men of high character and ability, who will be glad to "do their bit" in this way.

Respectfully submitted,

FRANK O. LOWDEN, *Governor.*

FIRST REGISTRATION UNDER SELECTIVE SERVICE ACT, JUNE 5, 1917

Appeal addressed by State Council of Defense to the People of Illinois, June 3, 1917.[2]

The purpose of registration day is that all men between the ages of 21 and 31, inclusive, shall be enrolled for actual and early employment in the nation's business, the nature of that employment— whether in the army, in the workshop, in the mine, or on the farm— and exemptions therefrom for cause, to be determined later.

The people of the state are solemnly invoked to remember their home land is at war. It isn't talking war; it isn't about to go to war. It is at war—now. It thus becomes the duty of every citizen to help all young men of registration age to understand these three fundamental reasons why each should register next Tuesday.

First, registration is the law of the land—a just law and one that cannot be evaded, for it is supported by all the nation's power and all its resources for law enforcement. To wink at attempted evasion is to give wilful encouragement to law breaking that will bring swift punishment.

Second, their country having called them, registration is the

Illinois State Journal, June 4, 1917; *Chicago Tribune*, June 4, 1917.

solemn and patriotic duty of those summoned to register. The one fixed obligation of a citizen is to respond when his country calls in time of need.

Third, registration will be a mark of honor for each man whose name is on the rolls, proclaiming that he has heard the first call of duty and has answered "present!"

Employers in particular are charged with the duty of seeing that their employees realize the significance of registration day and have unrestricted opportunity, without loss of pay, to comply with the law.

Each man, woman, boy and girl can help in this great national task. Friend speaking to friend and neighbor to neighbor, each doing his part to the limit of his influence, will set in motion a flood of impulse and action which even the shirker will be unable to resist.

Take registration to your conscience. Think registration, talk registration, see that registration is performed.

AN ADDRESS BY GOVERNOR FRANK O. LOWDEN, REGISTRATION RALLY, SPRINGFIELD, JUNE 4, 1917[3]

Ladies and Gentlemen:

Tomorrow will give Illinois a chance to show of what stuff it is made. Tomorrow is a day which will be writ large in the annals of this unhappy time. If our young men shall go gladly to the places of registration; if, throughout the length and breadth of the state, with solemn and orderly deliberation, they shall record their names; if, when night falls tomorrow ten million young men of America shall be found upon the list from which the army of democracy and humanity is to be recruited, tomorrow will be a proud day in the history of this state and this nation.

As you have been told by the other speakers, this is no ordinary contest between two nations. It has become a war to the death between two systems of government—the divine right of kings to rule and the divine right of men to govern themselves. When this war is over, wherever you may go upon the face of this old globe, one or the other of these contending principles will rule, and rule absolutely.

[3] From a manuscript copy in the possession of Governor Lowden.

I could not help but think, as these little boys came in upon the platform tonight—boys with all their lives before them—that this contest means more to them than it does to these old veterans on these front rows. More, Senator Magill, more, Mr. Chairman, than it means to you and me, because when this war is over they will be entering upon their manhood free and happy with the flag of their country above them, or they will be slaves of a military autocracy. In the latter event, we, my friends, are vastly happier than they, because we shall not have so long to endure the ignominy of that triumph upon the liberties of our fathers and ourselves.

Just think for a moment what it means to all the world. They say, the representatives of autocracy, that self-governing peoples are not able to defend themselves against their powerful foe. They say we haven't the manhood, they deny that man—just the plain, common man anywhere—has the patriotism from principle to support his country's flag, but insist that it is only when the iron hand of militarism has been laid upon the average man that he will respond to his country's call, and tomorrow, thank God, we have a chance to prove that in America this is a lie. And if we fail, if we fail, what is there of hope anywhere in all the world? In the past when men have struck for liberty and been vanquished, there has been some place else to go. We owe much of our best citizenship to that very cause. Among our peoples we have none more patriotic, as I believe, better citizens, as I am sure, than those who have come to our shores because they have been vanquished by tyranny abroad. And among all of that number there is none who surpasses in good citizenship those Americans whose fathers came from Germany after the revolution of '48 to gain for themselves and their children the liberty they had been denied at home, and I for one, am sure, that though they bear German names and have German ancestry, they will be found in the front ranks of true Americans fighting for the institutions which we love.

But, if we should fail—the most oppressive thought, as it seems to me, that ever weighed down man—if we should fail there will be no corner in all the earth, go where you will, to which the vanquished lover of liberty may flee, to enjoy even in exile independence and liberty, for all the world will be under the iron banner of military autocracy, in the Orient and Occident alike.

And then there is another reason why Illinois, particularly, should distinguish itself tomorrow. Did you know that more men have voluntarily gone to our colors from Illinois in the last few months than from [any of] the whole sisterhood of states? She has a reputation to maintain and I know that she will maintain it. There is another big reason, a reason that should influence Springfield especially, why we should tomorrow lead the sisterhood of states in proportion to our population. The greatest exponent of self-government in all times lived his life in Springfield and sleeps out to the north, and year by year, the just and gentle and lovers of liberty from all over the earth come, more and more, to make a pilgrimage to his tomb. If we are to guard that sacred dust successfully, we must tomorrow maintain to our utmost ability the cause for which Lincoln so nobly lived and heroically died—the right of man to rule himself.

And so, on the eve of the most significant day, it seems to me, in all our history, let us gird ourselves for a successful day, because when in future ages the history of this day is written, June the fifth, in the year of our Lord nineteen hundred and seventeen, will be found to have determined largely the destiny of America, for tomorrow democracy in America has a chance it has never had in all history, here or elsewhere, to show to all the world its majesty and might.

And if for any reason any one should despair, let him recall the meaning to all the world of this thing we call the American republic. It has been the inspiration of every statesman looking to an enlargement of human liberty in other lands. It has been the solace of the dying patriot fighting for liberty, wherever that fighting has been staged, for through the mist which dims his dying eye he has seen the flag of America and has had the faith to believe that one day men should be free throughout the earth.

And if we should fail, what hope for humanity anywhere? It took two thousand years to produce conditions under which our own republic was possible, and if we should fail, I tell you, my friends, from the bottom of my heart I believe that the world will enter again upon a longer, darker night than the dark ages from which humanity so slowly and painfully emerged. Tomorrow is the day when we shall show in America that we are worthy of our forefathers; that we are worthy of these veterans of the greatest war the world had ever seen up to that time; that we are worthy of the institutions which Almighty God with generous hands has heaped upon us.

Good-night, and let us remember tomorrow and nothing else.

AN ADDRESS BY HUGH S. MAGILL, REGISTRATION RALLY, SPRINGFIELD, JUNE 4, 1917[4]

This great concourse of people here tonight is a compliment to the city of Springfield, for it shows a genuine interest in questions of vital importance to our national life. It is an expression of a wholesome, patriotic, public sentiment which is the strongest support of a free government. In a monarchy the people may blindly follow their leaders, but in a republican form of government no great movement can succeed that does not have the sanction and support of at least the thinking people of the nation.

Events of momentous importance—without precedent in the history of our country—have followed in such rapid succession during the past few weeks that it is difficult for us to grasp the full import of the conditions that surround us, and the full meaning of what we must now undertake as a nation. For more than one hundred years America has been quite free from the influences and dangers of European diplomacy and European wars. A liberty-loving and peace-loving people, our nation has prospered until it has become the richest nation in the world. We have not felt the need of a large army nor of great fortifications, for we have felt confident that because of our friendly attitude toward all nations no nation could have any just cause for attacking us. Our security has been in our consciousness of justice and a fair dealing to all.

When our people became aroused by the inhuman treatment of the Cubans by Spain, we drove Spain out of the island; but, true to our principles, we did not appropriate one foot of Cuban territory,

[4] *Illinois State Journal*, June 5, 1917. Hugh S. Magill, of Springfield, was director general of the Illinois Centennial Celebration, 1917-1918.

but established a republic. The Philippine Islands, which fell into our hands as an accident of that war, were not ruthlessly taken from the conquered nation. Instead of levying war indemnity upon Spain, we paid her $20,000,000 for these possessions. In fact, all of our actions as a nation have been in the interest of humanity, never for conquest and exploitation.

Under these conditions it has been hard for us to comprehend the military plans of the Pan-Germanic league. Now we know that for more than a score of years the war lords of Germany have been planning definitely for a great world war which would make Germany a world empire. It has been the policy of the Prussian war party to get the nation thoroughly ready and then strike out to conquer the other nations, one at a time, and levy upon them [such] crushing war indemnities as would make it impossible for them to recover, while the German Empire would be made richer and stronger by the tributes which they would exact.

In 1898 the German Admiral von Goetzen told Admiral Dewey at Manila that in about fifteen years his country would begin a great war, and that soon after they had finished the business in Europe they would come over to America and capture New York and Washington and would exact one or two billion dollars in tribute. It is a striking fact that the great world war began sixteen years after the date of this statement. It is commonly stated in the German papers today, in order to encourage the German people to continue the war, that Germany is sure to win from her European foes and that she will then fall upon the United States and demand a war indemnity which will more than repay all the cost of the war and make Germany, not America, the richest nation in the world.

In the presence of these actual conditions our peaceful nation has been forced suddenly to begin gigantic preparations for the defense of our liberties. We recognize that we are sadly unprepared for the fearful struggle that confronts us. Within a week Germany mobilized her millions with every soldier fully and perfectly equipped. When our government called 5,000 boys to Fort Sheridan, it was weeks before they could all be supplied even with uniforms. The question is, how long will it take us to equip an army of a million men and train them for the serious business of modern warfare?

Tomorrow the young men of the nation between 21 and 31 are called upon to register, that from these an army may be raised to go forth in defense of our liberties. However much we may regret the necessity for this conscription, no thoughtful person, unless he deliberately refuses to consider existing conditions, can doubt that such action is imperative. No choice remains for us but to fight or meekly submit to the domination of a cruel military autocracy.

I think I know, in a measure at least, the sacrifice which the fathers and mothers must make in giving their boys in our country's service at this time, particularly when we consider the fearful destruction of modern warfare. Our only son, who graduated last June from Dartmouth College, and who since that time has been pursuing his law studies in the University of Chicago, has laid aside his books and is now at Fort Sheridan learning the use of the rifle, the bayonet, and the sabre. Throughout his life thus far he has been trained in the arts of peace. Now, in the service of his country, he is to be trained in the fearful science of war. Our experience is in common with that of thousands of homes of our land.

Our people are called upon in this great crisis to prove their loyalty by service and sacrifice. It is beautiful to sing "America" and "The Star Spangled Banner," and to have our hearts thrilled with high patriotic emotions, but we are called upon today to give more definite proof of our love for liberty and our devotion to our common country. If we emulate the example of those who followed Washington in the days of the Revolution, and those who, under the leadership of Lincoln, paid the last full measure of devotion to preserve this Union, we will count no sacrifice too dear in defense of our liberties and the priceless heritage which our fathers have left us.

Those who cannot go to the front may show their patriotism by upholding the government and supporting those who bear the burdens of battle. Our nation must be supplied with abundant funds. Every citizen ought to be glad of an opportunity to purchase a liberty bond. This loan ought to be oversubscribed in order that it may be clear to our leaders at Washington and to our foes abroad that we propose to furnish all the funds necessary to prosecute this war to a successful termination. Every effort possible must be made to increase the food supply in order that there may be an abundance not only for our own needs, but for our allies as well. He who toils to supply us with food performs a patriotic service, but he who seeks exorbitant profits in such a crisis as this should be dealt with as a criminal, if not as a traitor. There will be opportunity for deeds of mercy, which can best be performed through the magnificent organization of the Red Cross society. Those who can help in no other way should give the fullest support to the work of this organization, whose mission is to alleviate suffering and sorrow.

There is a work for us all to do, and every American citizen loyal to his country, cherishing the sacred principles for which it stands, should give himself in whole-hearted service. Let the motto erected here tonight be the solemn pledge of each one of us. Let us here in the home of Abraham Lincoln and under the influence of his hallowed memory, dedicate ourselves to the service of our country and the cause of humanity.

NATIONAL ARMY MOBILIZATION DAY, SEPTEMBER 5, 1917

Statement issued by Governor Frank O. Lowden, August 21, 1917.[8]

The President has designated Wednesday, Sept. 5, 1917, as mobilization day for the National Army. Let all honor be paid to the men who have been selected to form this army. They go to join the colors in order that we may be safe at home. They are the pick of our young men. The rigid examinations they were required to pass were such that only the names of sound, clean, wholesome young Americans will be found upon the muster rolls.

It was not a draft that placed their names upon the rolls. They were selected because the great republic found them fittest to serve in this hour of need. A volunteer army may appeal more to the imagination, but an army composed of men who were selected because they were found of all men within the republic the best fitted for soldiers, is a hundred times more inspiring. When a republic can designate for national defense those of her citizens best qualified to defend it, the republic has found itself.

[8] *Illinois State Journal*, August 22, 1917.

All honor to these young men. Though they go to fight upon foreign battle fields, they go to fight an American war. Our forefathers of the Revolution fought one great European empire to win freedom for the colonies. The greatest republic of all time has been the result of their efforts. We now find ourselves engaged in war with another great European empire to hold what our forefathers won. The men who go forth today with the battle cry of the soldiers of the Revolution upon their lips deserve as much of their country as did the men of Lexington and Valley Forge.

I earnestly urge that our people, at such time before the fifth of September, and in such way as they may locally determine, shall publicly show their appreciation of these young patriots. Let them go to the colors with the assurance that the gratitude, the admiration and the prayers of Illinois will accompany them wherever they may be.

PROCLAMATION BY WILLIAM HALE THOMPSON, MAYOR OF CHICAGO, SEPTEMBER 19, 1917[6]

WHEREAS, in the creation of a national army in its many branches of service and the recruiting of our navy to a war footing, in accordance with the law of the land, many thousands of our young men will be called to the national colors; and

WHEREAS, it is the duty of all patriotic citizens to stand by our country in times of controversy with any other country, and to show in an unmistakable way that the American people stand behind the army and the navy which represent the majesty of our government; and

WHEREAS, in obedience to law, many of our citizens already have gone, and 3,000 others are leaving today, and still others will leave hereafter to go into training in order to prepare themselves to give such service as their government may call upon them to render; now

Therefore, I, William Hale Thompson, mayor of Chicago, call upon our citizens to show to our soldiers and sailors who are leaving for the front that our hearts, our hopes, our prayers go with them and

6 *Chicago Tribune*, September 20, 1917.

will abide with them in their camps, on the fields and on the sea where their deeds shall shed further luster on the flag of freedom; and, in the name of our two and a half million people, united in a common love for the blessings of our free government, and with assurance of our fondest hopes for the success of our arms in any conflict in which they may engage, I bid our soldiers and sailors Godspeed.

RETENTION OF DRAFTED MEN IN EMPLOYMENT

Resolutions adopted at a meeting of the State Council of Defense of Illinois, August 28, 1917.[7]

RESOLVED: That all employers be requested to retain in their employ all drafted men until the time arrives for such men to leave for military duty, and that they be officially requested to do so; and that a copy of this resolution be sent to the Council of National Defense.

PUBLICATION OF EXEMPTION LISTS

Resolutions adopted at a meeting of the State Council of Defense of Illinois, December 14, 1917.[8]

Believing the publication of the total number of exemptions from army service by those in the United States who claim citizenship in, or who are subjects of, the countries associated with the United States in the prosecution of this war has brought about a situation in Chicago and Illinois which demands the active co-operation of all citizens and organizations of labor and business, the State Council of Defense pledges its assistance in the work of getting volunteer recruits for the forces of all countries associated with the United States in the prosecution of this war from among the men exempted from the United States draft by reason of such claims.

We call to the attention of all patriotic business houses among the employes of which there be those, few or many, claiming to be such citizens or subjects that assistance given to the work of enlisting those eligible for military service in the forces of the other countries

[7] Minutes of State Council of Defense, August 28, 1917.
[8] Minutes of State Council of Defense, December 14, 1917.

associated with the United States in the prosecution of this war not only will help to recruit the forces of our associates in this war against autocracy but will relieve American industry of a problem which gives cause for concern because there now exists a status unjust to loyal Americans and to those claiming to be citizens or subjects of other countries associated with the United States in the prosecution of this war alike.

ABSENT VOTING OF PERSONS IN MILITARY SERVICE

Senate Bill Number 508, Fiftieth General Assembly.

AN ACT *to enable qualified electors of this State enlisted in companies or regiments organized in this State and absent from their election precincts because engaged in actual military service, to vote as a unit in certain elections.*

SECTION 1. *Be it enacted by the People of the State of Illinois, represented in the General Assembly:* That qualified electors of this State enlisted in companies or regiments organized in this State and absent from their election precincts on the day prescribed by law for the holding of any general election because engaged in the actual military service of the State or of the United States, shall be entitled to vote for all State officers and on all State-wide questions in any such election. The qualified electors of any such company or regiment shall vote as a group or unit, as hereinafter provided. The commanding officer of any such company or regiment shall, in his discretion, fix the number of polling places for any such election.

§ 2. Thirty days before any such election the Adjutant General shall furnish the Secretary of State with a register containing the names and addresses of all qualified electors enlisted in companies or regiments organized in this State and absent from their election precincts because engaged in the actual military service of the State or of the United States.

§ 3. The Secretary of State shall, as soon as possible after the nominations for the various State offices shall have been made, prepare official war ballots in such number as shall be necessary to supply such absent voters. Such ballots shall be sent to the commanding officer of any such absent company or regiment, together with the registry of such absent voters prepared from the report of the Adjutant General to the Secretary of State. Such ballots shall contain only the names of the candidates for State offices. If, at any such election, any proposed amendment to the constitution or other proposition or question is to be submitted to the voters of the State, the Secretary of State shall furnish in the form prescribed by law, an equal number of ballots for the question or questions so submitted.

§ 4. The Secretary of State shall also cause to be prepared and printed, at least twice as many official envelopes as there are voters absent from election districts, as shown by such register. Such envelopes shall be gummed, ready for sealing. Upon one side of said envelope shall be printed endorsements in substantially the following form:

"OFFICIAL WAR BALLOTS FOR GENERAL ELECTION.

November .... 19....

Name of voter...

Residence (street and number, if any)........................,

County of ....

City or town of..

....

Secretary of State."

Upon the other side of said envelope shall be printed the following oath:

"OATH OF ELECTOR.

I do solemnly swear (or affirm), that I am a citizen of the United States, and am now of the age of at least twenty-one years, or will be on the .... day of ...., 19....; that I will have been an inhabitant of the State of Illinois for one year next preceding this election, and ninety days preceding such election, a resident of the county of ...., and am a qualified voter residing at (street and number, if any)................, in the (city or town) of..................; that I am in the actual military (or naval) service of the State of Illinois, or of the United States, and at present attached to............(here state the principal command to which attached), and that I have never been convicted of any crime (or if convicted, state the time and when pardoned by the Governor of any State).

....

Subscribed and sworn to before me this.......day of............,
A. D. 19....

....

Title of Officer."

The Secretary of State shall also furnish poll books and necessary poll lists, tally sheets, copies of this law, and any and all other blanks and forms necessary for the conduct of such election.

§ 5. Elections in the camps shall be held not less than five nor more than twenty days prior to the general election day. The date of such election shall be fixed by the commanding officer of any command where the poll or polls of such election shall be held, by proclamation duly made. Such polls shall be opened at such hour of the day as shall be most convenient for such voters, and shall remain open not less than three hours, and as much longer as shall, in the opinion of the officers of election serving at such polls be necessary in order to receive the votes of all voters of this State entitled to vote at such poll, but no poll shall be kept open later than sunset of the day on which said election shall be held.

§ 6. At the hour and place for the opening of the polls, the qualified voters of this State then and there present, shall, by a *viva voce* vote, select three of their own number to act at such election as judges of election. Such judges shall, so far as possible, be so selected that they shall represent the leading political parties of this State. When so elected, they shall choose one of their number as chairman and another as clerk, by drawing lots. Such chairman shall then administer the oath of office to the other judges, and one of the judges shall then administer the same to the chairman. The oath to be administered shall be as follows:

"I do solemnly swear (or affirm), that I will support the Constitution of the United States and the Constitution of the State of Illinois, and that I will faithfully discharge the duties of the office of judge of election, according to the best of my ability."

Such oath or affirmation shall be written or printed, or partly written or partly printed, attached to or entered upon the poll books used at such election, subscribed by the persons taking the same, and certified to by the person administering the same.

§ 7. Immediately upon the organization of the board of judges the commanding officer to whom shall have been delivered any official war ballots, poll books and envelopes, shall deliver the same to the judges of election and shall take a receipt therefor, which receipt shall be forwarded by mail by such commanding officer, to the Secretary of State. Said judges shall produce and have at the polls before any votes are taken by them, a box for the reception of the ballots to be voted at such election. Before proceeding to take any votes, they shall open said box and publicly exhibit the inside thereof, and the same shall be entirely emptied. They shall then close and securely fasten the same, and said box shall not be opened again until the close of the polls at such election. Each such box shall have an opening in the top thereof for the reception of voted ballots.

The chairman of the board shall have charge of the ballot box during the election and shall receive from the qualified voters, their envelopes containing ballots, and shall deposit them in the ballot box. The other two members shall keep the poll books.

§ 8. Before any person shall receive an official ballot or be permitted to vote, he shall make and subscribe the oath printed upon the official envelope, as provided herein, and any one of the judges of election is hereby authorized to administer and attest such oath. If any voter shall refuse to take the oath so tendered, he shall not be allowed to vote, but if he shall take the oath tendered him, his vote shall be accepted. Upon subscribing to the required oath, the voter shall state his name and residence by street and number, if any, county, city or town, which information shall be entered upon the poll books. He shall also give such other information as is required to be entered in the poll books. When such voter has given such information, the judge in charge of the polls and envelopes, shall write in the proper blank spaces upon such official envelope, the name and residence, by street and number, if any, of such voter, and the county, city or town in which he claims to reside, and shall deliver such ballot or ballots and such envelope to such voter. Such voter shall then retire to some convenient place and shall prepare his ballot and envelope for voting. After preparing his ballot, the voter shall fold his ballot in such a way that the contents of the ballot shall be concealed, and enclose the same in such envelope, which he shall securely seal. He shall then deliver such envelope to the chairman of the board of judges. Before such envelope shall be deposited in the ballot box, the chairman shall state the name of such voter, his residence, whether or not he is entitled to vote and whether or not the envelope is securely sealed. If the voter's name and other information hereby required, appear upon the poll books, the judges keeping such poll books shall so announce and record such voter as voting. The chairman shall thereupon deposit such envelope in the ballot box. Any person so voting shall not in any manner vote again for any candidate or on any question in such election.

§ 9. As soon as the polls of such election are closed, the judges shall publicly destroy all official envelopes and ballots not voted and shall then publicly open such ballot boxes and count and ascertain the number of voters voting, and shall not adjourn or postpone the count until it shall have been fully completed. The judges shall number each voter whose name is recorded in such poll books as having voted, beginning with the first name entered therein, and numbering the same in consecutive order, and shall fill out and sign the certificate to be made by them as to the whole number voting at such election. If the envelopes containing ballots found in such box shall be more than the number of such envelopes so shown by the poll books to have been deposited therein, the judges shall compare the names upon such envelopes with the names recorded in such poll books, and all such envelopes so found in said ballot box purporting to have been deposited therein by a voter whose name is not duly entered in such poll books, as herein provided, shall, with their contents, be immediately destroyed, without opening the same, and if more than one such envelope shall be found in said ballot box purporting to have been deposited therein by the same voter, then all such envelopes and their contents purporting to have been deposited in such ballot box by such voter, shall be destroyed. No such envelope without an official endorsement, as herein provided, shall be counted.

§ 10. At the completion of the count, the judges shall certify the correctness of the same upon the poll books, and shall publicly announce the number of votes cast. They shall, thereupon, enclose all such envelopes containing ballots, without opening the same, in a sealed package, with the poll books, and shall forward them to the Secretary of State, at Springfield, Illinois, as soon as possible after such election.

§ 11. Upon the receipt by the Secretary of State of the packages containing the envelopes and poll books, he shall at once forward such envelopes to the county clerk of the respective counties wherein reside such voters absent in military service. Each county clerk shall deliver all envelopes so received from the Secretary of State to the county canvassing board at the time of its regular meeting, and such board shall count all the ballots enclosed in such envelopes and make abstracts of the same, which abstracts shall be sent to the Secretary of State, to be canvassed in the manner provided by law for the canvassing of other votes. Such abstracts shall be made and sent to the Secretary of State in accordance with the provisions of Sections 71 and 76 of an Act entitled: "An Act in regard to elections, and to provide for filling vacancies in elective offices," approved April 3, 1872, in force July 1, 1872, as subsequently amended.

Any such ballots may be rejected for cause by the county canvassing board.

§ 12. If any person shall wilfully swear falsely to any affidavit herein provided for, he shall, upon conviction thereof, be deemed guilty of perjury, and shall be punished as in such case by law provided. If any election officer shall refuse or neglect to perform any of the duties prescribed by this Act, or shall violate any of the provisions thereof, or if any officer taking any of the affidavits provided for herein, shall make any false statement in his certificate thereto attached, he shall be deemed guilty of a misdemeanor, and upon conviction thereof shall be punished by a fine not exceeding one hundred dollars ($100.00) or by imprisonment in the county jail, not exceeding thirty (30) days, or by both such fine and imprisonment.

§ 13. The general election laws to the extent that the same are not inconsistent with the provisions of this Act shall govern and control all elections under this Act.

Approved June 22, 1917.

PROPOSED WAR RISK INSURANCE ACT

Resolutions adopted at a meeting of the Woman's Committee, State Council of Defense of Illinois, August 21, 1917.[9]

Whereas: Men risk their lives and their economic future at their country's call and, Whereas, they leave their dependents uncertain of their future livelihood and Whereas, the Government is under obligation to give to these soldiers and sailors the assurance that their dependents need not become objects of charity, we therefore, urge the necessity of passing the bill H. R. 5723 at this session of Congress so that when this new national army moves it shall carry with it the morale that comes from confidence in the Government that called them to patriotic service.[10]

And we, therefore, urge all organizations and individuals to send letters or telegrams to our State Senators and Congressmen.

Mrs. Frederick A. Dow,

Acting Chairman.

Martha K. Wood,

Secretary.

PLACES OF AMUSEMENT FOR MEN IN CAMP

Resolutions adopted at a meeting of the State Council of Defense of Illinois, September 12, 1917.[11]

It is necessary that our soldiers and sailors at Rockford and at the other cantonments in the United States should be furnished with inspiriting and clean amusements, in order to help maintain a spirit of good cheer and contentment, and reduce the dangerous temptations that frequently follow and entrench themselves near camps.

There soon will be, at Rockford (Camp Grant) forty thousand men. At this cantonment and at the fifteen others in the United States there should be immediately erected adequate auditoriums or amusement halls with large seating capacities. Arrangements should

[9] Minutes of meeting held by Woman's Committee, State Council of Defense, August 21, 1917.

[10] War Risk Insurance Act, approved October 6, 1917.

[11] Minutes of meeting held by State Council of Defense, September 12, 1917.

be made for the production of patriotic and elevating dramatic and musical plays at the cantonments, by high-class travelling companies. This can be more readily accomplished if like and uniform steps are taken in connection with all of the sixteen cantonments. Public-Spirited booking agents can be readily found who will without charge engage professional travelling companies in sufficient numbers so that there can be daily performances in rotation at the different camps. By charging a nominal admission fee, the necessary expense of the entertainments can be defrayed. The cost of constructing and equipping the sixteen auditoriums (which will be of only a temporary nature) at the different cantonments, will, it is estimated, not exceed $500,000.

THEREFORE, BE IT RESOLVED by the State Council of Defense of Illinois, that the Secretary of War be respectfully urged (out of appropriations already made by or to be secured from Congress) to cause to be immediately constructed auditoriums and places of amusement at Rockford and other cantonments, and to perfect arrangements so that during the present autumn and coming winter attractive, clean and first-class musical and dramatic entertainments can be furnished to the men in those camps.[12]

RESOLVED FURTHER, that a copy of these resolutions be forthwith sent to the President of the United States, to the Secretary of War, to the Secretary of the Navy, to all the Senators and Members of Congress, to the National Council of Defense and to the State Council of the different states, with the request that they cooperate in this movement.

[12] Under the direction of the War Department Commission on Training Camp Activities, "Liberty theaters" were subsequently erected at a cost ranging from $5,000 to $50,000 each in thirty-four camps throughout the country, including Camp Grant.

CALL TO CANDIDATES FOR SECOND OFFICERS' TRAINING CAMP, FORT SHERIDAN, ILLINOIS[13]

Issued by Col. J. A. Ryan, commanding officer, Second Officers' Training Camp, August 23, 1917.

To the Candidates of the Second Training Camp:

You have been selected from some twenty thousand applicants because your qualifications indicate you can become efficient officers in the armies of the United States.

The success of the first training camp[14] was due to the spirit that moved its members to apply themselves from the start to the work in hand. You will have with you as instructors officers of the regular army and officers who have just completed their course of training in the first training camps. Their whole object will be to give you the best instruction, practical and theoretical, that is possible, within the three months' time allotted. The success of their work will depend on your hearty coöperation, which means close attention to study and drill and strict compliance with all the regulations of the camp.

Most of the candidates who come here have already achieved success in civil life—success in military life is achieved by the same means—namely, work and study. You know the methods, and the very fact that you have come here shows your intention to apply them.

The two qualities in men which brought about the greatest returns in the last encampment were patience and teamwork. Patience enables us to examine with care the requirements of any problem, and teamwork brings the united efforts of all to achieve success.

---

[13] *Chicago Tribune*, August 24, 1917.

[14] Four officers' training camps were held in military establishments in Illinois during the war. The first and second camps were conducted at Fort Sheridan during the periods May 15-August 13, 1917, and August 27-November 27, 1917, and a third camp was held at Camp Grant January-April, 1918. Candidates enrolled in the fourth camp at Camp Grant, begun on May 15 and originally intended as a division school, were for the most part transferred to central officers' training schools established June, 1918, in certain permanent replacement camps. On September 15, 1918, an infantry central officers' training school was established at Camp Grant. The capacity of the school was 5,600, and the course continued for four months.

Cheerfulness, good humor, and the habit of looking at the bright side of things will be of great assistance. The man who can retain his cheerfulness under the most trying circumstances is the man who wins in the end.

Remember you are, in a way, going back to school, and the comradeship which you will find among your fellow-candidates in the various companies will be an incentive to effort. The friendships you will form here will be lasting, and one of the greatest results that will come under your observation will be the many good qualities you will discover among your comrades during these three months which you little suspected when you first met them.

Remember this is the world's greatest problem, and everything you do each day here contributes to the final results as if you were in the trenches in Flanders.

LEADERSHIP, AN ADDRESS BY LIEUTENANT COLONEL C. A. BACH, CAVALRY, U. S. A.[15]

Delivered before the candidates enrolled in the Second Officers' Training Camp, Fort Sheridan, Illinois, November 20, 1917.

In a short time each of you men will control the lives of a certain number of other men. You will have in your charge a greater or less number of loyal but untrained citizens who look to you for instruction and guidance. Your word will be their law. Your most casual remark will be remembered. Your mannerisms will be aped. Your clothing, your carriage, your vocabulary, your manner of command will be imitated. When you join your organization, you will find waiting for you, or you will receive, a willing body of men who ask from you nothing more than the qualities that will command their respect, their loyalty and their obedience. They are perfectly ready and eager to follow you so long as you can convince them that you have these qualities. When the time comes that they are satisfied you do not possess them, you might as well kiss yourself good-by. Your usefulness in that organization is at an end.

[15] From a mimeographed circular distributed to the candidates enrolled in the Second Officers' Training Camp.

From the standpoint of society the world is divided into leaders and followers. The professions have their leaders, the financial world has its leaders. We have religious leaders and political leaders and society leaders. In all this leadership it is difficult if not impossible to separate from the element of pure leadership that selfish element of personal gain or advantage to the individual, without which such leadership would lose its value. It is in the military service only where men freely sacrifice their lives for a faith, where men are willing to suffer and die for the right or the prevention of a great wrong, that we can hope to realize leadership in its highest, most exalted and disinterested sense. Therefore, when I say leadership, I mean military leadership.

In a few days the great mass of you men will receive commissions as officers. These commissions will not make you leaders; they will merely make you officers. They will place you in a position where you can become leaders if you possess the proper attributes. But you must make good, not so much with the men over you as with the men under you.

Men must and will follow into battle officers who are not leaders; but the driving power behind these men is not enthusiasm but discipline. They go with doubt and trembling and with an awful fear tugging at their heart strings that prompts the unspoken question, "What will he do next?" Such men obey the letter of their orders but no more. Of devotion to their commander, of exalted enthusiasm which scorns personal risk, of *their* self-sacrifice to insure *his* personal safety, they know nothing. Their legs carry them forward because their brain and their training tell them they must go. Their spirit does not go with them. Great results are not achieved by cold, passive, unresponsive soldiers. They don't go very far and they stop as soon as they can. Leadership not only demands but receives the *willing,* unhesitating, unfaltering obedience and loyalty of other men, and a devotion that will cause them, when the time comes, to follow their uncrowned king to hell and back again if necessary.

You will ask yourselves "Of just what then, does leadership consist?" "What must I do to become a leader?" "What are the attributes of leadership and how can I cultivate them?"

Leadership is a composite of a number of qualities. Among the most important I would list self-confidence, moral ascendency, self-sacrifice, paternalism, fairness, initiative, decision, dignity, courage. Let me discuss these with you in detail.

Self-confidence results, first, from exact knowledge, second, the ability to impart that knowledge, and third, the feeling of superiority over others that naturally follows. All these give the officer poise.

To lead, you must know—you may bluff all your men some of the time, but you can't do it all the time. Men will not have confidence in an officer unless he knows his business and he must know it from the ground up. The officer should know more about paper work than his first sergeant and company clerk put together; he should know more about messing than his mess sergeant; more about diseases of the horse than his troop farrier. He should be at least as good a shot as any man in his company. If the officer does not know and demonstrates the fact that he does not know, it is entirely human for the soldier to say to himself: "To hell with him. He doesn't known as much about this as I do," and calmly disregard the instructions received. There is no substitute for accurate knowledge. Become so well informed that men will hunt you up to ask questions; that your brother officers will say to one another, "Ask Smith—he knows." And not only should each officer know thoroughly the duties and responsibilities of his own grade but he should study those of the two grades next above him. A two-fold benefit attaches to this. He prepares himself for duties which may fall to his lot at any time during battle; he further gains a broader viewpoint which enables him to appreciate the necessity for the issuance of orders and joins more intelligently in their execution.

Not only must the officer know, but he must be able to put what he knows into grammatical, interesting, forceful English. He must learn to stand on his feet and speak without embarrassment. I am told that in British training camps, student officers are required to deliver ten-minute talks on any subject they may choose. That is excellent practice. For to speak clearly, one must think clearly, and clear, logical thinking expresses itself in definite, positive orders. While self-confidence is the result of knowing more than your men, *moral ascendency* is based upon your belief that you are the better man. To gain and maintain this ascendency you must have self-control, physical vitality and endurance and moral force.   You must have yourself so well in hand that, even though in battle you be scared stiff, you will never show fear.   For if you by so much as a hurried movement or a trembling of the hands or a change of expression or a hasty order hastily revoked, indicate your mental condition, it will be reflected in your men in a far greater degree.   In garrison or camp many instances will arise to try your temper and wreck the sweetness of your disposition.   If at such times you "fly off the handle," you have no business to be in charge of men.   For men in anger say and do things that they, almost invariably, regret afterwards.   An officer should never apologize to his men, also an officer should never be guilty of an act for which his sense of justice tells him he should apologize.

Another element in gaining moral ascendency lies in the possession of enough physical vitality and endurance to withstand the hardships to which you and your men are subjected, and a dauntless spirit that enables you not only to accept them cheerfully, but to minimize their magnitude.   Make light of your troubles, belittle your trials and you will help vitally to build up within your organization an *esprit* whose value in time of stress cannot be measured.

Moral force is the third element in gaining moral ascendency. To exert moral force you must live clean, you must have sufficient brain power to see the right and the will to do the right.   Be an example to your men.   An officer can be a power for good or a power for evil.   Don't preach to them—that will be worse than useless.   Live the kind of a life you would have them lead and you will be surprised to see the number that will imitate you.   A loud-mouthed, profane captain who is careless of his personal appearance will have a loud-mouthed, profane, dirty company.   Remember what I tell you.   Your company will be the reflection of yourself.   If you have a rotten company, it will be because you are a rotten captain.

Self-sacrifice is essential to leadership.   You will give, give all the time.   You will give of yourself physically, for the longest hours, the hardest work and the greatest responsibility is the lot of the captain.   He is the first man up in the morning and the last man in at night.   He works while others sleep.   You will give of yourself mentally, in sympathy and appreciation for the troubles of men in your charge. This one's mother has died and that one has lost all his savings in a bank failure. They may desire help, but more than anything else they desire sympathy. Don't make the mistake of turning such men down with the statement that you have troubles of your own. For every time that you do, you knock a stone out of the foundation of your house. Your men are your foundation, and your house of leadership will tumble about your ears unless it rests securely upon them. Finally, you will give of your own slender financial resources. You will frequently spend your own money to conserve the health and well-being of your men or to assist them when in trouble. Generally you get your money back. Very frequently you must charge it to profit and loss.

When I say that paternalism is essential to leadership, I use the term in its better sense. I do not now refer to that form of paternalism which robs men of initiative, self-reliance and self-respect. I refer to the paternalism that manifests itself in a watchful care for the comfort and welfare of those in your charge. Soldiers are much like children. You must see that they have shelter, food and clothing, the best that your utmost efforts can provide. You must see that they have food to eat before you think of your own, that they have each as good a bed as can be provided before you consider where you will sleep. You must be far more solicitous of their comfort than of your own. You must look after their health. You must conserve their strength by not demanding needless exertion or useless labor. And by doing all these things you are breathing life into what would otherwise be a man machine. You are creating a soul in your organization that will make the mass respond to you as though it were one man. And that is *esprit*. And when your organziation has this *esprit* you will wake up some morning and discover that the tables have been turned; that instead of your constantly looking out for them, they have, without even a hint from you, taken up the task of looking out for you. You will find that a detail is always there to see that your tent, if you have one, is promptly pitched; that the most and the cleanest bedding is brought to your tent; that from some mysterious source two eggs have been added to your supper when no one else had any; that an extra man is helping your stryker give your horse a super-grooming; that your wishes are anticipated; that every man is "Johnny on the spot." And then you have arrived.

Fairness is another element without which leadership can neither be built up nor maintained. There must be first that fairness which treats all men justly. I do not say alike, for you cannot treat all men alike—that would be assuming that all men are cut from the same piece; that there is no such thing as individuality or a personal equation. You cannot treat all men alike; a punishment that would be dismissed by one man with a shrug of the shoulders is mental anguish for another. A company commander who for a given offense has a standard punishment that applies to all is either too indolent or too stupid to study the personality of his men. In his case justice is certainly blind. Study your men as carefully as a surgeon studies a difficult case. And when you are sure of your diagnosis, apply the remedy. And remember that you apply the remedy to effect a cure; not merely to see the victim squirm. It may be necessary to cut deep; but when you are satisfied as to your diagnosis, don't be diverted from your purpose by any false sympathy for the patient.

Hand in hand with fairness in awarding punishment walks fairness in giving credit. Everybody hates a human hog. When any one of your men has accomplished an especially creditable piece of work, see that he gets his proper reward. Turn heaven and earth upside down to get it for him. Don't try to take it away from him and hog it for yourself. You may do this and get away with it, but you have lost the respect and loyalty of your men. Sooner or later, your brother officers will hear of it and shun you like a leper. In war there is glory enough for all. Give the man under you his due. The man who always takes and never gives is not a leader. He is a parasite.

There is another kind of fairness—that which will prevent an officer from abusing the privileges of his rank. When you exact respect from soldiers, be sure you treat them with equal respect. Build up their manhood and self-respect. Don't try to pull it down. For an officer to be overbearing and insulting in the treatment of enlisted men is the act of a coward. He ties the man to a tree with the ropes of discipline and then strikes him in the face, knowing full well that the man cannot strike back. Consideration, courtesy and respect from officers toward enlisted men are not incompatible with discipline; they are part of our discipline.

Without initiative and decision no man can expect to lead. In maneuvers, you will frequently see, when an emergency arises, certain men calmly give instant orders, which later, on analysis, prove to be, if not exactly the right thing, very nearly the right thing to have done. You will see other men in emergency become badly rattled; their brains refuse to work, or they give a hasty order, revoke it, give another, revoke that, in short, show every indication of being a blue funk. Regarding the first man you may say: "That man is a genius. He hasn't had time to reason this thing out. He acts intuitively." Forget it. Genius is merely the capacity for taking infinite pains. The man who was ready is the man who has prepared himself. He has studied beforehand the possible situations that might arise; he has made tentative plans covering such situations. When he is confronted by the emergency, he is ready to meet it. He must have sufficient mental alertness to appreciate the problem that confronts him and the power of quick reasoning to determine what changes are necessary in his already formulated plan. He must have also the decision to order the execution and stick to his order. Any reasonable order in an emergency is better than no order. The situation is there. Meet it. It is better to do something and do the wrong thing than to hesitate, hunt around for the right thing to do and wind up by doing nothing at all. And having decided on a line of action, stick to it. Don't vacillate. Men have no confidence in an officer who doesn't know his own mind. Occasionally you will be called upon to meet a situation which no reasonable human being could anticipate. If you have prepared yourselves to meet other emergencies which you could anticipate, the mental training you have thereby gained will enable you to act promptly and with calmness. You must frequently act without orders from higher authority. Time will not permit you to wait for them. Here again enters the importance of studying the work of the officers above you. If you have a comprehensive grasp of the entire situation and can form an idea of the general plan of your superiors, that and your previous emergency training will enable you to determine that the responsibility is yours and to issue the necessary orders without delay.

The element of personal dignity is important in military leadership. Be the friend of your men, but do not become their intimate. Your men should stand in awe of you; not fear. If your men presume to become familiar, it is your fault, not theirs. Your actions have encouraged them to do so. And above all things, don't cheapen yourself by courting their friendship or currying their favor. They will despise you for it. If you are worthy of their loyalty and respect and devotion, they will surely give all these without asking. If you are not, nothing that you can do will win them.

It is exceedingly difficult for an officer to be dignified while wearing a dirty, spotted uniform and a three days' stubble of whiskers on his face. Such a man lacks self-respect, and self-respect is an essential of dignity. There may be occasions when your work entails dirty clothes and an unshaven face. Your men all look that way. At such times there is ample reason for your appearance. In fact, it would be a mistake to look too clean—they would think that you were not doing your share. But as soon as this unusual occasion has passed, set them an example of personal neatness.

And then I would mention courage. Moral courage you need as well as physical courage. That kind of moral courage which enables you to adhere without faltering to a determined course of action which your judgment has indicated as the one best suited to secure the desired result. You will find many times, especially in action, that, after having issued your orders to do a certain thing, you will be beset by misgivings and doubts; you will see or think you see other and better means for accomplishing the object sought. You will be strongly tempted to change your orders. Don't do it until it is clearly manifested that your first orders were radically wrong. For, if you do, you will be again worried by doubts as to the efficacy of your second orders. Every time you change your orders without obvious reason you weaken your authority and impair the confidence of your men. Have the moral courage to stand by your order and see it through.

Moral courage further demands that you assume the responsibility for your own acts. If your subordinates have loyally carried out your orders and the movement you directed is a failure, the failure is yours, not theirs. Yours would have been the honor had it been successful. Take the blame if it results in disaster. Don't try to shift it to a subordinate and make him the goat. That is a cowardly act.

Furthermore, you will need moral courage to determine the fate of those under you. You will frequently be called upon for recommendations for the promotion or demotion of officers and N. C. O. in your immediate command. Keep clearly in mind your personal integrity and the duty you owe your country. Do not let yourself be deflected from a strict sense of justice by feelings of personal friendship. If your own brother is your second lieutenant and you find him unfit to hold his commission, eliminate him. If you don't, your lack of moral courage may result in the loss of valuable lives. If, on the other hand, you are called upon for a recommendation concerning a man whom, for personal reasons, you dislike, do not fail to do him full justice. Remember that your aim is the general good, not the satisfaction of an individual grudge.

I am taking it for granted that you have physical courage. I need not tell you how necessary that is.

Courage is more than bravery. Bravery is fearlessness—the absence of fear. The merest dolt may be brave because he lacks the mentality to appreciate his danger; he doesn't know enough to be afraid. Courage, however, is that firmness of spirit, that moral backbone which, while fully appreciating the danger involved, nevertheless goes on with the undertaking. Bravery is physical, courage is mental and moral. You may be cold all over, your hands may tremble, your legs may quake, your knees be ready to give way— that is fear. If, nevertheless, you go forward, if in spite of this physical defection you continue to lead your men against the enemy, you have courage. The physical manifestations of fear will pass away. You may never experience them but once. They are the "buck fever" of the hunter who tries to shoot his first deer. You must not give way to them.

A number of years ago, while taking a course in demolitions, the class of which I was a member was handling dynamite. The instructor said, regarding its manipulation, "I must caution you gentlemen to be careful in the use of these explosives. One man has but one accident." And so I would caution you. If you give way to the fear that will doubtless beset you in your first action; if you show the white feather; if you let your men go forward while you hunt a shell-crater, you will never again have the opportunity of leading those men.

Use judgment, in calling on your men for displays of physical courage or bravery. Don't ask any man to go where you would not go yourself. If your common sense tells you that the place is too dangerous for you to venture into, then it is too dangerous for him. You know his life is as valuable to him as yours is to you. Occasionally some of your men must be exposed to danger which you cannot share. A message must be taken across a fire-swept zone. You call for volunteers. If your men know you, and know that you are "right," you will never lack volunteers; for they will know your heart is in your work, that you are giving your country the best you have, that you would willingly carry the message yourself if you could. Your example and enthusiasm will have inspired them.

And lastly, if you aspire to leadership, I would urge you to study men. Get under their skins, and find out what is inside. Some men are quite different from what they appear to be on the surface. Determine the workings of their minds. Much of General Robert E. Lee's success as a leader may be ascribed to his ability as a psychologist. He knew most of his opponents from West Point days; knew the workings of their minds. He believed that they would do certain things under certain circumstances. In nearly every case, he was able to anticipate their movements and block the execution. You cannot know your opponents in this war in the same way. But you can know your own men. You can study each to determine wherein lies his strength and his weakness. Which man can be relied upon to the last gasp and which cannot. Know your men, know your business, know yourself.

ENLARGEMENT OF GREAT LAKES NAVAL
TRAINING STATION

Resolutions adopted at a meeting of the State Council of Defense of Illinois, May 3, 1918.[16]

Whereas there is in the Naval Appropriation bill, now pending before the Congress of the United States, an item for the appropriation of money for the purchase of additional land at the U. S. Naval Training Station, Great Lakes, Illinois, (land which is already under lease and occupied by the force at the station)[17] and

Whereas it is of the highest importance that the station shall be maintained at least at its present capacity, and

Whereas it is vital to the welfare of the young men in training there, and to the Navy itself, that they shall be properly and adequately quartered, with ample room for their training, and

Whereas the U. S. Naval Training Station at Great Lakes is the largest in the country and should be permanently maintained as such for the reason that the largest number and best quality of Naval recruits come from the territory tributary to that station, therefore be it

RESOLVED, by the State Council of Defense of Illinois that it is the sense of this Council that the item in the Naval Appropriation Bill, appropriating money for the purchase of additional land at the U. S. Naval Training Station Great Lakes, Ill., should be retained in that bill and passed, and be it further

RESOLVED, this Council urgently appeals to all members of Congress from Illinois, Senators and Representatives to support the item referred to and use their influence to secure its passage.

[16] Minutes of the meeting of the State Council of Defense, May 3, 1918.

[17] The Naval Service Appropriation Act approved July 1, 1918, authorized the President to acquire additional land for the Great Lakes Naval Training Station and appropriated $887,500 for that purpose.

A MODERN BATTLE AND WHAT IT MEANS, AN ADDRESS BY COL. HENRY J. REILLY[18]

Delivered before the Chicago Association of Commerce, June 6, 1917.

During the three weeks I have been home from Europe I have been more and more impressed with the fact that while our people are more than willing to do what they must in the war, there is a failure to understand the magnitude of the war in its present state, and the magnitude of the burden which must be ours if we are going to do our part. There is no doubt that everybody intends we shall do our part. Therefore, the only thing to do is to find out what that is, and what the doing of it really means. The only way to do that is to face the truth of the war to date. Why conditions have been as they have to date, and what they really are to-day, are the two matters which we must determine.

It is no time to spare anybody's feelings; it is no time to get our own feelings hurt. We must boldly face the truth. Our enemy to-day is still in possession of a large, well-equipped, well-trained fighting army. That army is on the territory of our allies; it has not yet been beaten, and it does not think it is going to be beaten.

During the two years and ten months this war has been going on, and prior to that when war was mentioned, both the public and the press have always emphasized everything in connection with war, excepting the one thing which counts in war, and that is fighting on the battle field. We must have ammunition. Of course, we must have ammunition. We have got to have men, money and supplies and enough of each, but no matter how great the quantity of each, all these things are insufficient unless we have a fighting army.

There is only one way to win this war, and that is to get the German army on the battle field and trounce it. The only way that can be done is by putting up a better and a stronger army in front

[18] *Chicago Commerce*, June 8, 1917. Col. Henry J. Reilly, U. S. Army, was commanding officer of the First Illinois Field Artillery, which became the 149th Field Artillery, 42d Division, from May 23, 1917, to October 16, 1918, and from November 23, 1918, to May 12, 1919. He was made a brigadier-general, Illinois National Guard, April, 1921.

of it, and continually maintaining it in a better state as regards number, supplies, and above all fighting efficiency. That is the simple truth of the whole matter. We can travel around in as many circles as we may wish, but we must always come back to this truth. If we will not face it, if we are not willing to produce such an army, we will not win.

Probably the best way to explain what I mean is for me to attempt to give you some idea of what modern battle really is.

The first thing to remember is that the day has absolutely passed when the individual example of heroes, no matter how brave they may be, has any material effect on the issue in any way, shape, or form. The day is absolutely past for any kind of carelessness. The day is absolutely past for any of the "hurrah boy" spirit. The day is absolutely past for "Up, boys, and at 'em." That is all gone.

The waging of war is a scientific profession. If we will not wage it that way, and the other side does, there is only one answer: We are going to be beaten.

The chief trouble today is, first, to know exactly where your enemy is. In the old days two armies were out in the open, confronting each other with the infantry in double rank within three or four hundred yards of the enemy's infantry; and with artillery ranges of but a thousand yards. That is past. Due to the extreme range of modern heavy artillery brought onto the battle field today, the men first come under fire at anywhere from seven to eight and nine miles. No matter how great the range of the artillery, no matter how many bursting shells may be scattered over the battle field, if when they explode they do not hit their target, not very much damage is done. The battle field is so deep that any talk of smothering all of it with fire is absurd. It cannot be done. In other words, you have got to know where your targets are. You must find the enemy, locate him accurately, and therefore the preparation for battle depends in the first place upon the reconnaissance performed by airplanes.

Before our airplanes can go over the enemy's territory to perform that very necessary reconnaissance, they must get rid of the enemy's airplanes, as these naturally will do everything possible to prevent such a reconnaissance being made. While the airplane is new, the principle involved in their use is the old, old principle of combat. We must fight and win. This means not only the highest type of airplanes, but also the highest type of fighting men to put in them if the enemy is to be beaten in the preliminary air battles. If we do not provide the best kind of airplanes and the best kind of fighting men, we are not going to be able to fly over the enemy's territory to perform the preliminary reconnaissance which must be the basis of our attack. In other words we will be put on the defensive and robbed of the initiative. The possession of the initiative is the first step in winning the war. This because the first thing we have got to do to win is to put the enemy on the defensive. Then after we have him on the defensive, we have got to lick him.

At the present time this country is unable to take the initiative, because while we have "good enough" machines, and aviators whose courage is certainly above reproach, "good enough" is not sufficient. We must have better machines or we will be beaten. If our enemy can fly higher and faster than our aviators can, they will be above ours, with the result that the "good enough" machine will go down before the one just a little better. There is no such thing as "good enough" in aviation. We must have the best. If we do not have the best, we cannot chase the enemy out of the skies even temporarily.

Supposing the enemy is chased far enough back in the skies so that our machines can go over his territory. What is to be done? Literally hundreds and thousands of photographs have to be taken so that every point in the enemy's position is shown. Those photographs are taken back to the various headquarters where they are examined very carefully. Every bit of information found on them is put on maps. Incidentally, in the French service when these photographs are taken showing a series of trenches directly in front of a division, the division commander has the photograph in his hand four hours later. After weeks, or perhaps months, of this work a map is produced on which is every bit of information about the enemy; all his trenches, his batteries, line of supplies, headquarters, and every possible item of information being shown. The artillery is assigned its targets from this map.

The artillery having been assigned its targets, the next thing is for each of the batteries to determine exact firing data so that they can hit the targets assigned them. A six-inch shell may be sent out and will raise a cloud of dust twice as high as this room, but if it does not hit the target it is aimed at, it does not do any particular damage. The pieces flying some hundreds of yards in every direction may kill somebody, it is true, but the gun or trench assigned as a target is not destroyed.

To get the exact data, our aviators must go out, circle over the trenches and watch while the batteries fire and report the shot short, or over, to the right, or to the left, until the battery commander knows the exact firing data. This takes a great deal of time.

When the determination of firing data is finished, the next step is the artillery preparation. The artillery preparation is primarily to smash all enemy shelter of all kinds; to smash all machine guns; to smash his batteries; to so muss him up that he will be unable to resist when our infantry attacks him. The heavy artillery does the smashing. Incidentally, the heaviest field gun we have is the six-inch. Over there they use nine-inch and larger calibres by the hundreds. Trench mortars, which throw large charges of high explosives short distances to tear and smash the front-line trenches and cut the barbed-wire entanglements in front of them, are used in the preparatory fire also. High explosives is the most satisfactory way to cut barbed-wire, though no way is always satisfactory. The line of light field guns, consisting of three-inch, seventy-five and seventy-seven milli-meter, and the British eighteen-pounders, all about the same thing, often has as its mission during this preparation the establishment of a line of bursting shells called a barrage fire in rear of the enemy's first position.

The object of this barrage is to prevent any reinforcements, any food, any water, or any ammunition being brought up to the enemy's infantry in the front line. It is to prevent any of the wounded or well men from getting out. While the heavy artillery tries to smash them, the light artillery keeps them penned in, without help.

During that preparation, reports must be had by the chief of artillery and the general in command of how the destruction is pro-gressing. If it is not satisfactory, our infantry, when it gets out of their trenches to attack, will suffer.

In the battle of the Somme, in 1916, the British artillery preparation was not what it should have been. This was not due to lack of material, nor lack of bravery, nor lack of hard work, but due to exactly the same causes which will make our artillery preparation at least in the beginning, not what it ought to be. You cannot make artillery soldiers and officers in a few weeks. You may make them, but they cannot do the business as it should be done. What is the result? The Somme is a good example. Over a good many parts of the line, when the British infantry came out of their trenches, they were held up by machine gun and rifle fire, and hand grenades, and every other kind of fire, because the artillery preparation had not been sufficient. It was not their fault that they could not go ahead, and that, therefore, the Somme battle was indecisive.

During the preparation, the aviators must again fly over the enemy's position. Depending upon the reports they bring back the general decides when the smashing has gone far enough, and sets the day and the hour for the assault to begin.

The assault no longer consists of a lot of men rushing out of their trenches in the direction of the enemy. It consists of a very carefully planned attack in which every single platoon of the infantry has a prescribed order and a prescribed objective. Those plans have to be made up in advance. In advance you cannot tell when the exact day or hour of the assault is going to arrive. Therefore, in the order the day of the assault is put as "X" or some other letter, and the hour of the assault is "the hour H on the day X." In the order everything is dated "the day X, and the hour H." In that way all arrangements can be made for the attack without giving away the day and the hour on which it is to be made. When the time is decided upon, it is only necessary to send out word that such a day is "X" and such an hour "H."

The infantry which is to make the assault has generally been kept in the rear for several weeks. Here the men have been given plenty of outdoor exercise, plenty of food, and everything done to make their spirits as high as possible. Men who have been in the trenches a long while do not display the same desire to leave them and chase the enemy out of his as do men who have been kept out of danger and with attractive living conditions. However, before the infantry can get up into the trenches from which they are going to make the assault, they have got to move from the rear of the battle field through seven or eight miles of artillery fire, as the enemy, of course, does not rest quietly in position while this preparation is going on. He does everything possible to silence the batteries, to stop the preparation, or failing that to make it less effective. They particularly endeavor to make the infantry which is to attack suffer as much as possible while on the way to the front line trenches. Thus, before the infantry can ever reach the point from which it is to start the assault, it has already been through a very trying period.

When the hour "H" arrives, all watches having been set at the same time, the infantry leaves the trenches and the attack is carefully and methodically carried out in accordance with the prearranged plan, unless the enemy's resistance is still sufficiently great to disarrange and stop it.

Just before "H" hour the field artillery has to establish a moving barrage, which is so planned that the shells drop two hundred yards in front of the attacking infantry. Now, a barrage is a fire in which each gun is assigned a front of, say, fifty yards, in which it has to put five bursting shells every minute. So that on that front of fifty yards you will see five shells, one, two, three, four and five, and then again, one, two, three, four and five. Every piece of every battery does the same thing. It is called a barrage, because the average man has no desire to walk through any part of a line every fifty yards of which has five bursting shells in it every minute.

Sometimes at Verdun in barrage fires one piece would have but ten yards of front. When the barrage is established, it moves forward probably at the rate of, say, fifty yards every two minutes. The rate varies. The infantry follows the barrage, not at a run, but at a walk, carefully maintaining their order. There must be no confusion; everybody must be in the place which belongs to him, and must stay in that place, and must move exactly as he is supposed to move. What does that mean? It means just one thing: It means discipline; and it means the highest kind and the real kind of discipline. All this individual initiative stuff, to be slangy, but expressive, is "bunk."

Now, the infantry follows behind the barrage. As a rule, it is a succession of lines of groups in open order. The men are armed with hand grenades, some with rifles, some with Lewis machine guns, and some carry rifle grenades. The order for the attack lays down exactly how far each line has to go, and what it has to do when it gets to its objective. Attempts made so far to change missions while fighting is going on have practically always resulted in failure. I want to emphasize that fact, because I want to emphasize the necessity, first, to know how to plan the attack, second, to see that everyone concerned understands exactly what he is supposed to do, and third, that what is planned, is done. All this can only be done by discipline.

If the attack succeeds, each line settles down wherever it was told to settle down. When a trench has been passed over, it is necessary to see that none of the enemy are left behind. All corners, all bomb proofs must be examined and every enemy individual found either killed or captured. Otherwise, after the attacking groups have passed, the enemy individuals overlooked will rise up and shoot the attacking infantry in the back. In a number of cases, where the artillery preparation has not been sufficient, and the infantry did not have men detailed to do this particular work, the attackers have been completely cut off.

As a rule, while the infantry is following the barrage, the enemy does not know exactly where they are. They are afraid to fire for fear they may hit their own infantry. But once our infantry has settled down, the enemy readily finds out where it is, and will do the best he can to make it miserable. They generally succeed. Here is another part of the fight where a good many losses occur.

I have tried to describe a typical modern attack. On the Allies' side it was first initiated by the French in the Champagne offensive of 1915. That attack has been enlarged and improved upon. The British have copied it. It is the method we must copy. If we do not copy it, we will suffer, as there will be another German victory.

I have tried to bring out three things. The first is the importance of aviation and the fact that we have not a sufficient force of it. I have tried to bring out the necessity, secondly, for an enormous mass of artillery. Our lack of such a mass is best explained by saying that we have not got enough to give five regular divisions the amount which the tables of organization prescribed last year. When we entered the war, the French told us that this amount ought to be practically tripled. Outside of these five regular divisions, which have not enough, we are going to have sixteen divisions of the national guard, and sixteen divisions of the new national army. Where the artillery is going to come from I do not know. No attack can be even prepared, much less made, without this artillery not yet in existence.

Now the third, and most important of all—men! You may have the finest aviators and the greatest number of them in the world; you may have the most powerful artillery in the hands of the finest shots, but if you have not got the infantry soldiers to follow up the path the artillery has blown out, in order to seize the enemy's territory and hold it, you cannot win victory.

When I tell you that the British lost, in the battle of the Somme, in the seven or eight months that it lasted, over 800,000, perhaps you will get some idea of how much infantry you have got to have to fight a modern battle. In each of the first weeks in Verdun, the French used up sixteen infantry divisions. A French infantry division consists of 12,000 rifles. I do not mean they were all killed or wounded, but do mean that the sixteen divisions were so used up that they had to be replaced by sixteen other divisions.

So far we are planning just enough to carry us through the first two weeks of a Verdun. However, to do what the French did in those two weeks we would need more, because ours will be untrained soldiers, and they will not be able, in the beginning, to stand as the French stood at Verdun. That is no reflection on the courage of the individual American, which I believe to be second to none. It takes time, discipline and leadership, as well as courage, to make a first class soldier.

So that, in summing up, I say that there are three things that we have got to have, and we have got to have them all of good quality and in enormous quantities, and so far we have made no provision for them: Aviation, artillery and infantry.

AN ADDRESS BY WILLIAM C. GORGAS, LATE SURGEON GENERAL, U. S. ARMY[19]

Delivered before the Chicago Association of Commerce, October 26, 1917.

The actual administration of the care of the sick and wounded is probably the most important element in that care. Before the commencement of this war we knew that the great effort of administration should be to get the soldier's wound dressed at as early a date as possible, so that it would not become infected—to get the first-aid dressing. Then when that was once on, there was no very great pressure for three, four or five days to have him operated upon, or to get him back to the operating hospitals. But the great preponderance of large, mutilating shell wounds in this war has changed that proposition. A first-aid dressing, a first-aid packet put on as we have done up to the present time, will not protect these great wounds from infection, so that the tendency seems to be to have the man operated upon at as early a point as possible.

It is purely a matter of administration. If it is decided that it is necessary to get every wounded man operated upon as soon as possible, that is a pure question of administration. If we could get our operating organizations in the trenches, that would make it most simple; and if we could get them at the field hospitals, that would be the next best thing. If we could get them at the evacuating hospitals, that would be next best to the field hospitals. Probably that is the point where we will have to do the operating.

The infection occurs within the first twelve hours, and if the man is operated upon within the first twelve hours, in general his wound will heal just as an operative wound would in one of our civil hospitals. We avoid the infection which is now causing so high a rate of mortality and giving so much trouble in Europe. The administrative measure would be to concentrate at these hospitals the whole operating force of the army. If it is necessary to have the men operated on within the first two hours, it could be done, but probably twelve hours will be time enough.

[19] *Chicago Commerce*, November 1, 1917. The death of General Gorgas occurred on July 4, 1920.

The medical department, with the base hospitals at the concentration camps as they are now, has to deal with a class of sick and injured very much as any civil hospital does in Chicago. We expect to bring back from France only those who are permanently disabled. We are so far from our base that it would not be feasible to bring all the sick and wounded over here and return them when they are well.

We expect to bring about one hundred thousand men home every year for every million men in the field. These men will be men who are going to be discharged and men we can see will never be able to return to the firing line. The care that will be given to them will be principally to fit them for their vocations in civil life. They will be kept in the army so that a certain amount of discipline can be maintained, but all these hospitals will be more teaching centers than surgical or medical centers.

The idea will be that when a man loses his right hand, for instance, we know, as far as military service is concerned in general, he will be permanently disabled; but in a week after that amputation teaching should be commenced to teach him to do something that he can do with his left hand, typewrite, for instance. He will be gotten as rapidly as possible to the special hospitals in France and be brought as rapidly as we can get transportation to the special hospitals in the United States, where he will remain.

In the same way our organization will be modified in France. Now a country like France, which is doing its whole work in its own territory, necessarily needs a different organization from ourselves and from England. We all commenced this war with much the same organization. The French and the Germans have retained in general the organization they had at the beginning of the war. The English have modified theirs considerably, and we will expect to have to modify ours somewhat more than the English have done.

In general, the armies of all civilized nations, war-like nations, the Germans and ourselves, the English, the French and the Japanese—I expect the Germans would smile at our classifying ourselves among the war-like nations—all have adopted a similar organization. The basis of our army organization is the company, and the companies are formed into regiments and the regiments are consolidated

(21)

into brigades and brigades into divisions. Beyond the divisional unit divisions will be brought into corps, and the corps of the army will be consolidated into field armies. The smallest great unit of all armies is the division. Now, our medical department only goes as far as the field medical organization for a division.

That illustrates the front line of a division. The infantry and artillery regiments of the front line of a division are engaged right in the trenches. Next behind come the dressing stations. Now each regiment, each brigade, each division, has so many medical officers and medical personnel right with the troops. Each regiment, for instance, has six medical officers that serve right with the troops, and the personnel of the medical department, who, when the battle comes on, do the first dressings. The wounded are then sent to the rear as rapidly as they can be gotten there, to the next medical organization, but both of these organizations are under fire and the wounded are kept just as short a time as possible. The next organization that comes is the evacuation hospital. The evacuation hospital is behind, just out of fire. Behind that come again the base hospitals, where the men who need special treatment are sent, generally as near as convenient, but they may be in any part, and behind them will come the various special hospitals where the men who need special treatment are sent.

The French, when the war commenced, used the organization we used, but they have found that the preponderance of wounds are so large and so easily infected that their first-aid dressing does not protect and they want to operate as soon as possible. They have advanced their operating center, therefore, to the evacuation hospital, and there do all their operating. If it is necessary to operate in the first twelve hours, as now seems to be desirable, all of us can change our administration so as to meet this requirement. It is a mere matter of administration.

To witness some of the operations that occur in present military surgery is very gruesome. The wound is such that a large amount of tissue through which the missile passes is killed. If there is a delay beyond twenty-four hours in the general operation, the wound has become thoroughly infected. No matter what the injury is, the man is in a very precarious condition. Outside of a general infection he is likely to contract gas, gangrene or tetanus and the several infections that are liable to occur where there is a large mass of lowly organized tissue due to severe injury.

Now for the method of our great Dr. Carrel,[20] of the Rockefeller Institute. We will take what would occur with a gun shot wound on a man shot through the thigh. He comes into the evacuation hospital, say within twenty-four hours after injury, with a first-aid dressing put upon him at the firing line. The thigh has a small puncture that our modern rifle ball makes and a little larger puncture on the other side. It does not look very serious, but in this passage through the tissue that ball has killed a large amount of muscular tissue. It has crushed the bone and splintered it up and down for some distance. Now, it is necessary in operating to get all dead tissue out, to get all the broken bone out, everything that can give a place for the infection germs to develop.

Such a wound as that, not very severe, maybe, in appearance, would have to be laid open from the knee to the abdomen generally, and there is a tremendous amount of tissue exposed. All the little passages that have been injured by bone being driven into various parts have to be laid wide open and the tissue that has been killed cut away. So that when Dr. Carrel, for instance, or any other surgeon— all the methods have that in common—starts to treat that wound, he must take away everything that can lead to infection. When Dr. Carrel gets through with that thigh, preparing to put the solution in, you see an enormous wound in comparison with the bullet wound which the man had when he came into the ward, and you are impressed with the idea that the man was very unfortunate in falling into the hands of the surgeon and that he is very much worse off by the time the surgeon is through with him than he was when he came in.

The advantage of that operation is this: All the tissue that has become infected because of clothing or dirt of any kind that has been carried in—I have heard surgeons who were at the front tell that sometimes a mass of mud as big as an egg has been forced through

[20] Dr. Alexis Carrel, member of Rockefeller Institute for Medical Research, 1909—,was in the medical service in France during the years 1915-1919. He was awarded the Nobel prize in 1912 for success in suturing blood vessels and for the transplantation of human organs.

the skin by the explosion of a shell—all this material has been taken out and that wound is perfectly clean. That wound is in the same condition as the wound after appendicitis as it occurs in a civil hospital at home. The consequence is, when the surgeon gets through, that wound can be brought together and sewn up. Of course, I am referring to the period when he is sure there is no infection there.

The various methods differ. Carrel puts his solution in, and it takes several days before he can be sure the infection is gone; but if the surgeon is sufficiently sure that he has a clean wound lying there on the table, he closes the wound as you would an abdominal wound for appendicitis and the man is well within a week or ten days. Now it doesn't take any explanation to show the enormous advantage of such a condition of affairs if it can be brought about. We, all of us, think from the man's point of view, of the saving of life, of the saving of suffering that is brought about by such a condition. The military surgeon really has to put first the getting of the man back to the firing line, and the commanding general has to give that first place, but fortunately such methods are most effective in getting the man back to the firing line. Many a man thus wounded— take the one [wound] through the thigh, that results in death from infection within a few days, or permanent disability as the result of infection in the course of two to six months—will be saved and the man will be back on the firing line within two or three weeks if the wound can be kept free from infection.

Now, the difference that the French are making in their administration is that they have stopped as far as they can operating at the base hospital and have gone one step forward to the evacuation hospitals. The English are doing the same thing, and we will, no doubt, do the same. The French, when they have had their man operated on at the evacuation hospital, bring him back as rapidly as they can to the base, where, if there has been a successful operation, he is kept until he is ready for duty again. If it has been such an injury as the loss of an arm or leg or a knee joint, where more extensive treatment is required, which makes him obviously unfit for military service, he is sent back to the various special hospitals which are located all over the country. The base hospital feeds the special hospitals.

Orthopedics we have specialized [in] very extensively and the

French have. When a man has a stiff knee, if he is sent to that special hospital, the possibility of getting him fit again for service is very much greater. Some of the most successful special hospitals the French have are those pertaining to aural surgery, to injury to the face, of which there are a large number comparatively where a man has had the whole lower jaw taken off, carrying away all the tissues. The great drawback that such a man has, if he recovers, is his deformity, the horrible impression it makes in going upon the street or in meeting people he knows. . . . Aural surgeons have been enormously successful in doing plastic operations in cases of that kind. The French have one of those special hospitals beyond the base to which these men are sent. The object in their organization will be to settle that [whether plastic operation is feasible] as soon as possible, and it is not very difficult for the general surgeon to tell [it] when a man gets into the evacuation hospital. If he will eventually have to go to a special hospital, let us get him back there as soon as possible. He is sent to the base hospital and there is kept just long enough until he gets transportation to the special hospital. There are a great many other classes of special hospitals.

The eye men will have special hospitals over there to which a man who is totally blind will be sent rapidly, not that they can restore him to sight, but that he may begin to learn some vocation that will enable him to make a living. It is remarkable what ingenuity has brought out in this line and how useful a totally blind man can become if he is properly taught.

Shell shock, which will frequently disable a man for five or six months, the man will eventually recover from, but he does not get the proper care and attention in the base hospital, which is a general hospital. Those cases will be rapidly run to the rear for such special treatment as such hospitals will give. The French have to have many more special hospitals than we will have because they will have to treat all their special cases. Take a shell shock case that is going to disable a man for six months—we probably would bring such a case home for various reasons. His prospects for recovery are better at home with surroundings he would have here than they would be in France away from all his customary pleasant surroundings.

Take a tuberculous case. As soon as it is discovered it would be gotten first to the special hospitals in France, but would be kept there merely till they could get transportation. We will have special hospitals for the insane, which is a fair share of the disabled. . . . The idea with such a man would be that they would determine the treatment over there. Some would be much more likely to recover if kept there three or four or five months than if subjected to the strain of transportation at the time. All those problems would be determined locally.

The English have still further modified their old organization to meet special conditions. They are so near home that they take all their sick and wounded home as soon as they can get transportation, even those that are going back to the firing line in a few weeks. Therefore they cut the organization off at the base hospitals. They have no special hospitals in France. Everything of that kind is attended to in England.

That, in general, is the scheme that we have adopted, and France and England and the fighting nations in Europe have adopted for the care of their sick and wounded.

Manifestly the hospitals will be varied in various parts of our country. One base hospital need not be organized exactly like every other base hospital. A base hospital in our country here as we have it at the camps would not need a special man in the various surgical or other specialties any more than they would at one of our civil hospitals. We will have the various special hospitals scattered around the country to which men who need special treatment can be sent, but a base hospital at one of our camps should be organized and carried on very much as one of our large civil hospitals.

The large number of what we call reconstruction hospitals, the hospitals where these disabled men in Europe are going to be brought for treatment, represent another kind of organization. It would probably be better to bring all the men who have been blinded to the special hospitals here, and all the men who have stiff joints and injuries of that kind who need special training to loosen up the joints, or, if it is a permanent injury, to fit them for a vocation that will enable them to make a living, rather than to leave them in the general hospitals in contact with others.

So our organization in this country will necessarily include a large number of special hospitals, and if we bring back 100,000 such men a year you can see how rapidly our numbers will increase as has been the case in Canada, and what a large number of these special hospitals we will have to have.

In our present organization we look forward to having not less than 1,000 beds in a hospital because we have found that hospitals smaller than that are expensive and difficult of administration. Suppose we make our minimum 1,000 beds. That would mean that we would have to put up every year 100 hospitals and I don't mean to limit ourselves to a million men in France. I don't want to commit the army or the medical department to any such number. I heard Secretary Daniels, since I have been in Chicago, make the statement that we would soon have an army of ten million men and if that was not enough to bring us out all right in this war we were going to take every able-bodied man in the United States and put him into the army.

In the medical department of the army we have not laid our plans for any such sized army as ten million men, but we will probably have a pretty big number.

One hundred thousand beds for reconstruction in the United States is not going to be near enough. We would have to go on and increase that in the second year, probably as much more. Our preparatory work in this country will be probably no greater than that now in hand at the forty concentration camps, and not near as great because we have the great national guard camps and the regular army camps which have ceased to be used as our troops have gone abroad. What we contemplate now is the same number of permanent camps that we have now.

When the present army gets abroad, the sixteen divisions of approximately 25,000 men will have gone from each one of these camps; but the camps will be immediately filled by 25,000 fresh men who will be trained and ready to go over there to replace the wastage that occurs in all armies in the field, so that those camps will be permanent and our hospitals there will be permanent. Our permanent organization here in the United States from now on will be much smaller than it is now, but the reconstruction hospitals will more than make up the difference. A year from now we will probably have three or four times the numbers in the medical organization in the United States than we [now] have, and a medical organization in Europe very much larger than we have at present.

We do not intend, as the English do, to bring our sick and wounded home as rapidly as we could. We could, probably, if it were desirable, bring all the sick and wounded home, as the English do, because our transport system of taking the troops over and taking supplies could be readily fixed up as the English have so successfully done, so as to bring the wounded home very comfortably, and it would be more than enough, but the trouble would be the delay in getting the men back in the firing line.

The whole efforts of the general commanding are bent upon keeping his army filled, and he hopes to do this in great part by getting the slightly wounded men who are only incapacitated for one, two, three, four or five weeks, back to the firing line within that length of time. To bring one of these slightly wounded men home would mean an absence from the firing line for five or six months, so we have looked upon that as being undesirable and impracticable.

That, however, may be changed as the exigencies of the war develop. It may be found that the fact of giving a wounded man a little rest at home would make him a much more efficient soldier than if we got him back a month earlier and did not let him come home. I can see a great many psychological questions coming in there. I imagine it would stir the enthusiasm of us all much more, and our interest in the war, if we had the 200,000 wounded men, the 20 per cent that occur after some of the great battles, if we brought them back home, and [if] as soon as they were well enough [they] were to get around in the hamlets and cities in the different parts of the United States.

But at present that is not our plan. We have not yet been convinced that the psychological question would overrule the practical application. I expect I would have to talk a great deal of psychology to General Pershing to get him to consent for us to bring 200,000 men back home and keep them away from the firing line three months in order to effect a psychological condition in our country.

It is a matter of vast importance to the medical department to get the whole country interested in the first place in the army, and of course we naturally think the medical corps a very important unit. I am very glad to have the business men interested in the various phases of our administrative details, which naturally they understand better than the surgical and technical professional points.

AN ADDRESS BY MEDILL McCORMICK, MEMBER OF CONGRESS FROM ILLINOIS[21]

Delivered at a patriotic meeting, Springfield, Illinois, November 27, 1917.

I have heard often that this was a war not of armies, but of people, but I had to see with mine own eyes before I understood how the souls and bodies of whole nations were given to the conflict.

It is beyond my prosaic power to picture to you as it should be pictured the struggle which absorbs the energies of the democratic peoples of western Europe. I would have you conceive at the outset that four-fifths of the men between twenty and forty years of age are not to be found in their ordinary vocations of labor, or recreation. They are uniformed, the great majority of them in the zones of the armies, a few on guard duty or at administrative posts, a very considerable number of them at home on short leave, where they are everywhere in evidence with their wives, their mothers, their sisters, their sweethearts, in the parks, on the boulevards, at the play, in the restaurants. Four-fifths of the men between twenty and forty years are gone from their normal pursuits. That means of itself a revolution in the social and economic life of a country, but the absence of the men has been accompanied by the intrusion of great new industries for the supply of the war. The civil population, robbed of the labor of those best able to labor, must maintain those very same men and supply them with almost incalculable quantities of munitions and of engines of destruction. So it has come to pass that boys are advanced to men's places, old men have been recalled to young men's work, while in England and France alone some two million women are engaged in work for the war.

I don't know how many more of girls and women have added to the sums of their peace-time labors, and so have assumed part of

[21] *Illinois State Journal*, November 27, 1917.

the burden laid down by their brothers at the front. They are everywhere, the women and the girls—lassies from humble homes and daughters of the aristocracy, side by side, rivals, friends and companions in the new democracy of toil. They have taken the railway stations, as conductors of omnibuses, as porters at doors, running elevators, driving motor trucks. This last year two hundred thousand of them went out upon the land. Girls from all walks of life are working side by side, caring for the farmers' stock and guiding the power lathes in the shell shops. No wonder that the ablest of their political opponents join with the old friends of equal suffrage to enfranchise the women, who fight for the nation and for the new democracy as truly as their brothers and lovers and husbands in the trenches.

The eye is struck by the disproportion between the sexes, on the streets and in the places of business. You are aware at once that great peoples are husbanding their resources; lights are diminished to save coal; clothing is saved that the looms may weave uniforms; vehicles are few; housewives are sparing—very sparing.

I have said that the women are sparing of food. That is true of all the peoples but the first duty of saving rests upon the women. There is no longer an abundance, but there is not starvation. There is more to eat in France than in Switzerland, while German officers on furlough go to Switzerland to feast. But if there is no starvation among the Allies, they have learned by a harsh and unkind experience to husband for the future.

There were serious storms in western Europe this year. The wheat crop in Italy and France is short by a half. That is very grave in these countries, for the peasant farmers and workmen, during generations, have lived upon bread and cheese, a little meat and a few vegetables, in a sense of which we know nothing.

Effort—intelligent, energetic effort—is being made to diversify the food of the people, to teach them to cook in ways which are new to them. But, my friends, when the ready hands and the most plastic minds of the young have gone to the mills to labor for the war, it is the grandames who tend the cradles and prepare the food for the table. Those old hands cannot learn new ways. In this country we must spare something of our plenty to make good something of their want, not that they may eat white bread, for there is none in Europe, excepting in the camps of the American army; not that they may eat white bread, but that there may be barely enough of the coarse war bread for the mouths of all.

But do not think that because whole peoples are engaged in terrific labors, that because they have been bled by great sacrifices and are stricken by great losses that the atmosphere is one of gloom. France, England—neither of them was ever more heroic than she is today.

There are things which I saw and which I heard, of which the sad and glorious memory will wound and exalt posterity. Of such was the phrase of the nurse, torn by a broken shell, as she laid blenched upon her bed, while General Pershing saluted, as he saw bestowed upon her by the Generalissimo the cross of war. "General," she whispered, "I am happy to have been struck, that you may know that the daughters as well as the sons of France would suffer and die for her." A little later there was cited for decoration in the orders of the ministry of war at Paris, the name of a lieutenant of a line already dead, killed as he hurled from the trench a live shell, which would have killed his comrades, if he had left it where it had fallen.

An old friend of my mother's, the widow of an American of distinction, a splendid American herself, Mrs. Whitelaw Reid, sent for me to ask me about the front and about our men. She had come from the bedside of a young British officer, merry in his misery, glad, though he could walk no more and though he only had one arm, for he had thrown himself on a bomb, which, though it forever crippled him, did not touch one of the men of his command.

I spent a day with the Irish division—marched into the famous Hindenberg trench with the Dublin Fusileers, and came out with the Irish Fusileers—rollicking, laughing, as if they were going to a fight at a Donnybrook fair. With that indifference to paradox, with that subtle understanding of the spiritual truth which transcends any prosaic logic, the Irish division has blazoned on its banners the motto which Louis the Great conferred upon the Irish guard at Fontenoy. The gallant Irishman who commands them turned the pages of the roll of honor of the division, until he came to the name of a simple private. He had been lying wounded in a shell crater, when he espied over the lip of a ridge in the near distance a German machine gunner turning his deadly fire upon the scattered ranks of the Fusileers, seeking sparse cover on the muddy slope. Hughey jumped from the shell crater, dashed limping forward and with one blow of the butt of his rifle brained the machine gunner and carried the machine gun back to the crater. In a moment, he was up and gone. "Begorrah," he said, "the old man will give me hell for leaving me rifle where the Fritzer can find it," and dashing again over the lip of the ridge, he discovered two of the enemy in possession of his arm. He jumped into them with such fury that both surrendered, and then compelling one of his captives to carry his gun for him, Hughey drove the two prisoners back to the Irish lines.

There are no comparisons in gallantry. You cannot say that among the French, Breton or Gascon, Norman or Savoyard is more brave. Among the British, the Canadian, or English, Welsh or Irish, Scotch or Australian, none of them have been more daring than the others.

It is as true on Vimy Ridge or on the blood-stained "road of the ladies," as it was before Calvary, "that greater love hath no man than this, that a man lay down his life for his friend."

There is a great deal which you must want to know that I cannot tell you. There are many important things of intense human interest of which I am ignorant, because I traveled from capital to capital, and from front to front; because I went from statesman to general and from general to statesman with one preoccupation: "What must we do to win this war in the shortest possible time, and with the smallest possible loss of life?" There are not many men even in Europe, I found, who have thought of this, to me the whole problem, in terms at once general and definite. But among the few most responsible statesmen, among the few generals of real distinction, which the war has produced, I found a general agreement that cannon and coalition are essential to success; that time is the essence of victory.

It is really not so very long ago, although it seems months rather than weeks, since I traveled along the Italian front from Trieste to the Trentino, over the dry and broken wastes of the

Carso, upon the steep roads toward the Dolomites, through the very country which the Austrian and German armies have captured, along the very highways which now have been traveled by the German emperor and his allies, the Austrian emperor and the Bulgarian czar.

When I was there the Italian armies were short of cannon and still shorter of ammunition; in a country which produces no coal, less coal had been imported than in times of peace, though more was needed to keep the munition factories busy through every hour of the day and night. The wheat crop had failed in great part, and too little wheat was coming in. Hunger was too near.

If Italy holds the present line of the Piave, I am not certain but that we shall count the German thrust as a disguised blessing. It has shortened the Italian line. There is no evidence that it has weakened Italian resolution, and it has driven home to every thinking man, what only a few appreciated, the unity of the front from the Adriatic to the channel. A reverse, or a success, whether Italian, British, French or American, is of consequence to us all in common conflict with a common enemy. We cherish a unity of purpose, the enemy likewise, but the enemy also has a unity of command and action, because the imperial staff at Berlin dictates to Turkish, Bulgarian, Hungarian and Austrian, as well as to German army commanders. That attack in Italy was admirably done. It was triumphant proof of the value of unity. German divisions from the Russian and western fronts, Hungarian divisions from Bukovina, joined artillery from both fronts and drove at Italy, when a way in for them was opened by the treachery of a few Italian regiments.

In a statement published a week ago, I suggested that if the Germans hoped for a military success in Italy, they could not have believed that they would secure one. Doubtless they hoped to create a reaction against the war in Italy, but chiefly they were intent on making a great camouflage, to conceal in Italy their steady retreat and terrible losses on the Meuse and in Flanders.

The Central Empires were everywhere in the west on the defensive until the Russian collapse. They had even summoned Turkish infantry to the support of the Austrians in front of Trieste. On the western front from Switzerland to the channel, the Germans are out-manned and out-gunned. There has been a significant and steady deterioration in the morale of the German infantry, and in the quality of war material.

I would not have you believe that there are not splendid German divisions. I would not have you underestimate the genius and the strategic skill of German generals. I would not have you think that they can be driven from the trenches by the gallantry of America, or any other infantry. They cannot. The thing which is important is that Germany has developed the maximum of her military resources and must diminish in strength, however slowly. German troops come through the lines to surrender in increasing numbers, complaining that their officers leave them and go back during bombardments. They include in their numbers boys of seventeen and sixteen, whose tear-stained faces wring the hearts of their captors. The German brass shells show an insufficient and diminishing proportion of copper, as the German cannon show a grave lack of nickel —the necessary alloy of steel for the manufacture of artillery. But the German armies are now fighting on the defensive, behind the trenches, and all authorities with whom I talked agreed that they could not be dislodged for two years; that it would be impossible to hope for a military decision until then, when the Allies would not merely have the help of American troops, but more important still, the artillery, the transport and the air craft which American resources alone can supply them.

Heavy guns in this war are what the steam shovel was to the Panama. When the French company under DeLesseps sought to pierce the isthmus with picks, shovels and petty machinery, men died by thousands beside the scratched tropical hillsides. So died the men who fought at Verdun and on the Marne, because they had no weapons equal to the task before them. Now we know that advances can be made and victories can be won with little loss, when the armies advancing have their ways blazed for them by the fire of thousands of cannon.

I was at the last battle of the Chemin des Dames, in the midst of the artillery park, during the greatest bombardment which the French have carried out during the history of the war. That fight epitomized the three years' experience and the skill of the French high command, as Verdun symbolized the heroism and the democracy of the armies of republican France.

The Chemin des Dames—"the road of the ladies," the bloody road of the ladies, the highway on which the armies have fought for months and months. It was the scene of the bloody losses and the terrible repulse which the French met last spring under the command of a general now disgraced. He thrust his infantry forward, without artillery support, into the mouths of the enemy guns. It was that which dashed the spirit of our old friends in the republic across the Atlantic, before we came into the conflict. Those fruitless losses cost something to half the villages in France. How different was it this time, when the general-in-chief sent for me to go forward to the headquarters of the division which was attacking the key of the enemy's defense.

The road of the ladies runs along the flat crest of a range of low hills, their sides covered with half-grown forests and pierced by a multitude of caverns—quarries driven into the limestone for the building of Paris. Picture, I say, the long ridge of hills, with a flattened top, a sort of elongated butte, such as you might see in our western country. Here and there the narrow ridge broadens, where, from a larger central mass, spurs run out into the valley on the other side. On either side of the valleys, which are divided by the slopes of the Chemin des Dames, are other ridges. The one to the west held by the French and affording emplacements for some of its artillery. The one to the east crosses the little river, held by Germans, the ground upon which the greater part of their artillery is placed. Doubtless, some day, a master of description will paint in English the roads leading to the front, with horse-drawn light artillery, motor engines heavily dragging forward the ammunition trains for the supply of the heavies and middle-heavies, ambulances, food convoys, field kitchens, soldiers from every province of embattled France, yellow-skinned colonial troops from Annam and Cochin China, African blacks from the Senegal, bronzed tribesmen of Morocco, ten years ago hostile, now become loyal legionaries under the benign and ordered government of the French republic. And then a little distance from the roaring roads, the headquarters of the commander-in-chief of all the groups of armies in France, the headquarters of the commander of the army of that particular front and the commander of the army corps on that sector, each differing from the other only in size, each housed in a quiet villa, linked to the front and to the other commands by wires, so that each commander could follow and direct every move under him, telephone to his ear, and his eyes upon a relief map which pictured to him every hamlet and hillside, farm house and stream, mountain slope and precipice, highway, battery and entrenchment.

It was not until we drew near the headquarters of the key division, that we heard the voice of the battle. Then all the traffic which had choked the highway melted along the narrow gauge rails and the wagon roads to the actual front. We come suddenly upon a hut, half dug out of the hillside and half built of sand bags—the bomb-proof headquarters of the calm little man who was immediately responsible for the success or the failure of the pending attack. The air roared not loudly, as reckless writers have said. There were no ear-splitting detonations, unless you were by a battery itself; but as far as you could hear, and even farther—as far as the senses could suggest hearing—there rolled along the horizon undulating reverberations of sound as if thousands of noises were overlapping one another, while overhead the aeroplanes looked like a flock of birds and sounded like a sawmill.

"Permit me," said the general of division, "have the goodness, Mr. McCormick, to permit me to introduce to you our wrecking contractor." I looked at a second general in some wonder. "This general," he said, "is the chief of artillery, charged with wrecking the enemy batteries and the many defenses, so that our infantry may not be cut up when it goes forward to attack." I started eagerly to question the wrecking contractor, but my host, for such the general of the division had made himself, suggested that first we should lunch, as the artillery fire slackened, while the men ate their noonday meal, and then that we go to the artillery headquarters. The windows of the sandbag dug-out hut, which was headquarters and mess hall for the division staff, rattled with the shock of the guns. You could hear the occasional scream of a shell. I heard my old college mate, Gouverneur Morris, talking with a distinguished French artilleryman, a member of the Academy, and now a staff colonel, about the qualities of the French language. Morris explained that he hoped at the end of a year in France to complete the education which he had acquired during the years he spent there as a child, and to learn to write French accurately. This statement was concluded by [a] terrific explosion, and then I heard Colonel Marcel Prévost, answering that he had received his degree at the university some thirty-five years ago and had been fifteen years a member of the Academy; that he hoped that if he lived another ten or fifteen years by that time to learn to write French well.

Then hell echoed again and Prévost sought to dissuade Morris from trying to do in one year what not more than a dozen living French could do, what Prévost himself hoped to do not for a dozen years—to write the French language as it should be written. And then, as we arose to go forth, to overlook the battle, I heard the general say that nevertheless a knowledge of two languages was useful, as Paul Verlaine had beautifully translated into French the verses of Edgar Allen Poe; and then we went through a hole in the ground, into the office of the wrecking contractor. Here he had maps and tables and little reports, not unlike those of the number of square yards excavated and the number of tons of steel produced under the direction of the superintendent or general manager of an American enterprise. The photographs were carefully classified in groups for they came continually from the aeroplane observers and marked the progressive destruction of the German batteries. Certain officers were expert to read them, as certain physicians are cunning in making a diagnosis from a radiograph. Photographs of the result of the artillery fire were supplemented by the reports of pilots and observers, who occasionally came and went, and more often by wireless messages from aircraft equipped with Marconi instruments who notified headquarters to sprinkle the fire a little more to the left, or to drop it a little more to the right, and when they located 3,000 Germans hiding in a cavern, sent word to drop asphyxiating bombs on the cavern, so that the gases, as they went through the cracks, would destroy the men within. The French guns won the battle. They blasted away the enemy's batteries, overwhelmed, stunned, slaughtered the enemy infantry, and then the French infantry advanced at a walk and took, almost without losses, the ground

(22)

which their generals had planned for them to take last June. That is the secret of all successful advances.

If I have spoken at length of the battle of the Chemin des Dames, it is not to slight the tremendous efforts which I witnessed on the British front, but because the French attack epitomizes the importance of artillery as completely as it illustrates the science of the modern artillerist.

I saw something of the steady pounding by the British armies, the consequences of which are noted in this afternoon's dispatches. What is happening in Flanders and what is happening on the ridges between Aisne and the Ailette is not foreign to the events in Italy. The British and the French have proven that artillery is the weapon of first importance.

Lloyd George has spoken of the cavalry of the air. I would not underestimate the significance of aircraft, but they are only the servants of the great guns, which are the masters of modern battles, and the Germans are unable to summon reserves to hold the French or the British. As yet they have been able to bring from the Russian front only enough to drive into Italy. They preferred that use of their forces to an effort to stop the resistless advances of the British and French armies.

The tide has turned. By ever so little, perhaps, but the tide has turned. There may be backwashes, when the Germans bring still more divisions and more guns from the Russian front, when they add to their batteries in France and Flanders the cannon which they bought from Russian traitors during the period of fraternization. The tide has turned. It rests with us to see that it does not ebb again, but flows resistlessly to the full flood of victory.

Have I made myself clear? Have I presented the problem intelligibly? I have lived with it so constantly night and day, that I am conscious that in telling what I have seen and heard I may omit something of great importance.

Time is the essence of victory. Coalition and cannon are the means by which we may win a victorious peace. With them we can win, if American help does not come too late.

I cannot go without leaving with you a summary of the front. To the south from the Adriatic to the Swiss Alps runs the shortened

Italian line, about two hundred miles long, where Turks, Hungarians, Austrians or Germans are joined in battle with Italian, French and British; then from Switzerland along the mountains of the Vosges, over the rolling hills of central France and the plains of Flanders to the channel. Here, the British hold a fourth of the whole, one-third, let us say, of the active front in France. The British guns in proportion to the length of their line are three or four times as many as those of the Italians, and even more numerous by far.

France, God save her, cannot manufacture guns to make good her own inadequate supply, for she is manufacturing for us, the greatest steel producers in the world, because we are not able to turn out guns for our own armies. In France and Flanders our friends hold the enemy, out-manned and out-gunned. But we may look for some redress of the balance of power as the growing chaos in Russia permits the withdrawal of infantry and artillery from the east, to strengthen the lines on the western front.

We are sending men. We must send men; but at best they can cross the seas in slowly growing numbers to join the little army— the gallant little army—which is encamped about the spot where Joan of Arc was born and grew to womanhood and from which she went out upon the mission which was to end in her death and in the rebirth of France.

Men we must send, but still more urgently must we send guns, weapons, to our friends, that they may defend themselves; that they may win victories, while they await our coming.

"For God's sake send us great guns and munitions." I can hear the greatest of the French generals, as if he had but spoken. "We are grateful for your little army. Its coming was a pledge to us that you had not forgotten the old friendship, when the soldiers of Rochambeau and LaFayette mingled their blood with that of your forefathers across the ocean. But now, my friends, tell your countrymen to send us guns, many guns, and quickly, so that two years from now, when at last you are ready, we may have men enough to bear our share of the burden in the hour of victory, in order that you may not have to win this fight alone."

It is as if two great giants—Democracy and Empire—were

locked in a death struggle, cramped horribly in the bottom of a pit. Empire lies a little under Democracy, but better placed to gouge and to thrust. They are both terribly bleeding, suffocating, choking—the one from the blockade and the other from the submarines. But Democracy so lies that we may staunch his wounds, open a way for him for air and nourishment. You understand that if we bring Democracy what he must have, he will choke Empire into submission.

I have but one fear, that we shall not act swiftly enough. All through the war the allied democracies have done that which should be done, but too often they have done it too late. Already we have done things too late, because, with the lesson of the war before us, they might have been done sooner. . . . We wasted weeks, when we might have been building great numbers of sea-going destroyers. I hope that the new head of the war industries may impart decision and energy to the making of engines of destruction.

If we would do our part, we must create a war cabinet, a war council, which, in contrast to the partisan mediocrity of the present as of other peace cabinets, will summon to conference, will charge with chief responsibility the greatest men in the union, without reference to past rancors, without regard to difference of faith or faction.

Yonder across the seas the white host of patriotism has fused old hates in a common purpose; old enemies, embittered by years of personal and political strife, have put aside bitterness, to sit at the common council table, to share together the common burden, to divide among themselves, without jealousy, the tasks which are to be done.

As I walked along the outer battlements which defend the first approaches to the citadel of Verdun and gazed over the waste where fell a million men, there surged up in my memories the words of Abraham Lincoln:

"We cannot dedicate, we cannot consecrate, we cannot hallow this ground. The brave men, living and dead, who struggled here have consecrated it far above our power to add or detract. It is for us, the living, rather to be dedicated here to the unfinished work which they who fought here have thus far so nobly advanced. It is rather for us to be here dedicated to the great task remaining before us, that from these honored dead we take increased devotion to that cause for which they gave the last full measure of devotion; that we here highly resolve that these dead shall not have died in vain. . ."

Across the seas, the national spirit has been shot through with a new fire. In Italy, England, France, there is a new solidarity, a new and more real democracy than ever before, a consecration of purpose, born of the struggle and the sacrifices which they have made. They have learned to know the voices of those who speak out when things are not going well, from the voices of those who would weaken the government and the armies in the struggle.

We shall do no less. The resolution of the people, the industrial talent and the political genius of America will not prove unequal to the task.

Fired by old memories, united by new trials, roused to the full stature of citizenship by the task before us, we shall seek efficiency, as we shall seek victory, and with American steel eagerly arm our allies' forces and our own that they may strike down the enemy and not be stricken.

AN ADDRESS BY GOVERNOR FRANK O. LOWDEN BEFORE THE ILLINOIS MEN AT CAMP GRANT, NOVEMBER 1, 1917[22]

MAJOR GENERAL THOMAS H. BARRY:

Soldiers of Illinois: We are all honored by the presence here of the war governor of your great state. He needs no introduction to you, nor do you need any introduction to him. He emphasizes his interest in you by coming here to say a word of greeting and encouragement and Godspeed before you leave your native state in fulfillment of your great mission abroad.

Governor Lowden, I cannot speak in too high praise of these men of your state. They are imbued with a proper spirit, have shown it on all occasions, and have made unusual progress since they came to this camp; and notwithstanding the reputation of former soldiers of Illinois and the great commanders that the state has pro-

[22] From a manuscript copy in the possession of Governor Lowden.

duced, I am satisfied these men and officers will live up to the best traditions of the former soldiers of Illinois.

You, sir, have a right to be proud of them, the state should be proud of them, and the country should be proud of them, and I believe before their mission is fulfilled you will have occasion to be prouder of them than you are now. Your devotion to the cause and your courageous and most efficient administration of your great office in the interest of the great cause we are now engaged in are matters of history. And now, soldiers of Illinois, as you say in Illinois, here is your own Frank Lowden.

GOVERNOR LOWDEN:

Soldiers of Illinois: The last few days have been depressing to all of us, because of untoward events on the Italian front, and so today I come to you, not so much to encourage you as to receive inspiration from you, because those of us who are in official life, those of us who see troubles from day to day, who see sometimes pettiness of spirit on the part of those who ought to show greatness of soul instead, who see shrinking from the awful tasks this war has imposed, can go nowhere for inspiration and receive it in such full measure as when we come to a scene like this and look into the faces of twenty thousand loyal, great-hearted American young men, who are offering the supreme sacrifice, the sacrifice of life itself, that our nation may endure.

If it were not for scenes like this we might well despair. But here in this beautiful northern Illinois, in a camp which bears the illustrious name of the greatest captain of his century, surely we may take new courage for the future of our country and the future of mankind.

I want you to know, soldiers of Illinois, that we who remain at home are not unmindful of the fact that you are going to fight in a cause nearer to our hearts than any cause in which our fathers or their fathers before them ever fought. There were dark hours preceding our Civil War; there was a time that tried men's souls; but even in the darkest hour of that time we knew that whatever the issue of that war, we still would have some sort of fragmentary country left. It might be inglorious, if you please, it might be defective, if you please, but there would be still some soil above which would float the American flag and underneath whose folds we might then find a home. But if this war, in which you draw your swords, if this war go against us, there will be no spot in all America we can call our own and where we can enjoy the blessings of liberty, of our institutions and justice, those great heritages of our fathers; because democracy is in its last battle with military autocracy. When this war is over, wherever you may go, either the whole world will be altogether free or altogether under the heel of military autocracy. Not only that, but in all the world there will be no nook or cranny anywhere where defeated and worsted lovers of liberty may find a refuge.

So, men of Illinois, I want you to know that we appreciate the solemnity, the importance of the cause in which you are engaged. I want you to know that wherever you may be, on whatever foreign field, whatever dangers may confront you, the great heart of Illinois will beat in sympathy and love for you, and when you return—as God grant you may—Illinois will bring to you her gratitude with unstinted hand.

Some of you will not come back, but will find graves on foreign soil. But I want to say now that if we do not win this war, as I believe in my very soul, they who find graves in foreign soil will be happier than those of us who survive to face our country's shame and ruin, and those graves you fill will be attended with the love and tears of a grateful people. You may know if we win, I am sure somewhere you will be conscious, while not permitted to enjoy the fruits of your great victory, that you [have] saved America, you have saved Illinois, you have saved humanity everywhere from its everlasting ruin.

God go with you and keep you; our prayers will attend you; our gratitude is yours; we are proud of you today; and looking into your faces we may renew our faith that this great republic shall not go down in the great cataclysm of the world, but shall endure forever and ever to the blessing of humanity.

I thank you.

AN ADDRESS BY GOVERNOR FRANK O. LOWDEN[23]

Delivered before the 58th Field Artillery Brigade, 33d Division, Camp Merritt, New Jersey, May 22, 1918.

BRIGADIER GENERAL H. D. TODD:

The Governor of Illinois has kindly consented to talk to the men of the Fifty-eighth Brigade, and there is no necessity of introducing to you Governor Lowden.

GOVERNOR LOWDEN:

General Todd, Officers and Men of the Fifty-eighth Brigade Field Artillery:

I have not seen you for six months and I want to tell you that, though you are conscious yourselves of much improvement during that time, you cannot appreciate how great that improvement is because it has come gradually; but I, who have not seen you during that period, can say today that a magnificent brigade of trained and soldier-like and upstanding men has been created during that time, and I congratulate you with all my heart upon the progress you have made.

I come here today bringing a message of pride, of gratitude, of love, from the people of Illinois to this great organization. As you know, the Prairie Division, of which you are so conspicuous and so brilliant a part, is an Illinois organization, and it seems to me entirely appropriate, therefore, that I should remind you of not only the high privilege you have in serving Illinois, but all the splendid traditions of the state from which you hail and which you will represent in this greatest war of all time.

I see before me sons and grandsons of the old heroes of the Civil War. I want to remind you that at the beginning of the war it was an Illinois captain, not as well known then as many of you here today, who hailed from Galena, who led a regiment from Springfield, who received Lee's sword in surrender at Appomatox, and who, in four brief years, marched from obscurity on the banks of the Mississippi to immortal fame, and held aloft the American flag, redeemed,

[23] From a manuscript copy in the possession of Governor Lowden.

and for that was written a new luster and a new glory indeed—
Ulysses S. Grant of Illinois, the greatest captain of his country.

And may I say that it would not surprise us of Illinois, if, in the
strenuous months which lie ahead, great names may be evolved by
this organization which will match in luster that great name of which
Illinois is so proud. I want to remind you that though in that war
Illinois was only a fraction of its present size, yet it sent more than a
quarter of a million men to the front to fight the battles of freedom
and of union. And so, officers and men, you come from a state which
has great memories of the past, and Illinois knows, and knows full
well, that her honor and her reputation are safe in the keeping of her
own Prairie Division.

A little over a year ago I went from the Capitol at Springfield
to Lincoln's tomb in the cemetery there, in company with that old
hero of the Marne, Marshal Joffre. I saw him, with reverent hands
and tear-dimmed eyes, lay his wreath of flowers upon the coffin which
contains Lincoln's immortal dust. The Prairie Division also has
the matchless life, the uncounted sacrifices of that greatest exponent
of the people's government of all time to maintain in this war. I
knew that day, as I saw the old Marshal bend above Lincoln's immortal dust, that he, too, had gathered new inspiration for the
strenuous years that lay ahead of imperishable France's tragedy and
heroism. As he refreshed his courage and renewed his inspiration at
that hour, you of this great brigade, if you will but recall what Lincoln stood for, will yourselves fight with a stronger arm, with a
clearer eye, with a fuller heart, because Lincoln, in his lifetime, was
the greatest advocate the world had ever seen of the rights of man,
just common man. That is the cause for which you are fighting today.
In his death he became democracy's saint. His tomb became its
shrine. More and more liberty-loving men, from all quarters of the
world, make pilgrimage to Lincoln's tomb, there to pay their homage
to him and there to renew their own resolution to fight to the last
dollar and the last man for the sacred cause for which Lincoln lived
and in which he gave his life.

Oh, officers and men, Illinois is proud of its past. Its hundred
years of statehood are rich with great achievements. But Illinois

looks bravely into the future, because she knows that you and her other sons, who are offering all in the greatest cause for which men ever fought, are going to the battle fronts in Europe. Your fathers and their fathers before them have made her past secure, and she knows, she has full faith, that you will make her future equally glorious.

. . . .

You go to fight, not only for Illinois on its material side, you go to fight for the honor of your wives and mothers and daughters and sweethearts; you go to fight for the sacred cause of the common man in Illinois and everywhere, because at last the two old principles, the one that government must come from above, imposed by the few upon the many, and that other, that man, just man, created in the image of his Maker, can rule himself, are at grip in the final contest for the final mastery the wide world round. When this war is over, not only Illinois and America, but all the world will be either one thing or the other, will either be free with the rights of the people to rule established, or will be under the iron heel of military despotism and autocracy everywhere. No knights of old ever went forth to battle in as holy a cause as that which is calling you across the seas today, and I want you to know that I shall count that day happy indeed when some opportunity comes that I can do something, no matter what, to show my appreciation of you brave boys who are going to those battle fronts to fight our battles for us. I want you to know that, difficult though it may be for the people of Illinois to communicate to you all their pride in you and all their love for you, that they will follow you from the moment you sail, they will go with you across the seas, they will be with you in your training camps there, aye they will be with you in the trenches and in the hospitals. Illinois is proud of you, Illinois sends her love; and I shall take back to Illinois the message that I have been face to face with her Prairie Division, and that Illinois may know that her honor and her future are safe in its hands.

Good-by, God bless you, one and all. God keep you in this, the greatest year of all time in its significance to man everywhere.

AN ADDRESS BY NEWTON D. BAKER, SECRETARY OF WAR[24]

Delivered before the 86th Division, Camp Grant, Illinois, July 4, 1918.

Ladies and Gentlemen, Men of the Eighty-sixth Division:

It gives me pleasure to greet on this birthday celebration of our nation young America in arms. What I have to say is chiefly to these young soldiers. They are selected out of the body of the citizenship of this great republic. They have assumed the uniform of their country's army and they are about to sail overseas to defend, on new frontiers, liberties which our fathers acquired for us and transmitted to us for safekeeping and enlargement.

In the early days of this republic we believed it was enough for us to set up an example of freedom and by establishing free institutions among ourselves so to win men to their attractiveness and value that the mere force of our example would democratize and liberate all the peoples of the earth, and we were not much wrong about that. The spirit which was kindled in 1776 has in fact conquered the earth and one after another of the great autocracies and ancient and traditional empires of this world have given way before the spirit of 1776.

And yet here at the beginning of the one hundred and forty-third year of our republic we find that the American spirit and the American principle require new vindication on fields far away from home, and we are obliged to take the young manhood of our country and join it with the heroic manhood of Great Britain and France and Italy and to carry that young manhood for that purpose to a country which in many ways is the mother of liberty and the very founder of the romance of freedom.

There are reasons why you young soldiers should feel a special sense of inspiration and elation at your calling. In ancient times men were summoned into the armies of the countries of the world at the behest of rulers who derived their power from no consent given by those over whom they ruled, and those armies went forth for purposes of national aggrandizement. But you are a different army

[24] *Chicago Tribune*, July 5, 1918.

from that. You are the army of a free people, yourselves free men; you are fighting for a cause which is almost a romance in its purity and freedom from selfishness or taint of any kind.

Your country is sending you to rescue France from the heel of an invader who represents the last, we hope, the last manifestation of the autocratic and despotic principle upon this earth of ours. Your victory, when it is finally won, will mean no acres or square miles filled with servient populations to be governed by victors, but it will be a victory which rescues from the dust the very essentials and vital principles of liberty. Through it future generations, your children, the children of France, the children of Great Britain and those of Italy and of all peoples everywhere, may be baptised with the new spirit and have the new opportunity, which means the greatest possible development for each individual under institutions of his own fabrication and in his own power to change.

Let me be a little more intimate with you. I am not speaking about any individual in this group, nor to this group, but I am speaking to the whole company of 2,500,000 men, who comprise the army of the United States today. You have been selected by a democratic and free process for this service. You are going to join your fellows on the other side, where from the day you touch French soil, until you come home victorious, you will feel the intoxicating inspiration of a great ideal and the inspiring presence of a population which has been sanctified by sacrifice and by suffering.

Have no fears about France. The British and the French armies, for three long years, have withstood the greatest military machine ever contrived in the history of man. Day by day they have battled back this conscienceless invader, who has not stopped at any violation of the customary rules of lawful warfare, or of the principles of humanity. They have held the Germans and now there is a gathering of the forces from the great, free peoples of the world; Great Britain is strengthening her forces; France is strengthening hers; Italy is strengthening hers and a panoramic stream of ships across the Atlantic is carrying you and your fellows, until the allied army is becoming triumphantly superior in numbers and in force.

You are going to have the great privilege of seeing the final vindication of right on the very frontiers of freedom.

When you get there you will see a country in which the invader has destroyed homes and churches. You will see great stretches of the country a desolation and a ruin. Wherever the German has been able to go or reach with his destructive implements, he has utterly destroyed; and back of that line you will find the people of France, after three years of suffering, every woman in that nation in black, every mother in that nation made motherless of some of her sons by the sacrifices which this cause has demanded. You will find all scattered through France men, women, and children who have been driven out of their homes, and it is your high privilege and calling to take those exiled families and to lead them back to the homes from which they have been driven, to place them again on the soil of their birthplace, and to see France reconquered for liberty and rededicated to freedom. And when you have done that you will come home and all America will be waiting for you.

Young men, this is the great adventure. This is what youth is made for. This calls for and glorifies the qualities of youth.

The thing that distinguishes us, that makes this celebration of our Fourth of July an era in the history of the world, is that our army, young and brave and free, knows why it is entering this contest and realizes that the rescue of the principles of freedom and liberty, upon which our own country has in these years grown so great and so strong, counts more than life—counts more than any other thing—and that whatever the cost or sacrifice it must be made. It will not be long until you go. I wish you a safe journey across the seas, I wish you a full measure of the uplift and inspiration which comes from seeing this conflict in that great place. I envy you.

But those of us who must stay in this country, watching your progress, know in advance the heroism with which you will meet that struggle.

I bid you celebrate this Fourth of July. The God that rules nations made this nation, little and despised in 1776, grow great for this purpose and this mission. You are the emissaries of that nation. I bid you Godspeed.

AN ADDRESS BY GOVERNOR FRANK O. LOWDEN[25]

Delivered before the Sons in Service Organization, Highland Park, Illinois, August 10, 1918.

Mr. Chairman, ladies and gentlemen, particularly mothers and fathers of our soldier boys in camp, upon and across the seas, and the mothers and fathers of all who are yet to be called to the colors:

It is a very great pleasure to me to appear today at the first function of this kind of which I have heard—a reception to the fathers and mothers of our soldiers in the service. It is a great privilege, because I realize, as do you all, that lonely and sometimes dark hours come to the mother and to the father of the absent son, and I want to tell these fathers and mothers some of the things which ought to bring solace to their hearts, some of the things which make the rearing of those boys to have been infinitely worth your while.

When the boy is born, the parents begin at once to speculate upon what his future will be. If the little chap of twenty or twenty-five years ago learned to play with a mimic gun, we wondered if he would some day be a soldier, not that the mothers of America were rearing their boys to be soldiers, but they were rearing them to be men. Today, when the civilization of the world is threatened, to play a man's part means to take a place on the battle front of this, the greatest of all wars. That little boy, perchance, who twenty years ago loved to play with a toy gun, is now a soldier of an infantry organization abroad. Or, he may have preferred the tiny ship, and if so, today you may be thinking of that boy on one of our great men-of-war on some side of the sea. It is possible that he loved the locomotive. It is possible that all mechanical things appealed to his young fancy. If so, it may be that today that boy is a member of one of the great engineer organizations, which are accomplishing just as great wonders on the battle front as those other organizations which bear arms. But whatever the predilection of that child was and whatever, now that he is grown up, he is doing in this great world war, the parents may know that one of the questions which they asked themselves as the little chap first began to notice things, will he succeed in life, is answered; because I tell you, my friends, that if that

[25] From a manuscript copy in the possession of Governor Lowden.

little chap is now but twenty years old and is fighting for that flag and under that flag, he has already achieved a greater success and has already lived a more rounded and complete life than octogenarians in ordinary times.

It may be that the little fellow of twenty years ago took no particular interest in guns or ships or mechanical toys. It may be that he was a sort of a dreamer. It is possible that there flowered in his tender soul a gentle love for all good things. It may even be that that boy was chided by his schoolmates with being effeminate, because he did not love these other things; but if he was a dreamer, if he was gentle, because his mind was dwelling upon the gentler things of life, you may be sure he is in this war, in the very forefront of the battle, because that soul would know as it matured, that in this war which we are fighting today, all that every gentle soul of all the past has achieved for humanity, all the progress towards better, finer, more spiritual things that the centuries that lie this side of Calvary have brought, are in peril, and therefore the gentle dreamer of twenty years ago is somewhere at the battle front. Where, I do not know. He has only asked for that place, whether it is in the Young Men's Christian Association hut, whether it is with the Red Cross or whether it is in the battle line, he has asked only for that place where he could render the greatest service to humanity.

So, fathers and mothers of this beautiful north shore, I want you to reflect that however at times your hearts ache sorely because of the absence of those boys, I want you to take this comfort to yourselves, that those boys have answered and answered yes to the questions which in their earliest years you most often asked, will those boys lead useful lives. Because, as I said a moment ago, whatever the future may hold for them, or however brief their lives may be on the battle front, they have already lived a fuller and a completer life and to a nobler purpose than many long-lived generations of men in ordinary times.

I am going today to read to you from some of the letters that soldier boys have written to their homes. I have no doubt that many of you have received similar letters from your loved ones, if they have had time to write. I want to remind you, and this corroborates what Senator Parker told you, that the boys, not only the American boys, but the English and the Canadian boys and the French boys and the Australian boys, and the Italian boys are writing letters to their folks at home such as they would have been incapable of writing a few brief years ago. This also ought to be a comfort to your hearts. They are developing finer qualities than come in the ordinary times of peace. They are developing a finer religious sentiment than we have had. Not only is that true of our own boys, but France, which was becoming very rapidly at least an agnostic France, if not a godless France, France again under the influence of this war, has turned to her God. There is a revival of genuine religion in France such as had not been seen for a hundred and fifty years.

It may be, my friends, that we, too, before this war, were becoming very careless of the finer things of life. It may be that we too were becoming a materialistic nation. It may be that we needed to pass through the fiery furnace of war to purge us of our dross and give the spiritual forces within us a chance to come to life again. That may be the divine purpose of this awful war. Now, let me read you what some of these boys have said. Here is a letter from a boy of the 149th Field Artillery. That regiment belongs to the Rainbow Division and was recruited largely from Illinois men:

"My Mother: You have been so brave and wonderful in everything that this letter is very hard to write. The army idea of these letters is that the mothers need consolation. Now, I am not going to pretend that you want me to be here or that this is the place I most want to be, but I do know that my mother would not be satisfied to have her son any other place than where he is.

"I tell you when I get letters telling how well and happy you are looking and feeling, it makes me very proud of you and how can I crab or kick against my lot when you, who have the hardest burden of inaction and waiting to bear, are so brave."

Ah, that letter contains suggestions for us all. Let every one of these brave boys who is offering his all that our country may endure, feel from the tone of the letters which you write him that his mother, too, and his father, too, would not have their son any other place than where he is now. In that way, you help, as you could not help in any other way, these brave boys who are fighting our battle for us. Then when you write the boy, you tell him as this mother did, how well and happy you are and that everything goes well with you. When you write your boy that, it enables him, more than anything else you can do, to meet the stern duties of a soldier. I wish that every mother in this broad land might read this letter from one of our own 149th Field Artillery.

Now, here is another that came from an officer of the same division some months ago:

"No, dearest mother, there is something a great deal bigger than personal comfort and safety and affections concerned. I have had a big awakening over here, but I would not be anywhere else in the world just now had I the choice. It is patriotism, yet it is more than patriotism; it is pride, yet it is far more than pride. There is something at stake in this war bigger than the fate of the nation, even our own. It is a supreme test of might against right."

I want to ask you, how many boys of the carefree, thoughtless generation ago would have written letters like these? I want to ask you, how many men, engrossed in their own selfish gratification, living for pleasure alone, having reached the end of a dusty three-score years and ten, will have felt in all their lives as much generous, ennobling emotion as these boys expressed, who have but for a few brief months been at the battle front?

I want to tell you that this boy from whom I have last read, is right. It is something more than the love of his country involved; it is a pride, he says, and pride is a splendid quality of a soldier and of a civilian, when it is tempered by justice and mercy, but it is something more than pride. He says what I wish all our people at home could say one half as clearly and as well, that beneath all the outward seeming causes of this war, deep down, it is a war of righteousness against godlessness and injustice; that it is a war to preserve everything which all the good men of all the past have wearily and sometimes tearfully gained for the world. I wish that our people might know that if the ideas for which the Prussian autocracy stands today win, it doesn't matter what any of our ancestors in all our history have done for our beloved land. I wish our people might know that if this war goes against us, every noble emotion which has taken form for the benefit of civilization and the world from before the days of Calvary down, is lost, and that the world for another thou-

(23)

sand years at least will plunge again as it did once, into the dark ages, and that the black midnight of that time will have reappeared.

I wish our people might know, as this boy knows, that it is something deeper than even the welfare of our own land, because in all the history of time, there never was a war with the issues so clear and with the issues so vast as this war, fathers and mothers, in which your sons are fighting today. Don't forget that they too have a precious privilege. Don't forget that when this war is over and peace, a peace which shall endure, shall have come again, that these boys, most of whom will return, as statistics show, will have lived through the greatest event of all the years and we who have remained at home will then be the ones who will be entitled to sympathy. That also ought to be some comfort to you. If you will take to your hearts the spirit of this last letter, if you will learn what that youngster of that regiment has learned, that all that is fine, that all that is precious, and dear, that all the nobler and more spiritual things which have blessed mankind are involved in this war, you will thank God that you had a son or two sons or three sons to give to civilization.

Let me remind you of another thing. While our soldiers have gained in the finer things, the Prussian soldiers, the soldiers of autocracy, have gone the other way. Let me tell you the significance of that. Germany began to teach half a century ago that the state can do no wrong, that it is above all moral law, that it is not bound by any of the ethical notions which control individuals in their relations to one another. One of the consequences of that doctrine, which even she did not foresee, is that a nation cannot deny the obligation of moral law without all her people sinking down. One of the consequences is that her newspapers are now complaining everywhere that crime has never been as prevalent in the German centers as today; the increase is appalling indeed. You can't educate your people to believe that the state is above the moral law and still have your people obey the moral law. You can't serve a state that is unjust, you can't serve a state that breaks its plighted word, you can't serve a state that teaches that in war cruelty is permissible if it only helps achieve your end, without the people of the state also becoming false to their plighted word, without their also becoming cruel and relentless, without their also falling into the practices of crime. You can't have an immoral state and a moral people. You can't have a cruel state and a gentle, lovable people. Out of this war we have got to resolve that the state, at whatever cost, must observe in all its relations the moral law.

My friends, I have but a few more words to say, and then I shall close. I want to read from just one other letter which came to my attention. Before I do that, I wish to read to you what the *Deutsche Zeitung,* a leading paper of Berlin, has said recently on the subject of world conscience or world morality. "Away with 'world conscience'; enough of the world fraternity. The conscience of German power shall alone be our lord and master. Its motto is more power, more German Power—that is the legacy which our dead heroes have left us. See the letters of blood and fire; may the curse which arises from their graves fall upon those who trifle with that inheritance." That is the underlying inspiration of this war from the other side.

If this war shall go against us, we of America, just as much as those of Italy and Great Britain and France, will be under the iron heel of that military despotism which has forged and uttered this infamous denial of a God or of a moral law.

Now, let me come to the letter written by Lieutenant Newhall, of Minnesota, who resigned as instructor at Harvard University to go into the service. "Don't be unhappy, even if something happens to me. The Japanese point of view always appealed to me. They are proud when one of their relatives is lost in a patriotic struggle and put on festival clothes instead of going into mourning. I was pleased to see it suggested in the *Chicago Tribune* that we adopt the custom of wearing a badge, such as a star, instead of black. When we think of the bigness of the work at hand—and it is more than merely defeating Germany—any man can feel that even being killed is a small price to pay for having an active part in this great step forward, which the world is taking. It is the welding together of the liberty-loving peoples into a great coöperating society which is to be the triumph that will follow an Allied victory. The great weakness of our democracies has been that this liberty of which they were so boastful was a mere individualism which allowed every man to compete unscrupulously with all his neighbors. Now in the face of this German menace we are trying to learn how to curtail some of our individual 'liberties' in order to secure national unity. Germany and Japan have secured the spirit of coöperation through the action of autocracies. It is now for us to show that it can be achieved as well and in less dangerous form through democracy." And then to this honest soul comes this: "Perhaps it can't be. If that is so, it is better to be killed before that impossibility has been demonstrated. If it can be, then any one who contributes toward the achievement of that end can be proud in proportion to his contribution. Don't be anxious then. Be happy that I am over here as I am." Ah, that is the spirit. If we can't bring justice and victory and success through democracy, this young officer says, it is better to be killed than to survive the war.

As I look upon that service flag with its two hundred and seventy-one stars, two of which have already turned to gold, I want to say that if this war should go against us, they alone of all the people within your borders will have a right to peace and happiness and contentment. If this war should go against us, happy, infinitely happy, are the two represented upon that flag by golden stars, compared with all of us who survive the war; infinitely better off are they than we. . . .

So, fathers and mothers of these two hundred and seventy-one boys, I thank you, I thank you from the bottom of my heart, that you are making this contribution to the cause of humanity, to the cause of civilization. Illinois is celebrating her one hundredth year of statehood. Brilliant and splendid as are those hundred years, it is you, it is the mothers and the fathers of the boys of Illinois who are helping us in this hundredth anniversary of our statehood to be worthy of our mighty past, and so, with all my heart, I thank you again and again.

THIRD REGISTRATION UNDER THE SELECTIVE SERVICE ACT, SEPTEMBER 12, 1918— A PROCLAMATION

The President of the United States, by proclamation, has fixed September 12 for the registration throughout the United States of all men between the ages of eighteen and forty-five inclusive, for military service, except those who have already registered and those who are not required under the law so to do.

Under the authority vested in the President, it has been ordered that State headquarters, local boards and other officials of the State will hold themselves in readiness to proceed promptly with their work of registration on the date fixed.

Existing draft machinery will be used with such increased facilities and additional registrars as are required for this enrollment under the President's proclamation. The Governors of all states have been called upon to supervise this registration, and the Adjutant General, or Draft Executive, will, under this proclamation, be the central administrative authority. All local boards will have immediate direction and supervision within their respective jurisdiction. The actual registration will be made in the customary voting precincts within the jurisdiction of each board or in such other places as the local board having jurisdiction shall designate by public notice.

Rulings issued by the Provost Marshal General as to persons who are required to register under the act are as follows:

"All male persons who shall have attained their eighteenth birthday and shall not have attained their forty-sixth birthday on or before the day set for registration by the President must register. The only exceptions are:

"(A) Persons, who, prior to the day set for registration by the President, have registered under the terms of the act approved May 18, 1917, (which fixed the original age limits at 21 to 30 inclusive) or under the terms of the Public Resolution of Congress approved May 20, 1918, providing for the registration since June 5, 1917, of those reaching the age of 21 years, whether called for public service or not; and

"(B) Officers and enlisted men of the regular army; officers appointed, and men of forces drafted. Under the provisions of the act approved May 18, 1917; officers and enlisted men of the National Guard while in the service of the United States, and the officers of the officers' reserve corps and enlisted men in the enlisted reserve corps while in the service of the United States; and

"(C) Officers and enlisted men of the navy and marine corps, and officers and enlisted and enrolled men of the naval reserve force and marine corps reserve while in the service of the United States; and

"(D) Diplomatic representatives; technical attachés of foreign embassies and legations; consul general; consuls and consular agents of foreign countries residing in the United States.

"Persons not subject to registration solely on account of being in the military or naval service of the United States become subject to registration, and are required to register, immediately upon leaving such military or naval service.

"Citizens of the United States, or persons who have declared their intention to become citizens of the United States, who do not register on account of absence from the territorial limits of the United States are required to register within five days after their return to the United States".

The regulations then warn registrants and all other persons charged with a knowledge of the regulations, that ignorance of the provisions will not excuse them.

"These regulations, it is set forth, have the force and effect of law, and all persons required by these regulations to be registered, and all persons who may claim any right or privilege in respect of any registrant, are charged with knowledge of the provisions hereof. Failure by any person required to be registered to perform any duty prescribed by these regulations is a misdemeanor, punishable by imprisonment for one year, and may result in the loss of valuable rights and privileges and an immediate induction into the military service".

Local police authorities in all parts of the country will cooperate with the Government in the enforcement of order on registration day. Regulations prescribed by the President and sent to draft officials of the various states, contain the following provisions:

"On the day set for registration all federal marshals, deputy marshals and investigating agents, and all police officers—state, county, township, municipal, and town—of whatever grade or class, shall hold themselves in readiness to render whatever assistance may be necessary in preserving order at places of registration and in assisting in bringing about a complete registration.

"All marshals, deputy marshals, investigating agents, and police officers shall examine the registration lists and report without delay to the local boards the names of any persons known by them to have failed to register themselves when liable to registration; and it shall be the duty of local boards to report to the proper United States District Attorney all cases coming to their attention of persons who have failed to present themselves for registration as required by law.

"Police officers may require any person subject to registration to exhibit his registration certificate.

"In every case in which a duly designated officer or agent refuses or fails to act, the Governor, Adjutant General, or member of a local board will proceed at once to name another officer or agent for such duty, and will bring the fact of such refusal or failure, and the circumstances connected therewith, to the attention of the proper United States District Attorney, with a view to the institution of prosecution of such officer or agent, as provided in Section 6 of the Act approved May 18, 1917".

It is essential that the people of this State shall accord the fullest measure of cooperation in the carrying out of this order. Ignorance of the law, and of regulations issued by proper authority under the law, excuses no one. All persons on the border line of the age of registration will be required to give adequate proof that they are outside of the age limit specified. The penalty failure to register is one year's imprisonment, and no man can exonerate himself by the payment of a fine.

GIVEN UNDER MY HAND AND THE GREAT SEAL OF STATE AT THE CAPITOL IN SPRINGFIELD, THIS FOURTH DAY OF SEPTEMBER, IN THE YEAR OF OUR LORD ONE THOUSAND NINE HUNDRED AND EIGHTEEN, AND OF THE INDEPENDENCE OF THE UNITED STATES THE ONE HUNDRED AND FORTY-THIRD.

(SEAL)

FRANK O. LOWDEN

By the Governor:

LOUIS L. EMMERSON
    Secretary of State.

IV. PRESERVING LAW AND ORDER IN THE STATE

NEED OF AN ORGANIZATION FOR HOME DEFENSE

Resolutions adopted at a meeting of the State Council of Defense of Illinois, May 19, 1917.[1]

It is the sense of this Council that during the existence of the war the State of Illinois be provided as soon as possible with a home guard to act as an internal defense body that can be officially called on at all times by the Governor of the State for local defense and protection, said home guard to be governed as far as practicable by rules and regulations similar to those which control the militia of the State when in the service of the State.

STATE MILITARY AND NAVAL CODE—ACT OF 1909 AMENDED

Senate Bill Number 592, Fiftieth General Assembly of the State of Illinois.

AN ACT *to amend section 4 of Article 16 of "An Act to establish a military and naval code for the State of Illinois, and to repeal all Acts in conflict therewith" approved June 10, 1909, in force July 1, 1909.*

SECTION 1. *Be it enacted by the People of the State of Illinois, represented in the General Assembly:* That section four (4) of an Act entitled "An Act to establish a Military and Naval Code for the State of Illinois, and to repeal all Acts in conflict therewith" approved June 10, 1909, in force July 1, 1909, being the same and is hereby amended to read as follows:

§ 4. Enlisted men of the National Guard and Naval Reserve shall receive per day, for services actually performed when on active service for suppression of riot and for the enforcement of the laws, according to their respective grades as follows:

[1] Minutes of the meeting of the State Council of Defense, May 19, 1917.

a. Sergeants major, quartermaster, commissary and ordnance sergeants, of or attached to the division, brigades, regiments or separate battalions; first class signal and hospital corps sergeants, chief trumpeters and principal musicians, first sergeants and company quartermaster sergeants, drum majors and color sergeants in the National Guard, and chief petty officers and petty officers, first class in the seaman branch of the Naval Reserve, $2.75.

b. Battalion sergeants major and trumpeter sergeants, chief mechanics of batteries, sergeants of the hospital and signal corps, and of the line in the National Guard, petty officers, first class except in the seaman branch, and petty officers, second class, in the Naval Reserve, $2.60.

c. Corporals cooks, musicians and mechanics in the National Guard and petty officers, third class, and buglers, in the Naval Reserve $2.25.

d. Privates and seamen, all grades $2.00, *Provided* that from and after the passage of this Act and until the determination of the National emergency as set forth in the Act of Congress entitled "An Act to authorize the President to increase temporarily the military establishment of the United States," approved by President, May 18, 1917, the pay of enlisted men of the National Guard and Naval Militia while in active service of the State shall be at the rate of $1.00 per day.

§ 2. WHEREAS an emergency exists, this law shall take effect from and after its passage and approval.

APPROVED June 25, 1917.

STATE MILITARY AND NAVAL CODE— RESERVE MILITIA

Senate Bill Number 589, Fiftieth General Assembly of the State of Illinois.

AN ACT *to provide for the organization of reserve militia from the unorganized militia of the State.*

SECTION 1. *Be it enacted by the People of the State of Illinois, represented in the General Assembly:* That whenever the Governor as Commander-in-Chief of the military and naval forces of the State, shall deem it necessary or advisable for the purpose of executing the laws of the State, or of preventing the actual or threatened violation thereof, or any other emergency or suppressing actual or threatened insurrection or riots, or when the nation is at war and a requisition or order has been made, or is likely to be made, by the President of the United States calling the National Guard, or parts thereof, into the national service, he may issue a proclamation or call for volunteer companies, battalions, regiments, brigades, or other units of land forces to be known as the Reserve Militia which shall be formed from and out of the unorganized militia of the State.

§ 2. The Governor shall determine and shall fix in any such proclamation or call the number of such volunteers, their term of enlistment, and the kind and number of such units to be called for and organized, and he shall appoint and authorize officers to recruit and enroll such volunteers under such rules and regulations as shall be fixed and promulgated by the Adjutant General with the approval of the Governor: *Provided,* that no such term of enlistment shall be for a longer term than two years; *And, provided further,* that any and all such units may be disbanded or mustered out, and any or all of such volunteers may be discharged, when in the judgment of the Governor the emergency or the conditions making such organizations necessary or advisable shall have passed or changed.

§ 3. Every person so enrolling or enlisting in the reserve militia shall sign an enlistment paper in the form prescribed by the Adjutant General and shall take the following oath or affirmation, which may be administered by any such duly appointed recruiting or enrolling officer or any commissioned officer in the reserve militia:

"I do solemnly swear (or affirm) that I will true allegiance bear to the State of Illinois, and that I will uphold its Constitution and laws and will serve it faithfully; that I will obey orders of the Commander-in-Chief and of such officers as may be placed over me, and the laws, rules and regulations of the reserve militia, so help me God."

§ 4. The Governor, as Commander-in-Chief, shall make all appointments to commissioned rank in the Reserve Militia. Commissions evidencing all appointments shall be signed by the Governor and shall be attested and issued by the Adjutant General. All non-commissioned and petty officers shall be appointed in accordance with the rules and regulations promulgated by the Adjutant General.

Commissions to officers shall read to a certain grade in a given regiment, battalion, company or other unit of the reserve militia, and assignment of such officers to duty in any unit shall be by the Commander-in-Chief. The validity of all commissions shall be subject to formal acceptance and the execution of oath prescribed by law or by the rules and regulations promulgated by the Adjutant General.

§ 5. Each and every enrolled man who shall leave or sever his connection with the reserve militia shall be entitled to and shall receive a discharge in accordance with the rules and regulations to be promulgated by the Adjutant General with the approval of the Governor, and such rules and regulations shall provide the conditions and circumstances under which he may leave, retire from, or be discharged from the reserve militia.

§ 6. The organization, equipment and maintenance of the reserve militia shall be without expense to the State:

Provided, that if the Governor, as Commander-in-Chief, shall call the reserve militia, or any part thereof, into the actual service of the State, or to assemble in State or district encampments for the purpose of drill, discipline and increase of efficiency, the State shall pay the cost of travel and maintenance and shall pay the officers at the rate which is now or hereafter may be allowed to the officers in the National Guard, while in similar service of the State, and the enlisted men while in the actual service of the State shall receive pay at the rate of one dollar per day.

§ 7. The uniforms, arms and other equipment of the reserve militia, the minimum number of meetings for instruction, drill and training of the various units thereof, the character of such instruction and training, and all other matters and things necessary or desirable for the complete organization, equipment, discipline and efficiency of the reserve militia, not otherwise provided for and covered in this Act, shall be prescribed and carried into effect by and through rules and regulations promulgated by the Adjutant General and approved by the Governor.

§ 8. WHEREAS, an emergency exists, this law shall take effect from and after its passage and approval.

APPROVED June 25, 1917.

CALL FOR 6,000 VOLUNTEERS TO ILLINOIS RESERVE MILITIA—A PROCLAMATION

WHEREAS, The General Assembly of the State of Illinois, by an Act entitled "An Act to provide for the organization of Reserve Militia from the unorganized Militia of the State" approved June 25, 1917, authorized "that whenever the Governor as Commander-in-Chief of the Military and Naval forces of the State, shall deem it necessary or advisable for the purpose of executing the laws of the State, or of preventing the actual or threatened violation thereof, or any other emergency or suppressing actual or threatened insurrection or riots, or when the Nation is at war and a requisition or order has been made, or is likely to be made, by the President of the United States, calling the National Guard, or parts thereof into the National Service, he may issue a proclamation or call for volunteer companies, battalions, regiments, brigades, or other units of land forces to be known as the Reserve Militia which shall be formed from and out of the unorganized Militia of the State," and

WHEREAS, said Act provides further for the organization and control of said Reserve Militia, and

WHEREAS, the President of the United States has called the National Guard and all parts thereof into the National Service that were eligible thereto, and

WHEREAS, it appears to the Governor as Commander-in-Chief of the Military and Naval Forces of the State that it is necessary and advisable for the purpose of executing the laws of the State preventing the actual or any threatened violation thereof that may arise and for the purpose of meeting any emergency and suppression of actual or threatened insurrection that may occur.

NOW, THEREFORE, I, Frank O. Lowden, Governor of the State of Illinois, as Commander-in-Chief of the Military and Naval Forces thereof, do hereby issue my proclamation or call for six thousand volunteers in such Reserve Militia, their term of enlistment to be for two years, such volunteers to be composed of companies, battalions, regiments and brigade formations with their appropriate commissioned and enlisted personnel as shall be prescribed in rules and regulations promulgated by The Adjutant General and approved by the Governor. And I further authorize by future appointment, through proper military channels, officers authorized to recruit, enroll and enlist such volunteers under such rules and regulations as shall be fixed and promulgated by The Adjutant General with the approval of the Governor, and I further authorize the enrollment and enlistment of the units of the State Council of Defense Training Corps as may be by the State Council of Defense tendered to The Adjutant General and approved by him for such service, all said forces to be regulated and controlled by said Act of the General Assembly and the general military laws of the State of Illinois.

GIVEN UNDER MY HAND AND THE GREAT SEAL OF STATE AT THE CAPITOL IN SPRINGFIELD, THIS NINETEENTH DAY OF SEPTEMBER, IN THE YEAR OF OUR LORD ONE THOUSAND NINE HUNDRED AND SEVENTEEN, AND OF THE INDEPENDENCE OF THE UNITED STATES THE ONE HUNDRED AND FORTY-SECOND.

(SEAL)

FRANK O. LOWDEN

By the Governor:
LOUIS L. EMMERSON.
    Secretary of State.

CALL FOR 11,000 VOLUNTEERS TO ILLINOIS RESERVE MILITIA—A PROCLAMATION

WHEREAS, The General Assembly of the State of Illinois, by an Act entitled "An Act to provide for the organization of Reserve Militia from the unorganized Militia of the State" approved June 25, 1917, authorized "that whenever the Governor as Commander-in-Chief of the Military and Naval forces of the State, shall deem it necessary or advisable for the purpose of executing the Laws of the State, or of preventing the actual or threatened violation thereof, or any other emergency or suppressing actual or threatened insurrection or riots, or when the Nation is at War and a requisition or order has been made, or is likely to be made, by the President of the United States, calling the National Guard, or parts thereof into the National Service, he may issue a proclamation or call for volunteer companies, battalions, regiments, brigades, or other units of land forces to be known as the Reserve Militia which shall be formed from and out of the unorganized Militia of the State," and

WHEREAS, said Act provides further for the organization and control of said Reserve Militia, and

WHEREAS, the President of the United States has called the National Guard and all parts thereof into the National Service that were eligible thereto, and

WHEREAS, it appears to the Governor as Commander-in-Chief of the Military and Naval Forces of the State that it is necessary and advisable for the purpose of executing the laws of the State and of preventing the actual or any threatened violation thereof that may arise and for the purpose of meeting any emergency and suppression of actual or threatened insurrection that may occur that an increment of the Militia Reserve in addition to that created by proclamation of date the Nineteenth Day of September, A. D., One Thousand Nine Hundred and Seventeen, should be created,

NOW, THEREFORE, I, Frank O. Lowden, Governor of the State of Illinois, as Commander-in-Chief of the Military and Naval Forces thereof, do hereby issue my proclamation or call for eleven thousand additional volunteers in such Reserve Militia, their term of enlistment to be for two years, such volunteers to be composed of companies, battalions, regiments and brigade formations with their appropriate commissioned and enlisted personnel as shall be prescribed in rules and regulations promulgated by The Adjutant General and approved by the Governor. And I further authorize by future appointment, through proper military channels, officers authorized to recruit, enroll and enlist such volunteers under such rules and regulations as shall be fixed and promulgated by The Adjutant General with the approval of the Governor, and I further authorize the enrollment and enlistment of the units of the State Council of Defense Training Corps as may be by the State Council of Defense tendered to The Adjutant General and approved by him for such service, all said forces to be regulated and controlled by said Act of the General Assembly and the general military laws of the State of Illinois.

(SEAL)

GIVEN UNDER MY HAND AND THE GREAT SEAL OF STATE AT THE CAPITOL IN SPRINGFIELD, THIS FOURTH DAY OF MARCH, IN THE YEAR OF OUR LORD ONE THOUSAND NINE HUNDRED AND EIGHTEEN, AND OF THE INDEPENDENCE OF THE UNITED STATES THE ONE HUNDRED AND FORTY-SECOND.

FRANK O. LOWDEN

By the Governor:
    LOUIS L. EMMERSON.
        Secretary of State.

STATE COUNCIL OF DEFENSE VOLUNTEER TRAINING CORPS

Circular Number 1 issued by the Committee on Military Affairs, State and Local Defense, State Council of Defense of Illinois.

1.—This organization shall be known as the State Council of Defense Volunteer Training Corps. Its object shall be:

A—The security of the State by cooperating with the military and police authorities in guarding bridges, public buildings and industrial plants, patrolling towns, surrounding country, rivers, harbors, etc., and in general act as an emergency body.

B—To assist in carrying out the object sought in the formation of the State Council of Defense.

C—The encouragement of recruiting in the regular service and the National Guard, and the Volunteer Army, Navy and Marine Corps of the United States and the assistance in the preparation of men subject to the selective draft, the dissemination of military knowledge and for the general upbuilding of the physical character of the citizens of the State.

2.—No city or town shall be recognized as a post of the State Council of Defense Volunteer Training Corps which does not organize and maintain at least one company of the minimum strength of 1 captain, 1 first lieutenant, 1 second lieutenant, 4 sergeants, 8 corporals and 65 privates.

3.—The State Council of Defense may consolidate, transfer, muster out, disband, muster in new organizations to replace those mustered out or disbanded, and make such other changes in the organization of the Volunteer Training Corps as the best interests of the service may require. The Volunteer Training Corps in all of its units, divisions, branches and officers, shall, at all times, and in all respects, be subject to the control, direction and orders of the State Council of Defense.

4.—All units to be organized and operated under recognized military methods, except that local units will report direct to the Military Committee of the State Council of Defense, and the organization, discipline, government and equipment, as far as practicable, not in conflict with law, shall conform to the regulations, customs, and usages of the Army and Navy of the United States or of the regulations of the Illinois National Guard.

5.—The State Council of Defense shall appoint and commission, upon the recommendation of the Adjutant General, officers to command the various units of this organization, and shall reserve the right to accept resignations or vacate commissions, and may accept the officers and men of completely organized units, if such organizations meet with their approval.

6.—Any able-bodied man of good character, between the ages of 18 and 55, and who is a citizen of the United States, or has declared his intention to become such, may be enrolled in the State Council of Defense Volunteer Training Corps. Any person so enrolled may, if in good standing, the question of good standing to be determined by the commanding officer of the unit, resign from the State Training Corps.

7.—A man who has been dishonorably discharged from any military or naval organization of this State or of the United States, shall not be eligible for enrollment, unless such dishonorable discharge shall have been removed by competent authority.

8.—In the formation of the Reserve Militia authorized by law, the State Council of Defense Training Corps units will be given preference by the Commander-in-Chief.

9.—Units must drill not less than one period of two hours per week and must maintain an average attendance of not less than 60 per cent. Failure to maintain this average may cause the disbandment of the organization by the Military Committee of the State Council of Defense.

10.—A distinctive uniform will be adopted, which shall consist of campaign hat, breeches, blouse, leggings and shirt.

11.—The organization, equipment and maintenance of the Training Corps shall be without expense to the State Council of Defense.

12.—The State Council of Defense may give to each man in the service an appropriate decoration which he shall wear at all times when in uniform and at such other times as he may wish. Such decoration to consist of the Seal of the State Council of Defense surrounded by the words "The State Council of Defense Training

Corps," to be made of such suitable material as the State Council of Defense shall decide. Upon determination of service and upon the receipt of an honorable discharge, such decoration shall become the personal property of such man.

13.—No military organization other than the Council of Defense Training Corps will be recognized by the State or allowed to drill in uniform or use arms, except such organizations as are now, or may be hereinafter recognized by law.

14.—Local committees of citizens may be organized to assist financially and otherwise in the carrying out of these plans. Service in the corps does not carry any other responsibility than state-wide service within the State of Illinois under order of the State Council of Defense.

15.—The only punishment for disobedience or infraction of discipline shall be dishonorable discharge from the service and publication of such discharge.

16.—No remuneration shall be paid to any officer or private of this organization, except such men as the State Council of Defense may decide necessary to the carrying out of its plans.

17.—The State Council of Defense will recognize as many units formed in the same territorial or municipal division as may comply with these rules and the orders of the State Council of Defense.

18.—All requests for approval of the formation of units shall be addressed to John G. Oglesby, Chairman of the Military Committee, State Capitol, Springfield, Illinois.

By direction of the State Council of Defense.

JOHN G. OGLESBY,
Chairman, Military Committee.

APPROVED:

SAMUEL INSULL,
Chairman, State Council of Defense.

PENALTIES FOR DESTRUCTION OF MUNITIONS PLANTS, ARMORIES, ETC.

House Bill Number 874, Fiftieth General Assembly, State of Illinois.

An Act *to amend an Act entitled, "An Act to revise the law in relation to criminal jurisprudence," approved March 27, 1874, in force July 1, 1874, as subsequently amended, by adding thereto three new sections, to be known as sections 54o, 185e and 188a.*

Section 1. *Be it enacted by the People of the State of Illinois, represented in the General Assembly:* That an Act entitled, "An Act to revise the law in relation to criminal jurisprudence," approved March 27, 1874, in force July 1, 1874, as subsequently amended, be, and the same is hereby amended, by adding thereto, three new sections, to be known as sections 54o, 185e and 188a, to read as follows:

§ 54o. Any person who shall by means of dynamite, giant powder or other explosives, or by the ignition of explosives contained in any powder magazine, mill or manufactory, or any munitions plant, fort, armory or arsenal, explode, burn or otherwise injure or damage any powder magazine, mill or manufactory, or any munitions plant, fort, armory or arsenal, shall be guilty of a felony, and on conviction thereof, if any death shall result from such explosion, damage or injury, shall suffer the punishment of death or imprisonment in the penitentiary for his natural life or for a term not less than fourteen years; and if no death shall result, such person shall be punished by imprisonment in the penitentiary for a term not exceeding twenty-five years nor less than ten years. If the accused is found guilty by a jury, they shall fix the punishment by their verdict. Upon a plea of guilty, the punishment shall be fixed by the court.

§ 185e. Any person who shall destroy, damage or injure, or render unusable, any gas, electric, telegraph or telephone plants, or interfere with the conveyance of transmission of the product thereof, may, upon conviction, be punished by a fine of not less than one hundred dollars ($100), nor more than five thousand dollars ($5,000) or by imprisonment in the penitentiary for not less than one (1) year, nor more than five (5) years.

§ 188a. Any person who shall interfere with, damage or injure any source of supply for water, food or provisions for troops in the employment of the State or of the United States, shall be punished by a fine of not less than one hundred dollars ($100), nor more than five thousand dollars ($5,000), and imprisonment in the penitentiary not less than one year nor more than twenty years.

§ 2. WHEREAS, an emergency exists, therefore this act shall take effect from and after its passage and approval.

APPROVED June 26, 1915 [1917].

EAST ST. LOUIS RIOTS

Resolutions adopted by a citizens' committee at a meeting called by the East St. Louis Chamber of Commerce, July 6, 1917.[2]

WHEREAS, Riots have occurred which have appalled our good citizens and brought shame and disgrace to our city and done incalculable injury to the prosperity and future welfare of the city; and

WHEREAS, These riots and unlawful acts attending them have brought upon us the severest condemnation from the entire country; and

WHEREAS, There is a feeling among our own citizens that there may be a recurrence of these tragedies, and this feeling is retarding the resumption of normal conditions; and

WHEREAS, We believe it is necessary that the law-abiding citizens of East St. Louis take such action as will reinstate us in the good opinion of our neighbors and friends, and to assure the entire country that steps will be immediately taken for the enforcement of the law and the preservation of life and property, and that assurance be given to all of our law-abiding citizens, irrespective of race or condition, that in the future they will be absolutely secure in our midst:

Therefore, the following declaration is promulgated:

We, the citizens of East St. Louis, who are in favor of law and

---

[2] *Chicago Tribune,* July 7, 1917. Prosecutions growing out of the riots which occurred in East St. Louis on July 2, 1917, were directed by the Attorney General of Illinois, Edward J. Brundage. One hundred forty-four indictments were returned by the grand jury. Upon trial fourteen of those indicted were convicted of murder.

order and the protection of life and property, in a meeting assembled, declare that:

First. Without undertaking to specifically account for the recent riots, it is necessary to state briefly what has occurred. About a month ago a riot took place, in which a number of citizens, under the pretext of driving from the city all colored people located here, marched down our streets and assaulted every colored person that came in their way, and it so happened that nearly all of the Negroes assaulted were of our old-time citizens and most of them law-abiding people.

A number of vicious and lawless Negroes took advantage of the excitement brought about by this riot, and, under their leadership and impassionate plea for revenge, the worst element began to organize and arm themselves for this purpose, and on Sunday evening, July 1, when it was reported among them that some one was riding through the southern portion of the city, shooting into their homes, this lawless and armed band met at a late hour of the night in one of their churches on an agreed signal given.

When the police officers learned that the Negroes were assembling in the church, believing that a riot was likely to start, a number of officers were sent to dispel them, and as they reached the church these officers, without any warning, were fired upon and two of them murdered. This greatly aroused the white people and was the immediate cause of the riot July 2, in which so many people lost their lives and so much property was destroyed.

Second. We, in the most emphatic terms, condemn the action of the rioters in the latter part of May. By their action they were defying the law and were administering punishment to innocent and unoffending people.

In the same manner we condemn the action of the lawless and savage Negroes, who, on Sunday night, July 1, armed themselves for the purpose of committing deliberate murder, and who carried out these intentions by killing two of the officers of the city.

We are at a loss to find language to express our indignation concerning the action of the rioters on July 2; their unwarranted acts stand without a parallel in the history of our country. These rioters, without the slightest effort to discover the persons who had murdered the East St. Louis officers, directed their wrath against colored people who they knew had nothing to do with the murder. They in the most savage and brutal manner set fire to their homes and shot them down as they were fleeing for their lives. Some were not permitted to escape and lost their lives in the flames of their burning homes.

Third. We believe that the principal cause of this riotous conduct was the laxity in the punishment of crime that has prevailed for some time past. On account of this indisposition to punish crime there has grown up in our midst irreverence for the law that has brought about the harvest that we have just reaped.

Many criminals, both black and white, have found a congenial home in our city and have carried on their criminal acts without the slightest fear of the pains and penalties of the law. For all of this the police department of our city and those officials charged with the conservation of the law are the most to blame. They have not taken the step that should have been taken to rid our city of this lawless element, and they are to be condemned in the severest terms for the helpless and inefficient manner in which they permitted these disgraceful riots to take place in our city.

We believe that this is largely due not from [to] a disposition upon the part of our various police officers to fail to enforce the law, but from [to] a lack of an organization and understanding on the part of the head of the police department that all violators of the law, irrespective of race, politics, conditions, or associations, should be apprehended and punished.

While we commend the action of Adjt. Gen. Dickson for the able and efficient manner in which he and the men under his direction are handling the present situation, and for which we feel extremely grateful, we must condemn the action of the militia who were in our city on the second day of July pretending to give to the city aid, but who were wholly inactive and in some instances aiding and abetting the rioters.

It is said that a municipality usually receives the government that it merits. We believe that the good people of the city of East St. Louis are not without blame for the terrible experiences through which they have just passed, they have not been ignorant of the reign of crime that has been going on in the city, and the failure on the part of the police officers and other officials to punish offenders, and yet they have been so engrossed in their individual affairs that they have entirely overlooked and neglected to perform a public duty, and it has taken this terrible tragedy to arouse them to a sense of the responsibility they are under to the community in which they live.

Fourth. The good people demand that our city be rid of the criminal class that has recently infested it, that the law be strictly enforced without fear or favor, and that there be no influence in the city that can screen or immune any offender, that all law-abiding persons in our city, be they ever so humble, white or black, rich or poor, be absolutely secure in their lives, property, and the pursuit of happiness; that all persons, hereafter, who have a grievance, be it real or imaginary, must resort to the law for redress, and we pledge that we will see that nothing be spared to punish persons, white or black, who attempt to take the law into their own hands.

Fifth. We demand that the police department of the city be reorganized upon such a basis that the law will be enforced as here-inabove stated. And we pledge to the mayor our entire support in so reorganizing the police department of our city and in bringing about every reform that tends to peace and good order.

Sixth. We demand that every effort possible be put forth to punish the persons who murdered the officers Sunday night, July 1, and to punish all of the persons guilty of murder, and arson and assaults on Monday, July 2.

RELIEF—EAST ST. LOUIS RIOTS

House Bill Number 380, Fifty-first General Assembly.

AN ACT *making an appropriation to reimburse and pay to certain persons, firms and corporations the sums of money paid out and advanced by them to defray the expenses of gathering evidence and defraying the expenses of prosecuting persons who committed crimes on July 2, 1917, in St. Clair County, Illinois.*

WHEREAS, On July 2, 1917, a race riot occurred between members of the white race and members of the colored race in East St.

Louis, St. Clair County, Illinois, in which many scores of people lost their lives and many scores of buildings were burned by incendiary fires; and,

WHEREAS, It became important that those who committed crimes in connection with said East St. Louis riot should be prosecuted and punished under the criminal laws of this State for the purpose of bringing about a reign of law and order in St. Clair County and act as a deterrent to others; and,

WHEREAS, The county officials of St. Clair County and the city officials of East St. Louis were not equipped to handle the vast amount of work necessary to be done to bring about successful prosecutions of those who committed crimes in connection with said riot; and,

WHEREAS, Said riot having taken place subsequent to the adjournment of the Fiftieth General Assembly and there having been no appropriation made to the department of the Attorney General of Illinois to handle this extra expense; and,

WHEREAS, Divers persons, firms and corporations subscribed and paid $27,550 toward the expense of gathering evidence and the general expenses incurred in the prosecution of crimes committed on July 2, 1917, in the said East St. Louis riot; and,

WHEREAS, The said persons, firms and corporations should be reimbursed and paid the several sums of money which each of them contributed to the purposes aforesaid; therefore,

SECTION 1. *Be it enacted by the People of the State of Illinois, represented in the General Assembly:* That there is hereby appropriated to the several persons, firms and corporations hereinafter named, the sum of $27,550 or so much thereof as may be necessary to reimburse and pay to them the money advanced by each of them toward the payment of the expenses of collecting evidence and the expenses of the prosecution of crimes committed July 2, 1917 in St. Clair County, Illinois, in connection with the East St. Louis riot. There is hereby appropriated to each of the persons, firms and corporations hereinafter named the several sums set opposite the names of each of them, which said amounts represent the amount contributed by each of said persons, firms and corporations for the purposes aforesaid:

D. B. Beatty	$ 275.00
James W. McRoberts	275.00
D. E. Parsons	275.00
Dan McGlynn	275.00
R. R. Thomas	275.00
E. C. Kramer	416.66
Robert E. Gillespie	416.66
R. J. Kramer	416.66
Bruce A. Campbell	416.66
C. H. Way	416.66
J. F. Reid	416.66
Aluminum Ore Co.	2,500.00
Missouri Malleable Iron Co.	1,500.00
Geo. S. Mepham & Co.	250.00
General Chemical Co.	250.00
American Zinc Co.	750.00
Bell Telephone Co.	400.00
Certainteed Prod. Corp.	750.00
East St. Louis Railway Co.	500.00
East St. Louis & Suburban Railway Co.	250.00
B. Goedde & Co.	250.00
East St. Louis Light & Power Co.	250.00
Armour & Co.	1,875.00
Morris & Co.	1,875.00
St. Louis National Stock Yards	1,875.00
East St. Louis Cotton Oil Co.	750.00
Swift & Co.	1,875.00
St. Clair County Gas & Electric Co.	875.00
Hammar Bros. White Lead Co.	250.00
Grant Chemical Co.	125.00
East Side Packing Co.	500.00
Elliott Frog & Switch Co.	750.00
East St. Louis & Suburban Railway Co.	750.00
American Steel Foundries	1,875.00
Laclede Steel Co.	150.00
C. Reeb	250.00
H. Albrecht	250.00

M. V. Joyce	$ 250.00
F. E. Nulsen	250.00
C. E. Pope	250.00
Albert Diehm	250.00
H. M. Hill	250.00
John E. Hamlin	250.00
W. H. Hauss	250.00
N. C. McLean	250.00

§ 2. The Auditor of Public Accounts is hereby authorized and directed to draw his warrants and the State Treasurer is hereby directed to pay said warrants in favor of the several said persons, firms and corporations above named for the several amounts set opposite each of said names.

Filed July 11, 1919.

The Governor having failed to return this bill to the General Assembly during its session, and having failed to file it in my office, with his objections, within ten days after the adjournment of the General Assembly, it has thereby become a law.

Witness my hand this 11th day of July, A. D. 1919.

LOUIS L. EMMERSON, *Secretary of State.*

EXTRACT FROM AN ADDRESS BY GOVERNOR FRANK O. LOWDEN[3]

Delivered in Rock Island, Illinois, April 6, 1918.

.   .   .   .

Early yesterday morning, Robert Praeger was taken from the jail at Collinsville by a mob and hanged, because it was said of him that he was a traitor to his country, and possibly a spy.[4] Awful as those crimes are in my view of them, they neither excused nor palliated the action of this mob. Our boys upon the battle front are fighting to uphold the principle that men are capable of governing

[3] From a manuscript copy in the possession of Governor Lowden.

[4] The office of the Attorney General assisted in the prosecution of the twelve persons indicted for the murder of Robert Praeger. The trial lasted from May 13 to June 1, 1918. A verdict of "not guilty" was returned as to all defendants.

themselves. That principle involves the idea that in our form of government the law is supreme above all men and all things. That principle recognizes that in every form of government there is something sovereign. In a monarchy we call the thing supreme king or emperor; in a republic we call it law. And he who offers violence to the principle of law is as much an enemy to his country as though he would betray it in war. There is no place in all the world where news of this mob action at Collinsville, in this state— I say it with shame—will be so welcomed as at the court of Berlin. There is no place in all the world where they want to see the mob rule so much as our enemies of the Central Empires want to see it. Why, they have said for years that men are incapable of governing themselves, and now by every act like this we help them to prove the case they have charged against us. Even if Praeger be all he was charged, even if he be not only guilty of sedition, but if he be also a spy, Praeger could not have lived long enough to have done as much injury to his country as did the mob which lawlessly took his life. I hope that I can make myself clear upon this question, and I want to say to the people of Illinois that patriotism will not be permitted to be used as a cloak for crime in Illinois if I can help it.

The real patriot, the genuine patriot, holds his country too dear to wish to tarnish its name or injure its influence, and, whatever the provocation may be, the patriot whose boys are in the trenches of Europe fighting for the integrity of self-government, and the integrity of law and the rule of order will not for a moment injure that same cause at home by taking the law into his own hands or by violating that law in any way. What will it avail us if we win battles on the other side if democracy shall break down at home? What will it avail us to give these boys in a cause abroad if we shall lose that cause at home? The patriot will be regardful of his country's flag, because that flag is but an emblem of the purity and integrity of the law as such. The patriot will not only help in every way he can against our enemies, but he will help to strengthen, not weaken, the authority of that great republic, and he can only do that by yielding full allegiance to the law in all respects.

I do not for a moment mean to say that there has not been much provocation to lawless deeds of this kind. I have urged for months a more vigorous prosecution of those who are guilty of disloyal acts and words. I believe that we have been too lax. This is a matter for the federal government. Laws relating to sedition and treason must be uniform and can only be made effective if they are written upon the federal statute books. If the laws are not strong enough, and if that is the reason why there have not been more prosecutions, I am in favor of strengthening the laws. But whatever the defects in the laws, there is no warrant for anyone in Illinois or the United States of America, while this war is on, which threatens our very existence, in taking the law into his own hands, and he will not be permitted to do [so] if I can help it.

.   .   .   .

V. VISITS OF FOREIGN MISSIONS

INVITATION TO REPRESENTATIVES OF FRANCE AND GREAT BRITAIN TO VISIT SPRINGFIELD

Senate Joint Resolution Number 23, Fiftieth General Assembly, State of Illinois.

WHEREAS, Distinguished representatives of France and Great Britain are now visiting the United States;[1] and

WHEREAS: Springfield was the home and is the last resting place of the world renowned statesman and humanitarian, Abraham Lincoln, and is the capital city of the great commonwealth of Illinois;

Be it resolved: by the Senate of the State of Illinois, the House of Representatives concurring herein, That an invitation be extended to the representatives of France and Great Britain now upon a mission in the United States, and that they be urged to visit Springfield during their stay in the United States;

Resolved, further: That a joint committee of the Senate and the House be selected; the members of such committee from the Senate to be named by the President of the Senate, and those of the House to be named by the Speaker of the House, to extend this invitation and to arrange for the reception of the distinguished foreign representatives in the event of the acceptance of this invitation.

Adopted by the Senate, May 1, 1917.

Concurred in by the House of Representatives, May 1, 1917.

---

[1] After the United States declared war on Germany, England and France immediately sent special commissions to this country to discuss methods of coöperation. The British Commission, headed by Arthur J. Balfour, foreign minister, arrived in Washington on April 22 and visited only cities in the east. The French Mission, which arrived on April 25, 1917, left for a tour of the middle states on May 4, spent May 5 in Chicago, proceeded to St. Louis and Kansas City and returned by way of Springfield on May 7. The members of the French Mission and their party who visited Chicago and Springfield included the following: Former Premier René Viviani, minister of justice, head of the mission; General Joffre, marshal of France; Vice Admiral Chocheprat, senior vice admiral of the French Navy; Marquis de Chambrun, a member of the Chamber of Deputies and a lineal descendant of Marquis de LaFayette; Capt. George E. Simon, aid-de-camp of Admiral Chocheprat; Lieutenant Colonel Fabry, chief of staff; Lieutenant de Tossan, M. Hovelacque, inspector general of public instruction.

SPEECH BY MARSHAL JOFFRE, CHICAGO, MAY 5, 1917[2]

Marshal Joffre spoke in French and a translation was read to the audience by Charles G. Dawes, chairman of the meeting.

I am happy today to salute the city of Chicago in this assembly, where all classes of society are represented. This assembly reminds me of France at the moment of the declaration of war in the beginning of August, 1914. The Germans had assailed us in a brutal attack, hoping within a short time to destroy France by many barbarous blows.

The danger was caught in the act. All the French people ran to the border. The countrymen, the workingmen, all Frenchmen were standing at the border. The fight was hard, but at last we were successful and stopped them, and the battle of the Marne stopped them completely at the time.

We were in need of munitions. We were in need of guns and rifles. We have taken from among the ranks of the army all the special workmen to make guns, to make bullets also.

For months they have sought to benumb you by saying this was the war of capital. Workmen, this is untrue. The truth is that nothing so great as what is being done today has ever been seen in the world. The struggle is for democracy, the freedom, the salvation of the world.

Therefore, you will all arise to enter this war; you will come and avenge the soldiers of the Marne, who fell for right and justice, to avenge those who hoped to push back barbarism. Let us rendezvous on the fields of battle; there will we meet again the greatness of Washington.

I bring the greetings of the whole French army to the population of Chicago, and above all, to the workingmen of this city, among whom I am happy to find myself today.

All French workmen are mobilized and all are working heart and soul in the common cause. Each is accomplishing his duty in a victorious way. I am sure that all American workmen are one in heart with their brother workmen in France and are ready, like them, to fight for the final victory of democracy.

[2] *Chicago Tribune*, May 6, 1917.

We owe it to ourselves for humanity, for right, for peace, for liberty.

Long live France! Long live America! Long live liberty!

ADDRESS BY M. RENÉ VIVIANI, CHICAGO, MAY 5, 1917[3]

Citizens: I desire as my first word in entering this hall to salute the army and the navy, represented by the brothers of those who are already in France.

I want to thank and salute also in the name of the French laboring classes all the laboring classes I see before me here today who have quit their work to come here today to hear the word of France.

I salute all these workmen belonging to different races who have come to this wonderful country, America, Slavs, Russians, Greeks, brothers of those who work now for the independence and the emancipation of Russia, and all those who have come to present us this salute.

I want in the name of France to take advantage of the opportunity given me to answer one of the greatest calumnies which have been made against us, that for a few months we have tried to put you to sleep, making you believe that the actual war was a war of capital, that we were fighting to make money.

Do you think if it was true all your brothers would have rushed to the front to fight for the flag? Do you think the French laboring men and all the working classes would have taken the interest in it that they did take?

It is not a war of conquest. It is not a war where France and her allies wish to acquire territory. It is a war for humanity and democracy. That is why, in answer to the call of the speakers you have heard here belonging to your nation, you will stand together to enter this war to help France and her allies to fight to avenge the soldiers of the Marne who fought for right and justice.

You will come and join the ranks of the people who have fought for three years against Germany. All the citizens who are ready to fight for justice go to the battle fields of liberty.

[3] *Chicago Tribune*, May 6, 1917.

As one of the speakers a few moments ago said, no man has got the right to die for himself; no man has the right to live for himself. He owes his life to liberty and to democracy.

Vive l'Amérique! Vive la France!

RECEPTION OF FRENCH MISSION BY THE FIFTIETH GENERAL ASSEMBLY

House Joint Resolution Number 18. Fiftieth General Assembly, State of Illinois.

WHEREAS, The distinguished representatives of the French Government, now in this country, in their tour of the middle west, will visit the city of Springfield on Monday, May 7, 1917; and

WHEREAS, The General Assembly is desirous of extending to them the welcome and hospitality of the People of the State of Illinois; therefore be it

Resolved, by the House of Representatives, the Senate concurring herein, That the two Houses meet in joint session in the Hall of the House of Representatives at 2:00 o'clock P. M., on Monday, May 7, 1917, for the purpose of officially receiving the distinguished visitors.

Adopted by the House May 4, 1917.

Concurred in by the Senate May 7, 1917.

VISIT OF FRENCH MISSION TO SPRINGFIELD

Account of joint session of the House of Representatives and the Senate of the Fiftieth General Assembly, 2 P. M., May 7, 1917.[4]

The hour having arrived, the time heretofore fixed by Joint Resolution, adopted by the House of Representatives and the Senate, for the purpose of officially receiving and extending the welcome and hospitality of the people of the State of Illinois, to the distinguished representatives of the French Government.

The Senate, preceded by its President *pro tempore* and Secretary, appeared in the Hall of the House of Representatives, and, by direction of the Speaker, took the seats assigned them.

[4] *Journal of the House of Representatives of the Fiftieth General Assembly of the State of Illinois,* May 7, 1917, pages 871-874.

The two Houses being convened in Joint Session, the Speaker of the House of Representatives, as presiding officer, announced that a quorum of the Senate and House of Representatives being present, the Joint Session was duly convened.

The doorkeeper announced the presence, at the door of the House of Representatives, of the Joint Ceremonial Committee, who were admitted and assigned seats.

The Doorkeeper announced the presence of the Governor, Hon. Frank O. Lowden, the Lieutenant Governor, Hon. John G. Oglesby, and the distinguished representatives of France, who were received and escorted to the platform, where they were welcomed by the Speaker of the House of Representatives, Hon. David E. Shanahan, who spoke as follows:

THE SPEAKER. Premier Viviani, Marshal Joffre and associates, your Excellency, State officers, members of the General Assembly and invited guests.

This is indeed an important and happy occasion for the people of Illinois, for it brings to them, in their official home—the State Capitol—distinguished representatives of that historic country to which they are under immeasurable obligations. (Applause.)

To France we must look for our first European backgrounds.

French explorers were the first white men to traverse the wilderness which is now Illinois. The legendary visitation of the Spanish, if it occurred, left little or no mark upon this part of the world.

The saintly Father Marquette and his companion, the trader Joliet, were the real discoverers of the Mississippi Valley in 1673.

It was a French missionary priest who first preached the gospel of Christ and brought the message of salvation to the soil of Illinois.

The first teachers in Illinois were French.

The first attempts at Government were French.

The first Governor of this territory was French.

All the foundations of our civilization and Government are French.

Our earliest citizens and lawmakers were French.

The first settlements in Illinois, Cahokia and Kaskaskia, founded in 1699-1700, were made by the French.

(25)

The greatest fortification which the French Government ever constructed on the continent of North America was built in Illinois, Fort de Chartres, the site of which is now a State Park.

The fort was built under the direction of a French Engineer, Jean Baptiste Saucier, whose descendents are to-day honored citizens of this State.

In 1682 LaSalle took possession of the whole of the Mississippi Valley in the name of the King of France and in honor of whom he called the vast territory Louisiana.

Illinois was under French domination until the treaty of 1763, a period of over eighty years.

It is not necessary to speak of the invaluable assistance which France gave to the cause of the American colonies during the War for Independence nor of the services of the peerless LaFayette, a descendant of whom to-day honors us with his presence. (Applause.)

In 1825 when LaFayette was on his second visit to America this great soldier, the beloved friend and associate of Washington visited Illinois, then on the frontier of civilization.

Edward Coles, Governor at that time, had known the great LaFayette in Europe and it was probably through his influence that General LaFayette accepted the invitation to cross the rivers and mountains and visit the new State.

General LaFayette, with his son, George Washington LaFayette, visited Kaskaskia and Shawneetown. Our people gave them a royal reception, primitive though it was in those days.

Our history is filled with French names and records of French deeds.

In 1909 another great Frenchman visited this State and this city. He came then, as our visitors come to-day, to lay a wreath and pay tribute to the name and memory of the immortal Lincoln. (Applause.) The occasion was the one hundredth anniversary of the birth of that wonderful man. The whole country—the whole world—observed the anniversary; but Jean Jules Jusserand, the brilliant Ambassador for France to the United States—(applause)— the world-famed statesman and scholar, came to the city of Springfield to add his personal tribute of veneration to the memory of that great name; his eloquent and inspiring words are a part of the records of that historic occasion. He was a welcome, an honored guest, as are the distinguished visitors of to-day.

America can perhaps never fully repay to France its debt of obligation, but the United States and the State of Illinois appreciate the valor, generosity and heroism of the French people, past and present, and delight to honor their official representatives here present to-day.

I now have the pleasure of presenting His Excellency, Governor Frank O. Lowden, who will extend Illinois' greeting to the representatives of the Republic of France. (Applause.)

GOVERNOR FRANK O. LOWDEN. Premier Viviani, Marshal Joffre and other illustrious guests: Almost a century and a half ago we opened in this country the battle which is now pending in Europe, the battle of human liberty. (Applause.)

In the darkest day of our Revolutionary War, the emblem of France appeared on our coast, and we won that initial engagement by the help of France, and now the cause for which we then fought is making its last stand, not simply in America but around the world. (Applause.)

It is a great honor to have with us to-day, that distinguished statesman of France, who has a right to lay a wreath upon Lincoln's grave, because all his life has been given to the cause of humanity. (Applause.)

We welcome with more of emphasis than I can speak, that illustrious soldier, Marshal Joffre. (Applause.) Because his distinguishing qualities are the qualities that made deathless the fame of our own Ulysses S. Grant. (Applause.) Modesty, simplicity and invincibility, in the presence of the enemy. (Applause.)

It is my great pleasure to now present to you Marshal Joffre of our sister republic of France. (Extended applause.)

MARSHAL JOFFRE. I come here to represent France and the French army. For them I thank you. In their behalf and for this reception of their representatives, I salute the citizens of the State of Illinois and the city of Springfield.

GOVERNOR LOWDEN. And now it is my very great honor to introduce the illustrious statesman, Rene Viviani, and I hope that your reception will be an assurance to him that as the

French nation was in at the beginning of this battle for human liberty, America will be in with France at its close. (Extended applause.)

RENE VIVIANI. Before coming to this Chamber of the Legislature of Illinois, we went not far from here and entered into the Chamber of silence and deposited a wreath upon the tomb of the immortal Lincoln.

"The homage of the entire French nation comes with us. I wish you to understand that no matter how far it is from your city of Springfield to France, the vision of this splendid modern democracy is understood by the French people.

"You know that born of the people and with the most meager of opportunities, Lincoln arose by diligent study and through the virtue of his own native intelligence to become the Emancipator of all modern civilization, attaining his ends by plunging the nation into civil war after exerting every other means within his power.

"Lincoln knew the human conscience; that is the reason he is proclaimed immortal by the entire world. He accomplished this triumph for civilization, and although he is now in silence, by his triumphs and deeds he still lives in the memory of his people and of all people.

"But permit me to say with justice to all, that the French Revolution of 1848 also proclaimed the equality of men as well as did your own civil strife.

"Three years ago the government of the German Empire, without any motive or right whatever, violated the rights of men, plunging almost the entirety of Europe in strife and bloodshed. Despite the fact that France was taken unprepared and was confronted with what seemed unconquerable foes, she has withstood all attacks and has now conquered, at least, temporarily.

"The United States, this great republic of yours, sister to our own beloved France, is now face to face with the same crisis. We of the French republic and you in this great nation are now together in this great world war, this war for liberty which started with the French revolution and now is continuing to defend liberty and the rights of men from the onslaughts of Prussian autocracy.

"A few minutes ago when we heard the words of your Governor, we heard told the bonds which have formed an inseparable relationship between America and France. The first French to your shores came to discover the valley of the Mississippi and died in the land upon the boundaries of that great river. But they founded the first government here in that valley, and it is here that we see the domains of our ancestors.

"As the Governor has said, we will take back to France the duty of gratitude you owe to them. But it is not to France that you will owe this debt of gratitude, but to liberty and equality. And soon our children, the sons of France and the stalwart sons of America will both be fighting side by side to maintain this equality of men to uphold the cause of liberty and equality.

"We of the French mission take back with us a remembrance of you, and when we return to our country we will be asked what we have heard and seen. And we will answer that we have traveled through a great part of America and have been acclaimed everywhere for the sake of France.

"And now that you have joined us in this fight for freedom, you will, when this struggle is over with, have aided in liberating not only France but the whole world."

THE SPEAKER. The people of Illinois, Lincoln's Illinois, deeply appreciate the visit of these distinguished representatives of France, and the sweetest momento [sic] they can give to the hero of the Marne is the Stars and Stripes and the Tri-Color of France. (Applause.)

AN ADDRESS BY BORIS BAKHMETEFF, AMBASSADOR TO THE UNITED STATES FROM RUSSIA

Delivered at a gathering in Humboldt Park before the statue of Kosciusko on the occasion of the visit of the Russian Mission to Chicago, August 3, 1917.[5]

[5] *Chicago Tribune*, August 4, 1917.

The Russian Mission to the United States arrived in Washington on June 19, 1917, and on July 3 resolved itself into a permanent Russian embassy, M. Boris Bakhmeteff, the head of the mission, presenting his credentials as ambassador and continuing to act as director of the special technical and purchasing missions. Among the members of the Russian Mission who visited Chicago on August 3 were the following: Ambassador Bakhmeteff; Prof. George Lomonosoff, member of the Council of Engineers; Prof. Nicolai Borodine, representing the Ministry of Agriculture; M. Vladimir Novitzky, representing the Ministry of Finance; M. Soukine, representing the Ministry of Foreign Affairs; Colonel Oranovsky, Eugene Omeltchenko.

*Members of the Polish Committee, and you men and women of
    Poland:*

I have come here, to this monument of your national hero, to
bring to you the brotherly greeting from free Russia. I have come
to tell you that the Russian revolution is bringing Poland new life,
and a future of independent, free existence.

The old regime of oppression, of national hatred, and injustice
is broken. New relationships between nations are created, old in-
justices corrected, and scorned rights reëstablished.

Brethren Poles: The Russian people recognize the full right
of the brotherly Polish nation to determine its own fate with its own
will. The provisional government considers the creation of an independent Polish state, formed of all lands inhabited in great part by
Polish people, a sure pledge of a durable peace in future renewed
Europe.

Two events, the Russian revolution and the entrance of the
United States into war, have removed doubts, have made clear and
lucid the object and aims of the contest. It is the aim of the democracies of the world to create and establish the future life of nations on the basis of liberty, peaceful development, to exclude invasion, oppression, bloodshed; such life to give safety and independence
to all nations, based on the unquestionable right of each nation to
define its own destinies.

To realize such purposes, to make free and independent life of
nations really possible democracy must win; more so, democracy must
rule. It is the triumph of democracy that lies in the pledge of the
national independence of Poland. It is as well in the triumph of democracy that can be consolidated the achievements of the Russian
revolution. That is why I can say that our cause is common. The
freedom of Russia is the freedom of Poland, and the freedom of
Poland means democracy in Russia.

AN ADDRESS BY GOVERNOR FRANK O. LOWDEN[6]

Delivered at a meeting held under the auspices of the National Security League on the occasion of the visit of the Serbian Mission to Chicago, January 27, 1918.[7]

Mr. Chairman, Honored Guests, Ladies and Gentlemen:

It is a great honor to be here today. Illinois loves heroism. Illinois has shown its devotion to the ideals of democracy, and the greatest shrine erected to democracy in all the world is within the borders of Illinois, because that shrine is also a tomb, the tomb of Abraham Lincoln.

We know something of the superb history of Serbia; we know that for centuries she has stood as the sole defense against the Ottoman Empire, when it sought to conquer Europe. We know something of the tragedy of the far-off centuries. We remember the battle of Kossovo, in which Serbia alone, although it cost her her king, checked the advance of the Turks for almost a century into farther Europe, and that nation whose supreme tragedy has come within the last three years, appeals to us, appeals to us almost more than it is possible for anyone to say. So I am deeply moved when I look upon these young men in front of me, who are going back to vindicate the courage that their fathers showed; who are going back, not discouraged by that sad but heroic retreat of three months, which, when the history of this war is written, will be regarded as one of the most extraordinary military achievements of all time, because, in history, thank God, heroic retreats, in the cause of right, surpass forever victories of wrong and injustice. As you return to the land of your fathers, you take our wishes, our best wishes, and our blessings with

---

[6] From a manuscript copy in the possession of Governor Lowden.

[7] Serbia followed the example of England, France, Belgium and Russia in sending a special mission to the United States, which arrived in Washington on December 20, 1917. The members of the mission who visited Chicago were as follows: Dr. Milenko R. Vesnitch, Serbian envoy extraordinary and minister plenipotentiary to France, head of the mission; Dr. Sima Lozanitch, minister plenipotentiary at London; General Mihailo Rashitch, commander-in-chief, Serbian Corps d'Armée in France; Lt. Col. Mihailo Nenadovitch, military attaché at the Serbian legation in Switzerland; Capt. Milan Jovitchich, aid-de-camp to the crown prince; Vladislav Martinats, secretary to the Serbian legation at Paris; Col. Milan Pribichevitch, chief of the Serbian recruiting mission in the United States.

you. You will find many of your compatriots among kindred nations represented here today, fighting splendidly and heroically under our own flag, the Stars and Stripes. Whether they are fighting under the Serbian flag or under the Stars and Stripes or the Tri-Color of France or the Union Jack of England or the flag of Italy, they will be your comrades, my friends, because they will all, like you, be soldiers of liberty and humanity.

Our Prussian friends have had the audacity to speak of small countries as if in the march of events they were of no value. This great assemblage gives the lie to that infamous doctrine, which would result not only in the destruction of small nations but of all nations which do not yield to the supremacy of the cannon and the sword. This assemblage today shows how deathless is the national spirit, because you have responded, many of you, from lands which more than a century ago lost their independence and their freedom, but the national spirit is burning as bright in your hearts as though your old flag still floated above your land. May not all lovers of liberty everywhere join in the aspirations that have been uttered hereto and pray that in the infinite goodness of God, these nations, so long deprived of their independence, may form into a union which will not only check the oncoming waves of Turkish despotism but also that equal despotism which is sweeping down upon you from Prussianized Germany.

I realize that there are those here who have a more important message than I can bear. I simply want to say to these young men who are going out to fight, whether they fight under the Serbian flag or ours, they are fighting for us just the same. I want to tell them of a battle that was fought in Belgrade more than four centuries ago, a battle fought there before the first white man had ever seen America. The Sultan of Turkey, who had conquered Constantinople, was marching northwest into the heart of Europe. When he reached Belgrade, the Belgrade army was away, but they heard of it and came down the river. In the bow of the first little boat that bore that army to stem this onset of their foe was a white-haired monk, Capistrano, I think he was called, and as he landed he said to the soldiers, "Have good courage, for the Christ himself is fighting at the right hand of our captain." And that heroic little peasant army stopped in that battle the further march of the Turkish despot, turned him back and saved Europe, perhaps for all time, to Christianity.

Soldiers of the United States and of Serbia, let me say, as the old monk said to that old peasant army of your forbears, "Be of good courage, the Christ himself is at the right hand of our captain."

Good-by and God bless you.

EXTRACT FROM ADDRESS BY DR. MILENKO VEST-NICH, HEAD OF THE SERBIAN MISSION, CHICAGO, JANUARY 27, 1918[8]

I am proud to speak before Americans, citizens of this great democracy, the great melting pot of all nations, and we all of us appreciate the great honor of visiting Illinois, the home of Abraham Lincoln, from which the martyred president's example went out over the borders of the United States, across the seas to all the nations of the world, preaching liberty and justice.

Let me tell you of the origin of this tremendous war. Its origin was a simple one. The reason for this war is the wish of the Central Powers to become master of small nations, to overrun the world. Both the Hapsburgs and the Hohenzollerns always have had this desire. They descended first from their mountain castles and waged war upon the free peoples about them.

The Hohenzollerns have made terrible war upon the Slavic people from the beginning. First they founded Prussia. Next they subjugated northern Germany, and then took provinces from Denmark, Poland and France, until they made the German Empire.

You know the history of the Hapsburgs. They have become the valets of the Hohenzollerns. The two have united to Prussianize the whole world.

But the civilized world is fighting to overcome this dread object. Serbia has fought bitterly, and we are not yet through. This war can have only one end—the victory of the Allies. Still, the military victory is only a part of the definite object—making the world safe for democracy. We are fighting for one nation for the Slavic peoples, and, lest we forget, for a free Poland. Happier days are coming, and the blood that is being sacrificed now means peace for future generations. To arms! On to victory!

[8] *Chicago Tribune*, January 29, 1918.

VI. THE ILLINOIS CENTENNIAL

ILLINOIS' CENTENNIAL—A PROCLAMATION

On December 3, Illinois will enter upon the hundredth year of her statehood. The General Assembly of Illinois has created a Commission to provide for the celebration of our Centennial. It already has plans well under way to make this event worthy of the greatness and the history of Illinois. But its work will not be complete unless the counties of the State shall also organize for this purpose. There is not a county in Illinois, which has not been the scene of stirring and important events, which should find a place in the permanent history of the State.

Now is the time to single out and record these events. It is common knowledge that a young and expanding community, absorbed in making history, is only too careless about recording the history it makes. Many points in Illinois—scenes of momentous happenings— which could have been sought out and marked half a century ago, and have become fixed landmarks, are now only vague traditions. And, so, while it is yet time, let our hundredth year be marked by fixing permanently the events of our first hundred years, so far as they may be fixed at this time.

It is thought by some that the time is not fitting for this celebration, because of the world-wide war in which we find ourselves. I do not share this view. I realize the greatness of the burdens this war imposes on us. We, of Illinois, will bear those burdens more lightly if we shall recall the first hundred years of Illinois' achievements. Our fathers before us, too, bore heavy burdens. They, too, knew what it meant to offer all for a great cause. They, too, faced danger and difficulty. But they triumphed over all, and this great commonwealth—the home of twice the number of free men the United States contained at the close of the Revolutionary War—is the result.

We have a hundred years of noble history as a back-ground. Whether we shall have another hundred years equally inspiring, depends upon the issue of this world-wide war. It will help Illinois to play a great part in this war, if her people will refresh their courage and strengthen their will by a study of our first hundred years.

NOW, THEREFORE, I, Frank O. Lowden, Governor of Illinois, hereby call special attention to December 3, 1917, as the ninety-ninth anniversary of the formal admission of our State into the Union, and as the beginning of the Centennial year, and urge the general observance of this day throughout the commonwealth; and I further urge that organizations be formed in every county to co-operate with the Illinois Centennial Commission in planning an appropriate observance of Illinois' Centennial Anniversary.

(SEAL)

GIVEN UNDER MY HAND AND THE GREAT SEAL OF STATE AT THE CAPITOL IN SPRINGFIELD, THIS TWENTY-NINTH DAY OF OCTOBER, IN THE YEAR OF OUR LORD ONE THOUSAND NINE HUNDRED AND SEVENTEEN, AND OF THE INDEPENDENCE OF THE UNITED STATES THE ONE HUNDRED AND FORTY-SECOND.

By the Governor: FRANK O. LOWDEN
    LOUIS L. EMMERSON.
        Secretary of State.

ABRAHAM LINCOLN, AN ADDRESS BY WILLIAM REN-
    WICK RIDDELL, JUSTICE OF THE SUPREME
        COURT OF ONTARIO[1]

Delivered at the Lincoln's Birthday observance, Springfield, Feb-ruary 12, 1918, conducted under the joint auspices of the Illinois Centennial Commission and the Lincoln Centennial Association.

At first sight there might seem an incongruity in a Canadian addressing this gathering, met to honor the memory of a President of the United States. But that would be a narrow view; the first

[1] *The Centennial of the State of Illinois—Report of the Centennial Commission* (Springfield, 1920), pages 108-121.

words spoken after the martyr President's death are as true now as when on that fateful April morn fifty-three years ago they were uttered by Stanton, "He belongs to the Ages."

The Great President who led his people amid terrible difficulties, cheerful in the face of apparently irreparable disaster, calmly saying before truculent foes as before doubting friend, "Whatever shall appear to be God's will I will do," the President who in the very hour of victory achieved was stricken down by the hand of the assassin, has become the treasured possession of the world; and my Canada claims her share in him.

A lad of thirteen years when he died, I well remember the horror and detestation with which the deed of blood was regarded by Canadians, for we had learned to look upon him as our own and we venerated him less only than our beloved Queen Victoria.

Canadian to the last drop of my blood, British to my finger tips, I too was born on this our Continent of North America, have from infancy breathed her free air, drunk in almost with mother's milk the splendid principles of democracy which are her glory and her pride— in common with my brother Canadians, in all things I am "sprung of earth's first blood," in the highest and best sense I am American.

And I cannot but feel that your invitation to me to speak to you shows that you agree with me in the thought which caused me to accept your invitation; that, notwithstanding our difference of allegiance, our status in international law of alien and foreigner, notwithstanding all outward appearance of separation, there is between American and Canadian an essential and fundamental unity, for we be brethren, nay in all that is worth while, American and Canadian are one.

The great bond, the eternal principle, which makes us one is democracy; and Abraham Lincoln is the finest type and the greatest example of democracy the world has ever seen.

What do we mean by democracy? Not a form of government— the republics of ancient and medieval times, many republics, so-called, of modern times, are as far from democracy as the nadir from the zenith. Monarchies, too, are different, ranging from absolute monarchy where the arrogant monarch can say, "There is but one will in my country and it is mine," to the monarchy under which it is my pride to live in which the King is content to reign, leaving it to his people, to whom it belongs, to rule.

A republic in form may be an oligarchy or a tyranny in fact; a monarchy in form may be in reality a true democracy.

Every people has the government it deserves, every free people the government it desires; and that free people which has chosen that there shall be government of the people, by the people, for the people, is a democracy.

Yet he who adopts that principle simply because it recommends itself to his fellow citizens, or simply as a matter of policy, is not a true democrat; the true democrat must love the people, the common people.

Washington, *praeclarum nomen,* loved the common people, but he was not of them, one would almost say he was an English gentleman; he would not have a commission given to any but gentlemen; Lincoln was of the common people himself, he knew them and loved them as his own, not as a superior and from above but as one of themselves and on a level.

And this was the cause of utter bewilderment, honest perplexity, to many in the East, to no few in the West, who could not understand that high station was not inconsistent with simplicity of manner; they thought the joke, the amusing story, undignified, unworthy of the occupant of the highest office in the Union.

Had this been mere frivolity, such strictures would have been pardonable, but the light manner covered deep feeling, the joke had its immediate practical application, and the story was often full of significance, like the parables of the Gospel, in which the Master taught profound moral truths in the guise of tales almost child-like in their simplicity.

This very want of affectation was symptomatic of the deep regard he felt for his fellow men and of his reverence for the people at large; democratic in his views of government, he was democratic in his manner toward others.

Wholly believing in the power of public opinion, with a perfect respect for the popular will, he did not seek applause, or to amuse the people, except with the end of convincing them. Was not this the real reason why he relied so much upon "the stump," upon the open oral debate, when face to face the champions of rival policies might give a reason for the faith that was in them? Loving the people as he did, his greatest ambition was to be esteemed by rendering himself worthy of that esteem.

He was not unconscious of the tremendous importance of the issues involved, for coming as he did from a small frontier town, lacking what the world calls education, with little grace of diction and none of manner, he knew that his seven meetings with Douglas were the successive acts of a drama enacted in the face of the nation and to no small extent in the face of the world. But during his whole life, even when he had become the people's attorney by being placed in the Presidential chair he was not self-willed, he sought the advice and counsel of others, he listened to all the myriad counsellors, bidden or otherwise, ever trusting that those who should know would help him in his perplexities.

From early life he pondered over and struggled with every proposition till he understood it and mastered it; he read every book he could to help him to understand, and in the end he made up his own mind as to the right. Public opinion more than once was against him, more than once would have destroyed his plan, but with all his respect for public opinion he recognized his own responsibility before God, and man, and made—not adopted—a decision.

That marks the distinction between the democrat and the demagogue.

So at all times he repudiated any arbitrary personal prerogative; as he was not a demagogue he would not be an autocrat—no royalty could be smelt on his train.

At all times and under all circumstances he felt the majesty of law. It may be that Seward lost the nomination in 1860 because he had boldly asserted that there is a higher law than the Constitution; but that assuredly was not the reason for Lincoln's devotion to it. He did not imagine that the Constitution was perfect, but he revered it because it was a contract, and his conception of right did not allow him to look upon a contract as a scrap of paper.

This reverence for compact explains his attitude towards slavery.

Convinced that where the white man governs himself that is self-government, but when he governs himself and also governs another that is more than self-government, that is despotism—convinced that slavery is a violation of eternal right and that that black foul lie can never be concentrated [consecrated] into God's hallowed truth; wishing that all men everywhere could be free, nay, convinced that the Republic could not endure half slave and half free, he nevertheless fought the radical abolitionists as he fought those favoring the extension of slavery; while he swore that the Constitution should not shelter a slave holder, he would not permit it to shelter the slave stealer; he declared in his first inaugural address that he did not intend to interfere with slavery; even in the midst of war he repudiated the proclamation of Fremont, and at length he freed the slave only as a war measure. *Inter arma silent leges.*

Devoted to principle, he fought all his battles on principle; and while the most kindly and placable of men, he gave way no jot on matters of principle, he made no compromise with wrongdoing. The attempts at compromise with the seceding states, which we now know were foolish, he would have nothing to do with—he stood firm— Blair, Dawson, Greeley, who not? Men of consequence in their day but now as stars lost before the sun coquetted with rebellion. Lincoln listened, smiled and moved not. Rebellion he knew was not the work of a day; it was deep-seated and required heroic measures; one could not fight it with elderstalk squirts filled with rosewater; and he pressed on the war more earnestly than his professional soldiers and with no shadow of turning.

Lincoln had utter faith that Right makes Might, the true democratic doctrine, as opposed to the autocratic creed Might makes Right; and in that faith dared till the end to do his duty as he understood it. In that belief he dared to defy almost the whole of the Northern States by releasing the Southern envoys taken from the *Trent* contrary to international law. Firm in asserting right he recognized correlative duties, national as well as individual.

Lincoln had (it would seem) no well defined religious views in early life, but as soon as his thought became clear he recognized that there is a God who governs the world and that if God be with us we cannot fail in the end; he revered the justice and goodness of the Creator and humbly acknowledged that "The judgments of the Lord are true and righteous altogether." He walked humbly, knowing God as the Father of all, and that very knowledge made him the better democrat. As it seems to me no man can be a true democrat who looks upon the world as without a Divine Author and Governor, the children of men but an accident here with a future of utter nothingness. The true democrat is he who knows that all men are like himself the children of God, and therefore his brethren.

Does not the love of his fellow man shine out in every line of that sad but kindly face? Compare it with the scowling face of the Kaiser, the outstanding example of the autocrat—a face indicating arrogance, contempt, brutal disregard of the rights and feelings of others.

Your President has said that the present war is waged that the world may be safe for democracy.

Truly the world is now in the crucible; the furnace is seven times heated, the tension well-nigh intolerable; in the welter of blood, the cry of agony, the horror of death, the world's destiny is now being wrought out—the white hot metal must soon issue and take permanent form—all this is terrible but it was inevitable.

The autocrat and the democrat must needs meet in deadly conflict, and determine what the future of the world shall be—there is not room enough on earth for both.

This is no dynastic war to establish a sovereign or a reigning house, no religious conflict to render dominant Catholic or Protestant, all but a very few peoples are wholly indifferent who is and who is not king; Protestant Prussia and Protestant England, Catholic Austria and Catholic France and Italy are not divided on religious lines, the Catholic American or Canadian stands shoulder to shoulder with his Protestant fellow-countryman with the same high resolve toward the same lofty ends. A people whose whole principle of government is autocratic, whose Kaiser is never photographed without a frown, his avowed models a people whose princes glory in military uniform, whose whole national atmosphere is enmity, hate and malevolence had been preparing for more than a generation for world dominion—not a world dominion where others would be treated with kindness and justice, but where they would be ruled with a rod of iron, having no rights which a German was bound to respect.

The rest of the world was strangely blind to its danger—the few who understood and spoke out were treated as alarmists; one I know in Canada was laughed at and ridiculed, and more than one in England had the same experience. No one in a civilized country could believe that any people had reached the depth of infamy required to make them disregard all justice and right in order to aggrandize themselves and their ruling house. Yet so it was; and the world had a terrible awakening.

To the amazement of the civilized world, the solemn contract to respect and maintain the neutrality of Belgium was ruthlessly broken; the nation which prided itself on its blunt honesty became a perjured nation—true, at first, the Chancellor expressed some kind of regret but soon the real spirit became all too manifest, the brutal aggressor was contemptible enough actually to attempt to justify the wrong by lying charges against crucified Belgium, enmity, hate, malevolence did their perfect work. France must necessarily resist, for she was attacked—but the land across the channel was safe, her navy ruled the narrow seas, and there was little chance of a successful invasion of her peaceful shores.

But she had made a bargain with Belgium, she wished well to Belgium, her heart went out to Belgium, and she threw her small army in the way of the aggressor.

The world did not know the Prussian, did not understand to what depth of brutality he could descend. Rules of decency were supposed still to hold even in war; but every vile thought that could be conceived by the vilest of men was carried into execution by the invading Hun—not sporadically, as may happen in any army who see red and are in the agony of battle, but of design, with fixed purpose and by command of cool, collected officers. Murder, rape, arson by wholesale; women and children massacred or tortured with a torture worse than death—the Indian on this continent never gave such a spectacle, the world stood aghast and the German smiled a smile of self-satisfaction.

For long the conflict raged, Canadians fought and bled and died, many gallant young Americans joined our army, many joined the forces in France—but the United States was neutral.

Murder on land was followed by murder on the sea; American lives went out in the waters as Belgian lives went out on the plain, and yet America held her hand.

But when the promise solemnly made was contemptuously broken, when it became manifest that a wild beast, a tiger was abroad to which a promise was but something to be broken, when it became manifest that the Germany which was at war was the enemy of the human race, there was no longer hesitation.

War was declared by America against the enemy of America because the enemy of every nation governed by humane and moral principle, an enemy determined to set at naught all principles of right, of mercy, of justice to attain his object.

And America is united—the un-American, disloyal, hyphenated, I disregard; they are annoying but ridiculous and will vanish from sight once the United States seriously turns its attention to them. Some day when Uncle Sam is not too busy, he will take a bath and have his clothes baked; and we shall then hear no more of the vermin.

Is this not in a large measure the work of Abraham Lincoln? Abraham Lincoln thought that in giving freedom to the slave freedom was assured to the free; in waging war against slavery he said "We shall nobly save or meanly lose the last best hope of earth." Britain grimly hanging on, France bleeding at every pore, Italy angrily and helplessly watching the Hun devastate her beautiful land, look eagerly across the sea for the coming American host who are nobly to save, not, please God, meanly to lose the last best hope on earth—and he who set free the slave for a united America half a century ago made it possible for a united America to keep free and democratic the weary nations fighting for life against the autocrat.

It is a favorite thought of mine that the democrat and the autocrat are typified in the leading characters in that war for freedom and in this man, the kindly Abraham Lincoln, the most perfect ruler of men the world has ever seen, the repellant, scowling Kaiser, the superman, one of the worst failures, the one fearing God and expressing ignorance of His will, the other patronizing the good old German God, congratulating Him on being a faithful ally and admitting Him almost to an equal partnership: Lincoln willing to hold McClellan's horses if he would but bring victory; William, arrogance personified, filled with overweening pride and insolence. Lincoln took as his models the fathers of the Revolution and the good of all nations. The Kaiser, Alexander, Caesar, Theodoric II, Frederick the Great, Napoleon—Alexander, who, after deluging the world with blood, wept because there were no other worlds to conquer; Cæsar, whose cold-blooded slaughter of the unfortunate Gauls horrifies even the school boys, who have to pick out their meaning with the aid of grammar and lexicon; Theodoric, who murdered his guest at the banquet and slew his great chancellor because he dared to insist on the innocence of one whom Theodoric had determined to destroy; Frederick the Great, the perjured thief whom all the rhetoric of Thomas Carlyle cannot make into even a decent barbarian; Napoleon, who also sought world power and cared little how he got it, who sprinkled kings of his own family over Europe like grains of pepper out of a pepper pot, who cared no more for the blood of the common man than for the life of a fly—such are the Kaiser's chosen models and he strives hard to better their example. If the President had a reverence for contract, the Kaiser treats it as a scrap of paper; Lincoln gave up Mason and Slidell though he thereby angered the North because the rules of international law forbade their retention, the Kaiser boldly says there is no longer any international law and murders at sea as on land. The American instructed Francis Lieber—a Brandenburger, be it said, one who never forgot that he was a Brandenburger, a Prussian, a German— to draw up rules for the conduct of his troops, a war code the best, the most humane known to its time and never improved upon. The Prussian! The cities, villages and plains of France and Flanders cry aloud his infamy, slaughtered noncombatant, outraged woman, starved child, ruined fane, poisoned well, the hideous story is all too well known, the world will not for generations forget the nightmare horror of Belgium, and so long as devotion to duty, sincere patriotism and unaffected piety and self-sacrifice command the admiration of the world, so long will be held in memory the name of that illustrious martyr to the German rules of war, Edith Cavell.

America is at war. Why? What is the real reason? It is the same as why Britain and her fairest daughter Canada are at war.

It is that the principles which were dear to Lincoln may prevail, that malevolence and overweening pride may have a fall, that the awful doctrine of the superman may be destroyed, that humanity may be vindicated, that the free shall remain free and the enslaved made free, that the people of every land shall say how and by whom they will be governed, that militarism may be shown to be not only a curse but also a failure; that it may clearly appear that contract breaking, lying, cruelty, do not pay.

Until that lesson is learned and thoroughly learned, the Prussian must remain without the pale of friendly converse with other nations unlike him; but the lesson when learned will be abundantly worth the pain experienced in learning it.   Let but the arrogant superman lay aside his intolerable assumption of superiority, let him lay aside the brutality symbolized by the scowl of his Kaiser, let him feel the moving spirit of democracy and benevolence toward others, let him in a word become human—and he may be met as an equal, esteemed and loved as a friend.

But until that time comes, we must fight on—if the Germans conquer then nothing else is worth while. All the silly attempts at a German peace must be received with the contempt which they deserve, the contempt with which Lincoln looked upon the efforts of many to compromise. He could not compromise with slavery, we cannot compromise with autocratic pretensions. We cannot lay down the sword till democracy and our civilization are safe. We will never accept the *Kultur* of Prussia.

We must expect reverses, bitter disappointments, loss of hard-earned ground, lukewarm friends, incessant spying, incessant attempts to weaken our resolve—but these must not discourage us, the goal is clear ahead and there is no discharge in this war.

Thirty-five thousand Canadian lads, three thousand from my own city, of high courage and high promise lie under the sod, having given their all for us, having made the supreme sacrifice for civilization—a hundred thousand are crippled or wounded in the various hospitals—tens of thousands of Canadian mothers are broken hearted—yet we must carry on.

So too, America must now take her share of the burden; hating war as she does she must fight as never before, for there never was a war like this before—every nerve strained, all her resources called out, man and woman and child each in his own way doing his very best, even so the road will be long and hard, and ever and anon the heart will be sick from hope deferred.

There cannot be any doubt of the final result—right must triumph and wrong be put down, but there can be no slackening of the efforts put forth for victory.

One Canadian soldier bard has sung with a *curiosa felicitas* not excelled, I think, since the times of Horace:

> In Flanders fields the poppies grow
> Between the crosses row on row
> That mark our place and in the sky
> The larks still bravely singing fly
> Scarce heard amidst the guns below—
> We are the dead.   Short days ago
> We lived, felt dawn, saw sunset glow,
> Loved and were loved, and now we lie
> In Flanders fields.
>
> Take up our quarrel with the foe,
> To you from failing hands we throw
> The Torch—be yours to hold it high!
> If ye break faith with us who die
> We shall not sleep though poppies grow
> In Flanders fields.

(The poet, my friend, Lieutenant Colonel John McCrae, himself now lies in Flanders fields, having made the last, the supreme sacrifice for God, for King and for the right.)

So your dead are calling you—few they are now but many they will be—your hearts will ache like ours but thank God your courage is as high, your faith as serene.

As Lincoln before the dead at Gettysburg, so you before your dead in France and we before ours in Mesopotamia and Syria, at Gallipoli and Saloniki and wherever on the western front the battle has been waged most fiercely—at St. Julien, Vimy Ridge, Passchendaele, Courcelette—must offer up now the vow "It is . . . for us to be . . . dedicated to the great task remaining before us, that from these honored dead we take increased devotion to that cause for which they gave the last full measure of devotion, that we . . . highly resolve that they shall not have died in vain, that the world under God shall have a re-birth of freedom and that government of the people, by the people and for the people shall not perish from the earth." May we be strengthened to carry out the like resolve to his, "With malice toward none, with charity for all, with firmness in the right as God has given us to see the right, let us strive to finish the work we are in . . . to do all which may achieve and cherish a just and lasting peace."

For those who mourn the dead will come the consolation:

> To yearning hearts that pray in the night
> For solace to ease them of their pain
> For those who will ne'er return again
> There shines in the darkness a radiant light—
> A vision of service at God's right hand
> For the noble, chivalrous, youthful band
> Who gave up their all for God and the Right.
>
> God will repay what we owe to Youth,
> Youth that sprang at their Country's call,
> Youth ready to give up their all
> For God and Country, Freedom and Truth,
> For love of home and a scatheless hearth,
> For all that ennobles this transient earth
> Imperilled, o'ershadowed by "woeful ruth."

For God and the right? Yes, we fight not for Britain, for France, for America alone, not even for the democratic nations alone. Just as Lincoln when pouring his hosts against the South knew that he was fighting for the South and the future of the South, so we, straining every muscle against Germany and her allies, are fighting for them and their future. We do not arrogate the right to dictate to them how they are to be governed. Our arms may persuade them by the only argument they can fully understand that there is no need of loss of liberty to hold the Fatherland secure, that democracy can wage a war and defend a land in the long run more effectually than autocracy; but if they resist our persuasion, that is their affair—every nation has the government it deserves. But they must learn that people of our race are not to be bullied, that we are not subdued by threat or by brutality and *Schrecklichkeit* has no terrors over us. Having learned that democracy has the will and the power to live they may choose their own form of government; but they must keep "hands off" ours.

Free America, America who more than a century ago fought that her sons might be free, who fought half a century ago that the helpless black might be free, we welcome you to the great Armageddon wherein you will fight that the world may be free. Germany must share the benefits of your victory. Once she has seen the light, has learned the truth of the apostle's words, "God has made all nations of men of one blood," when her people have learned that men of other nations are their brethren not destined to be their slaves, that "The earth is the Lord's and the fullness thereof" then may be seen on earth what the poet saw in his vision of the heavens:

> I dreamt that overhead
>   I saw in twilight grey
> The Army of the Dead
>   Marching upon its way.
> So still and passionless,
>   With faces so serene,
> That one could scarcely guess
>   Such men in war had been.
>
> No mark of hurt they bore,
>   Nor smoke, nor bloody stain;
> Nor suffered any more
>   Famine, fatigue or pain;
> Nor any lust of hate
>   Now lingered in their eyes—
> Who have fulfilled their fate,
>   Have lost all enmities.

A new and greater pride
So quenched the pride of race
That foes marched side by side
Who once fought face to face.
That ghostly army's plan
Knows but one rede, one rod
All nations there are Man,
And the one King is God.

No longer on their ears
The bugle's summons falls;
Beyond these tangled Spheres
The Archangel's trumpet calls;
And by that trumpet led
Far up the exalted sky,
The Army of the Dead
Goes by and still goes by.

Look upward, standing mute;
Salute!

(Note: I have read this beautiful poem of Barry Pain's on
many occasions. I make no excuses for reading it again.—W. R. R.)

THE CENTENNIAL YEAR, AN ADDRESS BY GOVERNOR FRANK O. LOWDEN[2]

Delivered before the Commercial Club, Chicago, March 9, 1918.

Mr. Toastmaster, Ladies and Gentlemen:

It is a very great honor for me to be here tonight. It carries me
back to my early years in Chicago when on rare occasions I was fortunate enough to be a guest of this club. At that time many of the
great builders of this city were still alive, and I recall that it was the
pride of each one of them that whatever other engagements he missed
if he was in the city, he did not fail to come to this club. I recall very
distinctly the important civic subjects which were debated here. I remember well that some of the most important movements looking to

[2] From a manuscript copy in the possession of Governor Lowden.

a better Chicago had their origin here; and, when I was invited to come, I made up my mind that I was going to discuss some of the things which seemed to me pertinent in Chicago at this time with reference to our own local and state problems. Yet I do not know whether now that I am here, I shall have the resolution to do that or not. It happens that our minds are so filled with this great conflict which is raging across the seas, we are all so intent upon efforts which are directly concerned with the winning of the war that it is pretty difficult for us to dwell upon even the most serious problems which are a year or two off at this time.

My subject, it appears by reference to your program, is "The Centennial Year." That subject was not given by myself, but was assigned by some officer of this club. If, therefore, I shall not keep very close to the text, you may charge it to the officers of the club and not to me. But it would be very appropriate at this time to remind you that Chicago itself is one of the achievements of the century. It does come to my mind as I stand here that though not at a very advanced age, as I like to flatter myself, I can recall the time when the mighty makers of Chicago were still upon the scene and attending the meetings of this club. And what a tragedy it would be if that mighty achievement for which these great men wrought, if that epoch, because the building of this city was really an epoch in itself, if it should so happen that that great achievement should fail, and fail it will unless we win this war.

Their labors will have been in vain. Their dreams will not have come true; their hopes will have failed; and all the great achievements of the less than one hundred years since Chicago had its dawn will have come to naught. Because Chicago, like all the cities of this continent, will be of no avail, will stand for no idea nor ideal unless we shall prevail in this conflict on the other side.

What a tragedy it would be if Chicago in its youth should reach its end! Even if the Central Empires should win and therefore doom France and England and the United States, even if Paris and London and these other cities should therefore have reached the last chapter in their life, they would have this consolation, that they have had glorious centuries of achievements behind them. They could point to noble things done, to noble words spoken hundreds of years before

Chicago was ever dreamed of. But, if we should fail, there would be the pathos and the tragedy attending Chicago's doom that all feel when the young in the first promise of their early life fall. There would be the difference which we have already noted between death to those of tender years, and death to those who have reached the ripeness of four score years and ten.

Illinois, we are celebrating our centennial, and we have proud things of which to boast in the history of this hundred years. There are many thrilling chapters of achievements in the history of our state, and yet how young it is! How in its infancy Illinois still is, and what a pathos and what a tragedy if this first glorious century of Illinois should be its last!

I recall that the very entrance into the Union was an event of far-reaching significance. Under the old Northwest Ordinance, as some of you will recall, it was assumed that the northern boundary of Illinois would be a line drawn through the southern point of Lake Michigan. If that had happened, Chicago would have been in Wisconsin. If that had happened, Illinois would probably have been a slave state. Yet it would have happened if it had not been for the far-sightedness of one man of those early days. That man was Nathaniel Pope, our delegate to Congress when Illinois was a territory. He saw afar into the future. He saw that Illinois was so situated that more than any other state when the Union was formed it was a natural keystone connecting the north with the south, because southern Illinois is really southern territory. Southern Illinois was inhabited by people from the southern states who brought their slaves with them. He foresaw that in the extreme crisis that might come to the Union some day, it would be reserved for Illinois, if he could extend the boundary north to where it now is, to hold the Union together and to hold this state in the interest of freedom.

I think many of our people do not realize how different the currents of history would have run if it had not been for Nathaniel Pope. If the northern line of Illinois had run through the southern point of Lake Michigan, Abraham Lincoln would have lost Illinois; without the population of northern Illinois, a population that loved freedom and hated slavery, the Lincoln-Douglas debates would not have occurred. The whole current of our history would have been changed.

Then a little later a strange figure came on, who became one of our early governors, Edward Coles. Born in Virginia, owning many slaves himself, he freed his slaves while he was on his way hither, and then settled in the southern part of our state and became one of its governors. When the great fight was on for making Illinois a slave state it so happened that Edward Coles was governor of the state and he fought on freedom's side, although he himself had come from a southern family and formerly had owned slaves, and he won in that battle. His career was a most picturesque one.

And so I could come down to the days of the Mexican War, to the time when some of the men who afterwards made our history so illustrious first came to public view. You all know the story of the Civil War; you know it was the soldiers of Illinois who first turned the tide of that great conflict which made freedom a fact and slavery a crime.

It was from Illinois that the first great commander of the Union armies came. Only the other day I attended a most interesting meeting of the Sangamon County Historical Society in the court house in Springfield to celebrate some of the events of those days. I do not know when I have spent a more instructive hour in all my life. There were some of the old men there who knew Lincoln intimately. There were men there who recalled exactly how Grant was put into command of that first regiment, the first command he ever had. I think perhaps some of you know the story, but I am going to tell it even at the risk of being tedious.

A regiment had been stationed out of Springfield, which was recruited in Decatur. There was a very boisterous saloon keeper who was its colonel, and the people began to complain out in that vicinity that their chickens had all disappeared, and that the regiment had begun to confiscate their pigs. At that point they began to protest, and so they came into Springfield and the question was to find some one to command that regiment. Finally Governor Yates recalled that there was a young man serving as clerk in the adjutant general's office whose name he had forgotten but who was said to have been educated at West Point. He made inquiry as to this young man and he found that he was down in Ohio visiting his father to see if in some way he could not get into the United States Army.

They sent for him. He came back. That young man was Ulysses S. Grant. He was given command of this regiment probably because there was no politician soldier in the state who dared to undertake to handle it.

The Adjutant General of that time asked this young colonel how many cars he needed to transport his regiment to Quincy, to which point it was ordered. The young man replied, "None." The Adjutant General felt that he was insulted, that the assistance that he proffered was being spurned. But Grant replied, "I propose to take this regiment to Quincy on foot. It is better for the regiment to learn how to obey orders while we are still within the boundaries of our own state than to have them undergo that instruction while we are facing an army." And so he led the regiment to Quincy.

There is a story in Springfield, which is full of interest, of Grant's introduction to his new regiment. Some famous orator of the time, as was the custom in those days, introduced Grant in a glowing oration. The custom was for the colonel thus introduced to respond. This was Grant's speech in reply: "Men, go to your quarters."

I could not help but think as I sat there, a listener, while these proceedings were going on in this court house of Sangamon County, that so far as I know, that is the most historic court room occupied by any court of the United States today.

It was in that room that Lincoln made his epoch-making speech, in which he declared that "a house divided against itself cannot stand," the speech which framed the issue upon which the Lincoln-Douglas debates were made, the speech that resulted finally in his election to the presidency of the United States.

It was from one of the rooms alongside of this court room that this young clerk in the adjutant general's office—not so very young, either, around forty—of whom I spoke a moment ago, started on that dazzling career which led him, in four years, from obscurity to the heights of immortal fame.

It was in that room from which Lincoln's body in its last journey to the tomb was borne. That room is now occupied by the circuit court of that district. Do any of you, my friends, know any court room as historic as that anywhere now actually occupied for the purpose of holding court?

That has been one of the few, one of the many, I should say, things of thrilling interest which this centennial year ought to disclose to the general understanding of the people of Illinois. We have been making history so fast in this state that we have not stopped long enough to ponder upon the things of interest which we have done.

And now the question is, shall the historian of a thousand years say of Illinois, "It had a brief but glorious youth," and shall his pen stop there? That depends, my friends, upon whether we win this war, because the history of Illinois has reached substantially its end unless we should triumph in these battles which are flaming around the world.

It cannot happen for a moment that any state in all this constellation of states shall be secure a moment after the defeat of the Allies by the Central Empires.

It is true that many of us thought a year ago that this war did not concern us much. It is true we were told that it was three thousand miles away and that although there might be danger to the cities along the Atlantic seaboard, no ill or harm could ever come to Illinois. But we have been learning during that year that there is no place so remote, there is no country so far away from these battle fronts, that it won't be affected equally with all the world by the results of the war.

We have learned—and it has been difficult to make our people believe the truth of this—that there never was a war in all our history which came so close to our hearth and hearthstone as this war in which we are engaged today.

As I have said a thousand times, I think, since the war commenced, it is closer to the people of Illinois than was the Civil War. Because, filled with the blackness of clouds as the days were before that contest opened, we all knew that whatever the result of the war we would have some kind of a country left when the war was over. That country might be incomplete; it might be fragmentary;

it doubtless would be inglorious; but still there would be some country which rested beneath the folds of our protecting flag. There would be some territory we could call our own; there would be some place where still in comparative security our homes could continue to exist. And that was true of the people of the south.

But in this war in which we now are engaged, there is no spot between the Atlantic and the Pacific, between the Gulf and the Great Lakes, big enough for the humblest cottage which shall be free soil, if we fail in this contest of arms. For when the war is over, all the world will be altogether free or altogether under the iron heel of military despotism. There is no compromise. We are fighting for everything. We are fighting for all we are, for all we have, for all we hope for our children. We are fighting for the sanctity of the graves of the patriots of our past. We are fighting for all the future of our children, and their children after them.

If we can only feel that this is not such a war as any of the past, if we can only free ourselves from the shackles of tradition and realize that not for the first time in the history of the world have all the currents of ordinary life swept backwards, if we could only feel from the depths of our hearts that this would not be the first time that civilization has been lost, then we might succeed. There was a magnificent civilization in old Egypt. Athens had a civilization of her own, finer, more beautiful in many respects than any we have known. Rome had her civilization, but she too aspired to conquest of the world. She, too, got into the mood in which it seemed to her that Roman arms should triumph and rule everywhere, and they did for a time, but that time was succeeded by the blackness of night, and for centuries this beautiful civilization of old disappeared, and the awakening was slow and painful.

We had just begun to approach a civilization which is worth while, and that civilization can be plunged into the blackness of night, just as those old civilizations were.

If the doctrine that "might is right," if the notion that there is no such thing as honor between nations, if the concept that force, brute force, is the only thing which will rule the world, if that shall gain an ascendency around the earth, there will be a brazen civilization for a century or two, a civilization glittering, beautiful, perhaps, in a way, but soulless, and heartless, and hopeless, and void of all spiritual graces, all finer things. It may be that there shall be a civilization of that kind for a century or two, but again the Middle Ages will return to the earth, and it may be two thousand years more before man, just common man, shall be recognized again as having any legitimate rights upon the earth.

It is not a war such as was ever fought before. It is not a war aroused by the jealousy of one nation over the prestige of another nation. It is not a quarrel over a strip of territory. It is not a war that is aroused by dynastic pride. It is a war between these two principles, whether or not man is worthy to rule himself, whether the earth was made by the good God for all men, or [whether it was made] for only a favored few, and the fate of the millions is simply to toil and spin and delve in order that a few favored sons of earth may enjoy all there is of freedom, all there is of beauty, all there is of independence.

That war is in the last stages of its last battle. It has been fought before. Our forefathers along the coast of New England and the Atlantic seaboard waged it for awhile, and they won. But that only affected a small territory. It has been fought here and there at different times through the centuries. But now, at last, all the forces of democracy on the one hand, all the powers that believe that there is a God of righteousness, justice and mercy, all who believe that this world was intended for something else than a mere footstool for kings and princes, are allied together against all the powers of evil and darkness, and all the worshippers of brute and material force on the other hand.

That battle is being fought wherever there are men who love liberty, and wherever there are men who believe in the divine right of kings. So, when the war is over, our fate will be the common fate of all the earth. We will either have our old freedom and our old independence, we will either be permitted to visit the graves of our fathers without shame in our hearts, or we shall be the slaves of a military despotism as wide as is earth. This war is different from any that was ever fought; and if we can only make our people understand that, if they can only be made to know the truth, there is no doubt about the result.

The Central Empires are making it easy for us, in a way. They are making this war so frightful, they are making it so cruel, they are so consistently carrying out these diabolical policies which their professors had brazenly taught for fifty years, that at last our people are beginning to realize that either we shall win, or that this earth will not be a fit place to live upon, and therefore we had better die than survive the shame of defeat by those powers of darkness.

A few weeks ago I saw in the daily press—and I have no doubt many of you saw it also—the account of the burial of the first three Americans who fell fighting in France for this sacred cause. They were Sergeant Gresham, and Privates Enright and Hay. A distinguished French general attended the burial service, and he said in very simple but touching language that that spot had become holy ground. I wondered, as I read that account, if, after all, those three young men are not infinitely better off than those of us who shall survive this war, if we lose. I felt then that they were to be envied of all men, if the fortune of battle should go against us in this colossal strife. I thought also that, if we did win, and if peace should come again to this distracted world, those of us who visited France in happier times, would be sure to inquire first of all, when our feet touch the shores of France, not for any of her wonderful monuments, not for any of her achievements in art, but the first question that we would ask would be: "Where is that sacred spot, somewhere in France,"—that is the only description of it that we know—"which holds the ashes of Sergeant Gresham and Privates Enright and Hay?"

Now, if anyone thinks for a moment that I have exaggerated this story in any way, or if anyone believes that I have painted the picture too dark, let him just follow, from day to day, the stories in the press. There is not a day that does not reveal, somewhere in Russia or Roumania, or on the western battle front, that every step which the Central Empires take is in complete harmony with and subjugation to these frightful doctrines which their professors—and I regret to say, their pulpit—have taught for fifty years. It is not the old Germany. It is not the Germany of Goethe, Schiller, and Humboldt. It is not the Germany which furnished to us, after the Revolution of 1848, thousands of the best and most loyal and patriotic

Americans we have ever received. It is the Germany of this new *Kultur,* this new doctrine which had its birth in the imperial court, which was foreshadowed by Frederick the Great, when in the testament he left for his successor, he said, "Religion is a good thing for the subject, but a poor thing for the king; and treaties must not be taken seriously." We find from day to day that very doctrine, which we ought to have known was pronounced in all seriousness for fifty years, being followed to the letter.

Now, who can hope that if that power triumphs in this war, America is removed from the effects of that triumph? Who can for a moment believe that we are not involved as much in every sense as they of heroic France, noble Britain and bleeding Belgium? It is our war. It is our war to a finish; if we only realize that, we shall win. My friends, it is hard for us, I know, to believe that we could lose our freedom. It is hard for us to realize what our freedom means. The average man does not realize what free air means. He has been so in the habit of breathing it, and he does it so unconsciously that it is only when the air is withdrawn, and he is stifling to death, that he realizes what free air means.

And so it is with liberty. We have been so accustomed to it; it has confronted us and surrounded us so in all our life, like the air we breathe, that we have not really known what it has meant. We have got to stop and ponder before we realize that every act of our daily life, every thought we have ever entertained, every ideal we have ever set up in our hearts, everything we have held sacred and beautiful, will be tarnished, ruined and utterly destroyed if our liberty is gone. It is only then that we shall have the courage to go on to the end, wherever that end may lead. Let us realize the sublime privilege which is ours now, in this crisis of the world— the privilege to preserve perhaps for all time the jeweled blessings of freedom and independence.

Let us recall what this country has meant to all the world, during the well-nigh one hundred and fifty years of its national life. Let us recall how it has been the inspiration to every enlightened statesman on every measure looking to an enlargement of human liberty in all the world; how it has been an inspiration to the soldiers dying on foreign fields for liberty, because that soldier in his mind's eye could see the flag of America, and know that one day men would be free throughout the earth; and so that patriot could die with a smile upon his lips, because he had this blessed hope in his heart for the future of mankind.

But if this war shall go against us, there will be no spot anywhere beneath the shining sun for the defeated, broken and exiled patriots fighting for liberty, anywhere. If we can only have this realization in our hearts, we are going to win this war. But we are not going to win it by just simply saying that we are great America, and shall therefore win; we are not going to win it by boasting of our superior prowess. We are going to do as your chairman says. We are going to win it when all of our people, forgetful of all past differences, racial, religious or political, are a unit under our one flag.

Now, a new liberty loan is about to be offered to the people of the country. Do you know what our German friends said of us at the beginning of this war? They said that we were a people who would not fight; that we were a money-grubbing nation; that all we cared for was to speculate upon the misfortunes of others. But we hurled back that lie into their teeth, when more than one million of our young men, the flower of the manhood of America, fell into line, answering their country's call beneath the starry flag.

And now, shall it be said of us who remain that these young men are willing to give their all that the nation may live, but in spite of that, we are backward in simply giving of our wealth that they may fight and die for us to a glorious purpose? Reflect for a moment that we have got no choice. We have either got to loan this money to our government, or pay it in tribute to the Central Empires of Europe. What shall our choice be?

I thank you, my friends.

THE ILLINOIS CENTENNIAL, AN ADDRESS BY GOVERNOR FRANK O. LOWDEN[3]

Delivered at the celebration of the Centenary of the Illinois Enabling Act, held under the auspices of the Illinois Centennial Commission and the Illinois State Historical Society, House of Representatives, Springfield, April 18, 1918.

Many people have wondered whether or not Illinois should attempt a Centennial celebration, in view of the great tragedy which enfolds the world; but after the most careful consideration which the Commission was able to give to the question, the decision was reached that the war was all the more reason for recalling the events of our first hundred years. It was believed that by recounting the achievements of our past we would be better able to meet the demands of the present. We knew that we had a hundred years of glorious history behind us, and we believed that if we had those hundred years and their achievements in our mind, we would more readily be able to meet the high duty with which we are confronted today, and therefore would be more likely to have another century equally glorious.

I am not going, of course, to make a speech to you tonight, but I do want to read a few words, before I introduce the first speaker, from the Annals of Congress, which, as most of you know, is the official record of the proceedings of Congress.

This state, a hundred years ago today, was told by the federal government at Washington that it might organize itself as a state, if it so wished. Twelve days before the President signed the bill the following proceedings occurred in the House of Representatives at Washington:

"The House resolved itself into a Committee of the Whole on the Bill to enable the people of Illinois Territory to form a Constitution and State Government, and for the admission of such State into the Union on a footing with the original States.

"Mr. Pope" (who was delegate in Congress from Illinois Territory) "moved to amend the bill by striking out the lines defining the boundaries of the new State, and to insert the following: 'Beginning at the mouth of the Wabash River, thence up the same, and

[3] From a manuscript copy in the possession of Governor Lowden.

with the line of Indiana to the northwest corner of said State, thence east with the line of the same State to the middle of Lake Michigan, thence north along the middle of said lake to north latitude forty-two degrees, thirty minutes, thence west to the middle of the Mississippi River, and thence down along the middle of that river to its confluence with the Ohio River, and thence up the latter river along its northwestern shore to the beginning.'

"The object of this amendment, Mr. Pope said, was to gain, for the proposed State, a coast on Lake Michigan. This would afford additional security to the perpetuity of the Union, inasmuch as the State would thereby be connected with the States of Indiana, Ohio, Pennsylvania and New York, through the Lakes."

I doubt if, in all the voluminous records of Congress, from the beginning until today, any event has transpired, recited in so few words as this, which has so affected the destiny of America as this simple amendment. Before it was offered, the northern boundary of Illinois was to extend from a point at the southern extremity of Lake Michigan, west to the Mississippi River. Without this amendment Chicago would not have been in Illinois; without this amendment Illinois would have been a slave state, because it was that part of the population of the state in the northern part of the state which saved it when the great trial came; without this amendment northern Illinois would have been a part of Wisconsin, the Lincoln-Douglas debates would not have occurred, and in all human probability Lincoln would not have been President, but would have died an obscure country lawyer!

So I read these simple, unpretentious lines from that rather dry and dusty record of the proceedings of Congress, to show to the people of Illinois that a hundred years ago a Providence seemed to be with her, shaping the great destiny that has come; and if there ever was a time in our history when faith in a Providence guiding the destiny of State and nations was needed, that time is now!

The first speaker of the evening, Monsieur Louis Aubert, a member of the High Commission of France, a distinguished scholar and writer, is doubly welcome to our midst. Illinois' early history concerns itself principally with French names. Marquette, Joliet, LaSalle and Tonti are among the great names of her early days.

One of the most beautiful of our early traditions is the visit of La-Fayette, upon his return to America. This state has cherished with affectionate pride every incident of that visit; and when you visit southern Illinois today the first things of which they will remind you are the spots and scenes of LaFayette's early visit.

I want also to say to Monsieur Aubert that Illinois' first constitution was probably the only constitution ever framed by any government which was expressly drawn so that a Frenchman might be a public official. When the fathers of a hundred years ago convened, they provided qualifications of citizenship for everyone else for whom an office was created, but expressly and purposely omitted to include the lieutenant governor as coming within those qualifications in order that old Pierre Menard might be the first lieutenant governor of Illinois.

Those early memories have been greatly strengthened for us of this generation, in Illinois, by the visit a year ago of Marshal Joffre and Monsieur Viviani. It seemed to us fitting then that the hero of the battle of the Marne should come to our city and with loving hands should bear to Lincoln's tomb a wreath and lay it upon his bier, because of all the peoples of all time who have battled heroically for the principles for which Lincoln lived and died, the French nation during these years occupies the forefront.

These are gloomy days. We have all of us been under more or less depression; and the best comfort I have had recently was coming across a report that another great Frenchman, General Foch, sent from the field of the battle of the Marne to General Joffre at perhaps the critical moment in that battle. I am going to read that order: "My right has been rolled up; my left has been driven back; my center has been smashed; I have ordered an advance from all directions."

I don't know—maybe at this moment they have rolled up our right, on the western battle front; they may have pushed back our left; they may have smashed our center; but while the spirit of France lives and while the Allied armies are commanded by General Foch, we will order an advance all along the line! And as heroic France, in the battle of the Marne, saved the day for civilization, so we, the Allies, in the most sacred cause for which men have ever fought or ever died, will save the world to the civilization which it has taken so many centuries to attain.

It is my great pleasure, ladies and gentlemen, to introduce to you the very distinguished Frenchman, Monsieur Louis Aubert.

A MESSAGE FROM FRANCE, AN ADDRESS BY M. LOUIS AUBERT, MEMBER OF THE FRENCH HIGH COMMISSION[4]

Delivered at the celebration of the Centenary of the Illinois Enabling Act, Springfield, April 18, 1918.

Mr. Chairman, Ladies and Gentlemen:

I thank you for the privilege of addressing you tonight in the name of France. In wishing that my country be represented at this commemoration, you have given once more an evidence of that charming virtue of the American people:—Gratitude.

From 1825, when General LaFayette came to this state, up to 1917, the date of the visit of M. Viviani and Marshal Joffre, America has welcomed many illustrious Frenchmen.

Today, the greetings of France are brought to you by a more modest soldier. I hope you will not deem these greetings less warm and less sincere.

Gentlemen, as it has been your delicate idea to give to our meeting of tonight the character of a family reunion, let us speak first of our ancestors.

A Frenchman cannot glance at a map of your state without being deeply moved by souvenirs from the old country. Names of cities, Joliet, LaSalle, Vincennes—names of forts, Fort St. Louis, Fort Chartres, Fort Crevecoeur, how sweet those names sound to a French ear especially when heard far away from France!

But, gentlemen, there is something more eloquent than these stones or these names, now dear chiefly to archaeologists: it is the dream, the magnificent dream of which they are the last humble witnesses.

The first white men to set eyes on the incomparable landscape of this great valley were Frenchmen: Marquette, Joliet, Cavelier

[4] *Report of the Centennial Commission*, pages 197-206.

de LaSalle. The grand empire, the creation of which seemed invited by these beautiful waterways flowing between the Great Lakes and the mouth of the Mississippi, had its inception in French minds.

What you realized in this, the most splendid cradle of energy and boldness in the world, was first the dream of French pioneers.

These stones, however, these French names scattered over your territory do not merely bespeak dreams of by-gone days; they attest the dominating and still enduring qualities which our race has manifested with a persistency of which any race might be proud.

The idealism of a Marquette, of a LaSalle, who were neither conquerors nor merchants, but merely explorers, impelled by a scientific curiosity or a religious proselytism—their bravery coupled with prudence, their tenacity, their love of peace which made them act as umpires between rival tribes, their spirit of kindness toward the natives, all these traits of our ancestors we find in our explorers and soldiers of the nineteenth century, and today we find them in Brazza, who won for France the immense region of the Congo without shedding a drop of blood, in General Lyautey, who, almost without drawing the sword, has given Morocco the benefit of French peace.

And now, in this hour of emergency, France is reaping the reward of this human spirit in this war in which all her subjects, black, white or yellow, have rallied with enthusiasm around her flag.

No, indeed, the descendants of Joliet, Marquette, Cavelier de LaSalle have not degenerated into the old stay-at-home decadent race that the Germans were so pleased to picture. They have proved it to these same Germans at the Marne, at Verdun, and they are proving it today in the Oise, the Somme and the Lys valleys.

Likewise, I can safely predict that the qualities of your frontiersmen will come out in the sons of Illinois who are to fight in France!

I well remember when I was in the trenches over there, how, in order to find an analogy to the strange existence I was thrown into, I, who had always lived in cities and whom war had surprised in a study, had to go back to a chapter of your historian, Frederick J. Turner, on "the significance of the frontier in American history." These trenches marked the farthest line of our civilization. Beyond the barbed wire was "No man's land." Every night, in our patrols or reconnaissances, we would creep always in the same direction towards the listening posts, guided only by the odors and the sounds brought to us by the wind. Gradually, the traces of our steps made a trail like the trails of the "coureurs de bois." Then, later on, when we pushed forward our lines and advanced into "No man's land," these trails which then were used to bring supplies were widened into paths, then wagon roads and finally into railroads. So, in our turn, we passed through the different stages of your frontier life. And when, later, I heard of the skill and eagerness of the American soldiers in reconnoitering, I was not surprised; they are the worthy sons of the frontiersmen.

Gentlemen, there is another trait of your ancestors that our ancestors helped to develop in addition to the spirit of boldness and energy: it is the spirit of freedom. Your historians have pointed out how your revolutionary spirit was stimulated by this large territory suddenly thrown open to the industrial conquest of a numerous, hardy and independent people. It is because the exploration by Frenchmen of the Mississippi Valley hastened the day of that Declaration of Independence for which fought LaFayette and Rochambeau. It is because some of the most brilliant qualities of your race were prepared and assisted by those Frenchmen who blazed the way for your spirit of enterprise and made it possible for you to satisfy your love of freedom, that from the very beginning up to today, the image of France has been firmly implanted, to use Dr. Finley's words, in the very heart of America. That true spirit of freedom of your West, no one better than your great fellow-citizen, Lincoln, has expressed when he said: "I never had a feeling, politically, that did not spring from the sentiments embodied in the Declaration of Independence . . ." Then speaking of the inspiration derived from that document, he went on to show that "it gave liberty not alone to the people of the country but hope to all the world for all further time."

Then it is not an accident if the so inspired words that Lincoln applied to the Civil War apply equally well to our great war of today.

When he stated the impossibility for America to live "half slave and half free," did he not define exactly our own position?

Has anyone ever written anything that fits more adequately the present situation than this sentence that one never tires of quoting:

"We accepted this war for an object, a worthy object, and the war will end when that object is attained. Under God, I hope it will never end until that time."

We were not the aggressors any more than you were. It was not our love of adventure which drove us into this war, but the necessity of fighting for our liberty. With the admirable patience with which, for more than two years and a half, you opposed German outrages, we, their immediate neighbors, opposed their exacting demands and provocations for forty-three years.

Challenged to a fight to death, we have sacrificed everything, land and men, without stint. For over three years and a half, out of a population that the invasion has reduced to thirty-five millions, France has mobilized seven and a half million men. Previous to the last drive, three million French soldiers in the army zone were holding more than two-thirds of the western front.

Before the present battle, that effort had already cost us: 1,300,000 killed in action or dead from wounds received in battle; about 1,000,000 maimed and invalided—that is a decrease of two millions and a half out of our adult population, which to America would proportionately mean a loss of nearly six million men.

All our forces have been thrown into the fight; the results are that our wheat crops have been reduced by two-thirds, our shipyards have manufactured only guns and shells instead of ships, and our export business has been practically stopped.

All those sacrifices we have accepted without complaint, not only to defend our homes, but also to defend a great cause.

We never fought a separate selfish war. Our reserves in man power and material we have always placed, in the hour of need, at the disposal of Serbia, of Italy; and today in Picardy and Flanders our divisions fight side by side with our gallant allies, the British.

With more than half of our coal fields and over 80 per cent of our iron deposits in the possession of the enemy, we have managed, not merely to set up entirely new industries to equip our armies, but we have been able to help our allies, to whom, up to October, 1917, we had sent 1,500,000 rifles, 2,500 guns, and 4,750 airplanes; and you know that when you came into the war we guaranteed that, provided raw materials should be supplied, we could equip with guns and airplanes all American divisions brought over to France before July 1, 1918.

That we did, and today we have full confidence in your co-operation to the end. Upon the occasion of the first anniversary of your entrance into the war, your newspapers have reviewed the extent of your effort. Your effort has been tremendous and its results are already very important.

General Pershing's action in placing all his resources in men and material at the disposal of General Foch, has deeply touched the heart of France. We know that your whole nation is at heart with that action and that all of you are ready to amplify it in placing all your resources at the disposal of our common cause. The success of your Liberty Loan will show it plainly. President Wilson's decision to brigade small American units into larger units of the French and British armies, reminds us of those of our revolutionary government amalgamating the young recruits of Liberty among old seasoned troops, and you know the lesson Austrians and Prussians were taught during the campaigns of the French Revolution at the hands of those troops that their love of liberty made invincible.

The present battle, cruel as it is, has already brought serious and lasting advantages to the cause of the Allies. The first is the unity of command. We now have a generalissimo, a common leader, who is alone responsible for the strategy of the battle. Be assured that, when the time comes, he will know where to strike the blow. The second advantage is a greater unity of judgment. We now cherish less illusions than formerly about the sufferings of our enemies, their revolutionary discontent, their disposition towards a negotiated peace. Such a peace the Germans mention less and less since they have treated with Russia, Ukraine and Roumania; they are gorged with lands to profit by and peoples to dominate, and, even those who voted in favor of a peace of conciliation in the Reichstag in July last, are the first now to speak of necessary annexations in Belgium and in the French region of Briey.

Each autumn since 1915 the military leaders of Germany have made her people feel that war pays: Serbia crushed in 1915, part of

Roumania in 1916, and Russia and Ukraine and the whole of Roumania at the end of 1917. The Germans' hands are full, one more effort and all these gains will be insured forever. The magnitude of the stake is worth the boldest venture. Let us not rely on Austria, either. Not that she would not like to make peace—all the recent revelations of the secret negotiations which for a year Austria has tried to bring about, clearly indicate her desire to come out of the war, but Austria in a military way and industrially and financially speaking is only a vassal receiving orders from Berlin.

Let us not rely on our enemies, on the diplomacy that might divide them. Let us rely on ourselves. Let us rely on the valor of our armies to bring about peace and let us take to heart the words of President Wilson: "Force, force to the utmost, force without stint or limit, the righteous and triumphant force which shall make right the law of the world."

Gentlemen, the spirit in which France entered this war, the spirit in which she carries it through is the best test of the spirit in which she means to conclude peace. You entered this war without territorial ambitions, you entered it for a principle. So did we! Do you believe that our country could and would have stood her enormous material losses and her frightful sacrifices in men if she had been prompted only by greed? Poor bargain, indeed!

No, the spirit that has animated the French soldiers since August, 1914, is a spirit of crusade, and if our national aspirations are summed up in the names of Alsace-Lorraine, it is because to us Alsace-Lorraine embodies the very spirit of this crusade.

Last October, before the Reichstag, Herr von Kühlmann exclaimed: "Alsace-Lorraine is the symbol of the German Empire." Yes, Alsace-Lorraine, annexed in spite of the unanimous protests of its inhabitants; Alsace-Lorraine, under German yoke for forty-three years, has been the symbol of this brutal empire which already before the war had enslaved all its neighbors, the Danes of Schleswig, the Poles of Prussian Poland, and, during this war has subjected Courland, Esthonia, Lithuania, Poland, Roumania, Servia, Russia, and through Turkey, Armenia.

The return of Alsace-Lorraine to France, on the contrary, would consecrate the victory of the principle for which we are all fighting! It has become the symbol of the right of people to dispose of themselves.

"Citizens possessed of souls and intelligence are not merchandise to be traded, and therefore it is not lawful to make them the subject of contract," objected to their new masters the newly-annexed Alsatian-Lorrainers, through their representatives in the Reichstag in 1874.

And President Wilson echoed the same sentiment when he said last February:

"Peoples and provinces are not to be bartered about from sovereignty to sovereignty as if they were mere chattels and pawns in a game."

Gentlemen, when Herr von Kühlmann or Count Czernin proclaim that Alsace-Lorraine is the only obstacle to peace, do not believe them. At the Peace Conference, there will be other questions to settle to make the world safe for democracy. Alsace-Lorraine is only one of the fourteen peace conditions enumerated by President Wilson. No, Alsace-Lorraine is not the only obstacle to peace. But no peace is possible without the return of Alsace-Lorraine to France, for the brutal severance of these French provinces was the first crime of the new German Empire against democracy, and out of that crime have come all the others that have astounded the world.

Listen to the final touching words of farewell that the populations of Alsace-Lorraine addressed to the French National Assembly in Bordeaux, forty-seven years ago, and remember that when they were repeated before the Reichstag in 1874, they were met with sneers and laughter.

"Your brothers of Alsace-Lorraine, now cut off from the common family, will preserve for France, absent from their hearths, a filial affection until the day when she shall resume her rightful place here once more."

Gentlemen, note these words—brothers, family, filial affection, hearths. . . . It is the whole question of Alsace-Lorraine!

And after forty-seven years, your President, whose only concern is a lasting peace through justice, has heard the protests and pronounced this verdict:

"The wrong done to France by Prussia in 1871 in the matter

of Alsace-Lorraine which has unsettled the peace of the world for nearly fifty years should be righted in order that peace may once more be made secure in the interest of all."

At present, the recruits of Illinois, your own sons, are perhaps occupying in French Lorraine, at St. Mihiel or Aux Éparges, the sectors which face the Lorraine still occupied by the Germans. If some day France owes to their gallantry the recovery of her children which were torn away from her, gentlemen, then you will know that your sons have been soldiers of Right!

Your forefathers and ours were empire builders. It is for us to show that their spirit may prompt us now to build up a world better than the one we have known.

In the first place, we will have to reconstruct France. You will help us. France feels that in the past as well as during this war, she has served mankind. In the interest of mankind you will help us to rebuild France.

We will have to reclaim "No man's land" and bring back life into the field of death. For this undertaking of peace, of civilization and happiness, I look forward to the coöperation of the descendants of the French and American settlers who raised your fair state of Illinois out of the wilderness of the prairies.

We will also have the world to reconstruct. This war has shown most plainly that there is no safety for a free state except in a close partnership with all other free states, respectful of each other's rights!

During this war, the nations most jealous of their national prerogatives had to sacrifice something of their pride and accept the control of international organizations.

After the war, something must survive of this union. We must discard the policy of "laissez-faire" and establish in its stead a better justice and a great efficiency. The antiquated conception of the balance of power must give way to a new regime. What will this regime be? We know already the one that the German *Kultur* would set up. It would control the whole of Europe and reach out to Persia and India, and the Far East. And once in control of Europe and Asia, the Kaiser, as he bluntly told you, would stand no nonsense from America. So, in the end, it would amount to nothing less than the domination by the Germans of land, sea, sky and man.

The American conception of the new order is quite different. You know what it is, you Westerners, who have the far-seeing eye of the prairies, you citizens of Illinois, who gave to America the man who saved the Union. You have realized on this continent a federal organization which, while respecting the rights of the states, is strong enough to insure fair relations between them. The society of nations is nothing else, gentlemen, but the American spirit extended to the world.

Perhaps our generation will see this League of Nations realized. Meanwhile, we must modestly begin by practicing its spirit among our two countries, whose mutual feelings for the last hundred years are the surest promise of a better world to come.

Let us set ourselves to this momentous task with the spirit of those builders and settlers who are our ancestors. When they cleared the forest in the wilderness, they dreamed of the city which would rise some day near that clearing. It would be a beautiful city, open to all, where all men of good will would have a chance, where all men respectful of the rights of their fellows would live free.

Gentlemen, let us carry this dream one step further—let us work for a society of nations open to all peoples of good will, and where all nations, great and small, will have the place they deserve.

AN ADDRESS BY THEODORE ROOSEVELT[5]

Delivered at the celebration of the Centenary of the adoption of the first Constitution of Illinois, State Fair Grounds, Springfield, August 26, 1918.

Governor Lowden, Mr. Chairman, Bishop Fallows, and you, my Fellow Americans, Men and Women of Illinois:

I am honored by the chance to speak to you today. And, friends, on this occasion of the centennial of Illinois' admission to statehood, it is a matter of good augury that we speak under a governor whom we all know has deserved what Dr. Schmidt has said of him. The American people will have had a mighty triumphant next century,

[5] *Report of the Illinois Centennial Commission,* pages 243-258.

if, on the occasion of the bi-centenary of Illinois, we have such public servants as you, Governor, to preside over our destinies.

Now, friends, I come here today to speak primarily of the things that are closest to the souls of all of us. For this is a great crisis at which time the men and women of the nation think not of little things, but of the great fundamental matters that most intimately concern all of us. We are passing through the third of our great national crises. In this case it is a part of a world crisis, the like of which has never been seen before.

I know that the rest of you will not begrudge my saying a special word of greeting to the men who wear the button that shows that over half a hundred years ago they showed their troth by their endeavor.

Now, men, we are here today under that flag. We are citizens of a great and proud nation only because those men and the men like them in their youth cast aside everything else for the chance of death in battle for the right. As we look back at those years, keener and brighter grows the fame of the men who fought for the Union and for liberty. And today from throughout our borders men in khaki have gone in their youth to venture everything with a proud and gallant recklessness of what may befall them so that you and I, you men and women here, that we and our children may continue to hold our ideals high among the nations.

I want to say just a word as to the form of advertisements which I see here, "Square Deal. Give us a Chance." Now, friends, I regard one form of advertisement for good causes, which I see here in Springfield, just as I have seen it in New York. There are a dozen A-1 movements in all of which I am interested. I am immensely interested in the Thrift Stamp Saving Campaign; in the Food Saving Campaign; in the Conservation Campaign; in the Food Growing Campaign, but I always object strongly when I see any picture or any advertisement that "food will win the war," or "money will win the war," or "savings will win the war." Tell the truth. Saving food will *help* win the war. Savings will *help* win the war. Money will *help* win the war. But the war will be won as the war was won at the time of Abraham Lincoln, by the fighting men at the front. Everything else is only auxiliary to the fighting men at the front. Shame, triple shame to us who stay at home unless we do all those things, unless we buy liberty bonds, buying to the limit, unless we subscribe to the Red Cross and all kindred organizations, unless we buy thrift stamps, unless we save food. Do all those things but don't get conceited about it. Recollect that when you have done all, you have just done a half of what you ought to do to put your strength back of the men at the front. Stand by the men at the front. And remember that the only people who have fulfilled the full measure of their devotion to the country at this time are the men who have gone and the women who have bravely bade them go to fight for their country. There is only one person I put as high as I do the soldier and that is the soldier's wife or mother who stands by him; she who takes care of the house, and takes care of the baby, and does whatever can be done at home. If she does her full duty and sends her husband or her son away with a smile, even though her heart is breaking, and writes him cheerful messages, I respect her as I respect the soldier. I have no use for the soldier who runs or for the woman who whines. Recollect, you women, that if you make it hard for your sons and for your husbands, if you fail in your duty, you are acting just as ill by the country as would the man who fails his country on the field of battle. Bear yourselves as gallantly as the gallant boys you have sent to the front. Remember that is the duty of all of you.

Now, the immediate duty of the hour is two-fold. In the first place, to insist upon a 100 per cent Americanism throughout this land. In the next place, to speed up the war and win it at the earliest possible date.

In the first place about Americanism. This is merely another way of insisting that we are a nation proud of our history, proud of our past and proud of our present; that we are a nation, not a polyglot boarding house. Unless we have a nation, we won't have anything to fight for. Nobody fights for a boarding house. If we treat this country or permit it to be treated as a land into which people from thirty different old-world countries crowd and squeal and struggle for the best place at the trough, while all their allegiance is to some land over seas, if we do that, we have no country at all. There isn't any possibility of a divided allegiance. Either a man is all American or he is not an American at all. Any kind of an alloy to loyalty makes it utterly valueless. At this time the man of German origin who says that he is loyal to Germanism, to Deutschtum, although he is not loyal to Germany, to Deutschland, is making a distinction without a difference. You cannot be loyal to Germanism and Americanism at the same time any more than you can be loyal to Germany and to the United States at the same time. Germanism is incompatible with Americanism. If a man has the slightest loyalty to Germany at this time, he is disloyal to the United States. There is no half way to it, of any kind or sort. It is exactly as it was at the time of the Civil War. You had to be all for the Union or all against the Union. If you were half Union and half Secesh, you were kicked out by both sides. Isn't that so? (An old soldier: "Sure.") It is just the same thing now. You have got to be all one thing or all the other. If you live in the United States you are not entitled to be anything except an American, pure and simple, and nothing but an American. If any man still looks back and wants to be a half or a quarter or a tenth something or somewhere else, send him back to that somewhere else. There can be in this country loyalty to but one flag—the flag of the United States. Loyalty to any other flag is disloyalty to that flag. And when I say any other flag, I mean not only the flag of any foreign nation, but I mean the red flag of anarchy or the black flag of international socialism. If any man follows the red flag or the black flag here, put him out. Make him go wherever the red flag or the black flag is, but don't let him stay here. And more than that, I want to have a man be United States and stand by the flag of the United States and talk United States. I am perfectly well aware that you can talk United States and still talk treason. At any rate we know what you are talking about in a case like that; whereas, if you are talking some language we don't know, then you can talk pretty much anything without our knowing it. We have room in this country, permanent room, for but one language—the language of the Declaration of Independence; the language of Washington's Farewell Address; the language of Lincoln's Gettysburg Speech and Second Inaugural—the English language. All other languages that are spoken here or printed or used in newspapers should be used only during the transition period, a period to be established by law, after which the newspaper shall be printed in English. In our schools there is only one language that should be used, and in our primary schools only one that should be taught—the English language. In our upper institutions of learning, study German or any other modern language as you do one of the ancient languages, but study it as a foreign language.

Let me illustrate what I mean in my own case. I have a right to talk against hyphenated Americans, because my ancestry is so varied that if you want to express me by a hyphen you will have to use seven of them. About 225 years ago certain Dutch traders came to the mouth of the Hudson and some German peasants (I have some German blood in me, but I am straight United States, however) to the Schuylkill, and some English and Welsh Quakers and Scotch and Huguenots or French Protestants who had been driven out of France because in France the Catholics persecuted the Protestants, and the Irish Catholics who had been driven out of Ireland because in Ireland the Protestants persecuted the Catholics. Their children grew and spoke the same language. If they had not spoken the same language, they could not have married one another. A young man could not have proposed in one language to a young lady speaking another. And, if they had not married one another, I would not be here.

Sometime ago I spoke in Wisconsin and in Minnesota. I had with me two Illinois citizens, friends of mine, straight Americans, Mr. Otto Butts, of Chicago, and Judge Harry Olson, of Chicago. Mr. Butts' father and mother were born in Germany and Judge Olson's father and mother were born in Sweden. I have told you of my ancestry already. The three of us were Americans and nothing else. At the meeting, the Judge presided and Mr. Butts introduced me and then I made a speech. Now suppose the Judge, when he presided at the meeting, had spoken in Scandinavian and Mr. Butts, when he introduced me, had spoken in German, and that I had then burst into eloquence in low Dutch. You would have needed three translators for every member of the audience. We all spoke English because you have to use one language and that is the language of the country itself.

Nobody is obliged to come to this country, but if he comes, he is to take our constitution and our flag and our language. If he does not want to do that, he can go straight back to the land from which he came.

Now having said that, I don't know how I could say it with any more emphasis than I have—whatever other defect of character may have been lodged against me, at least I have not pussy-footed—of one side of Americanism, I wish with no less emphasis to say that the other and the equally important side of Americanism is the imperative duty of treating all men who show their good faith in Americanism as on an absolute equality with everyone else without regard to their creed, their birthplace or their national origin. In this crisis, since our people became fully awake (I think our people remained asleep quite a time. I did my best to wake them up) the great majority of Americans of German origin have shown themselves as aggressively and absolutely and single-mindedly American as the citizens of any other stock. And when that is the case it should be recognized as being a high crime against the American spirit to fail to honor those men by putting them on an equality with the rest of us.

I can illustrate what I mean by referring to the Civil War. In the southern states, the bulk of the men joined the Confederate forces, but there were plenty like Farragut who stood for the flag. We are the fellow countrymen of men of German blood, in whole or in part, who have stood by the flag in this war, Americans, who, if we do not recognize them as such, we damn ourselves for not doing. Let me give you an example. At the front in the flying corps, two of the best American flyers are Rickenbacker and Meisner, both of them of German origin, one of them an ace. The more of that kind of men we get into our army the quicker we will get to Berlin.

Let me give you a couple of other examples. The other day I spoke at Martinsville, Indiana. I was introduced by Mayor Schmidt of German origin. He has two boys overseas in the army. One of them was in my boy Archie's regiment and was wounded about the same time that Archie was wounded. They were lying in the same hospital. Do you think they are not comrades? Don't put it to them if you don't think so. Major Simmons of the Red Cross told me the other day, just after he had returned, that he went into the hospital to see my boy Archie. The next cot to Archie's was occupied by a young fellow from Massachusetts, and the next cot to him was occupied by a young lieutenant. A bullet had gone through the point of his heart. They had to keep him there for eight days without moving a finger until the muscle could heal, because, if he had moved, it would have meant instant death. He was feeling pretty good when Major Simmons came to see him. Simmons began talking to him, getting messages for his family and for a young lady who did not belong to the family. He finally asked him his name and the boy turned with a grin and said, "My name is von Holzenheimer." Wouldn't the Huns feel good if they knew they had got a man with that name? There were three boys lying alongside in the hospital, wounded in the same cause. All three were of different race origin. All three Americans and nothing but Americans. And infamy shall be the portion of any one who tries to sunder one from the other two.

And remember—I wish to speak this to that small body of men of German origin who have tried to remain American and something else, who have tried to be half American and half German—the Germans, the newspapers and the officers in Germany feel more bitterness toward the Americans of German origin than they do toward any other people here. They are not placated in the least by any half-and-half loyalty. You cannot make yourself an ally of Germany except by doing Germany's bidding. If you act sulky, half and half, a little American, but not very much American, its only effect is that you do not remain American at all, and you do not become a German, because you lose all place in their country. Do one thing or the other. If you stay in this country, become whole-heartedly and absolutely and without reservation an American. If you are not prepared to do that, then get out of the country and go back to Germany. That is all, one thing or the other.

There is another point in connection with Americanism. There has recently been some talk about internationalism as a substitute for patriotism. It was talked about and indulged in by the Russian Bolsheviki a year ago, when they said they loved all mankind. They have shown their love by cutting the throats of 30,000 of their brothers and by betraying the free nations of the earth and by throwing Russia, bound and helpless, under the feet of German autocracy. Internationalism stands to nationalism exactly as the love of one's self stands to the love of one's family. It is an invaluable addition, but a mighty poor substitute. We are American nationalists. We intend to do justice to all other nations, but the professed internationalists during the past four years have played Germany's game exactly as the professed pacifists played it during the same time.

And I wish to say how glad and proud I am that we should sit here and listen to the invocation by a bishop who wears the button of the Loyal Legion, because, when the choice was between peace and righteousness, he stood for righteousness. Whenever you meet a man who tells you that he loves other countries as much as he loves his own, treat him as you would the very affectionate gentleman who tells you that he loves other women as much as he loves his own wife. Professional internationalism stands toward patriotism just exactly as that form of diffused affection stands towards an honorable family life. I like a good neighbor. I want him to treat me squarely. If any neighbor tells me he loves me as much as he does his own wife and children, I distrust him. If he does not care more for his family than he does for me, I am dead sure he cares very little for me. I want to have nothing to do with that kind of a man.

American pacifism has been the tool and ally of German militarism and in just the same way the professional internationalist has been the foe of nationalism of America. For the moment the pacifists and the internationalists are moderately quiet, but just as soon as peace comes they will begin to be noisy again. It is only four years and a month ago that those men were screaming that there was no more chance for war; that the capitalists would not allow it; that the socialists would not allow it. And they said that men like myself were poor maniacs because we asked this country to prepare, and they went on and said during the next three years, up to a year and a half ago, "No, don't prepare; if you prepare you will have war; keep harmless; if you are harmless enough, nobody will hurt you." Well, we tried it. We kept unprepared and we got into war. We tried being harmless and we are still busily engaged in trying to undo our harmlessness, notably in the matter of flying machines. We have been exceedingly harmless in aircraft.

Now that is what the pacifists said in the past. Don't trust them in the future. A pacifist does not keep you out of war. Even a pacifist will fight if you kick him long enough. The trouble is, when he does fight, he isn't any earthly good.   He has not been trained so as to make himself effective.   I asked for preparedness, not because I wished war, because I did not wish war.   Events have proved that I was right, for, if we had prepared our strength in advance, the chances are a hundred to one that no nation would have invited a trial of strength with us.

Now, when peace comes, do not trust the pacifists.   They are the enemies of righteousness.   Do not trust the internationalists. They are the enemies of nationalism—the enemies of Americanism. Do not trust the illusionists, the people who promise you peace with ease, with the absence of effort, and who say if you would only let your heart grow timid and your muscles flabby, you will be doing the Lord's will.   That is a poor type of Christianity, isn't it?   Not the Peter Cartwright type.

Take the view, you women, that you expect your husbands, the fathers of your children to take.   You expect them to be good neighbors, but you expect them to have their first thought for their wives and children, for their mothers.   Isn't that so?   Same way with a man in international matters.   Treat every other nation squarely. Behave toward every other nation as you would wish every other nation to behave toward you.   But remember, if you do not treat this nation squarely first, you cannot be any good to any other nation.

Let us accept any reasonable proposal when peace comes, whether it be called a League of Nations, or a League to Enforce Peace, or by some other title, any reasonable proposal upon which we can in good faith act, and which really does offer some chance of lessening the probability of future wars and diminishing their area, but never let us forget that a promise that any such league or other piece of machinery will bring about permanently the abolition of war is a sham.   No machinery will avail until by degrees the heart of man is changed. Use the machinery.   Take hold of it, but treat it not as a substitute for, but as a supplement to, preparing our own souls and bodies to protect our own hearthstones in time of need.

Agreements!   Every agreement that the mind of man could devise had been called into being to protect Belgium from Germany, but when the hour came that the ruthless Prussian German Hohenzollerns thought it to their interest to disregard those treaties, they treated them as scraps of paper, as they themselves said.

You cannot devise any treaty that will not be a scrap of paper in the future, unless the law-abiding nations have their strength prepared to put back of that treaty if it is violated. That is the way in which you can secure the greatest likelihood of peace for this nation. I would be willing to risk my case with the mothers of the land. I would be perfectly willing to prevent every one else from voting except the mothers, if I could put the case fairly before them and say "if you do not raise your boys so that they can be soldiers for the right, some time or other you shall see them go against the cannon unprepared, you will see your daughters turned over to the mercy of a foreign enemy."

I asked for preparedness, not because I wished war, but because I did not wish it. I asked it in the name of those who do not wish war, because, if war comes, their sons and they themselves will have to go. You don't find the pacifists doing that. The pacifists stay at home. They have important business elsewhere. It is the men who practice the fundamental virtues of the days of Washington and the days of Lincoln, upon whom you have to rest for safety in time of trial, and not upon the glib tongued creatures who try to teach you that rhetoric is an effective substitute for action.

And when I say prepare our strength, I do not mean to let George do it; I don't mean to stand by and plead while somebody else prepares—I mean for *us*. I mean that our sons and grandsons shall train themselves in times of peace, and that they so train themselves that an enemy shall know that it will not be eighteen months after the war has begun, but that it will not be longer than eighteen days after war is begun before they are ready for action. And if every nation understands that, you will not be able to get any power in the world to look crosseyed at us.

And as for the pacifists. I suppose you have had his type out here—the conscientious objector. You have heard of him? Yes. We had plenty of them in New York. Men used to write to me a year and a half ago and say, "Are you going to respect my conscience?" I would answer, "Certainly, only you have got to respect mine." I wanted to find out first what the man was conscientious about. If he is merely conscientious about shooting somebody else, I would say, "All right, I'll put you in the army and send you up to the front to dig trenches. After you have dug them, I will put other men in with rifles. You will not hurt anybody. You may get hurt yourself, but you will not hurt anybody else." Or, if he prefers the navy, I'll say, "All right, I will put you on a mine sweeper." A mine sweeper never hurts any other vessel. It hunts for mines. If it finds them—if it is not awfully careful, it is apt to go up. The man himself may go skyward, but he will not hurt anybody else. If a man will do that kind of work, he is all right. But if he says he is conscientious about risking his own worthless carcass to fight for his country, then I would say to him, "I am too conscientious to allow you to abide in a land that must be protected by the ones who are willing to fight for it."

We are in the war. Our duty is to speed up the war to the utmost limit of speed and be prepared to fight it through, no matter how long it takes to fight it through. We must insist upon a peace by a complete and overwhelming victory. Remember, that if you put an army in the field by driblets, the war will last four times as long as it will if you put your army in in the biggest possible mass at once. If you put it in en masse it is much more apt to end the right way.

Above all things, let us distrust the man who wants to fight the war a little but not much; who says raise an army but not too big an army, that will make us uncomfortable here.

I feel about nations as I do about individuals. I don't accept the view that there is one standard for national honor and another standard for private honor. Neither do I accept such a view in matters of courage and common sense. I would advise a nation as I would advise a man. Any one of us who has a son wants to feel that the son is not a brawler and is not a coward; that he never bullies a weaker man, but that he will stand up for his rights. When a man will stand up for his rights, the other man had better look out for him.

I would advise any man in private life just as I would a nation. Don't hit any man if you can honorably avoid it, but never hit SOFT. Nobody is crippled if you hit him a little, but not much. If you hit him SOFT, he will hurt you in response. Don't hit him at all if you can help it. If you do hit him, put him to sleep. I see the bishop gathers my meaning.

That's the same way with a nation. Don't go into war if you can honorably keep out of it, but make it understood that if any nation goes to war with you, it is a war. If you go into war, put it through, and do it NOW. Send our troops over by the millions. Accept no excuse if we do not have our cannon and our aeroplanes by the tens of thousands of them and our ships by the thousands. Remember that the longer the war lags, the more terrible the toll of bloodshed, of loss, of suffering, of misery, will be. Put the war through. Stand by every government official from the highest to the lowest insofar as he stands by the people in putting the war through and not one minute longer than he so stands.

That is the Abraham Lincoln doctrine. In this state (I am not at all sure it was not in Springfield—at any rate in one of your cities in Illinois) in 1854 when Lincoln was reproached for standing with certain men on certain things, although he was against them on other things, he answered: "Stand by any man who is right; stand by him as long as he is right, but stand against him when he is wrong." And to do less than that is to show yourselves less than a man and less than an American. Good sound doctrine. Any man who tries to get you to stand by any one who is wrong is trying to get you to do a servile, an un-American and an unpatriotic thing.

When we shall have won the war, when those of our sons who are to come back do come back, some of them sound, some of them crippled, when the young men of the nation, the flower of the nation who have fought for us and have done their work, when they come back, let us see to it that they have come back to a better country than they left.

This terrible war with all of its lamentable accompaniments may nevertheless be of lasting value to this nation, for it may scourge us out of the wallow of materialism made only worse by a mockish sham of sentimentality into which we were tending to sink. The finest, the best, the bravest of our young men have gone forward to face death for the sake of a high ideal, and thereby they have brought home to all of us the great truth that life consists of more than easygoing pleasure and more than hard, conscienceless, brutal strife for purely material success. We must rightly care for the body and the things of the body, but such care leads nowhere unless we also have fought for our own souls and for the souls of our brothers. When these gallant boys on the golden crest of life gladly face death for the sake of a high ideal, shall not we, who stay behind, we who have not been found worthy of the great adventure, shall not we in our turn try to shape our lives so as to make this country the ideal, which we in our hearts acknowledge, and to make that ideal and the actual work-a-day business of the world come a little corresponding, a little closer one to the other? Let us resolve to make this country a better place to live in for those men and for the women who send them to battle and for the children who are to come after them to inhabit the land.

When peace comes and even before peace comes, let us weigh and ponder the mighty spiritual forces called into being by this war and turn them to the social and industrial betterment of the nation. Abraham Lincoln, with his usual homely common sense and unerring instinct for the truth, bade our people remember that the dollar has its place, a place that no one but a fool will deny, but that the man stands above and not below the dollar.

Of late we have worshipped the dollar over much and have been smugly content with service to mammon, heedless of the fact that devotion to dollars is almost equally damaging to those who have too many as to those who have too few. For, when success is treated as tested and measured not by the achieving, self-respecting, hard-working family life and. the performance of duty to one's self and to others with pleasure as an accompaniment of the duty, but as measured simply by the mass of dollars collected, the result is inevitable that the successful greedy ones develop a mean arrogance toward others, and the unsuccessful greedy ones a mean envy toward others, and the envy and the arrogance alike are but the two sides of the same evil shield.

In this country let our purpose be to secure justice to humanity. At this moment we hold our heads high because our sons and brothers overseas have placed love of a great cause above material success. Let us see that that position is not reversed in this country for a long time to come.

The other day I read the statement that there were a hundred thousand undernourished children in New York City. If we had a like number of undernourished soldiers, what a cry would go up. Yet these children are the citizens of the future and the industrial army is of the same consequence as the military army; and if we do not realize this truth, some day this republic will rock to its foundations.   In achieving this purpose, we must be equally on our guard against the American Romanoffs and the reactionaries of industry and politics and against the vultures who appeal to the base spirit of envy and class hatred, who strive for disorder and anarchy.   The history of Russia during the last eighteen months teaches this country what to avoid.   If you avoid the Scylla of the Romanoffs and plunge into the Charybdis of the Bolsheviki, it don't help.   The fact that you have been wrecked on one side of the strait does not give you any cause for congratulation because you got away over this side of the strait.   Avoid both.   Avoid the man who is afraid of progress and avoid the man who would plunge you into the abyss in the name of progress.

One of the lessons we should learn is that the most sordid corruptionist can do no more harm—and heaven knows how much harm he can do—that the most sordid corruptionist can do no more harm to the nation than the conscienceless demagogue or the impracticable and fanatical visionary.   We must take the rule of justice and fair play as our guide in dealing alike with capital and labor; with the business man and with the working man, with the man who lives in the town and the man of the open country.

During the war there should be no profiteering, no unusual and abnormal profit.   Yet I would like to call this to the attention of some possibly well meaning persons—unless there are legitimate profits you cannot tax them.   If there are no profits to tax, there will be no taxes and no wages.   People will not permanently run a business when you do away with the profits.   Remember that.   In a very real sense we should see that the government supervises in this way.   It should be done, keeping clearly in view the fact that business must succeed or no good will come to any one and the fact that when it does succeed, there must be a reasonable share of the success go to the men who have put in the capital and to the men who do the labor, who are entitled themselves to the right of collective bargaining in their own interests and who are entitled to be treated as in a whole and now in an unlimited sense, partners in the enterprise. There must be the fullest recognition in honor and in material rewards. There must be the fullest recognition of this kind for successful, conscientious, intelligent, hard-working men. And when I say recognition, I mean recognition that they accept as such and not that that somebody says they ought to accept as such.

But there must be no limiting of production; no limiting of output; no insistence on reducing the efficiency of the skilled and hard-working to the plane of the shiftless and the inefficient.

So with the farmer. Our aim should be to bring about in this country not merely the maintenance, but the increase of the farmer who tills the soil he owns. Our legislation should be shaped to favor the growth of that class rather than the class of the great land owners who rent their land, or of the renting class itself. Our aim should be to use whatever means may be found necessary to put a premium upon the maintenance and upbuilding of the class which, in the past, has always been the bedrock of the nation, the class of farmers who live on the land, who till with their own hands, who, themselves and through their sons and through one or two hired men do the work on the farm on which they live. Make the farm more attractive for them, giving a chance to the tenant to own the farm. Make it possible for the man who wants to buy his farm to get the money from the nation on reasonable terms. Do all of that that we can. And when it has been all done, remember that nothing that the government can do can more than aid the man himself to do the work. No use of trying to carry any man. If you carry him and he lets himself be carried, you will exhaust yourself and you will kill him. There is only one efficient way to help any one and that is to help him to help himself.

So, while the government can and must do certain things, the farmer acting for himself and acting by and with the coöperation of other farmers, must himself do certain things. Let us try to introduce gradually and cautiously by adapting to our own needs, the helps, the coöperation and control that have been found effective in Denmark and elsewhere and that have revolutionized the status of the farmers in those countries, and proceed as regards all business men, as regards the wage workers, as regards the farmer, all alike, on the one safe theory in American life, that unless this country in the future is a pretty good place to live in for the children of all of us, it will be a mighty poor place for the children of any of us. Proceed on that assumption. Work together, in unions, in farmers' leagues, in coöperation. When you make class unions, don't work politically. You farmers, recollect if you call a nonpartisan league nonpartisan and yet make it a party league, it doesn't mean anything. You haven't called it what it is, that is hypocrisy. Work with the unions, work with organizations of any kind, business, labor, farmers, but don't forget that there is one union above any other union, and that is the union to which we all belong—the Union of the United States of America.

AN ADDRESS BY JOSEPHUS DANIELS, SECRETARY OF THE NAVY[6]

Delivered at the dedication of the statue of Stephen A. Douglas, Gilbert P. Riswold, sculptor, Springfield, October 6, 1918.

The two presidents of the United States who more than any other have typified the real American spirit and glorified the product of the frontier in the days of adventure and development were Andrew Jackson and Abraham Lincoln. They touched the life of Stephen A. Douglas, the first his hero and his political mentor to whose teaching he gave full proof of loyal allegiance; the second his political competitor with whom he contested for high honor, winning and losing, and with whom, in his last days, he was co-worker in the preservation of the indissoluble union of indestructible states.

Before Jackson's election, all our presidents came out of the schools of Virginia and Massachusetts and either in culture or in views illustrated the training of Old England. To be sure, they had been at war with what was then called "the Mother Country" before, out of all the stocks in Europe, the American became in the melting pot a composite of mingled blood and differing faith and the varying habits of all nations who have made it a mighty republic.

Jefferson alone of them all lived amid the foothills of the mountains of the Old Dominion and from the heights of Monticello looked

[6] *Report of the Centennial Commission*, pages 301-316.

toward the West with the enthusiasm and faith of the seer. He saw in the rolling prairies and mountains, then just opening to settlement, the home of a people over whom a free air would always blow, building a civilization that would make the republic as vast in territory as it would be truly democratic in profession and in practice with the latch-string on the outside, an invitation to all who wished to live in the atmosphere of equal opportunity.

That vision caused Jefferson to send Lewis and Clark on the journey of discovery where they trekked to the extreme West, where rolls the Oregon—but, impatient as he often was at the conventionalities in the seaboard colonies which sometimes fettered, cribbed and confined, Jefferson's education was not different from that of well-to-do youths of English birth.

But Jackson was the very incarnation of the day when the West caught the imagination and challenged the courage of young men to whom achievement is valued only when it overcomes obstacles. Born in the Scotch-Irish settlement of Waxhaw, North Carolina, before he attained his majority the unconventional and heroic Jackson began his journey to what was then the West—the unbroken wildness of the forests of western North Carolina, where he fought his duel, established his fame, and then moved on until he made his home in Tennessee, the farthermost western territory, into which men of adventurous spirit were moving from what, even then, men of his temperament were calling "the effete East."

In this congenial atmosphere, Old Hickory became the central figure and from the Battle of New Orleans until his death was the dominant figure in America.

Abraham Lincoln was akin to Andrew Jackson in his early struggles, in his unfettered mind, in his inflexible purpose, and in his devotion to the Union as evidenced by Jackson's vigorous steps to prevent nullification and Lincoln's like victory over secession. Where Jackson was a torrent of passion when aroused and none could stand before his denunciation, Lincoln was the incarnation of a patience born of power which was invincible and unconquerable. How much these men influenced the life of the illustrious statesman of whom I am to speak is a field that invites speculation and throws light upon the career of Stephen A. Douglas.

All youths of ambition are hero-worshippers. To the youthful Douglas, early orphaned and apprenticed to the trade of cabinet maker, the commanding and picturesque figure of Old Hickory was the perfection of the ideal American. Jackson's career as a soldier inspired his patriotism. His resolution to brook no opposition to his well conceived plans at New Orleans by arresting, imprisoning and banishing a Federal judge, challenged the admiration of the youth of the Green Mountain state, and his defiance of power by his veto of the charter of the National Bank so stirred young Douglas that he ever regarded Jackson as the embodiment of political wisdom and sound statesmanship.

During the twenty-five years that Mr. Douglas was in public life—and he held almost every office in the gift of the people—he followed the political paths blazed by Jackson, and was never so confident of the correctness of his position as when he felt he was taking the course that Jackson would have followed. Born in a far eastern state, his eyes early turned toward the expanding West, and, like his great examplar, he made his home on the frontiers of the American settlement.

The rolling prairies called him, they broadened his conception of the future expansion of the country, and he became as truly western as though his eyes had first opened on the Father of Waters. The career of Douglas, like that of Lincoln, is illustrative of American opportunity. From the rude cabin to the most exalted station on earth is the epitome of Lincoln's life—a life that has beckoned many a farmer boy to diligence and to study. New England training made Douglas a mechanic. As a boy he was a cabinet maker, and his greatness has been an incentive to the youth to labor to attain skill in his craft.

Illinois was "the West" in their youth. Its rich lands were giving reward to the industry of the farmer. The tide of immigration from Vermont and other New England states, and from Kentucky and other southern states, met in this commonwealth, already conscious of the coming greatness, which the new settlers were making possible. In this tide of on-coming makers of a state came the youthful and slender Douglas, with enough education to become a teacher, and Lincoln with less schooling, but with a latent power which was to give him immortal fame. Douglas early gave proof of the eloquence which later commanded listening senates. Lincoln matured more slowly. Both were nourished under the same sky, practiced in the same courts, won the admiration of men of like patriotism. Today the commonwealth which gave them welcome, when poor and unknown they knocked at its doors for admittance, pauses in its centennial to do honor to them—its two most illustrious commoners, statesmen and patriots. A distinguished son of a noble empire will voice the world appreciation of Lincoln, who is too great to belong to any state or any nation, to any age or clime.

The honor is mine to speak of the illustrious "Little Giant," who, dying at the age of 48, had for eighteen years been the most influential leader in the hall of Congress, of whom it may be truly said, he, like Lincoln and Webster and Clay and Benton, belonged to the only American aristocracy of

"Tall men, suncrowned, who live above the fog
"In public duty and in private thinking."

Mr. Douglas walked into the town of Winchester, Scott County, Illinois, in the autumn of 1833, with his coat on his arm, with thirty-seven cents in his pocket, all his earthly possessions. Within ten years he had been admitted to the bar, commanding a large practice, had been a member of the Illinois legislature, prosecuting attorney, register of the land office, judge of the State Supreme Court and member-elect to the National House of Representatives. The succeeding eighteen years of his life he served as representative and senator in Congress, defeated Abraham Lincoln for the Senate, was defeated for president by Abraham Lincoln and died in the middle of his senatorial term with the love and confidence of the people of Illinois of all parties and creeds, and with the respect of the whole country which he had served with ability, singleness of purpose and with a vision of its possibilities that few of his era had seen with the eye of faith.

I am to speak today not of the Douglas of the period of the Lincoln and Douglas debates when Greek met Greek, or of the epoch-making campaign for the presidency in which the victor of 1858 was defeated by his old-time adversary. In all history no debates so challenged the attention of the country. It determined the candidates of the two parties for the presidency in 1860. What the outcome of that election would have been if the party to which he belonged had given united support to Douglas is a conjecture that may be left to those who delight in reflecting upon what might have been. Rather, let us think today upon Douglas as the man, as the orator, as the political leader, as the champion of popular sovereignty, as the disciple of Old Hickory, as the masterful national party advocate, as the unquestioned leader in the Senate; but high and above all as the constructive statesman who more than any of his contemporaries contributed to national expansion, to internal improvements, to the Americanism that thinks in big terms and had the faith in his country's future which placed no limit upon its growth and greatness.

It has been popularly supposed because he was from early manhood engaged in the very thick of heated political campaigns, that politics was the breath of his nostrils. Superficial historians have failed to see that with him politics and office were never an end but always a means to securing the larger rights of the people and to promoting that national growth which were his earliest and latest dreams and his master passions. Other ambitions and loves had play in his busy life, but he ever shaped his course by the steady North Star of faith in the ability and right of his countrymen in each sovereign state to determine for themselves their local and domestic concerns, with the steadfast and fixed devotion to an indestructible union of indissoluble states. From these principles he never wavered.

The first public address Douglas made after his admittance to the bar was in defense of Jackson's veto of the National Bank charter. Small of stature, a briefless barrister, he attended a meeting in Jacksonville called to endorse President Jackson's action. In the very center of culture of the young state, the site of its only college, his eloquence, his argument, his sound reasoning so impressed his hearers that he stepped into state fame and retained this high place in forensic debate until the day of his death. As his first public appearance was in defense of Jackson's actions which changed the fiscal policy of government, so when at the age of thirty years he became a member

(29)

of Congress, his maiden speech in the House of Representatives was in vindication of the hero who inspired his boyish admiration and had profoundly influenced his political convictions and public life.

There are times when the ordinary civil processes must give way to emergency measures, but only for the period of national crises. Let us never forget that America places the military over the civilian government only to preserve conditions that insure the civilian supremacy.

No militarist could endure in our country. So deep-seated is our devotion to a government where military force is under civilian control that when, as happened in the case of Grant, a general is elevated to the position of president and as such is commander-in-chief of the army and navy, he must doff his military uniform and don civilian garb. But there are brief periods when national existence demands temporary military supremacy.

Such a time came when General Jackson was commanding the troops at New Orleans. He found it necessary in order to successfully execute his matchless strategy to declare martial law, and when opposed by a federal judge General Jackson found it necessary to arrest the judicial officer, imprison and banish him. Jackson stopped at no half-way measures to insure victory. Later when military rule was replaced by civil government, the judge fined General Jackson $1,000 for contempt of court. Civilian government was again supreme and General Jackson bowed to the decree. Though tenders of the money came from many friends, General Jackson declined to accept the offer and paid the fine himself. There was never a better proof that, while the American people welcome martial law to save the life of the republic, they displace it immediately when the peril that evoked it is over. For years a bill had been pending in Congress to repay General Jackson the $1,000 which he had paid out of his own pocket. It slumbered on the calendar, but party feeling ran so high it could not pass. The first act of the young Illinois Congressman was to call up the measure, and his first appearance in debate was in support of the bill. He and other friends of Jackson wished vindication of their hero. Douglas proved to the satisfaction of Congress that it was not only Jackson's right under the circumstances to declare martial law, but that he would have been recreant to his duty if he had failed to take such vigorous action. The action in that case was the precedent which has been followed from that day to this.

When Mr. Douglas met his hero face to face years afterwards, in a call at the Hermitage, General Jackson said to Douglas, "I always knew I was in the right at New Orleans, but I never understood just how and why until I read your speech."

The lesson of this hour which we draw from the life of Douglas is far removed from the forum of politics and the debates of questions which stirred the people in the fifties. They are valuable only in illustrating his convictions and consistency and the ability he displayed in defending them and winning the approval of those who heard or read his able addresses. It seems a thousand years since people grew heated over these differences. Now that the whole world is in the throes of a great war to decide whether the world can endure half democratic and half autocratic, in the clear retrospect we can appraise the heights of devotion to country in the example which Douglas set to his countrymen then and now. He had devoted his life to the settlement of radical differences over a question which could not be composed by an adjustment or compromise. Clay, with like love of a united republic, had postponed the conclusion. Douglas in his Nebraska bill and squatter sovereignty believed he had found a solution. Clay did not live to see that this remedy was a postponement. Douglas in sorrow saw the disunion which he had patriotically sought to avert.

But when war came, in spite of his blood-sweating attempts to avoid a clash between brothers, he had not a moment of hesitation as to the course he would pursue. His state called its sons to preserve the Union. With all the powers he could command he united his voice with that of Lincoln in calling the people, though it was a painful duty to one who gave twenty years to averting the sectional conflict, to take up arms, to maintain undivided the great republic upon whose solidarity he believed depended the hope of free government in the western hemisphere. As Senator from this great commonwealth, he stood behind Lincoln when he delivered his inaugural address. He stood behind him physically, and behind him with the full weight of his ability, his counsel, his eloquence and the leadership of a great party which had given him 1,300,000 votes, and which in Grant and

Logan and McClellan and Hancock contributed generals of distinction, and from its rank and file poured into the regiments, men who fought as valiantly for the Union as did the men of different political faith. It was a seemingly insignificant incident, which cheered all who were hoping war could be averted, when, as Lincoln was introduced, he looked about for a place to deposit his hat, Senator Douglas stepped forward and took it and held it. That act had a world of meaning as the future course of Douglas evidenced. "One blast upon his bugle horn was worth a million men."

When a people are at war, partisanship if it be based upon love of country bourgeons into patriotism. Mr. Douglas had been a partisan of partisans. The man to whom the reins of government had been entrusted had been his political foe. In the moment of the peril of the perpetuity of the Union, Mr. Douglas forgot his defeat, forgot political consideration, forgot any resentment or disappointments, forgot everything but the supreme fact that the united republic he loved was threatened with separation and all which that involved to American greatness. In that hour he made full dedication of himself and his powers, rallied the forces of defense of a united republic that should stretch from lakes to gulf and from ocean to ocean.

And he fell as truly in his country's cause, speaking and counselling for united support to Mr. Lincoln, as the men who gave their lives on the field of battle under the leadership of Grant and Logan. He died with the prayer in his heart, so eloquently uttered by Webster, with whom he was kindred spirit, "When my eyes shall be turned to behold, for the last time, the sun of heaven, may I not see him shining in the broken dishonored fragment of a once glorious Union; or states dissevered, discordant. . . . Let their last feeble and lingering glance rather behold the gorgeous ensign of the republic, now known and honored, throughout the earth, still full high advanced, its arms and its trophies streaming in their original lustre, not a stripe erased or polluted, not a single star obscured, bearing for its motto . . . spread all over in characters of living light, blazing on all its ample folds, as they float over the sea and the land, and in every wind under the whole heavens, that sentiment, dear to every American heart, Liberty and Union, now and forever, one and inseparable."

That classic from America's first orator was the utterance of the great son of the Bay State, who, though of an opposite party, was one with Douglas in endeavoring to find a way to preserve the Union and to avert the war whose coming shadow was to them a tragedy too awful to contemplate. Neither Webster nor Douglas yearned for continuing peace more ardently than did Abraham Lincoln, as is evidenced by the great Emancipator's inaugural address. That inaugural was the key note of his deep feeling and his administrative acts. To the southern leaders he held out the olive branch in the same spirit, if not after the manner of Douglas, when he declared: "We are not enemies, but friends. Though passion may have strained, it must not break our bonds of affection."

We have often been assured that the war between the states was inevitable and nothing could have averted it. That fatalism may be right, but I have never given my assent to such a doctrine either as to that war of brothers or to the present world war. I am one of those who believe war is not foreordained but comes only by man's disobedience of the laws of God. It is not for us at this distant day to assess the responsibility for that terrible nightmare. Today, as Illinois honors Lincoln and Douglas, it is sufficient that the state may have the distinction that both these eminent men, in differing ways, sought to the last to avert it without separation of the republic, and that both were free from hate, passion or revenge, and both cherished the hope we have lived to realize, that the sections once estranged are again friends, having no differences. Each is straining to contribute to the fullest of the flower of its manhood in this war to make the world safe for democracy, and afterwards to see to it that democracy is made safe for the world.

It was no new point of view, when in 1861, hurrying to Springfield after a conference with the President, Mr. Douglas addressed the General Assembly and summoned the people to united support of the perpetuity of the Union. After the "most straitest sect" he was a State's Right Democrat, but he was true in this, as in all things, to the example of Andrew Jackson, a Democrat of Democrats, who drew the line at secession or nullification or anything that impaired national existence, whether harbored in Pennsylvania, Massachusetts, South Carolina or by the confederacy.

He had no tolerance with the spirit that did not give whole-hearted support to his country when its lawful authorities had declared war. I think he held with the creed of that noble American, Admiral Stephen Decatur, who declared: "Our Country! In her intercourse with foreign nations, may she always be in the right; but our Country, right or wrong." To him "Our Country" embraced every foot of land from the Rio Grande to the Great Lakes and from his birthplace in the Green Mountain State to Oregon, to whose admission to all American rights he gave earnest effort. This life-long devotion to his country's cause in war impelled him to employ vigorous denunciation of those who not only gave half-hearted support to America when waging the war with Mexico, but who, while our brave soldiers were ready to make supreme sacrifice on the field of battle, denounced the war as "unholy, unrighteous, and damnable." Rising in hot indignation at what he regarded as their unpatriotic criticism, Mr. Douglas, when a member of the House of Representatives, thus vehemently denounced their course:

"I tell these gentlemen that it requires more charity than falls to the lot of frail man to believe that the expression of such sentiments is consistent with the sincerity of their professions—with patriotism, honor, and duty to their country. Patriotism emanates from the heart; it fills the soul; inspires the whole man with a devotion to his country's cause and speaks and acts the same language. America wants no friends, acknowledges the fidelity of no citizen who, after war is declared, condemns the justice of her cause and sympathizes with the enemy; all such are traitors in their hearts, and it only remains for them to commit some overt act for which they may be dealt with according to their deserts."

The Douglas of 1846 spoke the same language which was spoken by Judge Kenesaw Mountain Landis of Chicago recently when he sentenced to prison those Americans who, after war was declared, by voice and overt act gave aid and comfort to the enemies of their country. The climax of the address of Douglas in his address before the General Assembly of Illinois in 1861, "The shortest way now to peace is the most stupendous and unanimous preparation for war," is the admonition America has heeded in this day of its participation in the world-wide struggle.

Eliminating the controversial questions, upon which parties and men widely differed, Mr. Douglas' claim to fame may be said to rest upon these solid, practical contributions:

1. He pioneered the internal improvements which blessed Illinois with the Illinois Central Railroad and it is to his wise foresight that the State of Illinois derives a large revenue from its operation. In nearly every other instance, all profits accrued to the owners of the road without return to commonwealth or republic without whose aid the construction of the road would have been impossible. The precedent has been followed by other states and many cities without thought that they were following the precedent of Douglas.

2. He gave support and impetus to the construction of a transcontinental railroad, in keeping with his consistent optimism and faith in the West. He saw in his day, as with the vision of the prophet, the prosperity of the Golden West to whose government and development he was the chief legislative guide and to whose people he was the friendly mentor.

3. His unwavering, uncompromising, courageous advocacy of the right of the people to decide for themselves the kind of government they desired, and the ability of the people to decide for themselves better than any others could make decision for them.

That doctrine was his pillar of cloud by day and his pillar of fire by night, and he was ever ready to defend it whenever and by whomever challenged. In the defense of this principle he broke with the administration on the question of the Lecompton constitution upon the admission of Kansas as a state.

It required courage for a "thick and thin" party leader like Douglas to go to the White House and tell Mr. Buchanan that if the President pressed the Lecompton constitution he would oppose its adoption on the floor of the Senate, but this was not the first time Douglas had opposed measures of his own party administration that contravened his devotion to giving effect to the will of the people.

With him that duty transcended all others. The story of that interview in the White House has been often told. When all other arguments failed to secure the support of Douglas, the President said: "Senator, I wish you to remember that no Democrat was ever successful in opposing the policy of an administration of his party," whereupon Senator Douglas drew himself up with dignity and replied: "Mr. President, permit me most respectfully to remind you that General Jackson is dead," and withdrew.

Not only in his own state and in the republic did Mr. Douglas throw the full weight of his influence in behalf of full control of government by all the people and oppose all limitations upon their right, but he gave advice and counsel which helped to end borough representation and unfair discrimination, that existed in old commonwealths. Let me cite a concrete example of his healthy influence in my own state, North Carolina, with which Mr. Douglas was closely identified and which shares with Illinois the honors done him. When he was a young member of the House, Mr. Douglas formed a close friendship with David S. Reid, of North Carolina, afterwards governor and senator. Through this friendship Mr. Douglas met the lady who became his wife, Miss Martha Denny Martin, daughter of Col. Robert Martin, an influential planter.

His oldest son, Stephen A. Douglas, Jr., was born in North Carolina; his other son, the late Hon. Robert M. Douglas, justice of the Supreme Court of North Carolina, resided there from the time of his father's death, and all the descendants live in North Carolina, and I am happy to say his grandson, Robert D. Douglas, of Greensboro, and his daughter are here. She has been invited to unveil the statue here today of her illustrious ancestor. Mr. Douglas' intimate association with North Carolinians, after his marriage, and his knowledge of North Carolina politics, caused him to give wise counsel to Mr. Reid, which helped to make Reid governor and senator and convert North Carolina from a Whig to a Democratic state.

4. His large conception of American expansion, of the destiny of his country to exercise a constantly increasing influence as a world-power. "No pent-up Utica contracted" his vision. It thrilled him, as a partisan, that the Florida and Louisiana territories had been secured by Democratic presidents, and also under presidents of his party Texas and California and the vast expanse of territory that makes up the far West, were added to our domain. He ardently supported the Mexican War. As chairman of the Committee on Territories it gave him pride to see them develop and be carved into sovereign states of the Union. But, though he was happy that

through the agency of his party American territory and American opportunity had been enlarged, his chief rejoicing was because he believed, as a patriot, expansion would afford a larger plane upon which to demonstrate the superiority of popular government.

He dreamed of still greater expansion, and was one of the most aggressive advocates of the shibboleth "54-40 or fight," believing that the Oregon line should extend to that boundary. So profoundly was he convinced of this right of America that, when by an agreement with Great Britain less territory was secured for his country, he declined to vote for the treaty. Long before John T. Morgan was born, he had dreamed of an Isthmian canal, and he held with Humboldt's view, expressed in 1827, that the United States would see to it that this canal should be in American hands. Because Douglas believed, after California and the far West were incorporated into the United States, this government must undertake that great work, he fought the Clayton-Bulwer treaty on the ground that it might hinder or embarrass us when we were ready to build the Isthmian Canal, and might prevent annexation of any territory to this republic if time should show that further expansion would be advantageous to the United States, and any other territory desiring to be incorporated. His big Americanism, born of his full acceptance of the spirit of the Monroe doctrine, went further, and he took the grounds that under the Monroe doctrine, no European country should have a voice in the destiny of affairs of this hemisphere. In his argument against the treaty, Douglas told of a conversation he had with Sir Henry Bulwer. In response to Bulwer's statement that Douglas' position was unfair because the provisions of the treaty were reciprocal, Douglas said in the Senate: "I told him it would be fair if they would add one word to the treaty so that it would read that neither Great Britain nor the United States should ever occupy or hold dominion over Central America or Asia." "But," said he, "you have no interest in Asia." "No," answered I, "and you have none in Central America." "But," said he, "you can never establish any rights in Asia." "No," said I, "and we don't mean that you shall ever establish any in America."

The day came when Douglas foresaw that America would dig the Panama Canal. The Clayton-Bulwer treaty required negotiation before the vast work could be made national.   Happily Great Britain sought no other colonies on this hemisphere; happily our cordial relations made easy the negotiations, and none of the fears of Douglas were realized.   His position, wise or unwise, is illustrated to show his ambition for American domination on this hemisphere and his devotion to both the letter and spirit of the Monroe doctrine.

Today the ties between Great Britain and the United States have been cemented in blood, and if it be given to those who have gone before to know what transpires here, Douglas must be happy that the allied aims and purposes of these two great English-speaking races are in accord in their right to insure for all the world the same freedom and liberty to which Douglas devoted his great abilities.

It is particularly timely to call attention at this moment to the man who set perhaps the most noteworthy example in our history of the submergence of political rancor, of selfish ambition, of everything savoring of party politics, in order that a great war might be won.   There is no finer example for us to follow today than that of Stephen A. Douglas in what would have been to men of less broadness of mind and strength of character the bitterest hour of their lives.   To all of us tempted to let matters political, selfish ambitions or personal profit of any kind, cloud our clear vision in this trying hour, I would like to paint the picture of Stephen A. Douglas, defeated after the most notable political campaign in our history, a campaign filled with more bitterness, more personal rancor, than any presidential campaign in this country, standing by the side of President Lincoln as he took the oath of office, taking from him his hat as he bared his head for the solemn oath, and from that moment to the end loyally, faithfully and sincerely upholding the hands of Lincoln in the trying days of Civil War that followed.

There was much in the career of Douglas to prove that he was an able man, a brilliant man and a wise statesman, but this one act raises him in itself above mere brilliancy and ability, and entitles him to stand as one of the really great men of our country.   To forget self, to forget parties, to forget everything but the necessity of our country in her time of need, that is the acid test of real greatness.

When President Lincoln stood at Gettysburg he asked that we dedicate, not that historic ground to the nation, but that the nation dedicate itself to the principles for which men had there given their lives, to the principles of a united country, which were finally triumphant on that famous field. And it seems to me that we might in the same way here dedicate not this memorial to the man, but ourselves to the carrying out of the great example of unselfish patriotism shown by the man honored by this memorial. Let us here and now highly resolve to dedicate ourselves to the subordination of everything which can hinder or block or confuse the minds of our people, which can render uncertain, by unfounded doubts and suspicion, our fixed determination to win this war through the power of absolutely united effort on the part of every citizen of this country.

Let us forget, as this great man forgot, everything but our country.

AN ADDRESS BY LORD CHARNWOOD[7]

Delivered at the dedication of the statue of Abraham Lincoln, Andrew O'Connor, sculptor, Springfield, October 6, 1918.

In the first place I have a message to give you, which is from my countrymen, not in England only, but in all those self-governing communities from Newfoundland to New Zealand, from South Africa to Canada, which are linked with England in this war. It is a message, I would even say, from not a few men among those strange nations of the East, in India, which even today, under the guardianship of England and her colonies, are making their first steps in the path of self-government. I have no right whatever to speak also for the French, our masters, and yours, in so many ways, but I am going to speak for them.

On behalf of all of these, the self-governing communities of the world outside of this Union, I beg to offer the most heartfelt congratulations and birthday good wishes to the great Commonwealth of Illinois, older than some of those communities, and younger, again, it may be by some years, than England, which now completes a hundred years of vigorous life, which have won it so high a place among the free commonwealths of the world.

Ladies and gentlemen: Among the great dead who have spoken

[7] *Report of the Centennial Commission*, pages 317-321.

the English language, more and more as the years go on, two men stand out, eclipsing all others, not only by the loftiness of their genius, but by the appeal which they make to the common heart of men. One of them was William Shakespeare, and the other—by the way, a great student of Shakespeare—was Abraham Lincoln.

In this terrible struggle in which all civilization is involved, to what statesmen of the past can we turn in comparison for lessons of wise statesmanship, effectual and profound? Why, it is a singular fact that there is no statesman, however able, whose example is so often quoted in England today as that of Abraham Lincoln.

But there is more than that. Men are fighting, men are dying today, for ideas of democracy, of freedom, of equality. It is well, when our sons are dying for that, that we should sometimes consider a little deeply what these words mean. How can we govern ourselves, when some of us, God knows, are not wise? In what sense are men equal, ought they to be equal, when in certain obvious ways nature herself has fashioned them so unequal? Where shall we look for the answer to these paradoxes which sometimes baffle us? I speak as a student. There is no statesman, no poet, no philosopher, whose thoughts on these deep matters, are at once so profound and so far reaching, and put in a language so transparently simple, as Abraham Lincoln. And perhaps the deepest philosophy that was ever uttered on these momentous questions of democracy was uttered upon Illinois platforms in those wonderful debates which Lincoln held upon your soil with the great Douglas, his generous antagonist and when the great crisis came, his friend, who was so worthily commemorated this morning.

But there is something more than that. Beyond his statesmanship, beyond the profundity of his thought, beyond the poetry of his language, there was something interwoven with his genius, which brings it singularly near to the hearts of men of all conditions and characters and kinds, wherever their lot in life may be cast.

I might well, I think, ask first this question: How comes it that not only I, brought up as an English boy, but untold thousands of Englishmen, I can safely say, though we knew little of America, and understood nothing at all about the issues of your Civil War, nevertheless, quite early in boyhood fell under the spell of Lincoln's name?

I think in part it is for this reason: there is a type of manhood —it has, of course, its corresponding type of womanhood—but there is a type of manhood which at his mother's knee, every well brought up American boy has been taught to think of as American, and which every well brought up English boy has been taught to think of as English. It is the type of the man who can, when the occasion comes, be the most terrible of all fighting men, but who, in the main, and more and more as the years go by, is above all things gentle and pitiful in his dealings, absolutely honest, and in his inner heart, intensely humble.

It is a type which bears some resemblance to the old world ideal of the chivalrous knight, but it differs from it; it is more simple, more humble, more full of sound common sense, and more ready always to take life upon the amusing side. Well, of that type of manhood which I have described so poorly, but which all of us recognize, the very pattern in history was Abraham Lincoln.

Let me ask again, how is it that of all great statesmen, however much we revere their names, none has such a hold upon our affection as Lincoln has? Chiefly it is this: More than any of them he brought to bear on great questions of state just that sort of wisdom which every man and woman can apply in the common affairs of his or her daily life. There never was a great man who had so thoroughly learned, so heartily accepted, the hard and wholesome conditions of our common human life, set as we are in a world which is always very puzzling, and is sometimes very rough; set as we are to do the best we can, and not to dream about some impossible better; set as we are to do the best we can and yet be always awake to the better which may any day suddenly become possible. That is the union of the practical man and the idealist, a union without which practical qualities and idealism are alike—vanity. Of that union again the pattern for all time was Abraham Lincoln.

With the help of Mr. O'Connor's work, and that of other artists, with the help of some of those old friends of Lincoln, a few of whom I have had the privilege of meeting this day, we seem to see the man himself as we read his character in some of those simple sentences of his. "I am here," he seems to say, "I must do the best I can to bear the responsibility of taking the course which I feel I ought to take." "The subject is on my mind day and night; whatever shall appear to be God's will, I will do." "I see the storm coming, and I know that God's hand is in it. If he has a place and a work for me, and I think he has, I believe I am ready."

These are the unmistakable accents of a manly humility, which is, perhaps, the most uncommon of all the Christian graces, but which, when it is really there, gives to its possessor a tremendous power.

Humble he was, and we cherish his memory for every little thing about it, that to the unthinking mind might seem rough, for the little things that remind one that he had been and was proud to have been a day laborer upon Illinois soil. These things endear him to us. Don't let them hide from us the fact that he had the statesman's genius, and that he had the prophet's vision. And so, before I commence drawing to a close, may I read to you, and may I ask you to note their significance today, some words which he spoke on that last journey from Springfield on his way to occupy the President's chair at Washington.

He was speaking, as he said, and as I believe without preparation, in the Hall of Independence at Philadelphia. He said: "I have often pondered over the dangers which were incurred by the men who assembled here and framed and adopted that Declaration of Independence. I have pondered over the toils that were endured by the officers and soldiers of the army to achieve that independence. I have often inquired of myself what great principle or idea it was that kept the confederacy so long together. It was not the mere matter of separation from the motherland, it was that sentiment in the Declaration of Independence which gave liberty, not only to the people of this country, but a hope to the world for all future time." "It was that which gave promise that in due time the weight would be lifted from the shoulders of all men."

We are beginning to see that prophecy fulfilled. Of course I do not mean that in this war, or any single struggle, we shall perfectly achieve those ideals of human progress after which you, with your magnificent daring and dash, and we, in our persistent, blundering, faithful way, are striving through the ages.

Not one war will win that far goal. Every great work that is done is, in his familiar phrase, "a work thus far so nobly advanced." But the work which Lincoln accomplished when he saved the Union of these states was an indispensable step to the work which we and our sons have set our hands to do today—from which neither America, nor France, nor the British Empire, will turn back until our purpose is accomplished.

Governor Lowden, in his gracious telegram to invite me here, spoke of the fact that Americans and Englishmen are now fighting side by side on behalf of those principles for which Lincoln lived and died. Yes, we meet here in the presence of the dead. Thinking of that great man, we think all the while of the fields where my nephews have fallen, where, if the war lasts, my son may fall; where, it seems to me, all the best young men I knew at home have fallen, and fallen not in vain. Where lives, it hurts the heart to think how many, have had to be sacrificed by the French, and sacrificed not in vain. And where the sons of America and the sons of Illinois are now falling, and falling not in vain.

I cannot find words of mine fitting to sum up the feelings of this day, and I must turn to the words so often quoted, and never quoted once too often; words in which you will permit, and he would invite me, to make one trifling change: "We here highly resolve that these dead shall not have died in vain." "That our far-scattered, yet united nations, under God, shall have a new birth of freedom, and that government of the people, by the people, and for the people, shall not perish from the earth."

AN ADDRESS BY GOVERNOR FRANK O. LOWDEN[8]

Delivered at the dedication of the Illinois Centennial Monument in Logan Square, Chicago, October 13, 1918.

Mr. Chairman, Veterans of the Civil War, the Newest Recruits to the Present World War, Ladies and Gentlemen:

I do not recall that I have ever seen in Chicago a more impressive scene than this we behold today. Coming as it does at the end of our first great century of progress and civilization, staged at the

[8] From a manuscript copy in the possession of Governor Lowden.

meeting of these four great highways of Chicago, the Centennial memorial piercing as it does the blue above, this celebration makes a picture such as I do not recall to have ever seen the like of before in this great city of yours by the inland sea.

I want to pay my tribute to the genius which has wrought this triumph of art. They who help us build these monuments to our mighty past help to inspire us to a greater future.

Coming as this event does in the midst of this great war that is raging all around the earth, let us see if we can gather some lessons from our past which will help us in our perilous present. No one in Illinois can in this Centennial year recount the glories of our past without recalling the central figure of the last century, her own beloved Lincoln.

Today I want to remind you that Lincoln too had his great temptations to enter upon a premature peace; but Lincoln declared that war had been forced upon us, that we were compelled to take up arms for a certain object, and when that object was attained we would grant peace and not before.

So today in the presence of this great concourse of people, I am sure that I am right when I say that the President of today, when he answers this last peace note from Berlin, will insist that we too entered upon this war for an object, and that until that object is attained there can be no peace.

That object, my friends, what was it? Declared in clear and indisputable terms by the President himself, it was to destroy the kind of government which had wrecked the peace of the world. Until that government which had inflicted untold miseries and sufferings upon humanity throughout the earth is crushed, and in its stead there comes a government of the people and all the people, the peace of the future is not secure, and the object of this war will not have been accomplished.

This effort which emanates from Berlin is being made not so much because she desires peace as that she desires a few months' respite from our attacks on her western front, until she can gather up her shattered forces again and await us in her stronger fortifications upon her own frontier.

So, if we, misled for the moment, were to grant an armistice at this time, it would add to the sufferings of your boys who are at the front and would prolong this war.

Now, let us, in Chicago and Illinois, and the United States, imitate our sons upon the battle fronts and when peace is urged answer that plea by a renewed assault all along the line. They have the true idea of the only path that will lead to peace, and if we at home are worthy of those boys, we will meet every duty that comes to us, and the first and most immediate duty is to oversubscribe the fourth liberty loan.

I want to remind you that a few months ago we all asked nothing more of our soldiers on the battle front than that they should stay the enemy during the remainder of this year, hold them where they were, and with another year we might hope for victory. That is all we demanded of these boys ninety days ago, but they not only have stayed the enemy where he was, but have driven him back from day to day until, as I speak, all of the gains of our enemy for those four months have been blotted out and more besides.

The American soldiers in the battle line have not only met their undertaking, but they have more than met it—they have oversubscribed and overpaid their undertaking in this war.

Now, shall it be said of those of us who remain at home that we shall not oversubscribe our undertaking?

I want to read to you today, briefly, on this subject of peace, what a distinguished German journalist himself said of the German people in this war but a few weeks ago.

Dr. Rosemeyer, who was asked why he did not write something to move the German people to an understanding of the real issues involved in this war, said:

"Nonsense! Haven't I been writing my fingers off for thirty years! What those fellows need is not ideas for their brains, they need bombs on their skulls. Help can only come from one place— from Bethlehem—Bethlehem, Pennsylvania. They will cheat you yet, those Junkers. Having won half of the world by bloody murder, they are going to win the other half with tears in their eyes, crying for mercy."

That is what this great German writer, who knew the Prussian mind and the Prussian heart, said of the Pan-Germans themselves, and today, by their tears and their cries for mercy, and their professions of love for justice, they are asking for a peace with the spoils of their bloody crimes in their hands, without reparation for a single one of the infamies they have perpetrated upon an unoffending world.

My friends, this war is not over. Let us not delude ourselves. It is not over, because we cannot be true to our soldiers who have made the last supreme sacrifice for us, and make a peace short of unconditional surrender.

I want to give you a form by which to answer the next note that Berlin writes to us. I call some of you old heroes of the Civil War to witness the sort of correspondence which went on between General Buckner of the Confederate forces and General Grant of our forces, at Fort Donelson. Buckner only asked for an armistice of six hours, and for the appointment of commissioners to arrange the terms of a possible surrender. A note somewhat like the last German note, except that only a six hours' armistice was asked by Buckner, while if the armistice is granted in this case, it will be prolonged until the Germans have reorganized their shattered armies and are ready to meet us on another battle field.

Grant received that note, and this is his reply: "No terms will be accepted except immediate and unconditional surrender. I propose to move immediately upon your works."

So now, with the German armies in a condition of demoralization and despair, the time is not for an armistice, but the language of Grant. If you will let Pershing and his boys and our brave Allies alone they will move immediately upon the enemy's works.

I cannot tell you, my friends, how proud I am to be here this afternoon. I can't tell you how much hope brightened within me when I saw these hundreds of new recruits pass by. Three days some of them have been training, and you saw their martial bearing and their martial tread. When you see what we make of these American soldiers in seventy-two hours, is it any wonder that they are adding new glory to the American flag every day on every battle front?

A letter that I have received from an officer in France said that if every commissioned officer of an American regiment is killed or disabled and seventy-five per cent of the rank and file become disabled, the other twenty-five per cent will still go forward under the command of a sergeant or a corporal, if need be.

That is not possible under any other form of government than ours, where every man is the equal of every other man. In a military autocracy which holds that all the earth and the fruits thereof belong to the favored few, and that the great mass of mankind must toil in order that the few may enjoy the luxuries of life, you cannot develop an army which will move forward under the command of the humblest man in the force; but a democracy which recognizes no essential distinction between one man and another, is capable of producing armies like this. That is why Chateau Thierry is a name that will be remembered forever in American annals, and will be written along with those other great names in American history, Valley Forge, Yorktown, Gettysburg, Vicksburg, and Appomattox; because it was at Chateau Thierry that the American soldiers helped turn the tide of this battle which had been running against the Allies for four months; and it is now running so strongly against the Central Empires that they are trying to cajole us with honeyed talk of peace long enough to gather up their broken army, so that they may still offer resistance to us on another battle line.

Think of the glorious pages of history which our boys wrote at St. Mihiel, where Pershing's army as an independent unit first appeared.

So I am proud to be over here in the heart of this great west side, which is showing us the type of the new American. Something was said about Americanization by the distinguished chairman. It is a worthy work, in which we all must interest ourselves; but the most complete Americanization that is being wrought, is being wrought upon these battle fields. Take up our casualty lists any day, and note the names of a half dozen nationalities side by side. When a boy is fighting in the American uniform in the cause of the world's liberty and civilization, it doesn't matter how his name is spelled, that name is an American name forevermore. So when the sons of Poland, the sons of Scandinavia, the sons of Bohemia, the sons of Italy, aye, and the sons of Germany, too, are fighting under the same banner, the cause of civilization, those boys are Americanized in a very brief time; and no one will be heard to reproach them upon their return for any lack of true Americanism. There is no place in all the world where brotherhood can find surer home than in the trenches upon the battle front; because when men have undergone the hardships of war, side by side, awaiting the morrow to meet the common foe, they are not likely ever again to clash over race or religious prejudices. A real brotherhood is possible there, and you veterans of the Civil War know how dear to your hearts is the name of "Comrade." You know what that mighty tie means, how closer than a brother the real comrade is. So we will have two millions and more, when this war is over, of new comrades, formed in the furnace of this mighty war returning to America, and we will have a new spirit of brotherhood throughout the land as a result.

My friends, awful as is war, frightful as are the sufferings which our boys endure, mighty as the sacrifice is that we all must make, there will be some compensation growing out of this war. I am sure of that. Let me read to you a letter which I brought, and this is for the benefit of the mothers, for they have the hardest part to bear. I know something of the mother's heart; I know that in its deep and mysterious recesses every pain that her son suffers is reproduced within herself. I know that she not only suffers all the agonies that come to her son, but that she has not the stimulus of action to help her bear pain. The mother's part in war is always the hardest part. So I want to read this letter from a young lad who belongs to the United States Marines, written to his mother a few weeks ago:

"The past six months has made home and mother very dear and sacred to me, and to thousands of other boys. God helping me, I will commit no sin that by His help I can avoid. God bless and help you folks. Do not worry about me, morally or physically. If I should meet death, I will die like a man for the most sacred cause our country or any other country has ever called upon mothers to give their sons to; but I am certain that I am coming back, and coming back a man. I am sure that you will never regret that you signed your name to my enlistment papers last April. God bless you, mother. Your loving son."

Similar letters are coming from the battle front every day. Ah, imagine if you can a lad of sixteen or seventeen or eighteen, writing such a letter as that a few years ago! So, while as I have often said, we shall not have as many young men in this country when the war is over, we will have a finer body of young manhood than any country ever had in all the history of the past. That will be one of the compensations. Then, again, my friends, we are going to have a better country when the war is over. Things were not going altogether well with us before the war. We were becoming a materialistic people. We were devoting ourselves only to the things which you can touch and handle, the things of the senses. The finer, spiritual values were dying out of our lives. The spirit of discipline had fled from the home, from the church, from the school, and from the state, if you please. We no longer looked upon our citizenship under that starry flag as the most precious possession we had. We only felt, in some sort of a way, that the country owed much to us, but not that we owed everything to our country. So when this great calamity came upon the world, when this great tragedy of the ages was initiated by the cruelty and tyranny and heartlessness of the Hohenzollern dynasty, it wasn't upon an altogether satisfactory world that the tragedy came. Now, wherever I go, whatever audience I face, I see a new spirit shining out of the faces of the men and the women, aye, even the little children. Humanity is having a rebirth in this crucial time. Our citizenship is going forward and upward by leaps and bounds, so, when the war is over we are going to have a better world than we have had in all the past. The old idea of human brotherhood for which our fathers fought at Concord and Lexington, and for which these old heroes fought on a score of bloody battle fields, that sense of human brotherhood is coming back to the earth. You know, we all know in our hearts that we were becoming selfish, very selfish, before this war. We were separating into classes, we were thinking of ourselves, we had forgotten, aye, absolutely forgotten, the Master's definition of who our neighbor was. But now, purified in the fires of this war, new and spiritual things are coming back to the world, a new brotherhood will come to our land. We will have a better world when the war is over.

Now, in conclusion, for I have spoken longer than I expected, among the other compensations that this war will bring about, and

I feel it this afternoon as I have not felt it before, is going to be a new Chicago. We have, too, in this great city, divided into groups, according to nationality, or according to religion, or according to some other test. Now, our citizenship of this great city is being separated into only two classes: all who love their flag, who believe that it is the most sacred protection to humanity the world contains— those who believe that America is the best hope of humanity everywhere are arrayed on the one side, and all the others (and thank God they are growing fewer in Chicago every day), are on the other side.

So, when this war is over, we shall have a new citizenship, and the only test of a man in those days will be: did he do all that he could while the war was on to save and protect our land? That will be the only test. We will have a solidarity of citizenship for all good things that we didn't have before.

I received a letter just as I left Springfield, yesterday morning, from a corporal who is with our soldiers in France, Corporal Paul Salzman, of Bloomington. He writes me as follows: "You can tell our people at home that we are constantly thinking of them; that we will do all that is in our power to make the fame of Illinois still greater." That is the spirit of our boys on the other side. I do not know this young man. All I know of him is what is contained in this letter, and although he is only a corporal, I want to answer that letter when I return home.

I have delivered Paul Salzman's message to you, my friends, and I am going to ask you what your message through me to Paul Salzman and his comrades on the battle front shall be. May I tell him (and I feel sure in my heart that you will authorize me to do so) that the people of Illinois are proud beyond expression of the heroic services of our soldiers on the battle fields? May I also tell him, as he asks me to tell you, that we are thinking constantly of them? I am sure I may. I want to add that our dearest concern in these fateful times is not only that we shall constantly think of them, but how we shall constantly do for them that their comfort may be increased. I want to add that we are thinking and thinking constantly, to use his word, of what we can do, my friends of Illinois, to make this state of such splendid past, even a better state. May

I tell him that that is your message to me to our soldier boys in the battle line, wherever those lines are laid?

Our past century has indeed been a glorious one. It is as full of inspiration as any century of any nation, or of any state. More and more often pilgrimages are being made to Lincoln's tomb. When men have despaired of the future, they have there repaired to refresh their courage and to strengthen their arms. Only a year ago, I visited that sacred spot with Marshal Joffre, the hero of the Marne. As I beheld him lay a wreath above Lincoln's dust, and saw his tear-dimmed eyes, I knew that old hero had strengthened his determination that "They shall not pass."

So, splendid as is the first century of our history, great as has been its contribution to all the progress of all the world, let us hope that we, in these, the most crucial years of all our history, shall be worthy of our glorious past.

My friends, I thank you for the patience with which you have listened to me today, and I want to tell you that I have gained inspiration by being here. I am surer of the future of our citizenship and our beloved land than I have ever been before, and so I thank you again from the bottom of my heart.

CLOSE OF CENTENNIAL YEAR, DECEMBER 3, 1918— A PROCLAMATION

On December third, it will be a full hundred years since Illinois was formally admitted into the Union of States. We have celebrated our Centennial Year with fitting observance in every part of the State. These celebrations have been occasions whereon our people have found in our past achievements their highest inspiration for meeting the solemn duties of the present year.

Our Centennial Year now draws to a close. At almost the same time the world-wide war has also reached its end. Illinois has played a part in that war worthy of her first great century. Her sons have given their lives on a score of battle-fields that the principles of liberty and justice to all men, for which her Lincoln lived and died, may become the rule of all the world.

During this time within our borders party clamor has been silenced, religious differences have been hushed, and all classes of our people have shown equal zeal and equal patriotism in support of the war.

The gates of the new century swing ajar. The mighty problems of peace are upon us. With the reorganization of our State Government, with a new constitutional convention before us, with a new system of highways to be built, Illinois is preparing to meet these problems. So, on December third, grateful for our first great century, let us plan how we shall make our second century, in achievement, match the first.

(SEAL)

GIVEN UNDER MY HAND AND THE GREAT SEAL OF STATE AT THE CAPITOL IN SPRING-FIELD, THIS TWENTIETH DAY OF NOVEMBER IN THE YEAR OF OUR LORD ONE THOUSAND NINE HUNDRED AND EIGHT-EEN, AND OF THE INDEPEND-ENCE OF THE UNITED STATES THE ONE HUNDRED AND FORTY-THIRD.

FRANK O. LOWDEN

By the Governor:
 LOUIS L. EMMERSON.
  Secretary of State.

VII. BRINGING WAR ACTIVITIES TO A CLOSE

AN ADDRESS BY LIEUTENANT GOVERNOR JOHN G. OGLESBY[1]

Delivered at the Victory Massmeeting held at the State House, Springfield, on the evening of November 11, 1918.

Citizens of Springfield:

We are meeting to celebrate what will come to be the most historic day in the annals of history—the virtual cessation of the world's war.

It is fitting that we meet here in the shadow of the statue of the Great Emancipator—Illinois' magnificent gift to civilization. And were he here with us his countenance would shine with glorified joy. It is unfortunate that our state's splendid leader, who has kept Illinois in the vanguard of the nation from the point of patriotism and public-spiritedness—Governor Lowden—is absent from the state and unable to witness this splendid celebration.

The armistice is signed. Peace appears to be assured, but it is not yet actually at hand. As we have in the past year and a half been ready for every emergency let us not be careless, let us not be lulled to sleep, but let us continue our every effort until the final and positive treaties are signed and the world is once again fit and safe for free people. Our soldiers have about finished their duty. We at home must continue our work, and, if necessary, our sacrifices. The period of demobilization and reconstruction will soon be at hand, and it will be a period of deep significance and importance not only to America but to all the world. There will be many problems to be solved, but I feel sure that they will be met and adjusted with justice and fairness.

In these moments of jubilation let us mingle our joy with a solemn thought for those of us whose husbands, sons or brothers have

---

[1] *Illinois State Journal*, November 12, 1918.

made the supreme sacrifice. Although their joy is as great as ours over this final outcome, although their sorrow is a sacred one, still their hearts are bowed with grief; so let us not only give them the honor due them, but add our prayers to the Almighty to assuage their pain and sorrow. While the war is practically ended, still, we at home—women and men alike—have a duty to perform. Each one has his individual tasks to do and each of us must stick to that task, no matter what it may be. If our soldiers over yonder would send us a message, it would be in these bright days that have come to carry on as faithfully as we have in the dark days that are passed.

The United War drive is now in swing. We should give of our utmost for this purpose, because it represents the association of all the different societies and organizations that are helpful to our soldiers.

With the war over, some may think there is no longer need of these activities. This is not so. On the contrary, now as never before must we energetically pursue our endeavors. And so, may I urge, that all of us continue our every effort until the world has once more been put in order.

THE MAINTENANCE OF ORDER—A PROCLAMATION

TO THE MAYORS, PRESIDENTS AND OTHER OFFI-
CIALS OF THE MUNICIPALITIES AND TO ALL
OTHER CITIZENS OF THE STATE OF ILLINOIS:

WHEREAS, the Secretary of War of the United States of America has today advised the Governor of Illinois as follows:

"Signing of armistice in no way lessens responsibility of civil communities for protection of soldiers from prostitutions and sale of liquor. Our states and cities ought never to lose the control which has been established or stop so vital a work. The Government proposes to leave no measure unused in repression of these evils from now until demobilization is fully accomplished. War Department is determined to return soldiers to their families and to civil life uncontaminated by diseases. Laxity in your State after so much has been done would be a disaster to our soldiers and their families." And,

WHEREAS, The said Secretary of War has requested that this message be transmitted to the executives of all cities and towns, now,

THEREFORE, I, John G. Oglesby, Acting Governor of Illinois, do hereby direct the public attention to the foregoing message and request that every effort be made to keep all communities free from vices and evils as suggested by the Secretary of War.

(SEAL)

GIVEN UNDER MY HAND AND THE GREAT SEAL OF STATE AT THE CAPITOL IN SPRINGFIELD, THIS FIFTEENTH DAY OF NOVEMBER IN THE YEAR OF OUR LORD ONE THOUSAND NINE HUNDRED AND EIGHTEEN, AND OF THE INDEPENDENCE OF THE UNITED STATES THE ONE HUNDRED AND FORTY-THIRD.

JOHN G. OGLESBY

BY THE ACTING GOVERNOR:
Louis L. EMMERSON.
SECRETARY OF STATE.

THANKSGIVING DAY, 1918—A PROCLAMATION

The President of the United States has designated Thursday, November 28, 1918, as Thanksgiving Day.

In pursuance of the proclamation of the President, I, Frank O. Lowden, Governor of Illinois, do hereby urge our citizens to observe that day as a day of prayer and thanksgiving. I urge that our people assemble in their places of public worship, and there render thanks to Almighty God for the manifold blessings he has vouchsafed to us in this time of our great trial.

There is much for which we should render thanks on this Thanksgiving Day. Above all, the God of Righteousness and Justice, the God of our Fathers, again has vindicated His sovereignty over all the earth and has triumphed over the powers of evil and darkness. Our faith has been strengthened and we now see with a clearer vision that God rules the world. Let us return thanks for our surer knowledge of Him, and let us also thank Him that man, created in the image of his Maker, is proving his right to rule himself.

Our soldiers have shown their valor upon a score of battle-fields. We asked of them only that they, with our Allies, hold our enemy in check until another year. But they have surpassed all we have asked or hoped. They have swept on from victory to victory, until they hold the last of their foes within their grasp. They not only have proven their mettle as soldiers, but they equally have shown their fine quality as men. For all of this, we surely should return thanks to Almighty God.

And now that the clouds of war have lifted, Humanity faces a new and fairer day. Out of this great war there comes clearer than ever before two shining ideas that shall rule the world—the Fatherhood of God, and the Brotherhood of Man.

(SEAL)

GIVEN UNDER MY HAND AND THE GREAT SEAL OF STATE AT THE CAPITOL IN SPRINGFIELD, THIS EIGHTEENTH DAY OF NOVEMBER, IN THE YEAR OF OUR LORD ONE THOUSAND NINE HUNDRED AND EIGHTEEN, AND OF THE INDEPENDENCE OF THE UNITED STATES THE ONE HUNDRED AND FORTY-THIRD.

FRANK O. LOWDEN

By the Governor:

LOUIS L. EMMERSON.
Secretary of State.

AN ADDRESS BY GOVERNOR FRANK O. LOWDEN[2]

Delivered at the Thanksgiving services held at the State Arsenal, Springfield, Thanksgiving Day, November 28, 1918.

Mr. Chairman and Ladies and Gentlemen:

It gives me great pleasure to be here this morning and though I am asked only to preside, the gentlemen have been courteous enough to say that I might speak a few words.

The time in which we live is so wonderful that it is almost impossible to single out the important events of the days as they unfold. There are certain things, however, that are clear to the dullest mind. One of those things is, that although for the last two years, in many dark hours, we have doubted whether our form of self-government could prevail against the mightiest military powers of the world, and though at times we wondered if after all democracy had the vigor and the virility to defend itself against the encroachments of its foes, we now no longer wonder. We now see that the misgivings of those dark hours were needless.

You will recall, I am sure, that a few years ago many of the profoundest students of the French government had reached the conclusion that democracy had failed in France, and that her republic was doomed to a short life. I recall particularly a book called "The Cult of the Incompetent," published perhaps six or eight years ago, by a French academician, in which he reached the conclusion that democracy had failed in France. But during the last four and a half years, that nation which had stumbled, it is true, from year to year, has written a more glorious history than it had in all the centuries of its past.

Again we heard mutterings from our English friends, to the effect that England was decadent; that England had lost her old time virility and would be unable to cope with the more centralized and efficient military despotism of Berlin. But during the last few years that slander has been refuted. In the centuries to come, when despots think of hurling their thunderbolts against self-governing nations, they are going to recall the English at Mons, at Ypres, at Aisne, and they are going to stay their cruel and brutal hands.

[2] From a manuscript copy in the possession of Governor Lowden.

And so in our own land, a few years ago there were many who wondered if our young men had not lost the vigor which had distinguished their fathers in other wars, and whether or not, as was charged by some of our critics, we had not become a nation of materialists, who thought only of gain and nothing of the more strenuous things of life. That charge has been answered during the last few months by two millions of as fine young men as ever went forth to battle.

So today the fears that had filled us during the last decade have been stilled. But that does not mean that other dangers do not concern us. For let us recall this morning that the victory which the self-governing nations of the world have achieved against the powers of autocracy was not so much a victory of democracy over despotism as it was a victory of righteousness over evil, because during even those unhappy months that followed March twenty-first, when our enemies seemed to gain on every front, and when our allies appeared powerless to stop them, depressed as we were, it was not so much for the fate of democracy that we were depressed, but it was because it seemed to us at that time as though righteousness had not the power to assert itself against the powers of evil. It was not the loss of our government, sad as that was, which was the most depressing event of those days; it was the fear that the God of Righteousness, that the God of Justice, that the God of our fathers was no longer able to assert Himself against the powers of darkness which were represented in the battle lines of our enemies during those fateful months.

Now I am here to say to you this morning that the real triumph, the thing that makes this peace the most notable in all the history of the world, is that our faith is refreshed and reinvigorated in the invincibility of the God of our fathers. But, my friends, I am also here to warn you that righteousness is exacting just as much of a democracy as of a king. I am here to say that our dangers in the future—though we no longer have to fear the mailed fist—are no less than they have been in the past; because, unless our government is stamped all over with justice and righteousness to all men, we, too, shall suffer as the autocracies of middle Europe have suffered.

There is no law anywhere, moral or legal, which justifies the majority in committing a wrong any more than a king committing a wrong. A democracy through its majority may violate all those sacred things for which we have fought and which have been established, just as much as can an emperor or a king. Justice and righteousness and liberty are exacting just as much of the American republic, if it is to endure, as they have of any throne in the past.

We have a conquered peace; we have also won a great opportunity and it is for us to meet that opportunity. Our task is but half accomplished. In the heat of this great conflict new emotions and new ideals have been born, and, so far as they are true and pure, we must be loyal to them if we would enjoy the fruits of our great victory. We are going to have some newer concepts of life. Humanity has been touched to the very heart in these years and we are going to think a little more tenderly of the man, just the plain, average man, than we have in the past. We are going to have new standards for success in the industrial world. The time is coming, when a captain of industry dies, that the world will say not how many millions of dollars he left, but how many men he maintained in happiness, well-being and contentment in his employ. There will still be rivalry in the future as in the past. Men will seek leadership in industry as in other fields in the future, but there will be a new measure of success when those captains come to compare themselves with others, and the main measure of that success will be the well-being of the men in the employ of that great industry.

We shall have a newer idea, a more vigorous idea, as to our duty to the state. We have gotten into the habit of saying that the state owes us everything and that we owe the state nothing in return. We are going to abandon that old idea and we are going to say that our first duty is to the state, so far as the things of this earth pertain. That is going to give democracy efficiency in functioning—something it has not had in the past.

I have just another word to say—I am almost forgetting the fact that I am here to preside—but I want to say one word more. In these days our thoughts are of the fathers and mothers in whose homes the stars upon the little service flag have turned from blue to gold. I had a letter from the chaplain of a regiment belonging to our Prairie Division—the division which, as you know, achieved immortal fame on a score of battle fields and has added to the other names with which we of Illinois conjure, the names of Cantigny, Chateau Thierry,[3] St. Mihiel and the Argonne Forest.   The chaplain of this superb regiment wrote me a letter before the armistice was signed, but received by me only yesterday.   I am going to read a portion of this letter because I think I owe it to the fathers and mothers of these boys of whom I spoke a moment ago, and because I have not seen the thought so well expressed by any one during the war.   This is what he says:

"Governor, don't let our folks at home get the wrong idea about our boys who fall in the fight.   They, the boys I mean, have the best of the conflict.   Death is only an old humbug to them.   I have heard them laughing in his old red face where he stalks in the dark.   And I have actually seen that same laugh set in a smile on their dear dead faces; and in spite of the bitter tongueless ache in my heart, I have had to smile back at them and say, 'It's all right, old chap, you're not dead; you are alive, and you shall live forever in the grateful hearts of humanity's millions; you have only been transferred to the triumphant hosts of the Supreme Commander, to march on and on in step with all the God-led progress this old world shall ever make through all eternity.'   Death!   Why death is a negligible faker to our brave boys.   They don't even consider him.   Either they come back or they go West, that's all."

And, bearing that picture in our hearts, let us resolve this morning that only by performing our noblest duties as citizens of Illinois shall we be worthy of these heroic boys.   I thank you.

AN ADDRESS BY GOVERNOR FRANK O. LOWDEN[4]

Delivered at a meeting of members of the local boards of central and southern Illinois, held in Springfield, December 30, 1918.

General Dickson, Ladies and Gentlemen:

I am just here for a brief moment to express my appreciation, which I hope to do in a more public manner in my biennial address to the General Assembly, of the very great contribution you have

---

[3] No units of the 33d Division participated in the battles of Cantigny and Chateau Thierry.

[4] From a manuscript copy in the possession of Governor Lowden.

made to the distinguished part Illinois has played in this war. We had just twelve days from the time we were asked to recommend the Exemption Boards until those recommendations should be in the hands of the Provost Marshal General in Washington. It was a task of great magnitude. I remember when I was asked to make the recommendations, I appealed to the public and said, "What I want is the best men in the several exemption districts of this state. I want representatives of both parties and of all classes of society. I want men who will, with single-minded devotion, address themselves to this great work." And the results of the Illinois exemption boards show clearly that my appeal was not in vain.

In my opinion, the administration of the Selective Service law is our greatest achievement in the prosecution of this war and that achievement has been made possible by the unselfish, disinterested and patriotic service of the members of the exemption boards. From time to time reports have come from the Provost Marshal General's Office in Washington that in several particulars Illinois had led all the states in the promptness and the efficiency with which it had administered the law. That credit is due in a very large measure to the exemption boards of this state—boards which have met and worked day and night to discharge the serious duties of their important office. I have said recently that I do not know which to admire the most, the valor of our soldiers in the field or the solidarity of our people at home in the prosecution of this war; and that solidarity has been made possible largely by your devotion to your important work. And though you have not uniforms to distinguish you, nor service bars to denote where you have served, you are just as important a part of the armies of liberty as the soldiers at the front.

I realized in the beginning that this was a new experiment for America. Our people had been used generally to the volunteer method of enrolling armies, and so we wondered how we should succeed when we inaugurated this great work. In the name of Illinois, and in behalf of Illinois, I want to thank you with all my heart for making this great experiment a success in Illinois.

The record of our state in the Civil War was a glorious one. In this great war, Illinois has been worthy of her past. And when the history of this war shall be written, you will be entitled to a very

(31)

large share of the credit which belongs to Illinois. I thank you heartily for giving me the opportunity to come before you for a moment, and express the deep appreciation I feel for what you have done.

ILLINOIS' PART IN THE WAR

Extract from the Biennial Report of the Governor to the Fifty-first General Assembly from the *Journal of the House of Representatives of the Fifty-first General Assembly of Illinois*, January 8, 1919, pages 18-19.

· · · · · · · · ·

You will recall, with justifiable pride, the hearty response which your Honorable Body made to the government at Washington immediately upon the severing of our diplomatic relations with the German Empire. From that day until the armistice was signed, Illinois presented a solid front to our enemies, whether they were found on foreign soil, or within our own borders.

You will recall that in the early days of the war, we took counsel together over the creation of Exemption Boards for the administration of the Selective Service Law. The time, within which we had to act, was short. But twelve days intervened between the time we were asked to nominate members for these boards and the time when the complete lists of them were in Washington. Illinois was required to furnish 227 of these boards. The membership of the boards was 681. The duties, devolving upon these boards, were of the most delicate and exacting kind. It was to be expected that some mistakes would be made in the personnel of the boards. And yet, for the entire period of the war, only ten members were found wanting and compelled to resign.

The successful administration of the Selective Service Law is one of the greatest achievements of the war. Those who have served upon the Exemption Boards are largely entitled to the credit for this achievement. Their labors have been exhaustive, their embarrassments great, their tasks new and untried, and therefore, their accomplishment was doubly creditable and honorable.

Your Honorable Body also provided for a State Council of Defense. That body was promptly appointed and organized, and at once began its work. Through the generosity of the chairman of the

Council, an entire building in Chicago, with fuel, light and janitor service, was given without expense to the State for the activities of the State Council. You are all familiar with the business-like and efficient work of that Council. Its activities multiplied until they reached into every corner of the State. Although the Council was composed of representatives of both political parties, and of both capital and labor, though it was intended to be, as it was in fact, representative of all our people, it acted with complete harmony and efficiency during all the months of the war. It was a large factor in maintaining the solidarity of our people which so distinguished Illinois during this time. An appropriation of $50,000 was made for the expenses of this body by the last General Assembly. This small appropriation was found insufficient and the public-spirited citizens of Chicago raised voluntarily $100,000 additional. In other states, appropriations of a million dollars, and in one instance, I believe, of five millions were made for similar bodies. The comparatively small expenses of our State Council were due, first, to business-like methods; and second, to the fact that its vast work was mainly conducted by volunteer workers. Notwithstanding the disparity in amounts expended by our State Council of Defense and those of other states, it is generally conceded, I believe, that in the amount and quality of work done, our State Council stands among the very first, if not the first, in all the Union.

Illinois, during the present war, has furnished 314,504 soldiers and sailors to the forces of the United States, a number 58,207 in excess of all who went from Illinois to join the Union Armies in the Civil War.[5] She has met whole-heartedly and promptly every demand for money or men made upon her from the day when war was declared. Her soldiers have won imperishable renown upon every battle field whereon they have fought. And henceforth Belleau Woods, Chatillon, Chateau Thierry, St. Mihiel and the Argonne Forest will be named in our history alongside of Donelson, Vicksburg, Missionary Ridge and Appomattox. For upon all these fields, and many others besides, the valor of Illinois soldiers played a mighty part.

. . . .

[5] Final figures on the number of Illinois men who served in the military and naval service were not, of course, available at the time of this message.

RESOLUTIONS ADOPTED AT A MEETING OF THE STATE COUNCIL OF DEFENSE OF ILLINOIS, DECEMBER 13, 1918[6]

WHEREAS The State Council of Defense of Illinois has watched with keen interest the splendid work of the various departments and organizations under its supervision, and

WHEREAS By the signing of the armistice with the Central Powers, continuation of the activities of many of these departments and organizations has become unnecessary, and, as a consequence, they are gradually winding up the business on hand and retiring from service,

NOW THEREFORE, BE IT RESOLVED That the State Council of Defense of Illinois hereby directs the Chairman to extend its sincere thanks to each and all of such retiring departments and organizations, and to all connected with their activities, and to express its grateful appreciation of the effective and patriotic service rendered and the excellent results accomplished.

THE WORK OF THE STATE COUNCIL OF DEFENSE OF ILLINOIS, AN ADDRESS BY SAMUEL INSULL[7]

Delivered before the Commercial Club of Chicago, January 18, 1919.

The State Council of Defense of Illinois is a liquidating—almost a liquidated—concern. Hence, what I am to say may be considered as a forecast of some aspects of a final report to the shareholders. These shareholders are the people of Illinois, for the Council has tried, at least, to be representative of the patriotism and effort of all our people.

In this we have followed the lead of Governor Lowden. From the first, he set a pattern of undivided loyalty and unfaltering devo-

[6] Minutes of the meeting of the State Council of Defense, December 13, 1918.

[7] *Illinois in the War, An Address to the Commercial Club of Chicago by Samuel Insull, Chairman, the State Council of Defense of Illinois, January 18, 1919* (Chicago, 1919).

tion to the cause of America. He did not seek to curry favor with either pacifists or hyphenates by soft speaking. Nor did he recognize politics or partisanship as a factor in the prosecution of the war. He did not conceal his convictions nor camouflage his attitude.

Governor Lowden not only set the State Council an example to follow, but he made our work infinitely easier than it would otherwise have been. Frankly, if we had not had him as our bulwark, and also as the pioneer in what we undertook to do, our difficulties would have been tremendous, and we might not have overcome all of them.

With Governor Lowden to lead, it is our belief that Illinois made a record in the war in which all may take a just pride. Let me sum up for you some of the state's achievements—not in wearying detail, but in gross totals.[8]

First, the men our state furnished to fight the war, for the men who do the fighting rightly come first. Under the selective service act, Illinois registered a total of 1,559,586 men of fighting age— 646,480 on June 5, 1917, between the ages of 21 and 31 years; 44,106 youngsters who had just come of age on June 5, 1918; 689,000 on September 12, 1918, boys between the ages of 18 and 21, and men between the ages of 31 and 45.

Illinois put into the national service a total of 314,504 men and boys—24,663 in the navy; 3,678 in the marines; and 286,163 in the army. The figures for the army are to the end of the war; those for the navy and the marines are up to June 30th only; the several thousand volunteers who entered the service as officers through the various training camps are not included. But even these incomplete figures show that Illinois furnished for the defense of the nation in the great war 57,207 more men than it did for maintenance of the union in the four years of the Civil War.

Another interesting fact is, that while the Selective Service Act was adopted almost as soon as America was in the war, 56.6 per cent of the men who went from Illinois—178,143—volunteered, and only 43.3 per cent—136,361—were inducted into service under the draft law.

[8] Final figures were not, of course, available at the time that this address was made.

Next, money. To finance the war, the United States has borrowed on bonds and war savings stamps, in round numbers, $19,000,000,000. Of this sum, Illinois furnished in round numbers, $1,300,000,000—more than $1,209,000,000 for Liberty Bonds and the remainder for War Savings Stamps. In other words, with about 5.5 per cent of the population of the United States, Illinois has taken virtually 7 per cent of the nation's war loans. This sum is once and a half times the value of the great crop (the greatest of any state in the union) which we raised last year.

Illinois has given, as well as loaned, her money for the war. The total collections of the various war aid and relief organizations of which a record has been kept run well above $42,250,000. This is within $7,750,000 of the total of all state appropriations for the two-year period of 1917 and 1918. In other words, in the eighteen months we were at war, the people of Illinois voluntarily assessed themselves about once and a half as much per year for war aid and relief as they are assessed for state taxes.

This money was given as follows:

Red Cross	$16,165,100
Y. M. C .A.	4,896,187
Salvation Army	781,941
United War Work	13,935,452
War Recreation Board	550,000
Under State Council licenses	6,000,000

This last sum is partly estimated; it was money collected for local aid of all kinds, and our figures show it was all collected with an overhead charge of less than 10 per cent. These figures do not include the very generous first contribution to the Knights of Columbus, nor the fees of the two Red Cross membership drives.

Another of the great contributions of Illinois was in the products of the field—crops. Estimates of the Department of Agriculture show that the 1918 farm crop was third in volume in the history of the state, and the greatest in money value ever produced by any state in America—$879,679,000. Iowa comes second, with a crop valued at $821,920,000; Texas is third—$175,000,000 behind Illinois.

It was a war crop in the strictest sense, planted and apportioned according to a predetermined program. The government asked for more wheat, and Illinois responded with 60,991,000 bushels, an increase of 70 per cent over the 1917 crop, which was twice that of 1916; for more barley, and Illinois raised 4,750,000 bushels, twice the crop of 1917; for more rye, and Illinois raised 3,800,000 bushels, nearly five times the 1917 crop. Our oats crop was 244,000,000 bushels, or 45,000,000 bushels short of the 1917 crop; and our corn crop of 351,450,000 bushels was 68,000,000 below the great crop of 1917, but because of early frosts in 1917 the corn crop of 1918 (Providence must get the credit for this, not our farmers or the State Council) has once and a half the feeding value of the 1917 crop. And it should be remembered that the crop of 1917—the largest of any state that year—was also a war contribution of Illinois.

While we were making these contributions directly to the war, we also continued to do our part in the manufacturing field. Notwithstanding the drain upon the man power of the state, Illinois, in 1918, turned out manufactured products valued at $6,000,000,000 —$3,943,000,000 in Chicago, the rest down-state. Of these, about $2,000,000,000 worth were on direct war contracts, but virtually all were war contributions, for Illinois factories are not largely given to the production of luxuries or nonessentials.

If you will add to this staggering record of the production of Illinois in a war year, the great production of our coal fields and oil wells, figures for which I cannot give you now, when the details are finally written, I think they will reflect credit upon every industry, and virtually upon every individual, in the state.

This great achievement of Illinois, gentlemen, represents more than fertile fields and wide-spread industries; it represents a state of mind, civilian morale, and team work. The State Council of Defense—unlike political parties, which sometimes lay claim to the beneficence of sunshine and rain—claims no credit for the fact that our fields are fertile, nor because we have established industries directed by enterprising men. But we modestly hope that we helped to bring about the state of mind, the civilian morale and the cooperation which enabled Illinois, not merely to do well, but to do almost her best while America was at war. And I believe that had the war not ended when it did, we would have done quite our best this year.

What the Council set out to do was to direct the energies of the state wholly to essential war work, to accustom the people to the necessities of the war and to prepare them for its sacrifices. In this we followed the directions of the national government generally, but when occasion required, the Council took the responsibility of pointing the way.

Let me cite an instance. At our very first business meeting, on May 8, 1917, the Council passed a resolution urging upon Congress the immediate enactment of "a rigid food, fuel and commodity act that will vest in a commission, to be appointed by the President, full power to control the production, distribution, transportation and price of food-stuffs, grains, fuel and other basic commodities." Bear in mind that at this time the Lever bill had not been introduced. The public knew little of what such regulation meant. Probably the bill would have been introduced sooner or later anyway, but our Council was the first official body to demand such a law, and our action at least helped to prepare the public mind for the regulation which later occurred, which all now admit was essential, and which the people accepted without a murmur.

Again, starting while the Lever bill was pending, it was the Illinois Council which took the lead in getting the Fuel Administration established—through its own action and the action of the Governor, as well as the joint action of thirteen middle-west states— almost as soon as the Lever bill became a law.

But, I repeat, our greatest value was in preparing the people for their war duties, and in getting public acceptance of war conditions and war demands, rather than in advising the national government of its obligations. We undertook to help the government get done the things it wanted done, instead of telling it how to run the war. It was for this that we built up our great organization—and, if I may be allowed to say so, it was a great organization. We had 50,000 active workers, distributed through all the counties downstate, and 30,000 more in Cook County, not counting the 300,000 women Mrs. Bowen had under her committee, which was attached to the State Council of Defense.

Our Council took the requests of the national government as orders; in turn, our county organizations regarded the requests of our Council as orders. Let it be said further, that the people in each community—the men and women throughout Illinois—were mindful of the suggestions which came to them from the Council itself or from our county organizations. Thus, we had the whole state working upon a common plan to achieve a common purpose.

I do not say it as a boast, gentlemen, but it is my firm belief that it was because these 80,000 active members of the State Council organization—leading men and women in their communities everywhere—were amenable to orders, and because the 300,000 women of Mrs. Bowen's organization not only obeyed instructions themselves, but were continuously preaching sacrifice and discipline—it was because of this that Illinois was enabled to make the war record it did. Acceptance of the draft law, of the restrictions on food and fuel, of the food production program, of amusement curtailment and longer working hours, the contribution of money in unheard-of amounts— all these things were done not only without protest but heartily. And I do not believe they would have been done with such good feeling, if at all, had not the public mind been organized for their acceptance. If the State Council did anything in this war, it organized the public mind.

Let me cite another instance, this time of the team work achieved in Illinois by means of our state-wide organization. On September 17, 1918, the national government called upon the State Council to help shut off non-war construction work, so that all the energies of the nation might be devoted to essential war work. Within thirty days, eighty-nine of our one hundred and two counties had established non-war construction boards, and when the end of the war came—only fifty-five days after the creation of the bureau—nonessential construction work to the amount of $13,873,000 had been deferred until after the war, and few people even complained about it.

Again, the national government in August last called upon the Council to regulate deliveries by the stores of Illinois, to induce people to carry home their own parcels, and to limit Christmas presents to useful things. This looked like a tough job, but within sixty days the merchants of every town of 2,000 or more inhabitants in Illinois, including Chicago, had limited their deliveries to one a day; women everywhere, who had never done so before, were carrying home their own parcels; and the merchants themselves, in every town of the state, were appealing to their patrons, in the name of the State Council, to buy only useful gifts for Christmas, and to buy those early. Besides, there was a board in virtually every town to see that these rules were enforced.

Another manifestation of our team work was the organization of the Volunteer Training Corps, now converted into Reserve Militia. The absorption of the National Guard by the United States Army left Illinois practically without protection against the internal disorder, which the nation at war might invite. In response to the request of the Council, nearly 15,000 men—largely men exempt from the national service — enrolled in the Volunteer Training Corps, uniformed themselves and used their spare time for training. When they became fit and competent troops, they were converted into Reserve Militia—six regiments of them, with one company or more in every considerable city of the state—and are now, under the direction of the Adjutant General of the state, equipped and qualified to perform any service which may be required of them.

It was organization of the public mind, also, which made possible our enormous sale of Liberty Bonds, and our great contributions to the Red Cross and other war aid organizations, and it was organization of the minds of the farmers which made possible the great crop I have mentioned. The Council helped the farmers plan the program which brought it about, helped to provide the labor which planted and harvested it (21,000 lads from the cities and towns who were trained and sent out by the U. S. Boys' Working Reserve, among other agencies), and the Council even provided the seed for a good part of our corn crop.

Some of you know already that the Council, indirectly was a seed-corn purchasing agency for Illinois. The Chicago banks backed us with a pledge of $1,250,000 for that purpose. We borrowed only $495,000, with which, together with our seed-corn propaganda, we not only saved the corn crop of Illinois but made a profit of more than $140,000 for the national Department of Agriculture—which became our partner in the enterprise at a late day, and took all the profits.

Which brings me to a fact which I think is unique in the histories of all our state councils of defense throughout the country. Gentlemen, in addition to whatever it did to help win the war, the State Council of Defense of Illinois was a money-making institution. We cost the people of Illinois money, to be sure—between $150,000 and $175,000. Fifty thousand dollars of this the Legislature gave us, and the rest we secured by passing the hat—chiefly here in Chicago. It is our intention not to ask the state for any further sum. But notwithstanding this, we really made money for the people of the United States—made around $450,000, or nearly three times what we cost the state—in legitimate, patriotic enterprises—enterprises which we believe did a great deal of good in themselves, besides being profitable.

In addition to the $140,000 we made out of seed corn, and turned over to the government, we also made over $300,000 out of our Patriotic War Show on the Lake Front. We have turned over to the Committee on Public Information $300,000 already (I very much regretted having to do so, but under the Congressional enactment there was nothing else for us to do), and will have another small check. In fourteen days, 1,955,602 people attended the show, and I am sure its value in arousing patriotic sentiment was great, indeed.

We also made over $8,000 out of our Patriotic Food Show last January, despite two of the most terrific blizzards Chicago has had in thirty years, and, besides, that show served as a model for more than 250 like shows throughout America. We sold more than 300,000 copies of the recipe book we got out for the show, distributing them from Britain to China, at five and ten cents a copy, and made a profit of over $7,500 out of that cook book.

Had we been able to keep all we made, we should now be turning money back into the state treasury, despite our small appropriation of $50,000, whereas other states had appropriations running from $100,000 for the smaller ones to $5,000,000 in one instance, and $2,000,000 and $1,000,000 in others.

As we thus turned the State Council of Defense to actual, honest and legitimate profit, I wonder, gentlemen, if the people of Illinois may not turn the war itself, and what it taught us, to actual, legitimate profit? I do not mean, in any sense, to profiteering.

Consider the great Illinois crop of 1918. It was just the crop the needs of the world demanded; a crop calculated to bring the highest market price. We grew it because the federal government made known the demands of the war and the leading farmers of the state got together and laid out a program which would meet these demands; because the farmers of the state counseled together, and after that worked together, to achieve a common purpose. The farms were short-handed, the state's greatest crops was threatened for lack of seed, it was hard to get planting, cultivating or harvesting machinery, or fertilizer. Despite all this, the state raised its most valuable crop in history, and did it easily, because the needs of the time imposed an obligation to do so. Co-operation, team-work, was accomplished as a matter of course, when the safety of the nation required it.

The same thing occurred in every other industry. Why, there wasn't a strike of importance in the state after the war started. All war undertakings succeeded by virtue of this spirit of co-operation. A billion and a quarter dollars' worth of Liberty Bonds were sold in Illinois through team-work. Co-operation achieved our contributions to war aid and relief. Look what happened in the United War Work drive! The widest differences in our country, or in any other, are religious; yet in that drive we found the Y. M. C. A., the K. of C., the Jewish Welfare Society and the Salvation Army passing the same hat and dividing the collection. And no one grumbled— much.

If we could achieve this unity of thought and purpose under stress of war, why can't we do it in time of peace? We proved that team-work served best when the nation was in peril; are we going to forget the lesson now that the peril of the war is past?

I hope not, for, remember, gentlemen, patriotism is but a higher development of team-work. Americanization—which is such a common term in these days—is only the conversion of the foreign-born to applied co-operation. To Americanize our citizens of foreign birth or ancestry is simply to bring them to the realization and acceptance of an American program for the good of America, and to work to that program.

Upon this question I desire to say a further word. You cannot get team-work, gentlemen, if the people of the team speak different languages. I mean this literally. A confusion of tongues is the simplest and most effective method for defeating a common purpose yet discovered; it was the method employed by Jehovah himself to accomplish that end. And as long as we have a confusion of tongues in America, we cannot hope to get that complete co-operation which means Americanization.

In the nature of things, we cannot entirely avoid a multitude of tongues in the first generation of those who come to America as a refuge of the oppressed or a land of opportunity for the enterprising. Therefore, it is futile to talk of complete Americanization of the first generation of the foreign-born. Such talk is futile—and I am not sure but that it is undesirable—for another reason also. For let me tell you that however well an immigrant may come to love America, however well he may come to understand and however highly he may come to value American institutions, he isn't going to forget the land of his birth. He can no more do that than he can forget the mother who bore him. He cannot forego all affection for his homeland—the soil itself, the companions and kin with whom he grew up, and the customs of his youth—even if he would.

While this is true, and while to think of abolishing our confusion of tongues in the first generation is hopeless, there is no reason why we should go on maintaining and propagating this babel of languages through the second, and even the third and fourth, generations. Yet that is what we are doing—in the foreign-language schools of America. It is these which most need to be Americanized, in behalf of a sound and enduring patriotism.

I have no objection to the teaching of foreign languages in American schools. I do object to foreign-language schools in America. A foreign-born family in America begins with two—the husband and wife. We may find it difficult always to make good Americans of these, because they lack our language. But the children of a foreign-born family, usually from four to ten—why should we deliberately make them poor Americans by allowing them to acquire their educations in a foreign tongue? The language in which a child learns the elementaries of education—the three R's, common grammar and fundamental history—is the language in which he comes to do his thinking. You don't help to make a good American citizen of a child by bringing him up to think in a language which is not the common language of his country.

We can't make a foreign-born citizen a good American by law. But we can make the schools of Illinois American by law, and thereby make it easier for those born here to be good Americans.

The State Council of Defense thinks this should be done. The Council believes it would be the longest step in Americanization it is possible to take. Hence, to round out its work, the Council will recommend this step to the General Assembly at Springfield. And if that recommendation shall be translated into law, it is our belief that to have made it will not be the least service we have rendered Illinois.

AN ADDRESS BY GOVERNOR FRANK O. LOWDEN[9]

Delivered before the Commercial Club of Chicago, January 18, 1919.

Mr. Chairman and Gentlemen of the Commercial Club:

It is a great pleasure to me to be here tonight. I think it is all of twenty-five years since I was first a guest of the Commercial Club. Its dinners have always been occasions of good fellowship and good talk. I appreciate the truth of what your president has said of the character of the business men who compose this great and historic organization. I know your standing in the business world. I had supposed that I had selected one of the best business men among you for chairman of the State Council of Defense. I cannot tell you how greatly disappointed I am tonight to hear him confess that the federal government got that half million away from us.

When, at the beginning of the war, the duty devolved upon me to constitute this State Council of Defense, I knew, or I thought I knew, that the war would not be won by capital alone, or by labor alone, or by any one class within our midst. Therefore, I made that body representative of all our people, as nearly as I knew how. At the time I was subject, of course, to some criticisms, but I have been used to that for a great many years, and tonight, as you have

[9] From a manuscript copy in the possession of Governor Lowden.

listened to the very able and comprehensive speech by the chairman of that body, I think you will agree that my action in so making up this body has been justified by the great events that have come out of the State Council of Defense.

I doubt if even you, with all the activities you have shown during all the months of this great war, realize the magnitude of the task that fell to this lady [addressing Mrs. Bowen] and these gentlemen. It was not only Chicago, but it was these scattered communities, these smaller cities, towns, villages and rural communities all over the state that had to be taken into account. Our people arose a little slowly at first, but as they learned the tremendous significance of this war they in increasing numbers wished to do their part. Organizations sprang up everywhere. There were, of necessity, collisions between different organizations in the same communities. Therefore, it was not only necessary to mobilize these forces of patriotism, but it was equally necessary to thoroughly organize them, and that great work was done, as if by a master hand, by the Illinois State Council of Defense. Wherever you went in Illinois, you found that instead of confusion, instead of uncertainty as to the functions of this committee or that committee, there was coördination, there was system, there was no loss of energy because of misdirection, but you found efficiency everywhere, and that was the work of the State Council of Defense.

You can realize that with the large number of committees organized everywhere, it was necessary to evolve some plan by which there was a central body, by which there was some point of common contact of all these forces. That was accomplished through the organization of what was known as the County Executive Committee, composed of the chairmen of all of these various committees, with some competent individual at the head of the executive committee, and thus, coördination and order came out of chaos, which had theretofore existed.

The chairman of the State Council of Defense has told you something of the organization of the Reserve Militia. When I tell you that within a few weeks after the Council came into existence, although all our National Guard had been federalized and were beyond the borders of the state, Illinois had more troops under arms, equipped and ready for any emergency than it had before the war commenced, you will realize that this was a great accomplishment. That, gentlemen, was due largely to the movement set on foot by the State Council of Defense under the direction of the very able chairman of its subcommittee, the Lieutenant Governor of this state.

We were without arms when the first of July, 1917, came. We could get no response to our request from Washington. I felt that we were helpless. I sent the Lieutenant Governor of this state, with personal letters to friends of mine in Washington, and he stayed there until he got the arms. We were the first state in the Union to have our own independent state force ready for any emergency after war was declared.

I am not going into infinite details as to the accomplishments of this great body. I am here tonight rather to make public acknowledgment of the very great and unselfish and distinguished services this body has rendered to the State of Illinois and to listen to the admirable presentation of its accomplishments by its chairman. I want, however, to call attention to one or two other things which I believe, after all, are the most important of all the things done.

As I said a moment ago, representatives of labor and representatives of capital were brought together by me in my office at Springfield. These gentlemen met then for the first time. I have no doubt that there were misgivings in your mind, Mr. Chairman, and in the minds of others, just as there were in the minds of these gentlemen who represented labor as to how they should get on. Yet I am told that in all the months that have since come and gone, the records of the State Council of Defense disclose no single divided vote upon any question of policy by that body.

The other night, I had the pleasure of attending a dinner in Springfield, given in honor of the chairman of the State Council of Defense. I was exceedingly interested to hear the different representatives of different war activities describe their experiences during the time of war. The first gentleman who spoke, in trying to find, as we all do, some compensation for sacrifices and the cost of the war, was more impressed by this fact than any other: that the coal miners, of whom there is a large number in Springfield, who, in the years before the war, had lived in a measure to themselves, and the other elements of the community really got aquainted for the first time, and discovered, to their surprise, that they were the same kind of folks, after all. There developed a complete harmony among all the elements in the city during the period of the war. He ventured the hope and belief that the new feeling, which had come to Springfield because of this mutual acquaintance and understanding, would continue and thereby afford some compensation for the losses of this war.

The next speaker found compensation in this: He had to do with correlating the agencies of the County of Sangamon (which is the county in which Springfield is situated) outside of the city with the activities of the people of Springfield. He said that in all the years, as far as he could recall, there had been a mutual jealousy between the city and the districts outside, but as they came to coöperate in these war undertakings, those prejudices were broken down, and as a result there is today a new feeling of coöperation and a comradeship between the people who live out on the farms and in the byways and the people who live in the city.

The third gentleman had found this, which gave him great hope for the future: he was connected with the religious activities, and he said that before the war, there were misunderstandings between the Protestants on the one hand and the Catholics on the other, and with those perhaps of the Jewish faith, but that under the stress of this great war, with the idea of human brotherhood springing up anew in the hearts of all, all of the denominations had felt that in some sort of a way, they were serving the same God and the same great cause and thus a new feeling of brotherhood had arisen as among the religious creeds in the city of Springfield.

My friends, if that was true of Springfield and Sangamon County, it was true throughout all of the state, and so, today, we have a solidarity of our citizenship with which we have won the war that is worth all the war has cost, if we can only preserve that solidarity.

And, gentlemen, why can't we? We have only half won this war. We had two foes—the crowned despot of Germany and the unbridled mob as represented in Russia. Those were our two enemies, and I do not know which is the more dangerous of the two. I only know that to the American the tyranny of the mob is as little to be borne as is the tyranny of the mailed fist.

The battle is only half won, and if we would win the other half, if we would regain all the prestige and security which were our proud boasts during other years, we must, whatever our inclinations may be, preserve the spirit which those gentlemen around that little board at Springfield described the other night when they said that the workingmen and the people of the city of Springfield had come together, and that the people of the city and of the country had come together, and that the people of all churches which believed in a God of righteousness had united to work together. Preserving this spirit under the Providence of God we will win this other battle just as we have won on European battle fields.

And now a word and I am done. You have been told of the great contribution in men which we have made to the armies of freedom, and it is a magnificent contribution. We wondered, some of us, in the years before the war, whether our young men had the same fibre that they had had in other wars. We wondered whether or not they would make the same superb showing upon the battle field as their sires had made, and we have followed with love and sometimes with tears their course upon a score of battlefields. We have seen them at Belleau Wood; we have seen them at Chantilly;[10] we have seen them at Chateau Thierry, where they first turned back the tide of that great conflict; we have seen them at St. Mihiel, and we saw them up to the very moment when the armistice came into effect in the Argonne Forest, and we know tonight that Illinois' sons need not blush when their deeds are compared with the deeds of their most valorous fathers and forefathers.

There is one other acknowledgment I must make to this club, and that is one of the reasons why I departed from my practice and came here tonight. This is the first time I have been in Chicago for over a month, and I came simply to attend this banquet. As long as the Illinois legislative body is in session in Springfield, as the

---

[10] Cantigny is probably meant. Units in which Illinois men predominated did not participate in action there or at Chateau Thierry.

Speaker will tell you, the governor who is wise will stick pretty close to his desk, and so this is my first visit, as I said, in over a month.

As the Chairman of the State Council of Defense has told you, we appropriated but fifty thousand dollars for their use. No one knew then the extent of the activities they would assume. It was, therefore, a pure guess as to the amount they would need; but as the government day after day added to their functions, as has been described, it soon became apparent that fifty thousand dollars would not be sufficient. The legislature was not in session. I did not deem it wise to call it into extraordinary session simply to provide those funds, and I, therefore, came to Chicago one day and got hold of a group of distinguished members of this club, whom, to relieve of embarrassment, for I see them before me, I shall not name tonight, I told them that we needed a hundred thousand dollars; that the state under the law could not contract an indebtedness; that I wished they would raise that hundred thousand dollars so that this great body could continue its useful and patriotic work, but that if they did I could not give them any sort of hope that the state would ever pay it back, and it must be regarded purely as a gift. Instantly, they responded, and that hundred thousand dollars was raised within a very brief time, largely contributed by members of this club. So tonight I would not be comfortable if I did not make acknowledgment to you gentlemen for the very great and generous help you rendered in that particular, and that, as I know, is only one of a thousand instances in which the members of this club have contributed their part to the winning of this war.

I am sorry I am not a member of this club, but I once was a lawyer, and that is a crime which under the by-laws of this club no statute of limitations ever bars. I thank you, however, as heartily as I know how for the great and splendid part you played, and assure you that you have helped make the name of Illinois illustrious in the greatest war of all the world. I bid you good night.

WORK OF THE WOMAN'S COMMITTEE, STATE COUNCIL OF DEFENSE OF ILLINOIS, AN ADDRESS BY MRS. JOSEPH T. BOWEN[11]

Delivered at a state conference of the Woman's Committee held in Chicago, March 4, 1919.

We have met tonight, first, that we may give you a final and brief report of the Woman's Committee, State Council of Defense; second, that we may present for your consideration a plan by which the machinery built up by the men and women of the state for war emergency may be turned into an instrument for the promotion of social welfare in times of peace; third, and most important of all, that we may receive a message from your leaders, the Chairman of the Woman's Committee, Council of National Defense, and the Chairman of the State Council of Defense. From Governor Lowden I have received the following telegram:

"Nothing but the orders of my physician could prevent my being at your dinner tonight. I had looked forward for several months to the occasion. I had wanted very much to express my deep appreciation of the services rendered by the women of Illinois in the winning of the war. They were the most important factor in maintaining the morale at home. They created a community spirit everywhere and directed that spirit to the comfort and support of our armies in the field. They were the soul of every worthy movement connected with the war. By their arduous and unselfish labors during the entire period of the war, they became in fact worthy comrades of their brothers in the trenches. With deep appreciation of all they did, I send my heartiest greetings, through you, to the war working women of our state.—Frank O. Lowden."

The Woman's Committee, Council of National Defense, Illinois Division, was organized in May, 1917, when the heads of all the women's organizations in the state gathered together, formed the Illinois Division, and elected their officers. At the same time, the Governor did me the honor of appointing me on the State Council

---

[11] From a stenographic report of the conference. Mrs. Joseph T. Bowen, of Chicago, was chairman of the Woman's Committee of the State Council of Defense of Illinois.

of Defense, and I was made chairman of women's activities throughout the state.

The two organizations were thus combined in one, under one set of officers, but with two names—and I may say to you confidentially that I have found these two names to be of great use on occasions. For example, when the legal adviser of the State Council of Defense gave as his opinion that all the money raised by the State Council's various committees should be put in the hands of the treasurer of the State Council and requisitioned out only by the State Council, it was a great comfort to be able to say that our money was raised under the name of the Woman's Committee, Illinois Division.

We were told in the beginning to prepare for a long war, and we therefore built a very solid foundation. From Cairo to Rockford, from Quincy to Paris, every city, town and township has added its unit to make up the most complete organization of women that Illinois has ever attained, an organization including women of all classes, creeds and nationalities, united in one democratic force, under one standard—*Win the War!*

We have in the state 2,136 local units and 7,700 chairmen who direct the work of the eighteen departments—the active workers numbering 326,333. In addition, we have registered for war work 692,229 women. The registration cards of every city and town have been kept by that unit and have been of great value in furnishing workers for governmental drives, for the exemption boards, for nurses in the recent epidemic, and for many other purposes. In Chicago alone—where the registration was very small compared to the state—7,052 lists of women and 17,000 individual names of workers have been given to various associations seeking volunteers. The women who registered offered every type of service, from the stenographer who worked all day and offered to give two hours every evening to help win the war, or the little cripple, confined to her bed, who, because she had trained a canary bird, volunteered to train carrier pigeons for the army, or the woman who registered that she was willing, but nervous, and would pray if necessary, to the woman of wealth who offered her machine, her home with all her employees, as a hospital for wounded soldiers.

The Finance Department has raised most of its money in a very democratic way. Every woman who registered was asked to contribute ten cents, and this sum amounted to $73,000. Nearly $100,000 in addition was raised by subscription. Some of it was made in business ventures. At one time when the government was urging the use of potatoes instead of bread, the Finance Department put upon the streets of Chicago and in some of the towns throughout the state, bags of potato chips which they called "Liberty Chips," and these chips, selling for five cents a bag, netted in Chicago alone $7,000 in three days. In addition, $473,000 has been raised by tag days for various charities, and the committee sold $3,250,000 worth of liberty bonds. Expenditure to date has been $97,793.98.

The Speaker's Committee, numbering 565 speakers, has held 2,408 meetings and reached 600,509 people, carrying its war message as an offset to German propaganda to even the most remote hamlets in the state.

Of course, some of our requests for speakers were very absurd. One club wrote asking us to send an atrocity immediately, who would tell war stories set to music! But on the whole, the demand for information was genuine, and it was sorely needed. At one meeting at which the subject was thrift and war savings stamps—and the meeting was composed of educated and intelligent people—the idea seemed to prevail that war savings stamps and thrift stamps were much like the Red Cross tuberculosis stamps and were to be pasted on the outside of letters. At another meeting where the subject of liberty bonds was being discussed, a foreign woman arose and said she did not think it was right for the government to put out these bonds; they were the same kind her old man always used when he wanted to get out of jail, and she did not think the government ought to make it any easier for him!

The Speakers' Bureau has been quick to seize opportunities to get hold of people. One of the speakers—a very forceful speaker—recently in the southern part of the state (it was at the time of the influenza epidemic) wrote back to the chief of the department in Chicago saying that no meetings could be held there, only funerals, to which her chief rather lightly replied, "Better go to the funerals." The speaker was a literal person, and she went to the first large funeral. The church was full, and after the mourners had left the church, she stood up, and in a commanding voice said, "Stop, listen; I have a message for you from the government!"—and they stopped and listened, and she gave a message on the subject of child welfare, and she formed a Child Welfare League in that town!

At the beginning of the war we found that large numbers of women whose husbands or sons had gone to the war came to us for employment which was necessary in order that they might live. Our Employment Department has registered 9,082 such women, and it has found positions for 2,205. It is probable they found positions for more than that, but a great many did not report back again. Most of these women were over forty years of age and utterly untrained, and they hoped for positions of responsibility with no work! One woman said she would like the position of opening the mail and being responsible for the keys of the association. Many of them felt that they knew all about children—their reason sometimes being no better than the Irish woman's, who had borne ten and lost nine. Others who had kept their own house seemed to feel that the position of housekeeper grew on every bush. It was found that we had to have some kind of training for these women, and so classes of instruction were started in 65 cities throughout the state, and 90 courses were offered in Chicago, where women could get training to enable them to take some kind of clerical or other position.

In this connection it was found necessary to establish a mending shop for women over seventy, too old to take a regular position, and this shop has been very successful, is now self-supporting, and gives steady work to thirty women.

The State Council of Defense has done a magnificent piece of work all over the state, but its activities have largely had to do with questions concerning military matters, finance, crops, labor, business, etc., while the Woman's Committee has had to do more with the women and children and with the practical details of the home. It has dealt mainly with human beings.

The Child Welfare Department, financed and managed by the Elizabeth McCormick Memorial Fund, has weighed and measured 325,000 children, and has instructed the parents of these children as to their proper care. This department has succeeded in arousing the

whole state to the necessity of conserving its children. Even the
schoolboys have become excited on the subject. One boy wrote a
composition in which he said, "Now that we are at war, it is everybody's business to have a baby and to save it!"

The department is making this work permanent by the establishment of child welfare centers, the employment of community
nurses, the extension of medical examinations in the schools, and the
education of mothers in the care of children. During the war the
government called upon the women of the country to practice conservation, and our Conservation Department has given, throughout
the state, in almost every town and city, demonstrations concerning
substitutes for flour and sugar, the remaking of clothes, and the necessity for the elimination of waste. In Chicago 205,000 women were
reached by these demonstrations, which were held in vacant shops,
department stores, settlements, and even on a motor van which was
turned into a portable kitchen.

We have tried to reach the girls of our state by enrolling 12,000
of them into Patriotic Leagues, through our Social Hygiene Department, which has given them instructions (in shops and factories)
essential to their well being. The chairman of that department, who
has just been made instructor of health education for the State of
Illinois, in her lectures has already reached 54,000 girls and women
in shops and factories.

Our Food Production Department immensely stimulated the
raising of crops throughout the state. It had 110 school gardens,
and 90,000 war gardens manned by children reported to it.

At our farm at Libertyville, Illinois, we have been training young
women in agricultural and dairying pursuits. We have turned into
farmers 76 young women, and a thousand applications have been
received from girls who were interested. Forty thousand people
have been addressed on the subject of farming and agricultural pursuits.

Knowing that a singing nation is a winning nation, we have established throughout the state 265 liberty choruses, and have distributed 81,000 song books similar to the one you have been using tonight—and which we hope you will take home with you.

The Women and Children in Industry Department has bettered
the condition of women and children throughout the state.

Our War Information Department has supplied public school
principals and others throughout the state with war information,
sending 143,000 pamphlets to its 500 war information chairmen,
many of them postmistresses or proprietors of little stores, who have
written back that they not only distributed the pamphlets after reading them, but have made them a matter of gossip with all their
customers.

Our Publicity Department has not only conducted the publicity
for the Woman's Committee, but has sent a news letter throughout
the state every week, has published three camouflage recipe books,
and has conducted a "Do-Without Club."

Our Americanization Department has held three institutes for
the foreign-born, and although organized late in 1918, the department has already reached something like 50,000 people.

The Social Welfare Department has made connections between
1,516 volunteers and social agencies, has provided wool for the "shut-
ins" in the hospitals, insane asylums, old people's homes and prisons,
where the inmates for the first time felt that they were doing their
"bit" toward winning the war. In addition, this department has
saved social agencies, it is estimated, $100,000 in money which would
otherwise have been paid to paid employees.

Our Allied Relief Department has raised for relief $788,130.68;
and has sent to Europe 705,140 hospital supplies, 182,035 garments,
and 27,188 kits, and has adopted 8,844 fatherless children.

I wish that I had the time and the opportunity to express the
thanks of the Woman's Committee to all the people who have so
generously helped that committee. I especially wish to make public
mention of the State Council of Defense, which gave the Woman's
Committee, rent free, its rooms, light, heat, telephone, services of two
stenographers, supplies and postage approximating a thousand dollars a month. And then I want to say for myself how very
grateful I am to all the women on my Executive Committee, to all
the chairmen throughout the state, and to the women on the city
and state committees, who have so generously and so kindly upheld

my hands and have shown me such loyalty and such willing coöperation.

When we met in this room last spring and listened to the inspiring speeches which were made to us then, and which gave us courage to face the great struggle which lay ahead of us, we saw then in our mind's eye those shell-torn battle fields of France, the ruined homes, the desolate villages, the long, dusty highways filled with artillery wagons, motors, guns, cannon, ambulances, and all the paraphernalia of war, and that endless stream of khaki-clad men who had crossed the seas to fight for the most righteous cause for which any nation ever fought. Nine months have passed since that meeting—nine months full of the most momentous events, and we all know now that those boys of ours, with the smile on their lips and the spirit of the crusader in their hearts, went into the fight just at the crucial moment, and by the sheer weight of their will to win, turned the tide and pushed back the foe.

Most of these men, thank God, are coming back to us, but some of them sleep in France. All honor to them, and to the brave and noble dead of our allies, with whom the fields of France are sown. "They found their lives by losing them; they forgot themselves, but saved the world!" Toward the men who are returning we feel a deep sense of obligation. They gave up comfort, pleasure, home, family, everything they held most dear; they, too, were ready to give up their lives. They have put aside all the shams of life and have dealt only with its realities. They have learned all that suffering and sacrifice and death can teach; they understand the real meaning of fellowship, and these men today have a vision of better things, a vision of a happier home, a cleaner city, a better state, a greater nation. They have been fighting for democracy, but we will never have a real democracy in this country—that democracy of which we caught just a glimpse during the war when we were brought together by a common danger and by a common sympathy—until we once more continuously work together for the good of our community, until we learn to reverence, not the aristocracy of birth and wealth and position, but only the aristocracy of service—until we can assure to every citizen of our great republic the right to be well born, the right to health, to education, to work, to decent living, to love, to happiness. These men will look to us to help them realize their vision. Shall we fail them?

VICTORY LOAN EXERCISES, FIFTY-FIRST GENERAL ASSEMBLY

Senate Joint Resolution Number 28, Fifty-first General Assembly.

WHEREAS, The nation-wide campaign on behalf of the Victory Loan of the United States of America was launched on the twenty-first day of April, nineteen hundred and nineteen; and

WHEREAS, It behooves every American, individually and collectively, to do all in their power to further the success of this, the last Liberty Loan; now, therefore be it

Resolved, by the Senate, the House of Representatives Concurring therein, That the members of the Fifty-first General Assembly of the State of Illinois meet in joint session in the Hall of the House of Representatives, at the hour of 12:00 o'clock noon on Wednesday, the twenty-third day of April, nineteen hundred and nineteen, for the holding of exercises in the support of the Victory Loan.

Adopted by the Senate April 22d, 1919.

Concurred in by the House of Representatives April 22d, 1919.

VIII.   POST-WAR LEGISLATION[1]

MEMORIAL TO CONGRESS—EXTRA PAY FOR SOLDIERS

Senate Joint Resolution Number 6, Fifty-first General Assembly, State of Illinois.

WHEREAS, The most important problem of reconstruction is the individual readjustment in the lives of the men who willingly went forth to heroically serve our Nation and our Allies in the time when free institutions and the rights of free men everywhere were threatened, and

WHEREAS, No adequate provision is being made by the Federal government for these returning soldiers, sailors and marines, who have made tremendous sacrifices for our country, and

WHEREAS, There is a movement to secure national legislation guaranteeing to every soldier, sailor and marine his pay for some sufficient period after his return to civil life, until he can obtain remunerative employment, and

WHEREAS, Other countries which have suffered more and which have expended far greater sums of money that [than] has the United States of America, are making more ample and more just provisions for their soldiers,

Be it Resolved, by the Senate of the State of Illinois, the House of Representatives concurring therein, That a memorial be sent to Congress requesting the Federal government to pay at least six months salary to every soldier, sailor and marine upon his return to civil life, and,

Be it Resolved, That the Secretary of State be, and hereby is directed to transmit copies of this resolution to the United States Senate and to the House of Representatives and to the several members of both bodies representing the State of Illinois, and to Hon.

---

[1] For a summary of legislation enacted by the Fifty-second and Fifty-third General Assemblies (1921 and 1923) relating to matters of post-war interest, see *The War-Time Organization of Illinois, Illinois in the World War,* Volume V, pages 25-26.

Newton D. Baker, Secretary of War, and to Hon. Josephus Daniels, Secretary of the Navy.

Adopted by the Senate January 28, 1919.

Concurred in by the House of Representatives, January 29, 1919.

MEMORIAL TO CONGRESS — REDUCTION OF RAILROAD RATES

Senate Joint Resolution Number 14, Fifty-first General Assembly.

WHEREAS, Many public improvements for which there is an imperative need have been postponed on account of the existence of a state of war between the United States of America and the Imperial German government; and

WHEREAS, The necessity for the resumption of the construction of public works is fully recognized and is being urged upon all people in authority representing the various political units and subdivisions of the United States; and

WHEREAS, One of the greatest problems confronting the State and the nation at the present time is the furnishing of immediate employment to a large amount of idle labor released from other activities by the victorious termination of the war; and

WHEREAS, The embarking upon the construction of the much-needed public improvements will furnish immediate and profitable employment to idle labor; and

WHEREAS, The increase in freight rates on the heavy materials, entering largely into the construction of public works, which went into effect on June 25, 1918, was approximately one hundred per cent greater than the increase on other commodities; and

WHEREAS, In the judgment of the General Assembly of the State of Illinois, freight rates on materials designed for use in the construction of public works are excessive and tend unmistakably to discourage the resumption of the construction of such enterprises, thus defeating the effort to give employment to idle labor; therefore, be it

Resolved, by the Senate of the State of Illinois, the House of Representatives concurring therein, That the President of the United States, the Congress of the United States and the United States

Railroad Administration be and they hereby are memorialized and respectfully but most urgently requested to take such action as will bring about a reduction in the freight tariffs governing the shipment of the materials entering largely into the construction of public works, said reduction to be not less than the advance which went into effect June 25, 1918, and to be effective at an early date; and

That upon the passage of this resolution, certified copies thereof be forthwith forwarded by the Secretary of State of Illinois to the President of the United States, the presiding officers of both Houses of Congress and members from Illinois of both branches of the Congress of the United States, and the Director General of Railroads.

Adopted by the Senate, February 12, 1919.

Concurred in by the House of Representatives, February 13, 1919.

EMPLOYMENT OF SOLDIERS AND SAILORS

Senate Joint Resolution Number 11, Fifty-first General Assembly.

WHEREAS, The cessation of hostilities in the World War has come upon us sooner than anticipated, and in advance of plans or preparation for readjustment from war to peace; and

WHEREAS, The soldiers and sailors from the State of Illinois are daily returning in great numbers, and the return flow of soldiers from overseas has as yet scarcely begun; and

WHEREAS, There appears to be great difficulty in placing our soldiers and sailors in suitable employment; and

WHEREAS, The re-absorbing powers of peace industries are at present insufficient to take care of discharged war workers and soldiers and sailors; and

WHEREAS, Ample provision should be made for the employment of our soldiers and sailors, in order that they shall not be compelled to accept public charity; and

WHEREAS, The working people generally of this country, as American citizens, are entitled to living wages and good living conditions, commensurate with the vast wealth and enormous resources of this, the richest country in the world; and

WHEREAS, The State of Illinois is ready and anxious to provide suitable employment for all its citizens; and

WHEREAS, Labor and capital are united in urging that steps shall be taken to provide employment at once to tide over the dangerous transition from War to Peace; and

WHEREAS, Many public improvements throughout the State of Illinois have been postponed on account of the war; now, therefore, be it

Resolved, by the Senate of the State of Illinois, the House of Representatives concurring therein. That the Legislature will, upon request, render all necessary assistance and co-operation with the counties, cities, villages, towns, municipalities, park districts, drainage districts, boards of education, sanitary district, and all other public bodies in the State of Illinois, to facilitate said bodies in making necessary public improvements; and will pass whatever legislation is necessary to assist said bodies in making necessary public improvements; and, be it further

Resolved, That all counties, cities, villages, towns, municipalities, park districts, drainage districts, boards of education, sanitary district, and all other public bodies in the State of Illinois, be, and they are hereby urged to take immediate steps to start work at once on public improvements coming properly within their sphere and under their supervision, in order to give employment to the unemployed; and, be it further

Resolved, That a copy of this resolution shall be forwarded by the Secretary of State to the proper public bodies in the State of Illinois.

Adopted by the Senate, February 12th, 1919.

Concurred in by the House of Representatives March 6th, 1919.

WORK ON PUBLIC IMPROVEMENTS URGED

Senate Joint Resolution Number 12, Fifty-first General Assembly.

WHEREAS, The cessation of hostilities in the World War has come upon us sooner than anticipated, and in advance of plans or preparation for readjustment from war to peace; and

WHEREAS, The soldiers and sailors and United States marines

from the State of Illinois are daily returning in great numbers, and the return flow of soldiers from overseas has as yet scarcely begun; and

WHEREAS, There appears to be great difficulty in placing our soldiers and sailors and United States marines in suitable employment; and

WHEREAS, The re-absorbing powers of peace industries are at present insufficient to take care of discharged war workers and sailors and United States marines; and

WHEREAS, Ample provision should be made for the employment of our soldiers and sailors and United States marines, in order that they shall not be compelled to accept public charity; and

WHEREAS, The working people generally of this country, as American citizens, are entitled to living wages and good living conditions, commensurate with the vast wealth and enormous resources of this the richest country in the world; and

WHEREAS, Labor and Capital are united in urging that steps shall be taken to provide employment at once to tide over the dangerous transition from war to peace; and

WHEREAS, The people of the State of Illinois have voted for a bond issue of sixty million dollars to build good roads, to be paid for from the vehicle tax fund of Illinois; and

WHEREAS, The people of the State of Illinois have voted a bond issue of twenty million dollars for a waterway to connect the Great Lakes with the Gulf of Mexico; and

WHEREAS, The Legislature has authorized the building of a new penitentiary at Joliet; and

WHEREAS, There are many other public projects necessary for the betterment of the State of Illinois, that would give employment to thousands of people; now, therefore, be it

Resolved, by the Senate of the State of Illinois, the House of Representatives concurring therein, That we urge upon the Department of Public Works and Buildings the desirability of giving consideration to an early resumption of work upon the above named public improvements.

Adopted by the Senate, February 26th, 1919.

Concurred in by the House of Representatives, March 6th, 1919.

RECORDING DISCHARGES OF SERVICE MEN
Senate Bill Number 231, Fifty-first General Assembly.

An Act *to amend Section 9 of an Act entitled, "An Act to revise the law in relation to recorders", approved March 9, 1874, in force July 1, 1874, as amended.*

Section 1. *Be it enacted by the People of the State of Illinois, represented in the General Assembly:* Section 9 of an Act entitled, "An Act to revise the law in relation to recorders," approved March 9, 1874, in force July 1, 1874, is amended to read as follows:

§ 9. Every recorder shall, as soon as practicable after the filing of any instrument in writing in his office, entitled to be recorded, record the same at length, in the order of time of its reception, in well bound books to be provided for that purpose: *Provided,* that seperate [sic] books may be kept for the recording of different classes of instruments.

Certificates of discharge of honorably discharged members of the military, aviation and naval forces of the United States shall be recorded by each recorder, free of charge, in a seperate [sic] book which shall be kept for the purpose.

Every recorder shall keep his office at the court house of the county for which he is recorder, and shall keep his office open and attend to the duties thereof from eight o'clock in the forenoon to five o'clock in the afternoon of each working day, excepting such days and half days as under any law are or may be legal holidays or half holidays, in any part of his said county, as regards the presenting for payment, acceptance, maturity, protesting, or giving notice of the dishonor of bills of exchange, bank checks, promis[s]ory notes, or other negotiable or commercial paper or instruments.

The recorder of deeds elected as provided for in this Act, shall receive such fees as are or may be provided for him by law, in case of provision therefor; otherwise he shall receive the same fees as are or may be provided by law to be paid to the circuit clerk and *ex officio* recorder for like services.

§ 2. Because of an emergency, this Act shall take effect upon its passage.

Approved March 27, 1919.

(33)

DEMOBILIZATION OF SOLDIERS FOR FARM LABOR

House Joint Resolution Number 17, Fifty-first General Assembly.

WHEREAS, There exists at this time a very great scarcity of farm labor in this State and the demand for labor on the farm is continually increasing and will continue to do so as the harvest season approaches; and

WHEREAS, We are urged by Federal officials, by State officials, by proclamations of Congress, by resolution of State Legislatures, by demand for appropriations of money to carry on public improvements, by the voice of the press of the country, to furnish employment for the unemployed and especially for the demobilized and returning soldiers of the late world's war; and

WHEREAS, We are constantly informed through the press and by various civic organizations and employment bureaus and agencies that great numbers of released soldiers are in need of employment; and

WHEREAS, It is our wish and patriotic duty to do all within our power to give employment and dignified relief to all seeking employment, and to take such action as will meet the requirements of the employer, and those seeking employment; and

WHEREAS, Both from official sources and newspaper interviews and reports, it is found that great numbers of released and returned soldiers are not experienced in farm labor or adapted to its requirements; and

WHEREAS, Large numbers of men who are experienced and adapted to farm occupations are retained in the service; therefore, be it

Resolved, by the House of Representatives, the Senate concurring herein, That United States military and civilian officials having in charge the demobilization of the United States troops, both in home cantonments and in the overseas service, be requested through the two United States Senators and the members of the House of Representatives in Congress from Illinois to so far as possible and so far as may be just and consistent demobilize without delay such men as shall clearly prove by their records on entering the service that they are adapted to agricultural occupations and who are willing to return to such occupation.

Adopted by the House April 8, 1919.

Concurred in by the Senate April 22, 1919.

MONUMENTS AND MEMORIALS

Senate Bill Number 134, Fifty-first General Assembly.

AN ACT *to authorize cities, villages and incorporated towns having a population of less than one hundred thousand to erect monuments and memorials.*

SECTION 1. *Be it enacted by the People of the State of Illinois, represented in the General Assembly:* Subject to the provisions of this Act any city, village or incorporated town having a population of less than one hundred thousand shall have power to erect monuments or memorials in honor of their soldiers and sailors or in honor of any one or more of its notable or distinguished persons, and to defray the cost of constructing such monuments or memorials shall have power to levy a direct tax of not more than six cents upon each one hundred dollars ($100) of all taxable property within the jurisdiction thereof. The tax hereby provided for shall be levied in addition to the taxes now authorized by law to be levied and collected by any such city, village or incorporated town and shall not be included in the aggregate of all taxes required to be reduced under the provisions of an Act entitled: "An Act concerning the levy and extension of taxes," approved May 9, 1901, in force July 1, 1901, as amended.

§ 2. Upon the presentation to the clerk of any city, village or incorporated town having a population of less than one hundred thousand, of a petition, as hereinafter provided, the question of erecting any monument or memorial as provided in this Act, shall be submitted to the voters of such city, village or incorporated town at the next regular election therein: *Provided,* that such question shall not be submitted to the voters at any election held less than thirty days after the filing of the petition with such clerk.

The question of erecting any monument or memorial under the

provisions of this Act shall be printed on the ballot in substantially
the following form:

Proposition of erecting a monument or memorial in honor of.................(insert for whom to be erected) of the (insert name of city, village or incorporated town) at a cost not to exceed...........dollars.	Yes	
	No	

If the question so submitted shall be ratified by a majority of all
votes cast at said election it shall be the duty of city council or board
of trustees, as the case may be, to erect or cause to be erected such
monument or memorial and, if necessary, to levy and collect, in the
same manner as other general taxes are levied and collected, a tax
sufficient to raise the amount specified in the petition.

§ 3. The petition herein provided for shall be signed by not
less than one hundred legal voters of the city, village or incorporated town in which the question of erecting any monument or memorial under the provisions in this Act is to be voted upon. The petition shall state the specific purpose for which the proposed monument or memorial is to be built, whether in honor of the soldiers and
sailors of such city, village or incorporated town or in honor of any
one or more of its notable and distinguished persons, and shall specify
the amount of money to be expended for the construction of the
proposed monument or memorial: *Provided,* that the cost of any
such monument or memorial shall not exceed six cents on each one
hundred dollars ($100) of all taxable property within the jurisdic-
tion of such city, village or incorporated town.

Approved May 10, 1919.

HISTORIES OF THE WORLD WAR AUTHORIZED

House Bill No. 731, Fifty-first General Assembly.

An Act *to authorize the publication of the history of the achievements in the World War of the soldiers, sailors and marines from
the State of Illinois, and to make appropriation therefor.*

WHEREAS: More than 300,000 citizens of the State of Illinois nobly responded to the call of the nation during the great World War; and

WHEREAS: It is fitting and proper that the achievements and accomplishments of the gallant soldiers, sailors and marines of this State, and the story of their patriotism and devotion to their country's cause during that great crisis, should be recorded for the benefit of the present and future generations; and,

WHEREAS: Official manuscript histories of the achievements and accomplishments of the members of the Thirty-third Division[2] and the One Hundred Forty Ninth Field Artillery, units of the Army of the United States composed of citizens of Illinois, who served so splendidly under the flag of the United States during the great struggle, just victoriously terminated, have been prepared for publication and presented to the State: now, therefore

SECTION 1. *Be it enacted by the People of the State of Illinois, represented in the General Assembly:* The Illinois State Historical Library is hereby authorized and directed to edit and publish the manuscript histories of the Thirty Third Division and the One Hundred Forty Ninth Field Artillery which have been prepared for publication and presented to the State. A sufficient number of copies of said histories shall be published to supply, without cost, each member of said Thirty Third Division and One Hundred Forty Ninth Field Artillery, and the family of each deceased member, with one copy thereof.

§ 2. For the purpose of carrying out the provisions of this Act there is hereby appropriated to the Illinois State Historical Library the sum of $50,000.00 or so much thereof as may be necessary.

§ 3. The appropriation herein made shall be subject to all the provisions, conditions and limitations of an Act entitled, "An Act in relation to State finance" approved....................1919, in force July 1, 1919.

APPROVED June 28, 1919.

[2] Frederick L. Huidekoper, *The History of the 33rd Division, Illinois in the World War*, Vols. I-IV, Illinois State Historical Library, Danville, 1921.

MEDALS TO SERVICE MEN AUTHORIZED

Senate Bill Number 331, Fifty-first General Assembly.

AN ACT *to authorize the award of medals to persons from the State of Illinois who were engaged in the military or naval service of the United States during the war between the United States and the Imperial German Government.*

SECTION 1. *Be it enacted by the People of the State of Illinois, represented in the General Assembly:* Bronze medals with suitable device shall be awarded to residents of this State who have been engaged in the military or naval service of the United States during the war between the United States and the Imperial German Government.

§ 2. Such medals shall be awarded only to commissioned officers, noncommissioned officers and privates in the military and naval service of the United States:

(a) Whose service in the army or navy shall have been honorable, in case they are not discharged at the time such medals are to be awarded; or

(b) Who have been honorably discharged from such service.

§ 3. The medals provided for in this Act shall be of one design approved by the Adjutant General.

§ 4. It shall be the duty of the Adjutant General to prepare a list of the names and addresses of all persons entitled to medals under the provisions of this Act, and to award medals to all such persons.

§ 5. The Adjutant General shall have power to make reasonable rules and regulations pertaining to the administration of the provisions of this Act.

APPROVED June 28, 1919.

ENDORSEMENT OF THE AMERICAN LEGION

House Joint Resolution Number 28, Fifty-first General Assembly.

WHEREAS, The young manhood of Illinois enthusiastically and patriotically responded to the call of our Government in doing its great part in the late World's War; and,

WHEREAS, These our loyal and honored soldiers having performed such valiant and heroic service as to bring credit to themselves and to crown American arms with victory; and,

WHEREAS, These our honored soldiers, numbering more than 350,000 from Illinois, are now being demobilized and returned to civilian life; and,

WHEREAS, These men are now engaged with other millions of their comrades in arms from the other states of the Union in forming at this time their patriotic and permanent veterans' organization, known as THE AMERICAN LEGION; and

WHEREAS, We recognize that the proposed Illinois chapter of the said AMERICAN LEGION will wield a great and good influence for economic, social, political and patriotic advancement within our Commonwealth, therefore, be it

Resolved, by the House of Representatives, the Senate concurring herein, That the General Assembly of Illinois hereby declares and registers its approval of this patriotic movement, and that it extends to our soldier citizenship its endorsement, and that it hereby gives assurance of moral support in this undertaking which already has taken concrete form in Illinois and elsewhere.

Adopted by the House, June 5, 1919.

Concurred in by the Senate, June 10, 1919.

MEMORIAL TO CONGRESS—NATIONAL SOLDIER SETTLEMENT ACT

House Joint Resolution Number 32, Fifty-first General Assembly.

WHEREAS, There is now pending before the House of Representatives of the Congress of the United States, H. R. 487, "A Bill to provide employment and rural homes for those who have served with the military and naval forces through the reclamation of lands to be known as the 'National Soldier Settlement Act;' " and

WHEREAS, This bill appropriates the sum of five hundred millions of dollars for the reclamation and improvement of lands, to be sold to members of the military and naval forces of the United States and of her Allies in the World War, at cost, as farms, and for the employment of these soldiers and sailors in that work; and

WHEREAS, The provisions of this bill possess great merit as a part of a program of readjustment and reconstruction; now, therefore, be it

Resolved, by the House of Representatives, the Senate concurring herein, That the members of the Fifty-first General Assembly of the State of Illinois request the members of the Congress from the State of Illinois to endeavor to bring about the passage of H. R. 487 or of similar legislation at as early a date as possible; and, be it further

Resolved, That a copy of this resolution be sent to each member of the Congress from the State of Illinois.

Passed the House, June 17, 1919.

Concurred in by the Senate, June 20, 1919.

REHABILITATION IN INDUSTRY OF DISCHARGED SAILORS AND SOLDIERS

Senate Bill No. 121, Fifty-first General Assembly.

AN ACT *to authorize the Director of Labor to secure information for statistical purposes and to promote the rehabilitation in industry of discharged sailors and soldiers.*

SECTION 1. *Be it enacted by the People of the State of Illinois, represented in the General Assembly:* That every employer of labor, employing five or more employees shall annually between the 1st day of January, and the 15th day thereof, or, upon the request of the Director of Labor in case of an emergency, or where employment is in an occupation seasonal in character, file with the Director of Labor a statement on a blank to be furnished by the Department of Labor, which statement shall set forth facts substantially, as follows:

1. Name of employer......................................

2. Nature of business.....................................

3. Is ownership individual, corporate or partnership?............

4. Name of manager or acting executive officer................

5. Address ....

6. Furnish the following data:

	Over 16 Yrs.		Under 16 Yrs.		Total
	Male	Female	Male	Female	
Usual No. employees..	----------	----------	----------	----------	--------
Usual No. hrs. employment per day......	----------	----------	----------	----------	--------
Usual No. hrs. employment per week.....	----------	----------	----------	----------	--------

7. No. of employees who left your employment to enter naval or military service of the U. S., between April 25, 1917 and November 12, 1918...................................

8. No of such former employees who have been re-employed......

§ 2. The Director of Labor is hereby authorized and directed to investigate the matter of re-employment of soldiers and sailors honorably discharged from the military or naval service of the United States, in order to bring about and to promote their speedy restoration to the industrial status formerly occupied by them. To that end he shall make use of all available information disclosed by records and statistics of his office, and he shall wherever and whenever possible and practicable advise with, and mediate between, employers and such discharged soldiers and sailors and he shall co-operate with patriotic organizations in efforts to bring about a prompt rehabilitation in industry of such discharged soldiers and sailors; he shall from time to time make such recommendations to employers as shall be deemed fit and reasonable in order to advance and promote such replacements in industry as shall be most advantageous to soldiers and sailors discharged from the naval or military service of the United States.

§ 3. It shall be the duty of the State Department of Labor to enforce the provisions of this Act and to classify the information thereby received, for statistical purposes and for such other purposes as are authorized by this Act: *Provided* that in no case shall the statistics be so arranged, or information so used as to reveal the affairs of any single employer.

§ 4. Any employer failing or refusing to furnish the information as provided herein shall be deemed guilty of a misdemeanor and shall, upon conviction, be fined a sum not less than $5.00 nor more than $25.00.

§ 5. This Act shall become effective upon its passage and approval.

APPROVED June 21, 1919.

CIVIL SERVICE PREFERENCE TO FORMER SERVICE MEN

Senate Bill Number 4, Fifty-first General Assembly.

AN ACT *to amend Section 29a of an Act entitled, "An Act relating to the civil service in park systems," approved June 10, 1911, in force July 1, 1911, as amended.*

SECTION 1. *Be it enacted by the People of the State of Illinois, represented in the General Assembly:* That Section 29a of an Act entitled, "An Act relating to the civil service in park systems," approved June 10, 1911, in force July 1, 1911, as amended, is hereby amended to read as follows:

Section 29a. Persons who were engaged in the military or naval service of the United States during the years 1861, 1862, 1863, 1864, 1865, 1898, 1899, 1900, 1901, 1902, 1914, 1915, 1916, 1917, 1918 or 1919, and who were honorably discharged therefrom, and all persons who were engaged in such military or naval service during any of said years, who are now or may hereafter be on inactive or reserve duty in such military or naval service, and also all persons who are citizens of Illinois, who, during the World War, were engaged in the military or naval service of the allies of the United States, who were honorably discharged therefrom, not including, however, persons who were convicted by court-martial of disobedience of orders, where such disobedience consisted in the refusal to perform military service on the ground of alleged religious or conscientious objections against war, shall be preferred for appointment to civil offices provided they are found to possess the business capacity necessary for the proper discharge of the duties of such office,

and it shall be the duty of the examiner or commissioner certifying
the list of eligibles, who have taken the examinations provided for in
this Act, to place the name or names of such persons at the head of
the list of eligibles certified for appointment.

APPROVED June 28, 1919.

SCHOLARSHIPS TO PERSONS FORMERLY IN THE MILITARY OR NAVAL SERVICE

House Bill Number 733, Fifty-first General Assembly.

AN ACT *to amend an Act entitled, "An Act to establish and maintain
a system of free schools," approved and in force June 12, 1909,
as amended, by adding thereto two new sections, to be known as
Sections 166a and 173a.*

SECTION 1. *Be it enacted by the People of the State of Illinois,
represented in the General Assembly:* That "An Act to establish
and maintain a system of free schools," approved and in force June 12,
1909, as amended, is amended by adding thereto two new sections,
to be known as Sections 166a and 173a, to read as follows:

§ 166a. Any person who served in the army, navy or marine
corps of United States, not including members of the Students' Army
Training Corps during the World War, who, at the time of entering
upon such service, was a resident of this State, and who has been
honorably discharged from such service, and who shall possess all
necessary entrance requirements shall, upon application and proper
proof, be awarded a Normal School scholarship.

Any person who served as above stated, and who, at the time
of entering upon such service was a student at any State Normal
School, and who was honorably discharged from such service shall,
upon application and proper proof, be entitled to finish and complete
his course of study at such institution without tuition and matriculation charges, but such person shall not be entitled to more than four
years of gratuitous instruction.

§ 173a. Any person who served in the army, navy or marine
corps of United States, not including members of the Students' Army
Training Corps during the World War, who, at the time of entering

upon such service, was a resident of this state, and who has been honorably discharged from such service, and who shall possess all necessary entrance requirements shall, upon application and proper proof, be awarded a University of Illinois scholarship.

Any person who served as above stated, and who, at the time of entering upon such service, was a student at the University of Illinois, and who was honorably discharged from such service, shall, upon application and proper proof, be entitled to finish and complete his course of study at the University of Illinois without tuition and matriculation charges, but such person shall not be entitled to more than four years of gratuitous instruction.

The holder of any university scholarship or free tuition privileges, under the provisions of this section, shall be entitled to all the privileges and shall be subject to all the conditions set forth in Sections 174 and 175 of this Act.

The provisions of Sections 166a and 173a, however, shall not apply to persons who were convicted by court martial of disobedience of orders, where such disobedience consisted of the refusal to perform military service on the ground of alleged religious or conscientious objections against war.

APPROVED June 28, 1919.

PROHIBITION OF GAMBLING DEVICES IN VICINITY OF MILITARY POSTS AND NAVAL STATIONS

Senate Bill Number 161, Fifty-first General Assembly.

AN ACT *to protect all counties in the State of Illinois in which there are United States naval stations, and military posts of the first class from slot machines and other gambling devices.*

SECTION 1. *Be it enacted by the People of the State of Illinois, represented in the General Assembly:* That it shall be unlawful for any person, firm or corporation, as owner, agent or otherwise, to manufacture, sell, lease, or hold, or offer for sale, or lease to another any clock, joker, punch board, tape or slot machine, or any other device upon which money is staked or hazarded, or into which money is paid or played upon chance, or upon the result of the action of which money or valuable thing is staked, bet, hazarded, won or lost, in any county in the State of Illinois in which there is a United States military post, or United States naval training station of the first class carried.

§ 2. Every such machine described in this Act is hereby declared a gambling device, and shall be subject to seizure, confiscation and destruction by any municipal, or other local authority, within whose jurisdiction the same may be found.

§ 3. Any person, firm or corporation, who, by himself or another, his principal, agent or otherwise, shall violate the provisions of this Act, shall be fined for the first offense not less than $100.00, and shall be imprisoned for thirty days in the county jail, and for the second offense not less than $500.00, and shall be confined in the county jail not less than six months, and for each subsequent offense shall be fined not less than $500.00 and imprisoned in the penitentiary for one year.

§ 4. It shall be unlawful to bargain for the sale or lease of any gambling machine described in this Act, or to collect money, or to take compensation for such sale, or lease, or to take or accept money from any person, or from any such machine as a share or royalty, or compensation for any such lease, or sale. Proof that such machine or device when seized has not been used, or is out of repair, shall not constitute a defense to a prosecution under this Act.

§ 5. All places where slot machines and other gambling devices are held or operated shall be taken and declared to be common and public nuisances, and whosoever shall keep any such place by himself or his agents or servant, shall, for each offense, be fined not less than $100.00, and shall be confined in the county jail for thirty days, and for each subsequent offense shall be fined $500.00 and confined in the county jail for six months.

Exception] Vending machines by which full and adequate return is made for the money invested and in which there is no element of chance or hazard shall not fall under the provisions of this Act.

FILED July 11, 1919.

The Governor having failed to return this bill to the General Assembly during its session, and having failed to file it in my office, with his objections, within ten days after the adjournment of the General Assembly, it has thereby become a law.

Witness my hand this 11th day of July, A. D. 1919.

Louis L. Emmerson, *Secretary of State.*

IX. RETURN OF THE ILLINOIS SERVICE MEN

REQUEST FOR A PARADE OF THE THIRTY-THIRD DIVISION

Senate Joint Resolution Number 22, Fifty-first General Assembly.

WHEREAS, The Thirty-third or "Prairie" Division of the United States Army is composed exclusively of the Illinois National Guard, and

WHEREAS, The 149th Field Artillery of the United States Army is composed of officers and men from Illinois, and

WHEREAS, These organizations have been from the time they reached Europe engaged in the heaviest fighting upon the Western battle-front, and have greatly distinguished themselves, fighting up to the very moment the armistice was signed, and

WHEREAS, The people of Illinois desire to honor in a fitting way these organizations, as units, when they return to Illinois, and

WHEREAS, This can be accomplished only if these organizations are permitted to parade as such in the City of Chicago, and

WHEREAS, It is now expected that these organizations will return to America in the near future, therefore be it

Resolved, by the Senate of the State of Illinois, the House of Representatives concurring therein, That the War Department be urgently requested to permit the Thirty-third Division and the 149th Field Artillery upon their respective arrivals, to parade as unbroken organizations in the City of Chicago, and, be it further

Resolved, That a copy of the resolutions, signed by the Presiding Officer of the Senate and the Presiding Officer of the House be transmitted by the Governor of Illinois, the Honorable Frank O. Lowden, to the Secretary of War and to the Chief of Staff.

Passed by the Senate March 18, 1919.

Concurred in by the House of Representatives, March 18, 1919.

APPROPRIATION FOR RECEPTION OF 33D DIVISION AND 149TH FIELD ARTILLERY

Senate Bill Number 365, Fifty-first General Assembly.

An Act *to defray the expenses of the reception of the Thirty-third Division and of the 149th Field Artillery of the United States.*

Section 1. *Be it enacted by the People of the State of Illinois, represented in the General Assembly:* The sum of twenty-five thousand ($25,000) dollars is hereby appropriated to defray the expenses of the reception of the Thirty-third Division and of the 149th Field Artillery of the United States Army upon its return to the State of Illinois.

§ 2. The Auditor of Public Accounts shall draw his warrant on the State Treasurer for the sum herein appropriated and upon presentation of itemized vouchers, approved by the Governor.

§ 3. Because of an emergency this Act shall take effect from and after its passage.

Approved May 1, 1919.

AN ADDRESS BY GOVERNOR FRANK O. LOWDEN[1]

Delivered at a dinner given in honor of the 149th Field Artillery upon its arrival in Chicago, May 9, 1919.[2]

Mr. Chairman, Colonel Reilly and Officers and Men of the 149th Field Artillery:

This is indeed a proud day for Illinois. Before the famous 149th Field Artillery broke its camp at Fort Sheridan, I had the honor of visiting with you. I saw you in the pride of your young manhood, with resolution written upon your faces, and I did not fear for a moment that the honor of Illinois would not be safe in your hands. But I did not anticipate a thousandth part of the

---

[1] From a manuscript copy in the possession of Governor Lowden.

[2] The 149th Field Artillery on its return to Chicago from overseas service on May 9, 1919, marched in review before Governor Frank O. Lowden, Major General Leonard Wood, commanding officer of the central department, and other officials. The dinner at the Congress Hotel followed the review, after which the regiment entrained for Camp Grant for demobilization.

achievements which would be yours on a score of the most important and bloody fields of Europe. We did not know then that it would be given to you, and the splendid division of which you are so important a part, so early to engage in the world war. We did not then know that you would write upon your banner in such illustrious letters the words "Lorraine, Champagne, Ypres,[3] St. Mihiel, and Argonne Forest." We did not know when you should return and we should read the annals of your service on the other side, that we would have read of the great war, because you are a part of all of it, from February of last year until the last shot was fired on western battle fronts.

Officers and men, as I saw you march down Michigan Avenue this morning and looked into your faces, I could feel with a keenness I had not felt before the tragic days and weeks and months of your heroic service abroad; but I want to tell you now that I envy everyone of you, because, though your years are young, you have lived more—if life is to be measured by its high emotion, by its pure unselfish sacrifices—you have lived longer than those of us who are twice your years.

Illinois welcomes you home with pride, and mingled with that pride she feels in you are tears for those brave comrades of yours who will return no more to their home and their state. They lie in immortal graves that will be kept green through all the centuries to come, so long as America shall remember and reward heroism and patriotism, so long as the banners of liberty are still flying in the sky.

Welcome, welcome to our homes and to our hearts.

You have made it possible for us who stayed at home to preserve the institutions for which you fought and for which your comrades died.

God bless you, officers and men, every one of you. I thank you.

[3] Illinois troops did not see action at Ypres.

ADDRESSES MADE BEFORE THE 132D INFANTRY, 33D DIVISION, CAMP MILLS, MAY 18, 1919[4]

COLONEL DAVIS:[5] On the first day of our return to the United States it is our particular distinction to have the whole state and the majority of the officers and men of this regiment, represented by its Chief Executive.

So precious to me, and I am certain to you, will be every word that the Chief Executive of Illinois is about to utter to us, that I shall without further ceremony give way to him, present him to you and take great pride in presenting every one of you to him, with the full recognition of the splendid service which every one of you has rendered to our country, and in the name of our regiment and in the name of the great division of which it is our pride to have been a part. I shall ask you, after I present him to you, to remain at ease because the Governor wants you to be at ease while he talks to you. And now, officers and men of my regiment, Governor Lowden of Illinois.

GOVERNOR LOWDEN: Colonel Davis, officers and men of the 132d Regiment, a little over a year ago, upon this very island I saw this regiment start for foreign battle fields, and I want to tell you now that it is a lot pleasanter, that it is a lot more delightful, to welcome you home, than it was to bid you good-by. And in that year that since has come and gone you have brought distinction to Illinois and to your country, and you have surpassed all our fondest hopes of what you would do when you found yourselves facing the enemy of our country and of civilization.

We followed you officers and men in all the arduous months in which you have been away from us; we have followed you with love and pride; we have been waiting, oh, how anxiously, since the armistice was signed until we could welcome you home again. And this is a proud and happy hour for Illinois and you are getting now but a hint of the welcome that awaits you when you return to our state.

We are familiar with the great words that you have emblaz-

[4] From a manuscript copy in the possession of Governor Lowden.
[5] Col. Abel Davis, commanding officer, 132d Infantry, succeeding Col. John J. Garrity.

oned upon your regimental banner. We know something of Hamel; we know how you were among the first there to make all the world know what the American soldier was and what he could do; we know something of the Mort Homme sector; we remember the Bois de Forges, and those names will be treasured forevermore in the history of Illinois and the history of the United States. Mingling with the gladness we feel as we look into your faces again are tears for your fallen comrades who will come back no more. The three hundred or more brave men you have left upon the greatest battle fields of history will be cherished tenderly forevermore in the heart of Illinois and in the heart of our common country. For you our gratitude, our love; for them our gratitude, our pride and our tears. We know, too, that there are among you today many brave men who have come into this regiment to take the places of those fallen comrades. We sent across men from other states, but from whatever state you hail, you will always be welcome in Illinois, because we shall claim an interest and a part in every man who has fought with this great division which has brought such luster to American arms.

I am not going to make a speech to you today, boys; I just want to tell you how good it seems to us to look into your eyes again and to welcome you home. I couldn't if I were to speak for an hour half voice the pride, the gratitude of Illinois for what you have done and for what you are. Good-by.

COLONEL DAVIS: Let us give Governor Lowden a message that he may take to Illinois of our gratitude to our home state and to our home cities for the manner in which they followed every one of our steps. Let that message be brief and let our hearts go to them as we send that message in the form of three cheers to those whom we love and for whom Governor Lowden speaks to us this morning.

(Three cheers for Governor Lowden.)

COLONEL DAVIS: First sergeants or senior noncommissioned officers will take command of their respective companies and lead them to mess.

(Cries of "Colonel Garrity.")

COLONEL DAVIS: Gentlemen, we are not going to ask Colonel Garrity for consent in this matter. We are proud indeed that he is here, and particularly proud that there are enough of us here that remember the splendid work which he has done for this regiment and the manner in which he laid the foundation on which we have all built.

Men of the old Second and of the new One Hundred and Thirty-second, Colonel Garrity.

COLONEL GARRITY:[6] Colonel Davis, Governor Lowden, officers and men of the One Hundred and Thirty-second Infantry, it is indeed a great pleasure for me to greet you on this, your first day back on American soil.

As the Governor has said, we of Illinois have watched your movements throughout the entire campaign. There have been many names that have been read by me, whom I knew personally, who are left behind and who have my deepest and most sincere sympathy.

I am glad, men of the Second, and proud, of the record that you have made in this great conflict. I knew when I left you that it was in you, and it makes me doubly proud to hear of all that you have accomplished.

I did not expect to be called on to say anything to you today and was not prepared for it. However, I will say once more that I am glad to see you all back on American soil and will be glad when you all reach Chicago, as I know all Chicago feels the same way. Thank you!

AN ADDRESS BY GOVERNOR FRANK O. LOWDEN[7]

Delivered before the 131st Infantry, Camp Mills, New York, May 24, 1919.

General Bell, Colonel Sanborn, officers and men of the 131st Infantry:

When I saw you in Houston in preparation for the great work you have just closed I had the honor to present to you these colors. I told you then I knew you would bring them back without a stain, but I did not know at that time that you would bring them

---

[6] Col. John J. Garrity, commanding officer of the 2d Infantry, Illinois National Guard, and of the 132d Infantry until April 4, 1918, when he was transferred to the command of the 130th Infantry. He resigned his commission on April 24, 1918.

[7] From a manuscript copy in the possession of Governor Lowden.

back with this double decoration (Verdun Sector—France, Sept. 10-Sept. 25, 1918; Amiens Sector—France, July 1-Aug. 20, 1918; Troyon Sector—France, Oct. 26-Nov. 11, 1918; Meuse-Argonne Offensive—France, Sept. 26-Oct. 21, 1918) ; that you would carry them to every battle field on which you fought with ever-increasing courage and renown.

And now that you have returned to us I congratulate you with all my heart upon the new distinction you have brought to Illinois and to the United States. We knew you would do well; we did not know that you would form a part of the division which never met defeat, which never failed to attain the objective assigned on schedule time. We did not know that in rivalry with the veterans of the greatest armies of Europe you would win superior praise; you would stand the competition which you met with ever new luster and glory.

Illinois is on its very tip-toes awaiting your return. And mingling, officers and men, with the pride we feel in you, our tears for those names which were read and where no response was given, and for those other comrades of yours who sleep on the score of foreign battle fields to return no more. For them, too, we have pride and love mingling with our tears, and so long as Illinois shall exist it will cherish in its heart of hearts the memory of these brave men who have paid the supreme sacrifice that our civilization might endure.

Oh, I am proud—I am more proud than I shall ever be. I felt ever since I saw you go for foreign shores that in some sort of way I was not playing my full part in this great war, that I did not go by your side and under these colors. I hope, however, I have not lost the right to call you comrades in the years that shall come for that will ever be one of the proudest satisfactions I shall have in life.

And now, Colonel Joe and officers and men, I welcome you in the name of Illinois, to the country whose prowess, whose courage and whose character you have embellished forevermore. I bid you to our homes and hearts and I promise you that Illinois deserves you because she will show that she knows how to appreciate the brave. And you, my friends, we are awaiting over one thousand miles to the west. When you come again to your beloved state I know that the thrill of joy you there will feel will match the courage and the manhood you displayed upon the battle fields.

Good-by. Good-by until I shall see you again as under this proud banner you march down the streets of Chicago upon your return.

RETURN OF THE 33D DIVISION—A PROCLAMATION

Illinois was one of the three states of the Union which furnished the Government an entire National Guard Division. That Division officially designated as the Thirty-third, is popularly known as the Prairie Division.

The Prairie Division sailed for European battle-fields in May of last year. Almost at once it went into the battle line. And until the Armistice was signed it saw the hardest and most dangerous service to be found. It won imperishable renown on a score of bloody battle-fields. It never lost a battle. It never was assigned an objective which it did not reach at the appointed time. England, France and Belgium vied with one another to do honor to this Division. It returns with a spotless record, bringing new fame to Illinois. And yet, it does not all return. More than a thousand of its number sleep on foreign soil.

The first detachment of those who survive is expected to reach Illinois on Tuesday, May 27.[8] As these heroic men return to our State, let Illinois show them that she knows how to welcome home her brave. Let the flag under which they fought and which their sacrifices have sanctified float everywhere. Let service flags be displayed in every home from which a soldier went. Let us, with special tenderness, do reverence to those service flags whose stars have turned from blue to gold. As the different parts of this great Division enter our State, let it be the principal business of Illinois to show her superb sons that Illinois is on tiptoe to receive them back to her arms with love and pride and gratitude.

The soldiers of the Prairie Division are typical of the more than 350,000 men which Illinois sent to the front during the Great War.

[8] The Thirty-third Division returned to Chicago in three contingents, on May 27, June 2 and June 5, 1919. A parade, reviewed by the Governor and other officials, was held upon the arrival of each contingent, after which banquets were given to the officers and men. The units then entrained for Camp Grant for demobilization.

This great host was scattered through many different commands. Illinois soldiers and sailors were to be found upon every battle-front, and in every branch of the service. They, too, are entitled to the honor and gratitude of Illinois. In honoring the Prairie Division, we honor all these brave men.

GIVEN UNDER MY HAND AND THE GREAT SEAL OF STATE AT THE CAPITOL IN SPRING-FIELD, THIS TWENTIETH DAY OF MAY, IN THE YEAR OF OUR LORD ONE THOUSAND NINE HUNDRED AND NINETEEN, AND OF THE INDEPENDENCE OF THE UNITED STATES THE ONE HUNDRED AND FORTY-THIRD.

(SEAL)

FRANK O. LOWDEN

By the Governor:
LOUIS L. EMMERSON.
Secretary of State.

INDEX

fore Illinois State Teachers' Association, Springfield, Dec. 28, 1917, 82–97;

by Dean Eugene Davenport, before Chicago Association of Commerce, April 4, 1917, 134–138;

by Carl Vrooman, before Chicago Association of Commerce, May 9, 1917, 138–147;

by Dr. C. G. Hopkins, before state conference of Woman's Committee, State Council of Defense, Chicago, June 26, 1917, 150–158;

by Arthur Reynolds, before Chicago Association of Commerce, April 18, 1917, 162–172;

by W. G. McAdoo, Chicago, Oct. 2, 1917, 185–190; Chicago, Oct. 12, 1918, 238–242;

by Frank A. Vanderlip, before Illinois Manufacturers' Association, Chicago, Dec. 12, 1917, 207–211;

by Barney Cohen, Labor Day meeting, Springfield, Sept. 2, 1918, 225–231;

by Josephus Daniels, before American Bankers' Association, Chicago, Sept. 27, 1918, 233–238; Centennial Celebration, Springfield, Oct. 6, 1918, 417–431;

by Hugh S. Magill, Registration Rally, Springfield, June 4, 1917, 258–261;

by Lt. Col. C. A. Bach, 2d Officers' Training Camp, Fort Sheridan, Nov. 20, 1917, 273–282;

by Col. H. J. Reilly, before Chicago Association of Commerce, June 6, 1917, 284–291;

by William C. Gorgas, surgeon general, before Chicago Asso-

ciation of Commerce, Oct. 26, 1917, 292–301;

by Medill McCormick, Springfield, Nov. 27, 1917, 301–313;

by Newton D. Baker, before 86th Division, Camp Grant, July 4, 1918, 319–321;

by Marshal Joffre, Chicago, May 5, 1917, 354–355; Springfield, May 7, 1917, 359.

by M. René Viviani, Chicago, May 5, 1917, 355–356; Springfield, May 7, 1917, 360–361;

by Speaker David E. Shanahan, at reception to French Mission, Springfield, May 7, 1917, 357–358;

by Boris Bakhmeteff, Russian ambassador, Chicago, Aug. 3, 1917, 361–362;

by Dr. Milenko Vestnich, head of Serbian Mission, Chicago, Jan. 27, 1918, 365;

by William Renwick Riddell, Centennial Celebration, Springfield, Feb. 12, 1918, 367–380;

by M. Louis Aubert, Centennial Celebration, Springfield, April 18, 1918, 394–402;

by Lord Charnwood, Centennial Celebration, Springfield, Oct. 6, 1918, 431–435;

by Lt. Gov. John G. Oglesby, at Victory Massmeeting, Springfield, Nov. 11, 1918, 445–446;

by Samuel Insull, before Commercial Club, Chicago, Jan. 18, 1919, 456–466;

by Mrs. Joseph T. Bowen, at State Conference of Woman's Committee, State Council of Defense, Chicago, March 4, 1919, 472–478;

by Col. J. J. Garrity, before

French Mission, personnel of party visiting Illinois, 353n; reception by 50th General Assembly, 356; visit to Springfield, 356–361.

"Food Conservation," proclamation by the Governor, 158–159.

Food, fuel and commodity legislation, need of, resolutions adopted by State Council of Defense, 132–133.

Food production, plans for, 134–138; resolutions adopted by Illinois Farmers' Institute regarding, 203–207.

Food production and conservation, need of, 138–147.

"Formation of Neighborhood Committees," resolutions adopted by conference called by State Council of Defense, 125–126.

"Fourth Liberty Loan," proclamation by the Governor, 232–233.

Fuel situation, conference called by State Council of Defense to discuss, 176; report of Committee on Law and Legislation, State Council of Defense regarding, 173–176; agreement between Governor and representatives of Illinois coal operators, 177–178; resolutions of coal conference, regarding, 178–183.

"Functions of Community Labor Boards," statement by Governor, 220–221.

Funds, for Red Cross war work, first drive for, 128–130; for war aid and war charity, act to regulate solicitation of, 130–132.

Garrity, Col. John J., address by, 504.

General Assembly, Fiftieth (1917), addressed by Governor, 1–2; message from Governor to, 253–254; account of joint session of, on occasion of French Mission's visit to Springfield, 356–361;

joint resolutions adopted by, 2, 21–22, 110–113, 148–149, 353, 356;

laws passed by, 122–124, 130–132, 252–253, 264–269, 332–333, 333–336, 343–344, 347–350.

General Assembly, Fifty-first (1919), extract from biennial report of Governor to, 454–455;

joint resolutions adopted by, 113–114, 115, 117, 479, 480–484, 486–487, 490–491, 491–492, 499;

laws enacted by, 485, 487–489, 490, 492–494, 494–495, 495–496, 496–498, 500.

Gompers, Samuel, meeting called by, 22; address by, 73–78.

Gorgas, Surgeon General William C., address by, 292–301.

Governor, *see* Lowden, Governor Frank O.

Grand Army of the Republic, members of, addressed by Governor, 103–105.

Great Lakes Naval Training Station, enlargement of recommended, 283.

Histories of World War, authorized by act of 51st General Assembly, 488–489.

Home defense, need of an organization for, 332.

Hopkins, Dr. Cyril G., address by, 150–158.

"Illinois' Centennial," proclamation by Governor, 366–367.